Viral Media

Viral Media

A Digital Production Marketing Guide
for Advertisers, Journalists,
and Public Relations Professionals

First Edition

Written by Dr. Paul Fornelli and Jody Mahler

Edited by Dr. Paul Fornelli

California State University, Dominguez Hills

Bassim Hamadeh, CEO and Publisher
Mieka Portier, Acquisitions Editor
Tony Paese, Project Editor
Berenice Quirino, Associate Production Editor
Jess Estrella, Senior Graphic Designer
Danielle Gradisher, Licensing Associate
Jess Estrella, Interior Designer
Natalie Piccotti, Senior Marketing Manager
Kassie Graves, Vice President of Editorial
Jamie Giganti, Director of Academic Publishing

Cover image copyright© 2016 iStockphoto LP/franckreporter.

Printed in the United States of America.

ISBN: 978-1-5165-9056-8 (pbk) / 978-1-5165-9057-5 (br)

Contents

Introduction

VIRAL MEDIA GUIDE

It is a well-known if unspoken truth, that most digital media production textbooks are biased. These texts are typically designed with but a single target audience in mind—students seeking a full-time career in the Hollywood feature film industry or in cable television and broadcasting. Unfortunately, this focus on such a singular audience tends to overlook other students whose professional responsibilities will also require them to master digital media production skills.

For students going to work in media-centric fields like advertising, journalism, media studies, and public relations (PR), learning the basics of digital media production (scriptwriting, camera operation, lighting, video editing, etc.), proves to be just as crucial for their professional development, as it is for film and video students. The commonality is the shared need for all of these professions to find ways to tell stories that better engage the viewer, even if not all of those media professionals share the same aspiration of walking the red carpet at an award show one day. Some of these professionals just want to shoot a viral video to help improve market sales for the upcoming quarter!

Regardless of whether you hope to pursue a career in film or TV, or you are merely looking to work in a media-savvy industry like journalism or marketing, this book will bridge the gap in the existing literature and provide a relevant, how-to guide for digital media students from all disciplines. This text offers insights into a host of digital media production techniques designed specifically for use in the viral media age, including new approaches to developing story ideas and distributing that content across the gamut of social media networks. To guide you through the viral media production process, this text will incorporate commentary from some of the top minds in marketing and media, as they reveal insider tips into actual viral media marketing production methods, standards, and techniques.

This book also contains a detailed section clarifying the proper standards of ethical behavior required of professionals working in digital media production. While targeted at journalists, the "Ethics" section possesses information that is essential for advertisers, PR, and digital media professionals of all stripes. The text also contains over a half-dozen real-world examples of viral and social media campaigns executed by some of the largest business organizations in the world, including Unilever's Dove and Axe personal care brands, McDonald's, Coca-Cola, and *The Hunger Games* motion picture franchise. These case studies provide a unique opportunity for students to access the inner workings of PR firms and ad agencies as they plot out and then implement online viral marketing campaigns. For journalists, the material in this book will offer a glimpse into the creative process involved, and the specialized techniques being employed to help sway the public's perception toward a particular person, brand, organization, or product.

This *Viral Media Digital Production Marketing Guide* is a customized text intended for media students and professionals alike who require an understanding of how to integrate multiple forms of media (film, video, sound clips, music, social media, streaming video content, etc.) into a successful ad campaign, newscast, promotional event, TV show, or feature film. This guide serves as a resource for creative media artists who want to learn how to make their messages stand out in a world saturated with dense media content, round-the-clock programming, and a diverse array of programming choices. Whether you are a student or an already-established creative talent, this viral guide has been tailored specifically for individuals like yourself. It will provide you, the reader, with a better understanding of how digital media production is best utilized, both in terms of its cost-effectiveness and its ability to reach a vast audience. This is the one digital production text purposefully designed to be of equal benefit to all media professionals.

SECTION I

Digital Production Planning in the Viral Age

INTRODUCTION

The Internet has changed the nature of digital media production by forever altering many well-established and long-standing production protocols. Instead of relying on expensive marketing campaigns requiring heavy broadcast, network-TV exposure, producers now have the ability to connect directly with their audience via a number of online video sites, such as YouTube, Netflix, Facebook, Vimeo, and Hulu. The Web has also changed how we consume digital media, blurring the distinction between professional video and self-generated user content. This has also led to a new media paradigm in which Hollywood features debut online instead of at the cineplex, TV shows are released all at once for binge watching rather than for incremental seasonal playback, newscasts stream around the clock, 24/7, and *viral video* ads become trending, must-see attractions rather than the unwanted, program interruptions of old.

On top of all of these changes, the Internet has also made digital media production seem more accessible than ever before. Whether partaking of a major motion picture, a blogger's video post, or a trending viral video, the perception among many viewers is that they could produce something of equal value if they simply had access to the same production resources. The reality, though, is that making a digital media production is not nearly as simple as merely *watching* a completed digital media production. The main issue for most production novices is that they cannot meet the high-performance standards of an experienced production team, since mastering these skills takes considerable

KEY TERMS

- above-the-line personnel versus below-the-line personnel
- brand synergy
- character description
- collaboration
- inverted pyramid
- press release
- production stages: preproduction/ production/postproduction
- production triangle
- "Seven Cs" of successful storytelling
- shot lists
- shooting schedule
- single-column script versus two-column script
- storyboard
- viral videos

I

time and patience. For those who are dedicated to learning the ins and outs of digital media production, the first section of this text will supply you with the foundational principles and basic terminology used within the production industry.

Section I will provide the reader with an overview of the main stages of the digital media production process, detail the above-the-line personnel and the below-the-line personnel involved at various stages of production, explain how to develop collaborative team goals, and evaluate the worthiness of a news story or creative concept. Subsequent sections of this book will include more detailed descriptions of the digital media tools and the video equipment that are needed to successfully complete the final stages of the production process.

CHAPTER 1

Importance of Collaboration

Paul Fornelli

Toward the end of Barry Bonds's illustrious MLB career, his individual stardom had grown to the point that he mandated his own personal locker-room space equipped with not just one but four lockers; a private, big-screen TV; a group of two to three personal trainers who attended solely to the slugger's needs; and, as the coup de grace, a vibrating massage chair reserved just for Bonds (Shea, 2007). In both a literal and a figurative sense, the long-time major leaguer effectively created not just a physical separation between himself and his San Francisco Giants teammates, but an emotional one as well.

Understand that there is no denying Bonds's great accomplishments on the field, his home-run prowess, or his enormous individual talent. He was the alpha dog of alpha dogs for the Giants. However, it is also well documented that his feisty, even contentious, relationships with fellow teammates frequently led to interpersonal conflicts and strained group dynamics in the club. Despite achieving some of his sport's greatest individual honors and accolades, Bonds, for whatever reason, was never able to achieve baseball's ultimate team accomplishment: winning a World Series championship.

Before Bonds starred on the diamond, a young athlete from Lansing, Michigan, made his mark on the basketball courts of the NBA. Magic Johnson was the top draft pick of the Los Angeles Lakers in the 1979 NBA draft. However, some scouts had doubts about him athletically because when he entered the NBA he was a step slow as a defender and had an extremely poor outside shooting touch.

Although considered elite, Johnson was not considered as pure an athlete as the gifted Bonds. Nor could Johnson boast the athletic pedigree of Bonds, whose father, Bobby, had been a three-time major league all-star while playing with the Giants and the Yankees in the early 1970s.

Nevertheless, Johnson would go on to become a champion at every possible stage of his career: at the prep, collegiate, professional, and Olympic levels. He was a three-time NBA MVP and led the Lakers to five NBA world championships before an HIV diagnosis forced him into premature retirement.

In retrospect, what was it that made Johnson's career outcome turn out so differently from that of Bonds, his MLB baseball counterpart? How was Magic Johnson able to overcome his own initial limitations and improve not only himself but also the level of play of

FIGURE 1.1 Despite achieving some of MLB's greatest individual honors, Bonds was never able to achieve baseball's ultimate team accomplishment: a World Series championship.

those around him, while Bonds could never quite accomplish the same feat? Why is it that Magic Johnson, to this day, is recognized as perhaps the ultimate team player, inspirational leader, and unrelenting competitor within his or any other team sport, while Bonds's career continues to be mired in controversy?

The answer is simple. What made Johnson unique was his extraordinary sense of vision. Whether orchestrating a full-court fast break or spotting an unguarded three-point shooter, Johnson unerringly found his open teammates and provided them with easy, uncontested

FIGURE 1.2 Johnson became a two-time inductee into the Basketball Hall of Fame—enshrined in 2002 for his individual career and again in 2010 as a member of the USA "Dream Team."

FIGURE 1.3 Valerie Jenness moderating "A Conversation with Magic Johnson" at the University of California, Irvine.

looks. He boasted a truly uncanny sixth sense and an otherworldly ability to get the ball to just the right teammate at just the right time.

Fortunately, Johnson's vision also extended well beyond the basketball court, and he was able to use his accrued public good will, business acumen, and celebrity status to build a brand for himself as a successful businessman, promoter, and philanthropist. Johnson would go on to launch the Magic Johnson Theater chain, invest in inner-city communities via his partnership with Starbucks, found the Magic Johnson Foundation to help fund research into a cure for HIV, and was inducted into the NBA Hall of Fame in 2002 on the very first ballot. Ironically, Johnson would also go on to become part owner in the Los Angeles Dodgers, the hated baseball rival of Bonds's San Francisco Giants.

You're probably asking yourself right about now, "What does all of this have to do with me? What does this story of two famous athletes have to do with me working in media production or learning to make viral videos?"

The connection is this, and it's a potent one: You are preparing to enter a field where collaboration is key. The worlds of advertising, public relations, photojournalism, and digital media production require a coordinated group effort in order to be successful. Like a sports team, every member of the production crew must know his or her particular assignment and the role that he or she is assigned to execute. Individual excellence is certainly required, but good production teammates must also be willing to subjugate their individual egos in service of the overall team.

If you're a student reading this text, you know from your own personal experience that few things are more dreaded than hearing that you've been assigned to a group project by your parents, teacher, boss, or whoever it may be. The assignment comes with the trepidation of not knowing the people with whom you will be assigned to work. What are they like? Do they know what they're doing? Are they up to speed on the work, or are you going to be stuck having to do everyone else's work? (Even worse, what if some of these people actually know *more* about the assignment than you do? Are they going to show you up and make you look incompetent? They may take all the credit!)

FIGURE 1.4 For students, few things are more dreaded than learning that you've been assigned to a group project.

Admittedly, group work can be frustrating sometimes, most notably when others fail to pull their own weight. On the other hand, when things work out—when the real opportunity arises to work with a team of competent, creative peers, who all share the same goals and accomplishments—few experiences can be more rewarding. That is why building a competent and cohesive production team is the most crucial step of the entire production process; a smooth-running team will prove to be an invaluable asset to a producer—especially a

FIGURE 1.5 The production crew for the TV movie *Sherlock Holmes and the Case of the Silk Stocking* in London.

producer with a short time frame and an even smaller operating budget. Like a championship sports team, working on a production crew requires a common vision and a shared sense of purpose. Well-constructed teams that can work together amicably in the spirit of cooperation demonstrate increased levels of innovation and productivity, unleashing the company's full potential (Chen, Sharma, Edinger, Shapiro, & Farh, 2011).

Understand, as well, that in the modern business environment, teams play a larger role in day-to-day operations than they ever have before. Indeed, the majority of work done in most commercial organizations is now performed by a team, rather than by stand-alone individuals (Druskat & Wolff, 2001). A well-integrated team is now required to handle the overall scope and complexity of most organizational problem solving.

What size teams are we talking about? As we will examine in the next chapter, the scale of a media production can vary in size from a small team of just two or three individuals, all the way up to a feature film crew boasting hundreds of artisans and technicians. For our purposes, though, we'll focus on smaller-scale production teams with basic crew allotments of just a few primary staff, such as producer, writer, director, camera operator, sound recorder, and postproduction editor.

Remember, though, that your team doesn't stop there. As a producer, you must answer to a number of additional, third-party stakeholders. This is assuming that your viral production plans envision something more ambitious than merely posting a bland video of yourself on Periscope or Facebook Live. For example, casting agents will be needed to audition performers, location scouts to find suitable filming sites, craft services to help feed the crew, make-up artists to attend to your talent, costumers to prepare a wardrobe, etc. The list will seem endless at times.

For those of you still at the university level, accounting for additional stakeholders might require anticipating the demands of your instructor or following the specific parameters of a given course assignment. It might mean having to deal with your campus's technical support staff or equipment room supervisor when trying to reserve or check out equipment for your shoot. Let's not be too quick to erase Mom and Dad from the equation, because they yet may be asked to underwrite and finance your viral media sensation.

At the professional level, first and foremost, the client must be taken into consideration. What message is the client trying to send the world? What type of creative approach does the client wish to undertake? Is this client a blue-collar or an upscale brand? Does the client want a testimonial spokesperson or an appeal to action? Has the client presented you with a time constraint or budget limitation to add even more pressure to the creative process?

The truth of the matter is that all of these different stakeholders, from the client to the production crew to third-party contractors, have varying needs, presumed outcomes, a desired pace of progress, and individual standards by which they judge a project's success. Balancing all of these disparate demands and expectations is daunting, but it is a critical part of a producer's everyday job description.

Consequently, before taking on a collaborative project, a producer must know what the demands on the team will be. To accomplish this task, a producer must know how to navigate the "seven C's" of successful storytelling: *conflict, clarity, connection, characterization, challenge, credibility, and closure.*

CONFLICT

Conflict has been described as the essence of drama; in other words, without the conflict, there is no story. As a producer, it will be important to determine what the core conflict of your production entails. It will be important to establish exactly who the opposing forces are in the story. For example, is there a hero or an underdog to root for in the narrative, or is this a story with many shades of gray? What are the stakes involved or the hurdles that need to be overcome? What happens if this challenge is not overcome?

CLARITY

Here's an important question to ask yourself before taking on the storytelling task, is your team, in fact, the best one to tell the story? Will your team be able to make sense of the story's conflict and its many ramifications—whatever their size and scope—and then be able to relay that information in a way that won't confuse your audience? After all, some stories, especially those involving topics like technology, medicine, the law, or high finance, require a certain degree of sophistication. Do you have a team member, or will you be able to add a third party who can make sense of the information in a simple, straightforward way, while avoiding the use of unnecessary jargon or complex terminology? Ultimately, your job as a producer is to make sure that all of this information is communicated to your audience as clearly as possible, while still accounting for the realities of budgetary and time constraints.

CONNECTION

There is an old adage that states a journalist's work must appeal to many, while still speaking directly to the individual. The surest way of turning a complex or abstract story into something tangible and meaningful is by tapping directly into your audience's emotions, The goal is to not only get your audience to respond emotionally to the story, but also to help them identify with the participants who were involved, Without that palpable emotional connection, any real, meaningful engagement between the narrative the viewer becomes impossible. Human beings are very emotional creatures, to the point that our feelings often trump our sense of rationality. All too often, people make decisions, sometimes life-altering ones, based solely on a spur-of-the-moment impulse or whim. Think how often have you heard someone say that they made a decision because of their "gut feeling"? In light of this reality, establishing an emotional connection with the audience becomes an absolute necessity in order to tell a good story.

CHARACTERIZATION

The best way to make an emotional connection with the audience is by highlighting the human-interest aspects of the story in order to make it more relatable to the audience. Some stories are not inherently "sexy," so they do not automatically compel massive viewer interest. To make topics like changes to the city tax code or improvements to your favorite home laundry detergent more appealing to viewers, it will be incumbent on your creative team to find the means by which to personify your work. This is accomplished by keying in on an individual or individuals directly affected by this changing set of circumstances. For advertisers, that sometimes mean soliciting paid testimonials from celebrity spokespersons. For public relations professionals, journalists, and documentarians, though, this means finding the proper subject or subjects willing to tell their stories to the public and, in so doing, bring the topic to life in a way that resonates with the audience and allows the viewer to identify more closely with the individual character's situation. After all, if the audience can't tell what an individual is really like, ultimately, there will be nothing there for them to like!

CHALLENGE

In terms of meeting the challenges that are encountered along the way, understand right up front that those challenges will be both internal and external in nature. The external challenges, such as finding an audience for your work, getting those viewers to look at your production, and then having to endure some critical second-guessing, are to be anticipated because they come with the territory. However, while those challenges are apparent, what sometimes gets overlooked are the internal challenges that production teams face when putting a story together. As creative artists, it is always important to stay open-minded when first putting a project together. As an individual, can you put aside your own preconceived notions and expectations to observe and document a story in an objective and forthright manner? Can your team bring a fresh perspective to the storytelling, while still addressing the core concern of your production and connecting to your intended audience?

CREDIBILITY

Storytelling is a true craft. It is an art form that requires repeated efforts, via trial and error, in order to be perfected. In the process of building up your craft, you must also continually build up your own level of credibility by demonstrating your level of dedication to your chosen profession. Team members are quick to take note when someone does not display a consistent code of conduct or adhere to a strict set of professional standards. In a collaborative team environment, trust and individual responsibility go hand in hand. This means that personal credibility, along with your content's credibility—ensuring that your sources are verified and your facts are properly vetted—becomes enormously crucial.

CLOSURE

If everything else has fallen into place, the final step in the storytelling process is to deliver a resolution to the audience: a conclusion that goes beyond a mere summation of details. For example, have all aspects of story or production been resolved, or are certain details still in a state of flux? What is the ultimate goal of the story that you are telling? Is it being used to inform? To educate? To change minds? To issue a call to action to the viewer? Is there some positive element, or perhaps a future remedy of some sort, that can be highlighted? Ultimately, what meaning can, or should, the audience take away from the story's outcome?

By navigating these seven C's of storytelling, production teams can avoid many of the pitfalls that plague poor productions. If these concerns are not addressed beforehand, they can lead to problems later on, during the heart of production. Even worse, these creative conflicts, if allowed to fester over time, will undermine overall team cohesion and lead members to start playing the blame game, pointing fingers at one another.

Such an outcome is to be avoided at all costs. The driving force behind successful collaborations is the effective use of communication among all parties. Your crew's capacity to work together as a team will determine the production's ultimate success or failure. When internal team communications break down, dysfunction is the inevitable result, which quickly leads to diminished team performance and increased workplace tension. It's one thing to butt heads occasionally, but does that interaction generate a creative spark or does the constant friction lead only to self-immolation?

The reality of the situation is that the more complex the production, the more help will be needed. By the same token, production failure, in whatever area, for whatever reason, reflects badly not just on the individual producer but on the entire creative team and, by extension, the larger production company, advertising agency, or PR firm. This is especially true if the effort put forth by the team is genuinely subpar or if the creative backlash proves exceedingly severe.

FIGURE 1.6   TV studio with a full production crew at work in a multicamera production at Asahi Broadcasting Corporation.

To function in a high-pressure climate such as this and avoid unnecessary pitfalls, teams need a leader they can trust and rely on. To operate at their peak, team members must feel empowered enough to engage in open, two-way communications with one another, to engage in creative dialogue, and then to respond to feedback in a meaningful and productive way (Dyer, Dyer, & Dyer, 2013). To be a leader of a creative team, especially one working in an online media environment, fresh approaches and new ideas must be embraced.

This is not the time for some team member to try to take advantage of production strife by asserting dominance and attempting to take control of every position on the set or by barking out orders to others on the crew. What is not needed is a lone wolf trying to step into the alpha dog's role; what's needed is a faithful pack leader, someone who can unite the team and keep them focused on a common outcome. That is why the sports analogy is so apt here.

Just like one of Magic Johnson's championship squads, media production teams require collaboration and camaraderie. They require creative personnel and a leader with a vision, someone who knows how to coach and strategize while inspiring team members to perform at their maximum level. Highly functional teams thrive under leaders, who are both empathetic and flexible, professionals who stress teamwork and collaboration and understand that a talented crew, given enough freedom, will make the right creative choices all on their own, just as Johnson trusted his teammates to do on their way to winning yet another championship.

FIGURE 1.7   Earvin "Magic" Johnson's star on the Hollywood Walk of Fame.

REFERENCES

Chen, G., Sharma, P. N., Edinger, S. K., Shapiro, D. L., & Farh, J. (2011). Motivating and demotivating forces in teams. *Journal of Applied Psychology, 96*(3), 541–557. doi:http://dx.doi.org/10.1037/a0021886

Druskat, V., & Wolff, S. (2001). Building the emotional intelligence of groups. *Harvard Business Review.* Retrieved from https://hbr.org/2001/03/building-the-emotional-intelligence-of-groups

Dyer, W., Dyer, J., & Dyer, W. (2013). Team building: Proven strategies for improving team performance (5th ed.). Hoboken, NJ: Jossey-Bass Publishing.

Shea, J. (2007, September 22). Did Giants' special treatment of Bonds contribute to messy end? Pampered slugger delivered, but there was a big downside. *San Francisco Chronicle.* Retrieved from http://www.sfgate.com/giants/article/Did-Giants-special-treatment-of-Bonds-contribute-2521262.php

CREDITS

CHAPTER 2

Finding and Evaluating a Story

Josh Meltzer; ed. Kenneth Kobre

N ow that you've learned what makes great storytelling, how do you actually go about finding possible stories and evaluating their potential for your video and multimedia journalism projects? Sometimes a story comes from the videojournalist's own experience. Sometimes it comes from talking with other people. Story leads can grow out of news assignments. Following are some other possible sources for stories.

WHERE TO DISCOVER STORY IDEAS

Stories are all around you, but how do you get started? Watch for trends that might include shifts in the public's buying preferences, changes in lifestyles, or a technology revolution in an industry. For example, a news story about a new smart phone might result in a trend story that looks all the ways smart phones have changed how people communicate.

A trend doesn't start in one day; it occurs gradually over time. Gary Coronado, a staffer for the *Palm Beach Post*, read an opinion piece about the trend for Central American immigrants to jump on trains for a free ride to the United States. He filed the clipping and later pitched the story to his editor. His dramatic multimedia story is called "Train Jumping."

READ THE PAPER OR THE NEWS ONLINE

"Having worked at the same newspaper for 22 years," says Colin Mulvany, a multimedia producer at the *Spokesman-Review* in Spokane, Washington, "I feel pretty connected to my community. I know what is happening in my town. I know what people are talking about and this helps lead me to good stories.

"Many times at my newspaper, word editors would pitch stories about major community events. My approach is to think less about an event and more about the people at the event. Personalizing a big, sprawling story with compelling characters will make your video stories come alive.

"In order to find multimedia story possibilities, I troll the newspaper's lists of upcoming stories (a.k.a. story budget). The deciding factor on whether to commit to doing a video or

FIGURE 2.1 **Train Jumping.** From a newspaper story, the producer learned about the trend of Central American migrants hopping trains to reach the United States. (Photo by Gary Coronado/*Palm Beach Post*)

audio slideshow versus doing a still photo depends on two things: (1) is there a strong central character in the story and (2) is it visual? One without the other is usually a no-go.

"I'm always searching for that elusive emotional gem. When we package a daily video with a print story, I look for ways to tell the story a little differently than what the print reporter is doing. Instead of thinking broad, I think defined. That can mean focusing on just one or two subjects out of six the reporter might have talked to.

"Nearly all global stories have local impact," says Mulvany. "Nearly every small town has a soldier in the wars in Afghanistan or Iraq. Every rural county has families with unemployed parents due to the struggling economy.

"Reporting and producing stories like these to your local audience will help put global events into better perspective, and when you do so with a strong narrative and powerful characters, you can really draw in your audience and make a powerful connection with them."

Mulvany's advice on finding stories: "Find time every day to read and listen to news and information that you can use for story ideas in your work. Listen to NPR, read national and international publications like the *New York Times* and the *Wall*

Street Journal. Watch a variety of television news programs to stay informed. Write down your ideas and follow them up with research."

CRAIGSLIST, CLASSIFIED ADS, AND SOCIAL MEDIA

Today, online classifieds like Craigslist, and social media outlets like Facebook are exploding in popularity. We all know by now that social media is a handy tool for keeping up with friends and family, but that's not all its only use. It also allows us stay abreast of what's going on locally. Make use of your connections to people who are more in the know than you are. Participate in discussions. Check out those sites daily and maintain your connections by interacting. Social media sites make excellent sources for story ideas and subjects. You may find that an acquaintance is aware of a strawberry festival or a baton twirling contest, a beauty pageant or an important political gathering going on in your town. If you're always at the ready, you can quickly run out and cover it. Use tools like Facebook and Twitter to stay in touch. They might indeed lead you to some unexpectedly terrific stories.

ICU: Los Angeles Connections

Craigslist, the Internet's global classified website, can be a gold mine of story ideas. The *Los Angeles Times* produced an entire series of stories that were found in the "Missed Connections" section of Craigslist. In this section of the site, people describe a situation about how they almost met someone they had encountered. But, for a variety of reasons, they didn't get the opportunity to actually meet that person. The stories about these missed opportunities—called ICU, as in I See You—feature love, lust, loss, and intrigue and span the emotional spectrum from heartfelt to hilarious.

Videojournalist Katy Newton, the project's producer, came up with the idea. "I had a friend who was going to Trader Joe's for weeks at the same time hoping to see a guy again whom she hoped might be the perfect match for

FIGURE 2.2　**ICU: Los Angeles Connections.**

FIGURE 2.3　**ICU: Nice Guy I Hit with My Car.** The videojournalist found her subjects by searching the Missed Connections section of Craigslist. (Produced by Katy Newton)

her, based on the vegetables he was choosing," Newton explains. "I had never heard of Craigslist's Missed Connections, but when I checked it out the next day, my first reaction was that many listings in that section of Craigslist are real human interest stories. They contain drama, and they're all set up with engaging characters who have a pressing need they feel must be fulfilled."

The fact that all of these stories had built-in compelling narratives was just what Newton was looking for to apply to a regularly running series of online video stories.

After Newton came up with the idea and made a successful pitch to her editors, she began the process of weeding through hundreds of ads a week, getting up early each day to read the posts on Missed Connections. "Just by the way they wrote the ad," Newton says, "I could tell which ones would be good storytellers, and so I would email about a dozen people a day and hear back from a couple and narrow my choice down from there after talking on the phone."

"These narratives that unfold from Missed Connections have perfect built-in arcs," says Katy Newton. For example, one of Newton's stories is about a woman who hits a guy on a bike with her car.

First she sets up a normal day. A woman is driving in to get gas and then—wham!—she hits something or someone with her car. This moment creates speculation in the audience's mind. What or whom did she hit? Then, she inserts an amusing comment. The audience is taken quite by surprise when the woman says, "I thought I might have hit a baby." Then the truth is revealed. The driver has hit a man on a bike. One might expect the man to be angry or sustain a severe injury. The two characters might end up hating one another. Instead, Newton explains, the story has a twist. The guy isn't angry with the woman. Instead, he is worried about *her*. This comes as a welcome shock—not only to the woman, but also to the viewer. In a happy instant, the perpetrator, the woman has found the type of guy she has been looking for—someone who values the welfare of others before his own. Who wouldn't want to meet someone like that? Of course, the resolution of the story isn't that the couple lives happily ever after but that the main character finds the type of man she has been dreaming of meeting. The quirky part is that he disappears. Now, the young woman is left to wonder. She has no idea how to contact this man of her dreams again. Hence the original reason for her posting on Craigslist's Missed Connections.

So the story is set up with a need; there is a twist; the need is satisfied; and a problem is resolved. Newton explains that though each of the 52 stories produced in ICU that year were on different subjects, they all more or less followed this same arc.

Looking back, Newton tells us that the series was a success. Her audience wrote in frequently with positive feedback.

Obviously, the success of this series of stories was due to the fact that all people inherently want to connect and find love. Looking for love is a universal theme. So we can all empathize with the subjects' personal tales of missed connections.

Aside from Craigslist, make sure to check out blogs and websites on any and all topics you can think of. At this writing, there are over a 125 million blogs, 500 million Facebook users, and 255 million websites on the Internet. A search on Bing, Google, or Yahoo! on any subject that comes to mind will surely bring up a healthy list of story possibilities. You can research a topic internationally, nationally, or right in your own backyard. Learn from the experts how to hone in on your topics with more efficient searches.

Often you can even check facts for your story with a web search. Or you might be able to find contacts and potential subjects to interview that way. The Cision Survey found 89 percent of journalists turn to blogs for story research, 65 percent go to social networking sites such as Facebook and LinkedIn, 61 percent use Wikipedia, and 52 percent go to microblogging services such as Twitter.

BULLETIN BOARDS

Locating usable stories requires constant observation. Never walk past a bulletin board or utility pole covered in flyers again without at least scanning the notices. There is probably at least one story on every utility pole. Pick up neighborhood flyers and subscribe to email lists from clubs and organizations to find out what's going on. Often you can translate a group's activity into a lead for a genuinely compelling story.

LISTEN FOR OFFHAND COMMENTS

Take your eyes off your smart phone for a sec. Stories can be lurking in the environment through which you move every day. Stay awake and alert at all times in order to be ready for them.

Scott Strazzante, a photojournalist at the *Chicago Tribune*, says that his antennae are always up. "I find that while I'm shooting

FIGURE 2.4 **A Team Without a Home.** Scott Strazzante's path to find this story of a soccer team consisting of homeless players is a great example of finding for stories by keeping your ears, eyes, and—most important—your mind open. (Scott Strazzante, *Chicago Tribune*)

FIGURE 2.5 **Age of Uncertainty.** Sylvia Coleman lifts a cup of wine to help Hattie Brown take communion. The photographer suggested a feature story on this woman who assists her fellow church members. But a colleague encouraged him to think more broadly about what this lady did—caring for elderly people in general. (Photo by Josh Meltzer, *Roanoke Times*)

routine assignments, I'm simultaneously listening to people talking. I'm reading blurbs that are in every little neighborhood publication, forever fishing for ideas. In simple stories that my newspaper thinks are just a brief, I might find a great narrative angle to make a powerful audio slide-show from. I never discount even a passing idea."

For example, Strazzante was sent to a nearby community to make a portrait of a family living in a homeless shelter for a Christmas gift-giving story. The night manager of the shelter gave him a quick half-hour tour and Strazzante made his portraits. "On my way out, the manager said to me, 'Have you ever heard of homeless soccer? There's something called the Homeless Soccer World Cup, and there's no team in Illinois yet, but we're starting one here.' So of course my story lightbulb went off big time," Strazzante says.

Strazzante spent the next several months following the team from the Illinois shelter, shooting photos, recording audio interviews, and capturing ambient sound. He says it was a perfect narrative of a sports story. Would they succeed or would they fail? They trained and sweated and ran their legs off. Of course, there were ups and downs in their season, including many losses and even the death of an assistant coach. But the team members struggled on, all the while dealing with their own personal issues of homelessness.

CROSS THE TRACKS

To hunt down the best stories, do one thing everyday that makes you a little uncomfortable. Go to unfamiliar neighborhoods and attend meetings of groups that are completely new to you. When you go, hand out business cards. Sit down and chat with the folks present. Ask people what's been going on in their lives and communities.

> What is important to them now?
> What or who would make for an interesting story?
> What stories are the news media not covering in their lives?
> What are the local controversies?
> Who are the characters in the community?
> The standouts? The misfits? The community leaders?

"A Sunday morning without assignments led me to a small Baptist church that I had never been to," recalls this writer, who was working for the *Roanoke Times* at the time. "While there, I photographed a middle-aged woman who cared for a handful of elderly women during the service. Some of those women were widows, others had husbands with duties at the front of the church, and so the women had to sit alone."

"Sylvia Coleman helped the older women turn to the correct pages in the Bible. She told them when to stand and sit and when to drink their communion wine. Many of the elderly women suffered from Alzheimer's or dementia.

"The next week, while chatting with colleague Beth Macy, I suggested a feature story on this woman who helps her fellow church members. Macy encouraged me to think more broadly about what this lady did, about caring for the elderly. With a few weeks of brainstorming with our editors and experts on aging, we developed a plan for a nine-part series on people who voluntarily care for the elderly. The news peg was that our community in western Virginia was experiencing huge growth in its elderly population. This new demographic raised the question: 'Who will care for this rapidly growing population?'"

The photos and audio gathered at the church that morning never even made it into the final project. But they did become the spark for a series that personally and intimately related to members of the community who come from different backgrounds. The project, called "Age of Uncertainty," was made up of nine video stories, photo galleries, and interactive elements. And, accidentally, it was born out of a random Sunday morning foray to an unfamiliar church across the tracks from this writer's usual haunts.

LOCALIZE AND PERSONALIZE LARGE ISSUES OF THE DAY

Think of the biggest stories in the news going on right now. They might be playing out in Washington, D.C., and appearing on national news, or perhaps they are unfolding in the largest immigrant communities. But no matter where they are occurring, chances are they are affecting people who live in your community or town.

FIGURE 2.6 **A Locksmith's Tale and Other Health Care Stories.** To tell the complicated story of health care for NPR Online, Krulwich and Hoffman zeroed in on the personal tales of a few individuals. (Robert Krulwich and Will Hoffman, NPR Online)

The health care reform debate filled the news for endless weeks. Most of the video reports on television focused on town hall meetings and congressional debates, both important events related to the issue. Robert Krulwich produced "Four Stories on Health Care" for National Public Radio Online (the NPR website also features multimedia and video stories) that put faces on the news and presented four unique different viewpoints and situations of real Americans who will be affected by health care reform.

In one story, a locksmith reveals that he has never needed health insurance and doesn't want it. In another story, a man is thankful that he had insurance after a near-death accident at his home.

These unique stories of different individuals do keep the audience centered on the large issues of health care and insurance. But they go further by presenting personal stories that help the audience to better identify with the broader issues. Furthermore, because the audience experiences these stories through single characters, there is a better chance viewers will be engaged and the stories absorbed in their entirety.

STORIES ABOUT THE PAST

Telling a complete story about the past using still pictures only, though certainly not impossible, can be a challenge. However, using multimedia complete with interviews, graphics or archival footage makes the job of recounting a tale about the past much more manageable. Writers have always loved to tell narrative stories about the past. But photographers often struggled with what they should photograph when a story had already happened. Now, with unlimited access to the tools of multimedia, the subjects of our videos can take an audience back in time just as writers do for the written word.

Ben Montgomery, Waveney Ann Moore, and photographer Edmund Fountain from the *St. Petersburg Times* produced a story called "For Their Own Good" about the abuse suffered 50 years earlier at the Florida School for Boys. The men tell haunting stories of abuse and punishment and the lingering effects of that trauma.

Portraits of the men and landscapes of the now-abandoned school accompany the powerful video interviews.

FIGURE 2.7 **For Their Own Good.** A story about the past will require creative visuals because documenting the story with video is often no longer possible. Portraits, landscapes, and still-life photography as well as other creative visual approaches will help to cover a strong audio story. (Ben Montgomery, Waveney Ann Moore, and photographer Edmund Fountain/*St. Petersburg Times*)

LONG-TERM PROJECTS

In 2003, Chad Stevens, now an assistant professor at University of North Carolina at Chapel Hill, traveled with students from Western Kentucky University for a spring break workshop (the Appalachian Cultural Project) to the Eastern Kentucky town of Whitesburg, deep in the heart of coal mining country. While working there with a few dozen students, he first learned of a mining process called mountaintop removal, in which coal companies blast the tops off mountains to extract coal without having to mine underground. "I had grown up in Kentucky and had never heard of the practice," Stevens says, "but when we went to see it first hand, I was changed forever." Stevens had read a book called *Lost Mountain.* That book became the source for his master's thesis at Ohio University. Stevens says, "The genesis of

FIGURE 2.8 **A Thousand Little Cuts.** In one of the more extreme acts of civil disobedience on Kayford Mountain, an activist poses as a crucified Jesus on the edge of the Arch Coal mountaintop removal coal mine.

The first nonviolent protest on Coal River Mountain brought attention to the campaign to build a wind farm. Five protesters, including Rory McIlmoil, left, and Matt Noerpel, chain themselves to an excavator on a mountaintop removal preparation site. Chad Stevens, the photographer, has been working on the project for more than seven years. (Photos by Chad Stevens)

the project was to do a visual version of this book with still images only, which would symbolize the transition of a mountain through this drastic process."

That initial spark has now spanned into a seven-year (and counting) project that evolved into a film project that Stevens continues to shoot to this day.

While shooting, Stevens has simultaneously been raising funds intensely. There are many grants available to photographers and filmmakers, some more competitive and lucrative than others. Stevens has won a few and lost others. But, along the way, a few freelance licensing projects have come his way. He never expected these lucky breaks, he says, which have fortunately helped to fund his project.

"I've licensed blast footage to a broad spectrum from Al Jazeera to the BBC and most recently Spike Lee's film *If God Is Willing and Da Creek Don't Rise*," he says. "Without foreseeing or even trying, I became the go-to person for mountaintop removal footage."

Though Stevens considers that the risk of taking on a long-term personal project is personally and financially daunting, he feels strongly that "there is something in the universe that helps us when we risk. Risk is usually rewarded in one way or another."

Some of the most important and influential photographic and documentary projects have emerged from personal interests. These kinds of projects are neither easy nor cheap. But if you can find a steady support network for both financial sponsorship and editing assistance, you can pursue issues that are important to you. Your conviction and enthusiasm for your own personal subjects will often be reflected in a highly successful result.

KEEP A JOURNAL

Richard Koci Hernandez, former multimedia journalist at the *San Jose Mercury News*, has volumes of journals that he uses to take notes, record inspirations and thoughts, and make sketches and plans for future and ongoing projects. "If you really study some of the most creative artists and storytellers and writers or musicians, many of them have kept meticulous journals—everyone from Edison to Picasso—all at different levels and in different styles, but it's been critical to their success, and I've found that to be true for me, too," Hernandez says.

"Keep the journal with you all the time," he says. "You've got to be disciplined to write in it regularly. Even while I was working for the *San Jose Mercury News*, I would drive down a street a hundred times and all of a sudden I would see a store or a person and something would hit me on that 101st time for a potential story or a type font that I liked in my next project, and if I hadn't had the means and the notion to jot it down, I would've forgotten it. Now, more than ever, it's important to 'journal' because we're so inundated with info on the Web."

Hernandez says he finds his journals most useful when suffering from a creative block in editing. "I'll just pull out my journals to remind me of ideas and—boom!—problem solved. All this stuff we think we'll remember will inevitably slip through the cracks under the pressures of daily life."

Hernandez also uses the Internet to find inspiration. "In addition to a small physical journal you can use social networking, bookmarks and RSS (real simple syndication) feeds to keep up with and share work that inspires you," he says. "Google Reader is a great way to subscribe to blogs and websites that you want to keep in touch with. I visit

FIGURE 2.9 **Journal.** Richard Koci Hernandez's journal of ideas that he kept when he worked for the *San Jose Mercury News*.

STORY-FINDING TIPS FROM REPORTER BETH MACY

When the *Roanoke Times* ace reporter Beth Macy thinks she might be onto a good issue story, she often meets an expert for coffee to feel out the story and to start gathering a list of potential subjects and a plan of action. Macy is always on the prowl for ideas, pulling out her calendar as she browses bulletin boards or has a conversation with a public relations representative from a relevant organization. A friendly meeting in person over coffee or tea will often yield Macy more contacts, names and numbers for a variety of stories than she could ever hoped to have gotten over the phone. "When you're genuinely curious about the world, there isn't a topic that, with the right amount of probing and tweaking, can't make a great story," Macy says.

Macy's story-finding tips:

- **Be nosy.** Sniffing out a good story is like being paid to get a graduate degree in stuff you're interested in.

- **Get out of the office.**

- **Public relations representatives** can actually be great sources, if you prod them enough.

- **Pay attention to your own life.** Do other people experience the things that are going on with you?

- **Reserve judgment.** Don't knock down an idea before you give it a chance to mature a bit.

- **Be alert.** It's the old boyfriend theory. The only time you find a boyfriend is when you're not looking for one.

- **Read** the walls—bulletin boards, ads, and posters for upcoming events.

- **Listen to what your friends** are talking about; eavesdrop on strangers.

- **Collaborate.** Find reporters, photographers, producers, and/or editors you like to work with, can collaborate with and trust.

- **Trust your gut.** If I find myself talking to my husband about someone, or find myself ruminating about something, there just might be a story there.

- **Read** and take copious notes.

my Google reader list most mornings to see what's new when looking for inspiration. Furthermore, use Facebook, Twitter, and multimedia sites like **vimeo.com** to follow the work of artists and journalists you admire."

FINDING SUBJECTS

The subjects in a story are often dictated by the nature of the piece. Some stories are about a particular person or family, whereas others are about an issue for which you will choose topics that exemplify the issue you are focusing on. The themes that you choose must draw the audience into the story and make them feel a part of it for the entire time. You don't want viewers to feel like mere observers—outsiders looking in. If you can hunt down truly engaging subject matter, you'll have a better chance of creating an excellent piece of work.

THREE NECESSARY KEYS BEFORE SELECTING A SUBJECT

Pamela Chen, a senior communications coordinator in photography and multimedia at the Open Society Foundations says, "Often, we encounter the story of a person whose life journey encapsulates the metaphor for the bigger picture issue. But in order to produce a multimedia story, we need to know:

- **First,** is this person actively engaged on the issue and doing work that is visually dynamic?
- **Second,** do we have the access necessary to record this action? Is the person willing to show their face and record their voice for the camera?
- **Third,** will they allow someone to follow them around in their daily life for an extended period of time?

"These questions are about action, access, and time. They are all three key to the eventual outcome. If this trio of crucial criteria cannot be met, then we must seek another way to tell the story."

CHAT WITH YOUR POTENTIAL SUBJECT

While preparing to shoot a video story at an event, Evelio Contreras, a video photographer at the *Washington Post*, says he'll often casually chat with people at the event before shooting. This accomplishes two things. First, it allows him to understand the story better, and second, he can hold informal pre-interviews to determine whom he might want to interview for the piece he is about to shoot.

"I never go where I'm expected or assigned to go. I don't want to be where the main story is, but rather I choose to be on the sidelines. The main story is very often over-populated with people who aren't looking for stories but rather sound bites. They are not looking for a dialogue or a conversation.

"I'm looking to have a conversation with someone so that I can hang out with them ... so that they'll be loose and relaxed and be themselves. I want to be able to hear someone sound as if they actually want to be talking to me."

Contreras says he looks for people who are quirky or have something different about them. If they make a lot of hand gestures, he says, he'll see that as a sign of someone who might be a character in the story. "I'm looking for passion in their eyes."

Contreras tries to establish himself as a documenter up front so that he can start a one-on-one conversation as soon as possible. He says, "I'm not interested in a hodge-podge of voices. I see that as overload to the audience. And it can often be a gimmick. I feel that interaction with one character at a time is more deliberate storytelling. You really have to suss out the tale you want to tell ahead of time."

SEARCHING FOR GREAT CHARACTERS

Tim Broekema, a professor at Western Kentucky University, says, "You can't sit at your desk and speculate: 'Hmmmh. I wonder where that character might be lurking.' Captivating characters appear to you when you're out in the field asking questions. Allow characters to come and go in and out of your life until you find the just right one. Too many beginning videographers get stuck. They settle for a character they think is 'good enough.' But 'good enough' isn't going to cut it. The chances of finding a great speaker who is also visually pertinent to your topic are few. Characters who grab and hold the viewers' attention are pivotal. So the process of character search is vitally important. Magnetic characters are just plain gifts from God."

Leads from Public Radio International (PRI) and National Public Radio (NPR)

In *This American Life*'s "Going Down in History" video story for Public Radio International's (PRI's) website, Ira Glass and his visual reporting team attend a high school portrait day to talk about how a single image taken that day for the yearbook—a photo which really doesn't represent much of anything about you—is the image that becomes your permanent historical record. In this story, Ira Glass shows the audience dozens of high school yearbook portraits. He then selects a half a dozen students to interview about this odd situation. At the portrait day for class pictures, Glass gets students to open up while reflecting on the idea of the permanent portrait captured their yearbook. The students discuss boyfriends, gossip, and what they regret doing in their past. They are fantastic subjects and they certainly weren't picked at random. They're all great talkers. They aren't shy and they obviously enjoy elaborating on Glass's comments and questions.

Many excellent examples of character-told pieces can be heard on National Public Radio's (NPR) weekly feature *StoryCorps*. *StoryCorps* actually is a nonprofit devoted to recording people's stories of their lives. The group uses a radio booth housed in an Airstream trailer that travels about the country and invites volunteers to interview a friend or chat with a relative or simply to recount a personal story.

For more well produced stories on radio, check out *This American Life* and *Radiolab*.

LOOK FOR AN EXTROVERT

On the topic of finding a subject, Darren Durlach from station WBFF-TV in Baltimore observes, "Hopefully a great character is someone who is dynamic, open, and unafraid to say what they think. Viewers generally care more about those extroverted types. Of course everyone we talk to each day is different. But I have learned to use my gut to look for 'real' people. The more sincere they are about what they say, the more their message shines out through the television screen. I just jump right in and ask almost everyone who walks by a question or two off camera to put out feelers or lead me in the right direction. Oh ... and we always try to avoid making leading characters out of public information officers or stiff people in suits because that usually takes us out of the realm of sincerity."

In Marlo Poras's full-length film "Run Granny Run," the lead character, Doris Haddock, speaks eloquently about her motivations to run for U.S. senator of Vermont in her mid-90s.

She takes the audience through her entire range of emotions throughout the story, and is open, well spoken, and often very funny as she attempts to break many stereotypes of the modern-day politician.

Characters who are the most "interviewable" are not camera-shy. They even like the camera. They speak clearly and with appealing detail about their experiences. Additionally, you will find that the more interviewable people are, the more they will offer when you ask questions. It's almost as if they can sense what you're looking for.

There is a category of people who are overinterviewed. Their message often sounds a bit memorized, like a sound bite. Politicians and public figures often fall into this category. If you're faced with interviewing such a person, plan ahead and ask unusual questions—questions that won't elicit a sound-bite response. Hark back to 90-year-old politician Doris "Granny D" Haddock. That feisty woman politician certainly does not fall into your typical sound-bite category.

FIGURE 2.10 **Run Granny Run.** Doris Haddock, in her mid-90s, a true character, explains her motivations to run for U.S. senator of Vermont. (Film by Marlo Poras)

EVALUATING THE STORY'S POTENTIAL

All stories, regardless of the medium, should consider the following: strong characters, narrative tension, a take-away point to remember, strong visual impact, emotional engagement, broad appeal, narrow focus, cooperative subjects, and a reasonable deadline. It wouldn't be a bad idea to answer these questions: what does the story say about the human condition? Will it be a visually exciting story? Will the story have broad audience appeal? What emotions does this particular story tap into in order to engage your viewers?

STRONG CHARACTERS?

Strong characters in your online stories are like the friend that everyone wants to hang out with. They are funny, compelling, and interesting to listen to. They entertain us, enlighten us, and keep the focus on their story.

We have seen all kinds of stories covering the wars in Iraq and Afghanistan, from battlefield action to recovery, families at home, and even analyses of money spent during the war.

FIGURE 2.11 Ian Fisher: American Soldier.

FIGURE 2.12 Ian Fisher cradles his injured elbow during processing into the Army at Fort Benning, Georgia. Though he later has a change of heart, he sees a possibility only two days after arriving, to escape enlistment. From his first day in fatigues through his days driving a Humvee in Iraq, military life often doesn't mesh with his expectations. Sometimes the structure of the Army and the demands of training for war clash with the freedom he shared with his outside friends. (Photos by Craig Walker, *The Denver Post*)

FIGURE 2.13 Ian braces for his crossed-rifles pin, signifying his completion of training. Drill sergeant Eldridge holds the pin in place and prepares to secure it with a fist. "I hit him square on the chest," Eldridge says. "He had two holes, and blood dripping down from each—'blood rifles.'" A sergeant closes the ceremony: "You are now the guardian of freedom and the American way of life! A warrior!"

FIGURE 2.14 As his team prepares to secure a room during a training drill, Ian is the first man in a four-man stack. Echo Company is deep into three days of urban-combat exercises. Drill sergeant Tommy Beauchamp has a lot of experience to share: he served one tour of duty in Afghanistan and two in Iraq.

Craig Walker's Pulitzer Prize–winning story "Ian Fisher: American Soldier," for the *Denver Post*, contains all of these elements, including a strong lead character. In a ten-part video story, we follow the path of an average U.S. soldier, Ian Fisher, as he signs up for the military, trains, heads to battle, and returns. The narrative is powerful, with honest interviews with Fisher and his mother and father throughout the piece.

The story arc for Walker's piece is classic. It's chronological and follows Fisher through a major change in his life with twists and turns, ups and downs, and a variety of small setbacks and successes that keep the audience's attention. Furthermore, this story is playing out in every town and city in America where soldiers have been sent abroad to war, so it helps to explain who these soldiers are and what their individual stories might be, by telling it through the eyes of one soldier.

FIGURE 2.15   Ian shows his frustration during a counseling session with Sgt. 1st Class Joshua Weisensel. For the second time, Ian returned late from a weekend home. Now he has turned himself in for a drug problem. In the days to follow, Ian's failure to cooperate puts him in danger of getting kicked out of the Army. Instead, the commander assigns him to a new platoon and drops him in rank. It's a demotion. But it is a fresh start.

FIGURE 2.16   Three days after Ian's return from Iraq, he and Devin apply for a marriage license. The couple are married an hour later in a quiet courtroom. Driving away, Ian turns down the music. "Ya know, everyone gets counseled in Iraq that life is not going to be like your fantasy when you get back home," he says. "Well, I'm checking this off my fantasy list."

Walker begins the story as Fisher graduates from high school and follows him for 27 months through his return. And Fisher is a perfect character. Completely open and compelling, he offers insight into his situation and serves as one representative for the more than 100,000 soldiers serving in Iraq. The narrative has ups and downs and twists and turns that serve to keep an audience hooked, wanting to know what happens to the young unsung hero soldier.

Finally, Ian's story has relevance to current events, is reflective of how Fisher feels about being at war, why he joins and how it is to return. This impactful piece puts a face on a large issue in what is probably the biggest story in this period of American history. It is a personal and intimate look at one of the most important stories of the decade.

NARRATIVE TENSION?

Michael Nichols and J. Michael Fay's story "Ivory Wars," featured on MediaStorm, is the story of efforts to protect elephants, often hunted for their ivory tusks, both inside and outside of national parks in Chad. Though the issue of poaching certainly is important on its own, it still needs a narrative thread to which audiences can attach themselves. The filmmakers and producers found a narrative thread within the general report on a national park. They zeroed in on one elephant named Annie whom the researchers collared to track as she moved both in and outside of the park.

Now their story, which is still about the issue of poaching and protection of natural resources, contained a chase that followed both the researchers tracking Annie's every move and the poachers who aim to kill her just as she exits the safety of the Zakouma National Park's boundary. Annie wanders here, and the

FIGURE 2.17 **Ivory Wars: Last Stand in Zakouma.** A story with narrative tension about poaching. (Photos by Michael Nichols)

tension builds. Then she goes there, and the action grows even more compelling as she continues to move throughout the region in search of water. Finally, we learn that Annie has been shot by poachers.

The tension, not knowing what will happen to Annie, is precisely what keeps an audience's attention. The narrative tension that the storytellers create and build upon as the story progresses is the kind of vehicle that carries an audience through a piece.

COOPERATIVE SUBJECT?

One of the obstacles that can make or break a story is whether your subjects are in tune with your need to finish the story. This is one obstacle you must work out early. Your characters may simply see you as a photographer who wants to take a portrait and be done with it. But in fact, you have plans to hang around with them for the long term. You want to do several interviews and organize multiple follow-up visits. Have a conversation with the people you are filming early on in the reporting process so that they fully understand what might be expected of them during their participation.

Similarly, you should have a conversation about the depth to which you want your story to go. This is a delicate area, so you must tread lightly to avoid causing the subjects to think you are intrusive, which could ruin your chances for developing a more in-depth story. The message is: don't scare away your subjects.

Sonya Hebert from the *Dallas Morning News* produced a profoundly somber, emotional story about a couple that loses an infant son to a rare birth defect. Hebert gained the trust of the family, who allowed her to remain with them, video camera rolling, while their son actually dies. Photographing the moment of death indicates that a high level of trust has been established with family members.

There exists a delicate balance between scaring your subjects away by having them commit to giving their all from Day 1 and being utterly honest about what kind of commitment you need from them in order to satisfactorily report the story. Bob Sacha, a multimedia producer, photographer, filmmaker, and teacher whom we mentioned earlier, says he likes to be frank pretty early on in the reporting process. "I'll tell my subjects, 'I want to tell your story accurately, so I want to spend as much time here as I can.' I want the experience to be a pleasant and positive one for the people. Basically, it's all about building a good relationship with them. You don't want to be a colossal pain in the neck. But you don't want to waste time and go nowhere either."

Sacha says he frequently has to be persistent to get his subjects to be fully participatory. "When you show up more than once, the people may be impressed by your level of commitment to telling their story well. By the third, fourth or fifth time you visit them, they will be comfortable with and even flattered by your dedication to their story. Such proof of your dedication will often open the final door to the degree of intimacy you've been waiting for."

Dai Sugano, a multimedia journalist at the *San Jose Mercury News,* agrees. "It's all about maintaining a relationship," he says. "When a person sees that you are consistent and committed to the story, they tend be more accepting of your presence. You know you are in a good position when the subject stops asking, 'Why are you taking that picture?' If you have established good rapport, the people may even begin to contact you about upcoming events in their lives. This obviously precludes your having to constantly ask them probing questions.

"There is no magical way for you to know what people are thinking, especially when you first meet them," says Sugano. "It's really not a bad idea to put in the extra time to fully

FIGURE 2.18 T.K. Laux feels for Thomas's heartbeat during one of the many recurring episodes of silence followed by gasps. "We love you, big boy. Please go home," Laux kept saying. "Thank you, Thomas. Please go." "Just let him do it his way," Deidrea said with a sigh. Again, Thomas gasped after ten minutes of silence. "There's nothing we can do."

FIGURE 2.19 "Choosing Thomas" Deidrea Laux sits on her bathroom floor holding Thomas before making a plaster mold of his hands and bathing and dressing him for the last time. "I got to feel what it's like to be a mom. It was good, Thomas. Thank you. I needed you," Deidrea said to her baby. The video-journalist was able to capture this very intimate moment in a couple's life. (Photos by Sonya Hebert, *Dallas Morning News*)

explain what it takes for you to tell the story well. Don't be afraid to inform them that things might not always go as smoothly as you both hope at the outset.

"When you are making a documentary, you can't really predict what's going to happen next. Things have a way of just happening. And you simply don't have time to ask for permission when they happen—one more reason why it is so important to explain the ground rules early on. If not, later on you could find yourself in a situation where the person you're filming thinks you have crossed a line and are being intrusive or rude. Of course, you can always explain afterward why you needed to photograph the subject in a sensitive moment, but if the person knows ahead of time that you might eventually tread on some delicate territory or other, they will be more likely to allow for those awkward moments without resistance."

Sugano shot and produced a story called "Torn Apart," which chronicles the story of a family of immigrant parents and American-born children who are faced with the parents' deportation. He followed the family for close to a year. "I photographed many stressful situations, including an occasion where an eldest daughter was emotionally overwhelmed. I took the trouble to later explain to her why I had photographed her crying. That way, she better understood why the picture was so important as it showed the pain she felt over being forcibly separated from her father," Sugano says.

FIGURE 2.20 **Torn Apart.** Immigrant parents and American-born children face the possibility of the parents' deportation. This story took the videographer a year to complete. He explained the photographic process to the family before he started so they would accept him over the course of the saga. (Dai Sugano, *San Jose Mercury News*)

FIGURE 2.21 **Take Care.** The producer was first attracted by Virginia Gandee's brilliant red hair and dozen tattoos—but then went deeper. Inside Gandee's family's Staten Island trailer, she cares for her grandfather. (Photography and video by Gillian Laub, MediaStorm)

He adds, "It is important that the people understand what they are agreeing to when they give you permission to follow their journey. Otherwise, major misunderstandings can occur later, which can completely derail the story. That said, you may not want to go into extravagant detail or push for definitive ground rules in the beginning as when it works well, the process of filming peoples' lives quite naturally evolves as the gradual building of a trusting relationship."

A TAKE-AWAY MOMENT?

Once we have good characters and a sufficient narrative to keep our audience interested, a story should also have a take-away message. Perhaps there is a lesson or moral to the story, or maybe it just teaches us something we didn't know enough about. Maybe it serves to make us laugh or cry, but every story must have a purpose to it that will linger after the viewer absorbs the last picture.

MORE THAN STRONG VISUAL IMPACT?

The story is the most important part of a video or multimedia project. Without it, you have nothing. That said, we work in a visual medium, and your project should also have strong visual impact. Strong visuals on their own can't carry a multimedia story, but they most certainly will raise the level of its quality.

Eric Maierson, a producer for MediaStorm, says that sometimes the initial attraction to a story might be purely visual. "There are people who create interesting visuals," says Maierson, "and that's their thing and there's nothing wrong with that. But if you're a journalist, you need more than just interesting visuals. You must have a story."

A story that Maierson helped produce called "Take Care" was discovered by photographer Gillian Laub, who had noticed the story's main subject, Virginia Gandee, a 22-year-old woman covered in tattoos, waiting for the subway. The initial attraction to her came out of a purely visual interest. But the story that Laub discovered about the tattooed woman was that Gandee was not only a single mother, but she was also the caretaker for her dying grandfather.

"That is what's compelling about the story," says Maierson. "In addition to having great visual potential, a good story must have a narrative that an audience can connect with. Furthermore there is great contradiction in this piece. Gandee is a hard-rocking woman with tattoos, yet she cares for her grandpa," says Maierson. "That contrast shocks the hell out of your audience."

A story that has visual potential refers to the idea that at least part of the story is going to unfold in front of you and you will have enough opportunities to show rather than tell that story to your audience. With this approach, one is thinking like a still photographer. Other times, as in the story "Take Care," you might feel that your subject has a look about him or her that catches your fancy. That initial curiosity might lead you to find a terrific story. As storytellers, we must be perpetually on the lookout for opportunities to record real moments that we can bear witness to with our cameras and microphones.

Every story you do will fall somewhere along a continuum of either great visual potential or strong narrative potential, so logically part of your decision-making process has to be to make a choice about where you want to and are actually able to take the story. Many stories that seem to have little visual or narrative potential on paper can end up becoming great storytelling opportunities. This is due in large part to the thought process of the photographer or storyteller. Think about all of the options you have before writing a story off. There is no one way to tell a story.

CAN YOU CAPTURE REVEALING MOMENTS?

While a graduate student at Ohio University, Yanina Manolova produced a series of video stories on women living in the Appalachian region of Ohio—women who struggle with recovery from substance abuse and domestic abuse within their homes. She tracks the women every step of the way, following them through treatment, visits to prison and even during violent encounters in their own homes.

Simply interviewing the women about what had happened in the past would certainly have been powerful, but Manolova realized that whenever she could *show* rather than *tell*

FIGURE 2.22   Stephanie, 19, cries on her mother's shoulder after graduating from the Rural Women's Recovery Program. Due to drug charges that resulted in the loss of her two children, her probation officer ordered her to attend the substance abuse program. She started using drugs when she was with her ex-boyfriend, Carroll, the father of her daughter. "He beat me all the time, choked me, shouted at me, put a knife to my throat. I felt like shit. That's why I used—so that I could hide my feelings. I started out with lower doses of Vicodin and Percocet, then I went to Oxycontin and heroin," Stephanie says.

FIGURE 2.23 **Neverland: A Short Film.** Patricia, 27, smokes crack in Mansfield, Ohio. She graduated from the Rural Women's Recovery Program in the spring of 2009 but relapsed in June of that year. Sexually abused at age 14 by a middle-aged man, her father's best friend, she has been using alcohol and drugs (marijuana, crack, cocaine, oxycodone, and morphine) since. "I got pregnant with my daughter by a drug dealer, and I went for treatment for about nine months while I was pregnant. He is in prison and has never seen his child," Patricia reveals. (Photography by Yanina Manolova)

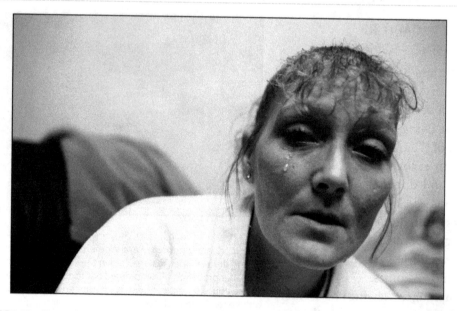

FIGURE 2.24 Deanna, 33, cries in her temporary housing provided by the Salvation Army Shelter in Newark, Ohio. She has been physically abused by her husband. Deanna lost custody of her son and although she completed a substance abuse treatment program, she could not stop abusing alcohol. She is on the waiting list for another substance abuse treatment program.

FIGURE 2.25 Clients of the Rural Women's Recovery Program practice yoga.

FIGURE 2.26 Jessica, 27, talks on the phone with her boyfriend during her relapse after having seven months of sobriety. She was abusing drugs and alcohol. She has survived several abusive relationships and has had five children from three different men and has lost custody of all of them. Jessica went for treatment at the Rural Women's Recovery Program.

FIGURE 2.27 Destiny, 4, poses in her stepfather's car in Mansfield, Ohio. Her biological father was a drug dealer and was recently released from prison. She has never seen him. Her mother, Patricia, went through substance abuse treatment and graduated. She relapsed and went back on the streets again. Destiny lives with her grandparents in Mansfield, Ohio. "Why mommy keeps leaving me? She promised she will never leave me again," Destiny asks.

FIGURE 2.28 Deanna, 33, left, cries following a visit from her husband and son at the Rural Women's Recovery Program, where she has been for two weeks. Her mother was an alcoholic, as are many of her family members. "I would get up and start drinking. Every single day. I will drink until I pass out," Deanna says. Lisa, 44, right, is sad after her boyfriend's visit at the Rural Women's Recovery Program. Another alcohol abuser, she has been part of the program for two weeks. Lisa was sexually abused by her father at age six; her husband, a drug addict, sexually abused her as well, and she has three children by him, all of whom are drug addicts. "After I left their dad, the kids left me. Then I started drinking a lot more," Lisa says. Hannah, 29, far left, talks to her mother, far right, during their family visit. Her alcohol problems began when she was fifteen. As a child, she was abused by her father.

the women's stories, the impact was tenfold. To tell their stories, she needed to actually document what was going on, including the drug use, the domestic violence and even sticky family situations.

EMOTIONAL ENGAGEMENT?

You are well advised to use emotion in your story. Does your story explore feelings such as humor, grief, passion, or rage (to name a few)? Though not everyone will think the same things are funny or sad or inspiring, there are certain types of characters and stories to which the majority of people will react strongly.

FIGURE 2.29 **Hammoudi.** (Directed by Anwar Saab, produced by Tima Khalil)

In Anwar Saab and Tima Khalil's story, "Hammoudi," the audience listens to the very frank voice of 12-year-old Mohammad Hajj Mousa, who lost both legs to a military bomb while living in a Palestinian refugee camp. His blunt and honest discussion of attempted suicide and depression, mixed with his look at his own friendships and family, are topics of mutual interest to a wide audience.

We as an audience have great compassion for this child, and the storytellers, through Mousa, have tugged on a variety of powerful emotions to keep us hooked.

BROAD APPEAL OR NICHE AUDIENCE?

If your story has broad appeal to wide group of people of different ages, ethnic backgrounds, and economic levels, you'll have the best chance of drawing in a large audience. The broader the appeal, the more people from varied backgrounds will have an interest in your work. You can't expect absolutely everyone to be interested; but as part of deciding whether to pursue a topic, you have to examine whether you think a large enough audience will be attracted and engaged in your story.

Are you hoping for wide appeal, or are you producing for a smaller niche audience? If you intend your audience to be small, you may want to include more pertinent details that would appeal to such an audience. If your intention is to reach a more vast audience, you will have to think carefully about the details and depth you put into the project and decide whether the subject will be more universally appealing.

High Click Rate

MediaStorm founder Brian Storm observes, "You want to do one of two things to successfully market your work and get it seen by a large audience. You either want cats spinning on a fan—something short and funny that gets 50 million hits on You Tube—or you want to produce the greatest series ever done on Darfur, for example. What you don't want to be is the noise in the middle."

Part of MediaStorm's success in terms of the numbers of people watching the stories there, Storm says, is due to the viral nature of the site's following. "We want people to see these stories and be so moved that the first thing they do is repost them on Facebook or Twitter. One person can create a huge trail of viral activity. But it won't happen for stories that don't move your audience in some emotional way."

IS YOUR FOCUS NARROW ENOUGH?

Don't attend events and merely cover them in a general fashion, stopping by here and there to shoot and interview a little bit of everything. Find a focus first. And stick to it!

In the *Time.com* story "Sudoku Master," producer Jacob Templin covers the Sudoku championships. Rather than feature everything going on at the event—clearly a visually rich environment with plenty of interesting characters—Templin focuses on two players, both former champions and good friends, as they compete in the weekend tournament.

FIGURE 2.30 **Sudoku Master.** Templin zeroed in just two players to tell the story of the Sudoku contest. (Produced by Jacob Templin)

Their friendship, partnered with their competition, helps provide a focus on what could have been a banal story about this event. Again, zeroing in on the human interest within a general subject often makes the story sing.

REASONABLE DEADLINE?

Many stories are produced in a few hours on strict deadlines; others take years or even decades to finish. How will your story fit into your schedule? Often, many editors do not understand the gobs of time it takes to both shoot and edit even a short piece. It takes even longer if you're a little green and inexperienced. Shooting low-quality stories is easy and quick. Making great ones is usually not so simple or rapid. So be wise and plan ahead. Calculate in advance how long the entire process will take you.

Director and producer Taggart Siegel shot "The Real Dirt on Farmer John," a full-length documentary, over several decades. He began photographing a college classmate in the 1980s and continued until he felt the story was complete. He documented several major transformations in his lead character's life. He followed him throughout the economic farm crisis of the 1980s. He documented his battles with local residents over his perceived lifestyle. And, finally, he brought to light the man's success at building up a large community-supported agriculture farm that now supports many families in the Chicago area.

FIGURE 2.31 **The Real Dirt on Farmer John.** The documentary took several decades to create. (Produced by Taggart Siegel)

Sometimes, as happened to Taggart Siegel, you can't put an end date on a story because you don't know when or how it will finish. As it turns out, this type of long-term story is very compelling to an audience. They watch the lives of the characters unfold in much the same way and at the same cadence the documentary maker did while producing the story.

Of course, we do not all have the luxury of following a subject over many decades. Most of us live in a world of deadlines. All the more reason to figure out the amount of time you'll need and discuss it with your editor so you both agree on a time frame. Many beginning video storytellers with too little experience in the medium make the mistake of underestimating the time they'll need to finish a story. They end up rushing or racing into the office at the last minute panting and pleading for more time. Remember that turning out high-quality storytelling in these media takes lots of concentrated application and oodles of time.

FIGURE 2.32 Alvin Stamper, 26, defends his title as the tobacco cutting champion at the Garrard County Tobacco Cutting Competition. Contests make good topics for multimedia and videos because they have a natural story arc built in. (Photo by David Stephenson/ZUMA Press)

CHAPTER 3

Preproduction Planning

Paul Fornelli

With a solid foundation of collaboration and story evaluation in place, it's now time to focus attention on the nuts and bolts of bringing the actual production to life. The most popular production strategy is an approach built on a three-step model, in which each step, or stage, acts as a prime structural building block within the overall production. Although there is some variance between production models, these three main stages are most commonly referred to as the **preproduction stage**, **production stage**, and **postproduction stage**. In the ensuing chapters, we will examine each of these production stages in detail, breaking down the tasks required at each stage, while providing deeper insight into the skill sets of the crews performing this work.

Let's begin in this chapter by dissecting the first of the three production steps: **preproduction**. The main purpose of preproduction is to plan out the logistics of a given production and calculate production costs, budgets, the length of a shooting schedule, and the project's likely success with a viewing audience. Once all of these factors have been weighed, a reasonable evaluation can be made determining the production's actual long-term viability. If the commitment is made to move forward on a given project, a score of duties and responsibilities will ultimately need to be resolved during the preproduction stage.

Before that work can begin, it is important that the driving force behind the project, usually the executive producer, understand that digital media production, above all else, is a business. It is expensive to produce quality storytelling, regardless of whether that storytelling comes packaged as a feature film, TV show, viral video, instructional how-to, or trade show promotional video. As important as creativity and artistic freedom are, the creative desire must be balanced by the realization that unless a production is being self-financed, there will always be expectations on the artist to deliver a viable product—preferably on time and under budget.

This dilemma is sometimes referred to as the "paradox of the production triangle." The origin of the **production triangle** model is uncertain, although it has been used in production management since at least the mid-1950s (Atkinsson, 1999). The production triangle model recognizes three basic, fundamental constraints involved within a production: (1) the artistic urge to produce a creative work of high quality, (2) the amount of money available to fully realize that creative vision, and (3) the amount of time required to complete that work

FIGURE 3.1 The three components of the production triangle are quality (how good is the idea/ property?), money (how cheap can it be made?), and time (how fast can it be made?).

properly. Put more succinctly, the quality of any work is constrained by the production's budget and timeline:

- Quality: How good is the idea/property?
- Money: How cheap is it to make?
- Time: How fast can it be made?

Unfortunately, the paradox that comes into play with the production triangle concerns the fact that while all three of these factors are crucial to a production, only two of the goals can be achieved simultaneously, leaving the third objective to be perennially subject to sacrifice. Expressed more colloquially:

- GOOD service CHEAP won't be FAST.
- GOOD service FAST won't be CHEAP.
- FAST service CHEAP won't be GOOD.

The dilemma for a producer becomes one of compromise: determining how best to balance these three complementary yet competing factors, all the time knowing that some of

FIGURE 3.2 Production team shooting footage for an episode of *Ocean Mysteries with Jeff Corwin*.

sacrifice will be ultimately required. The aim always remains the same: Find a way to maximize production value. Whatever the production budget may be, it should look as if every last penny of the production budget went directly into the quality of the finished work on display. Every shot, indeed every single frame of your finished work, should bear the appearance of quality and craftsmanship.

Accomplishing this delicate balancing act requires investing a good deal of time and human resources into planning and analytics. That is why it is important to take full advantage of the diverse backgrounds and skill sets possessed by your production team's members. Throughout the planning process, regularly scheduled production meetings with your team must be held in order to seek out their feedback and expertise. Production meetings are an indispensable part of the preproduction process, as they help to establish a creative culture that promotes collaboration and the open flow of communication amongst your team members.

Preproduction is also the stage where the most important production planning questions are addressed, including: What is the essential nature and purpose of this particular production? How will it be shot? Where will it be shot? What is the minimum size of the crew needed to shoot it? How long will it take to shoot? Will anyone want to see it? Where will they be able to see it? To deal with all of these disparate concerns, it's best to break the preproduction process down into four, easy-to-manage steps:

- Define the concept.
- Set realistic milestones and objectives.
- Investigate, research, and analyze.
- Target your audience.

DEFINE THE CONCEPT

This is the part of the creative process that requires a touch of alchemy, transforming an abstract concept into a tangible production. This is the time to think BIG, without constraints. There are no bad ideas when it comes to brainstorming new concepts or narrative approaches. At this nascent stage of the production, the focus should be on developing your story and finding new ways to connect with your audience, while breaking through all of the existing clutter generated by traditional media forms and their advertisers.

In order to transform an abstract story concept into a concrete reality, a script will need to be developed, in order to lay out production specifics like dialogue, characterization, and setting. Without a script there is no clear road map for a project, as the script provides the directions and landmarks necessary to get from the project's starting point all the way to its finish line. Much like a driver trying to traverse unfamiliar terrain without a map, projects that begin without a firm script in place typically suffer from a legion of production woes and invariably lose their way.

There are two basic production script formats to choose from and deciding between the two template styles is often predetermined by the nature and the scale of the production itself. For productions that shoot primarily with just a single camera, as most motion picture crews do, then a single-column script is used. A single-column script, sometimes referred to as a narrative script, is formatted to distinguish easily between descriptive passages set at normal margins (1.5 inches from the left margin; 1 inch from the right), with character names and dialogue centered in the middle of the page. Each new scene begins with a slug line, written all in capital letters, which includes information about where the scene takes place and whether it occurs inside or outside, in the daytime or at night.

```
                                              FADE IN:

EXT. DOWNTOWN PORTLAND - PIONEER SQUARE - MIDDAY

A CROWD has gathered in the square to watch as a group of
STREET PERFORMERS including a collection of street
musicians, jugglers and sleight-of-hand artists.

Among the crowd is SIANNA NESCI, a very attractive young
woman in her early 20s with keen, intelligent eyes and
light brown hair hanging loose at her shoulders

While watching the performers, her eyes wander lazily
through the crown until she happens to spot her ex-boyfriend
from college, JONATHAN "JOHNNY" BANKS(27).

BANKS is ruggedly handsome, with skin deeply-tanned from
working outdoors. He is tall, 6'2", well built and stocky..

                        SIANNA
                       (loudly)
                    Hey, Johnny!.

Sianna waves her arms to attract Johnny's attention, but he
doesn't notice her and he gins to move away from the crowd.

Sianna attempts  to follow him and sees him enter into a
local coffeehouse


INT. SHAMROCK COFFEE HOUSE - MIDDAY

Johnny is in line waiting for a barista. Sianna enters the
shop and approaches Johnny from behind, tapping him on the
shoulder.

As Johnny turns and sees Sianna a huge smile crosses his
face. He hugs her closely, and then kisses her softly on
the lips. They pull away and gaze into each other's eyes.


                        SIANNA
                   Hello, stranger!


                       JONATHAN
            How have you been? You look great. Even more
            beautiful than I remember


                        SIANNA
                  I've missed you.


                        (MORE)
```

FIGURE 3.3   A single-column script is formatted to distinguish descriptive passages, which are set at normal margins, from character names and dialogue, centered in the middle of the page.

For multicamera productions, a **two-column script** template is most often used. This two-column template, otherwise known as a multicolumn script, is most common in a television studio production environment, for shows such as newscasts, talk shows, sitcoms, and soap operas. The two-column script does offer some advantages because it simplifies all on-screen elements into either a video or an audio column. The video column, on the left, contains all visual content, including camera framing, shot lists, props, scenery, and any required on-screen graphics. The audio column, to the right, holds all of the dialogue and music cues, along with pertinent sound effect needs. Truth be told, the two-column format is a much more intuitive format to use, especially for beginners, because it doesn't require mastery of intricate margin settings or entail the expense of costly script-formatting software.

Approved : FINAL	"Sianna's Dilemma" • - • 1
VISUAL	**AUDIO**
FADE UP - EXTERIOR - PIONEER SQUARE - PORTLAND-OR	MUSIC UP - The sound of street musicians playing a rollicking version of *Sweet Georgia Brown*.
A CROWD gathers to watch a group of STREET PERFORMERS.	
Among the crowd is SIANNA NESCI, a very attractive young woman in her early 20s	MUSIC PLAYS along with NAT SOUND
While watching the performers, she happens to spot her ex-boyfriend from college, JONATHAN "JOHNNY" BANKS (27). Who is tall, 6'2", well-built and stocky.	
Sianna waves her arms to attract Johnny's attention, but he doesn't notice her.	SIANNA(loudly)- Hey, Johnny! MUSIC and NAT SOUND under
INT. SHAMROCK COFFEE HOUSE	MUSIC UP - A Kenny G sax solo plays in the background.
Sianna walks up to Johnny as he stands in line and taps him on the shoulder. He turns and gives her a hug and kiss.	SIANNA - Hello, stranger! JOHNNY - How have you been? You look great. Even more beautiful than I remember.

FIGURE 3.4 A two-column script simplifies the process by placing all on-screen elements into either a video or an audio column.

As part of the scripting process it can also be beneficial to create brief character descriptions for any scripted role; these are a brief overviews of each character's unique personality traits, motivations and their physical characteristics. Any unique abilities or talents that are required of the performers, such as an affinity for vocal dialects; musicianship; athletic ability; juggling; etc., should also be noted. The whole point of the preproduction process is to establish the practicality of your initial concept and to help you, as a producer, determine:

What makes the project unique?
Will it grab attention?
Can it create a stir?
Will it trend on social media?

Of course, the sky's-the-limit approach of early conceptual planning must give way, at some point, to the realities of time and budget. Accordingly, a determination must be made as to the essential nature of the production: Is it to be a viral ad, a traditional TV spot, or an in-house corporate promo? Is it an original, stand-alone concept, or is it part of some larger promotion or trending social happening? How large-scale a production is desired? Is a sizable crew ideal for this production, or is a core team of just three to four people enough?

Regardless of project size or stylistic approach, production crews are generally broken down into two broad groups: above-the-line personnel and below-the-line personnel. Above-the-line personnel are considered the creative part of the team, whereas below-the-line personnel are considered the technical crew. Above-the-line personnel include the executive producer financing the project, the director, the writer, any featured talent such as a major star or performer, and (depending on the type of project), possibly a well-known musical composer or special effects coordinator. Above-the-line personnel are usually connected with a project right from its inception and are often the ones who nursemaid the work through to its completion.

On the technical side, the below-the-line team consists

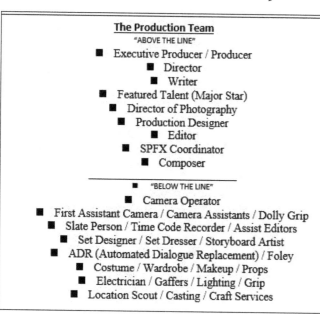

The Production Team
"ABOVE THE LINE"
- Executive Producer / Producer
  - Director
  - Writer
- Featured Talent (Major Star)
  - Director of Photography
  - Production Designer
    - Editor
- SPFX Coordinator
  - Composer

- "BELOW THE LINE"
- Camera Operator
- First Assistant Camera / Camera Assistants / Dolly Grip
- Slate Person / Time Code Recorder / Assist Editors
  - Set Designer / Set Dresser / Storyboard Artist
- ADR (Automated Dialogue Replacement) / Foley
  - Costume / Wardrobe / Makeup / Props
  - Electrician / Gaffers / Lighting / Grip
  - Location Scout / Casting / Craft Services

FIGURE 3.5 Production team members are often identified as either above-the-line or below-the-line personnel, depending on their specific crew assignment and overall level of responsibility.

of a host of different personnel. These diverse talents range from the location scouts to the casting agents, from the wardrobe manager to the first camera assistant, and from the set dressers to the sound recording technician. As specialists, these individuals' level of participation will vary, being used on an as-needed basis throughout different stages of the production.

FIGURE 3.6   Not all productions are created exclusively by prominent ad agencies or major Hollywood studios. Scores of smaller, independent productions are also in development.

Realize, though, that not all productions are created and financed exclusively by prominent ad agencies or major Hollywood studios. Any number of smaller, low-budget, independent productions are in development at any given time. These smaller-scale productions usually allow for a greater degree of creative freedom with little-to-no executive oversight. In these cases, directors tend to have direct control over production. The production teams also tend to be smaller, with a less-seasoned crew. For those lacking production contacts, a number of online sites and casting services specialize in providing production personnel, including *Production Hub*, *Backstage.com*, and *Assignment Desk*.

It is somewhat ironic that the earliest viral videos (from companies such as Red Bull, DC Shoes, Dove, and Old Spice) were designed to stand apart from the media pack, specifically because they rejected the overly slick production standards of Hollywood and Madison Avenue. The intent of those early videos was to give rebel marketers a way to distinguish themselves from the pack by presenting advertising content in an unconventional way, while doing so on a modest budget. The subsequent success of these ads has led major advertisers to mimic the homespun production qualities of these early videos—only at a much higher budget.

SET REALISTIC MILESTONES AND OBJECTIVES

With a script in hand, a true production breakdown can begin. A breakdown analyzes the number of pages in a script, the overall number of scenes contained within the script, the location of those scenes, and the performers and crew members needed on any given shooting day. A determination is also made as to the total number of shooting days required to complete the production, and exactly what accompanying props, sets, locations, makeup, wardrobe, and other amenities will be needed during each production day.

Actors and performers must also be cast. Does your production have a large enough budget to hire well-known talent, or will you be working largely with a group of unknowns hired through an open casting call process, in which actors are in invited to come in and try out for the role? As part of the initial scripting process it can be beneficial to create character descriptions for all of the major, scripted roles. These descriptions serve as a brief overviews of each character's unique personality traits, motivations, and physical characteristics. Any special abilities or talents required of the performers, such as an affinity for vocal dialects, musicianship, athletics, juggling, etc., should also be noted.

With a completed script in place, this is the stage of preproduction where the first accurate, real- world budget comes into play. What had once been an abstract concept now has

FIGURE 3.7   Octavia Wagner, age 9, a student at Fort Bliss Elementary School, dances for the judges during an audition.

taken solid form and the number of required shooting days can start to be calculated, a complete shooting schedule can be set, and a definitive production timeline put in place. Knowing whether the production period will stretch over two days, a week, a month, or half a year is a significant milestone. As a producer, it informs you as to how many cast and crew will be needed, over how many days, and at what kind of fixed cost. After all, it's easy to ask someone to participate in your project when that project is still just a vague idea, far away from actual production. It is something else entirely to tell a person that you need him or her for a week-long shoot in Phoenix that begins four days from now!

Where you decide to shoot can also have hidden ramifications for your budget. Shooting in a major media market like Los Angeles or New York City, for example, triggers studio zone rules, an agreed-upon boundary in which all productions are required to pay preset wages and fees to production personnel. In New York City, the studio zone rule is in effect for a 25-mile radius centered on Columbus Circle in Manhattan. In L.A., the studio zone extends out for a 30-mile radius from the corner of Beverly and La Cienega boulevards. (This 30-mile zone, often abbreviated simply as TMZ, is the origin of the name of the popular gossip channel and website.)

Although big cities such as L.A., with a robust production presence, may charge a number of fees to producers, there are now numerous regions, including southern U.S. states and even some foreign nations, that offer tax rebates or other financial incentives if you choose to shoot within their borders. Taking advantage of these tax breaks and filming subsidies can save a production a substantial amount of money. Fixing the shooting schedule and production timeline allows your team to explore these types of supplemental revenue resources.

FIGURE 3.8 The intersection of Beverly Boulevard and La Cienega Boulevard in Los Angeles. This is the center of the studio zone, that is, the 30-mile zone (TMZ).

A fixed timeline also allows production facilities to be reserved, equipment to be rented, talent to be auditioned, and locations to be prepared. For example, if the script calls for a jungle scene, how will that be achieved? Will the cast and crew be flown down to a Central American location for a week? That will give you an authentic look, but it could be very costly. You could elect to build a jungle set on a Burbank soundstage. It would be much more economical that way, but will the footage look realistic? Nowadays, another option might be to shoot the whole thing in front of a green screen and then add the jungle foliage later via 3D software, but how much time and expense will that add to the postproduction process?

This is where the aforementioned paradox of the production triangle comes into play. All of these various production techniques must be evaluated and a definitive decision made about how the production will proceed. It becomes a question of how your production can spend as little money as possible yet still achieve the proper lushness and vibrancy needed for a scene to appear realistic. Making the proper budget decisions for your digital video production now requires taking the next important preproduction step.

INVESTIGATION, RESEARCH, AND ANALYSIS

This is the point of your production in which the need for in-depth planning and logistics really comes to the fore. With the script serving as blueprint, we now have an understanding of anticipated locations, the budget and fixed costs, and all the finer details of preparation work can now begin. Early on, it will be important to address any permitting or licensing issues. Shooting in public, or on any kind of public property, almost always requires a film permit.

To use southern California as a case in point, filming within the city limits of almost any municipality (such as Los Angeles, Santa Monica, or Long Beach) requires obtaining a permit directly from the city in question. Shooting on property belonging to Los Angeles County requires a producer to navigate a variety of different departments, depending on specific needs (such as Los Angeles County Department of Beaches and Harbors, Los Angeles County Metropolitan Transportation Authority, Los Angeles Unified School District, etc.) because the permitting process is not centralized. At the state level, California has its own requirements for filming on a variety of state-owned properties.

Shooting in a different state or a distant country can present other concerns; travel documents, per diems, passports, work documents, and visas may all be required. There are also a variety of other legal documents to finalize and secure, including financial contracts for private investors, local business licenses, tax receipts and business expenses, and talent releases for performers. Simply staying in compliance with all of these permits and documentation requirements can be quite problematic, so attention to detail is an absolute must.

FIGURE 3.9   Shooting on public property, whether at a city, county, state, or federal level, often requires producers to navigate a variety of different government departments in order to obtain official film permits.

In addition to handling all of the legal and financial paperwork, this is also the time in preproduction to start viewing the project from a purely business perspective. Your viral video must be structured with a very narrow purpose in mind: How can you promote the client, organization, or product to the best of your ability? Part of this process means objectively looking at the best medium to use when it comes time to record your final production.

There are many viable recording options today. As it is, most "film" isn't even shot on film anymore. These pieces are shot on high-resolution digital video, and the images are then saved to digital storage cards. Some notable viral videos have been shot on nothing more sophisticated than a cell phone. A recent theatrical release, the independent film Tangerine, was the first feature film to be shot entirely on an iPhone! Videotape, conversely, has become obsolete in professional productions.

FIGURE 3.10   There are many viable production options when the time comes to record your production. As it is, most "film" isn't even shot on film anymore; it's recorded on high-resolution digital video.

FIGURE 3.11 Much of the Millennial and Generation Z demographics view media on their smart phones, using streaming apps such as Netflix and YouTube.

At the opposite end of the distribution pipeline, a producer also must take into account how the intended audience will consume the finished product. When a video achieves popularity online, it begins to trend on social media sites such as Twitter, Facebook, and Instagram. Although it's easy to anticipate that most viral videos will be watched via the Internet, the actual method of consumption varies widely. Rather than watching at a desktop, much of your audience, especially those in the Millennial or Generation Z demographic, will view your ad over their smart phones or encounter your video as it streams to their smart 65-inch television sets using a Netflix or YouTube app or a Roku or Chromecast device.

An older-skewing audience may not see your video until it makes onto a segment of the national news or on cable TV. Long-form videos sometimes achieve cult status and have a secondary life on DVD, pay-per-view, or premium cable. Some future audience may end up watching your videos via their yet-to-be-made, 3D hologram wrist projectors!

The point is that if one is able to tap into all of these media platforms simultaneously, the audience generated by the synergy of forces can be tremendous. Making sure that your video can be optimized for viewing on a variety of playback types is a crucial step to ensuring a maximum number of views, likes, and shares for your project, regardless of its method of consumption. For now, think back only as far as 2014, when the Amyotrophic Lateral Sclerosis (ALS) Ice Bucket Challenge videos became a sensation, involving more than 17 million participants and helping to raise more than $115 million in funds—money that was subsequently used to identify three different genes that contribute to the development of ALS (Rogers, 2016).

FIGURE 3.12 The ALS Ice Bucket Challenge viral videos became a sensation, involving more than 17 million participants and helping to raise more than $115 million in donations.

TARGET YOUR AUDIENCE

In order to understand who will be watching your video, first it will be necessary to adequately target your audience. The final phase of preproduction requires taking an honest assessment of your potential audience. Whom, exactly, is your project intended for? Have you created a video with mass appeal, or is it intentionally aimed at a narrower audience? Many video productions are created specifically for some type of specialty market, be it an in-house training video, a promotional marketing video, or a customized backdrop for a concert and trade show. Even some viral videos, despite their wide distribution potential, are aimed at specific markets: young adults, women, video gamers, etc.

To create a successful viral video, targeting a particular audience demographic becomes especially important. Online media usage is even more fragmented than broadcast or cable television viewership. Some sites, such as Instagram, Snapchat, and WhatsApp, skew heavily toward the under-30 crowd. Other sites are divided along political lines: liberal vs. conservative. There are even important gender distinctions, with Pinterest trending heavily toward females and LinkedIn more popular with males, while Twitter use is almost equal between the sexes (Clifford, 2014). Furthermore, the client or brand you are promoting may already have a targeted audience demographic in mind. If so, it is your job as a producer to use the proper techniques and stylistic approaches that most appeal to your desired audience. This requires understanding exactly what your audiences' expectations are: Wistful irony? Bold patriotism? Bawdy humor?

Does an audience already exist for the kind of production you are planning? It's not unusual for a project, especially a viral project, to try to ride the coattails of some popular fad or trendy genre. Recently in Hollywood we've seen a trend toward superhero films and television (Wonder Woman, The Avengers, Agents of S.H.I.E.L.D.); before that there was a wave of zombie-themed projects (Walking Dead, Zombieland, World War Z); and before that, it was vampire-themed productions (Twilight, True Blood, The Vampire Diaries).

Why all the copycats? Producers like to jump on trends while they're hot. It guarantees a certain level of audience interest and anticipation. If an audience is already tuned in to a particular brand, be it a film franchise, a trendy band, a new fast-food restaurant, or simply a model of radial tires, it makes sense to capitalize on that existing brand awareness and use it as a marketing tool to attract additional viewers to your own project.

In addition to judging the level of existing audience interest and awareness of a brand or organization, it's also important to gauge the audience's level of expectation. Is the audience looking for a faithful reproduction of a long-running theme or for a completely new take on an old favorite? Do they expect A-list talent and state-of-the-art special effects like those found in a feature film, or are they looking for a campy good time with a Sharknado movie of the week? Some brands build their image on class and prestige, whereas others aim for sass and snark.

Gauging your audience's expectations requires an understanding of exactly who makes up the core audience. On the macro level, audience demographics can be broken into

FIGURE 3.13   Shooting in progress in CCD studio in Christ University Bangalore with students Aishwarya Udaykumar and Akash Panigrahi.

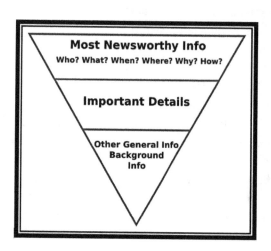

FIGURE 3.14   The inverted pyramid writing technique emphasizes the most newsworthy elements of the story the *lede* paragraph, while less important details are included in subsequent paragraphs.

large-scale groups on the basis of factors such as age, gender, income, level of education, spiritual affiliation, race, or culture. Indeed, entire genres and programming categories have been built around appealing to these mass-appeal demographics, but it is becoming increasingly hard to find untapped consumer markets. By microtargeting an already interested demographic via online networks and affiliations, viral advertisers can make sure that their work is seen by those who are most interested. They can also be assured of some return on their initial investment of time and energy.

With the logistics and planning complete, it can be a good be time to start building some buzz about your project. In addition

FOR IMMEDIATE RELEASE

Contact: Ellie Perry
(310) 243-xxxx
eperry@csudh.edu

2018 CSUDH EARTH DAY FESTIVAL

March 14, 2019 - California State University Dominguez Hills (CSUDH)'s Office of Sustainability in partnership with several other campus departments will be celebrating the 11th annual campus Earth Day Festival on Thursday, April 19th, 2018 from 10:00am-2:00pm. The event will be located on-campus at the East Walkway, 1000 East Victoria Street, Carson, California. This year's theme is "Root for the Planet," with an emphasis on root-to-table sustainable foods and community engagement.

This event will feature a variety of different educational activities such as a tree planting ceremony, e-waste drop-off area at the front of campus on Victoria Street (open to the public), a Farmer's Market, informational booths, guest speakers, and giveaways. Everyone is invited to enjoy this free event at CSUDH.

"The Earth Day Committee brings together a unique collection of campus departments together for this one event. As a result, the number of organizations and groups we're able to reach and bring to the campus simply grows year after year. This year's Earth Day is poised to be the largest one ever in this event's 11-year history, and we hope the on-campus community as well as residents from the City of Carson will come out in force to enjoy the festivities," said Ellie Perry, Sustainability Coordinator and organizing chair for the CSUDH Earth Day Committee.

Carson Circuit, Torrance Transit buses, and Metro and light rail provide direct service to most parts of campus. Visitors from outside Los Angeles can also use the Metrolink for quick and convenient connections to major bus lines. For more information please call the Office of Sustainability at 310-243-2303 or visit https://www.csudh.edu/sustainability/.

###

FIGURE 3.15   Example of a typical, AP-standard, press release.

to any online promotions that you might be doing, it never hurts to get some free coverage from traditional media entities such as local newspapers and broadcasters, by sending them a press release concerning the production. Press releases should always be written as a news story, following consistent journalistic style, known as the inverted pyramid technique, which is the style favored by the Associated Press.

The inverted pyramid writing style emphasizes placing the most newsworthy elements of a story in the opening or lede paragraph, these are the essential who, what, when, where, why, and how aspects of the story. Less important details (story background, supporting evidence, expert or eyewitness interviews) are included in subsequent paragraphs, depending on their significance. In order for your press release to reach maximum dissemination, it is very important to adhere to this journalistic writing convention.

This is because it is not uncommon for publishers or assignment desk editors to use press releases as a way of gleaning information for their own news reporting. It is estimated that about 10 percent of all press releases end up being retransmitted via the media exactly as they were originally submitted, without being subject to additional editing or content review. Therefore, when drafting a press release, it is always important to emphasize the newsworthiness of your production, in order for it to attract the proper attention.

A typical press releases has standard 1- to 1.5-inch margin, uses 12-point Courier or Times New Roman font, and has a 1.5 line spacing. For maximum impact, send out your press release on official company letterhead and include a release date (which identifies whether story is for immediate or delayed publication) and the name of the organization's media contact person. The main information contained within the release should include a bold headline, a dateline, an opening lede paragraph, and two or three additional body paragraphs, followed by a closing end mark.

With all of the preproduction planning and logistics complete, it's time to move on to the next crucial stage in the process, which is covered in detail in Section II—Digital Production & Postproduction in the Viral Age.

REFERENCES

Atkinson, Roger (December 1999). "Project management: cost, time and quality, two best guesses and a phenomenon, its time to accept other success criteria". *International Journal of Project Management*. 17 (6): 337–342. doi:10.1016/S0263-7863(98)00069-6.

Clifford, C. (2014, March 4). Women dominate every social media network—except one (Infographic). *Entrepreneur*. Retrieved from https://www.entrepreneur.com/article/231970#

Rogers, K. (2016, July 27). The 'ice bucket challenge' helped scientists discover a new gene tied to A.L.S. *New York Times*. Retrieved from https://www.nytimes.com/2016/07/28/health/the-ice-bucket-challenge-helped-scientists-discover-a-new-gene-tied-to-als.html

York, A. (2017). Social media demographics to inform a better segmentation strategy. Retrieved from https://sproutsocial.com/insights/new-social-media-demographics

SECTION I: WRAP UP AND REVIEW

KEY TIPS FOR HOLDING SUCCESSFUL PRODUCTION MEETINGS

- Hold regularly scheduled meetings at pre-established times.
- The meetings do not necessarily have to be lengthy; sometimes 5–10 minutes will suffice.
- Avoid cancellations; use the opportunity, no matter how brief, to keep the team informed.
- For lengthy meetings, do not skimp on your team's most basic needs; make sure that they have access to water, coffee, snacks, etc. Small details matter!
- Consider rotating the leadership responsibilities for each production meeting between different department heads in order to keep everyone involved and empowered.
- Encourage open feedback from all meeting participants; don't stifle creative thought. Be open minded about any thoughtful analysis supplied by your team members.
- Always take time to celebrate team successes as well as individual milestones. Such acknowledgements foster a sense of harmony and collaboration amongst the crew.

QUESTIONS

1. Discuss the merits and various aspects for all of the Seven "Cs" of story evaluation that are used to assign a value to the newsworthiness of a particular story idea. Based on your own observations, which of these seven elements do you consider to be most important in helping to judge the level of interest that a story is likely to generate?

2. Identify some of the reasons why collaboration is deemed to be so important in the viral media production and marketing industries. Before a production ever begins to shoot, what type of preparatory work must first be completed? What are just a few of the dangers associated with having to work with a disorganized or dysfunctional digital media production team? What steps can be taken to help keep crew conflicts to a minimum?

3. What are the three main stages of digital media production? What specific production-related activities take place during each of these three main stages? Which crew members are involved during each of these various production stages, and what are

their particular responsibilities? What typically distinguishes an above-the-line crew member from a below-the-line crew member?

4. For those working in online news or on media blogs that have to keep their sites constantly updated to attract fresh web clicks, the 24/7 nature of the Internet can be quite challenging. These sites must learn how to thread the needle of when it is justifiable to publish an unverified, breaking news story for the sake of being the first to do so, versus taking the risk of disseminating inaccurate information and being accused of spreading "fake news." Based upon your own personal observations, what are some of the unique problems and ethical dilemmas that both journalists and PR professionals have to deal with when making decisions about how to handle a sudden, trending, crisis management situation of uncertain origin?

RELATED PROJECTS AND EXERCISES

- To gain a better understanding of how the same narrative can be retold in multiple ways, have each individual student view two to three hours of competing newscasts, public affairs, or magazine-style programs sampled (or recorded) over the course of a single 24-hour news cycle. Have students compare the various approaches that are used to present the stories and how these approaches differ from one news source to the next. Ask the students to identify which stories were prioritized by each different content provider and how much time each provider allotted for the telling of those featured stories.

- In order to understand the importance of teamwork in a modern business environment, break the students into teams of four to six individuals. Assign the teams to conduct a research assignment on the importance of building competent and cohesive production teams in a contemporary work environment. Have each group answer the following questions:

  1) Why is it that in the modern business environment, teams play a larger role in day-to-day operations than they ever have before?

  2) Are well-constructed teams able to work together in a more cooperative environment, while demonstrating increased levels of innovation?

  3) What percentage of business work—not just in media production, but across all fields—is now generally performed in a team setting, rather than by lone individuals?

  4) How does the student feel about group-based work assignments?

  5) What expectations do they have when it comes to working within a group?

- Ask the teams to conduct a one-on-one interview with a person or organization of their choosing. Students will need to draft a list of 10–20 questions for the question and answer (Q&A) segment that will be converted into an open-ended, two-column script prior to the interview. The audio from the formal interview needs to be recorded, so the Q&A must take place in a quiet area that has very little background noise. Students in each group should use this project to focus on refining their interview skills, learn more about the story-evaluation process, and hone their basic microphone and audio-recording skills. The final project submission will take the form of an audio podcast or radio news report.

- Try a team-building exercise to help your student groups break the ice with one another. Here's a good one to start with: divide the students into teams with as equal a number of members as possible. Then, assign each team the task of creating a business from the ground up, in this particular case, let's make it a start-up commuter airline. Allow the teams a 10–15-minute planning meeting during which they will devise a name and the branding for the airline, create a marketing slogan for the company, and design an actual "aircraft" to successfully complete its "maiden flight" in order to secure a financial investment for their start up. The first team to successfully fly and land their aircraft within a designated area is awarded the start-up capital for financing.

To complete the "flight," simply have one of the team members stand behind an agreed-upon "launch point" when releasing their paper airplane for takeoff. Set up a receptacle of some kind, such as a clean trash can or basket approximately 25–30 feet away from the launch point. This process is repeated until one of the teams actually completes the requirements of the exercise. After each round, the group's planning time should be reduced by 50%. The only rule that must be followed is the requirement that the plane must take off from behind its designated spot and then land in the assigned area. Students are free to improvise any marketing materials, design elements, or in-flight instructions as needed. Creativity and innovation are encouraged throughout this exercise.

CREDITS

Digital Production & Postproduction in the Viral Age

INTRODUCTION

In many ways, Section II serves as the heart of this entire book as it concentrates on the two remaining digital production stages, *production* and *postproduction,* while also considering what it takes for media to be considered "digital" in the first place. This portion of the text deals with both theoretical and practical aspects of viral video production and postproduction. Section II transitions us from the open-ended possibilities of the initial preproduction phase into the more pragmatic applications of production techniques, equipment usage, and editing skill.

Section II supplies a complete description of the main production crew's essential duties and responsibilities over the course of the production stage. Remember that the production process requires a collaborative team effort, one in which *above-the-line* and *below-the-line* production staff come together to discuss scene layouts, storyboards, shooting locations, etc., in order to create a viable production schedule. As such, Section II reveals key aspects of the digital recording process, including proper camera composition, camera movement, and three-point lighting procedures, all detailed in full. Discussion of basic audio fundamentals is also included, with particular attention paid to microphones, including their transducers, connection types, and pickup patterns.

KEY TERMS

- codecs
- camera movements (pan, tilt, dolly, truck, and pedestal)
- camera framing (wide shots, close-ups, etc.)
- compositing
- depth of field
- electromagnetic versus mechanical waves
- focal length
- grammar of editing
- image resolution
- interlaced scan versus progressive scan
- lossless compression versus lossy compression
- microphone elements (dynamic, condenser, and ribbon)
- microphone polar patterns (omni, cardioid, etc.)
- motion graphics
- nonlinear editing
- three-point lighting

As part of the text's exploration of the viral production process, Section II also scrutinizes the underlying mechanics of digital media, providing a foundation for core concepts such as *electromagnetic* and *mechanical waves, analog versus digital signal types,* and the role that *bit depth* and *sample rate* play in determining the quality of a digital file. It is critical for viral content producers to have a fundamental understanding of how analog and digital media work, for although analog recording is rarely used in live production anymore, an enormous amount of archived content still remains preserved in analog format, waiting to be digitized and repurposed for modern consumption. To convert analog footage to a digital format, or, to maximize online playback and download speeds, it is first necessary to have a solid understanding of how sample rates, frame rates, *video and audio codecs*, and *image resolution* formats all work. Mismatching any of these digital properties can result in the generation of unstable or incompatible media files.

Section II concludes with insights into the final phase of the production process—*postproduction*. Let us not forget that most viral content is not made up of live, streaming video footage; rather, most productions require footage to go through a lengthy editing process in which the best performances, or most appropriate soundbites and visuals, are selected by an editor, often employing fundamental techniques known as the *Grammar of Editing*, that date back to the earliest film pioneers.

What has changed, quite drastically in fact, is the advent of nonlinear editing (NLE) software which allows editors to assemble digital media together in a nondestructive manner (meaning that no actual cuts or physical wear and tear have occurred to the source material), and then place that media randomly into any desired point on a timeline. In the past, editing had to be done sequentially, laying one clip immediately after another, because the footage could only be played back in a linear fashion. Other aspects of postproduction, including the use of music scoring, motion graphics, and special effects are also assessed. With these steps complete, all that remains is for your final edit to receive approval and then your viral video can finally be uploaded for public unveiling.

CHAPTER 4

Production Primer

Jody Mahler

INTRODUCTION

In this chapter we will explore the second component of the three-stage production model: *production*. In the preproduction stage we learned that the main tasks centered around writing a script, acquiring locations, auditioning actors, and forming a production team. Now that the *production* stage is about to commence and principle filming is ready to begin, the collaborative process really kicks into high gear. You will learn that viral video production, like any other creative art form, has its own unique vocabulary, methodologies, strategies, and techniques which must be mastered in order to produce a worthwhile final product. This chapter will explore all of these various production elements in greater detail.

PRODUCTION AS A COLLABORATIVE PROCESS

As pointed out in the previous chapter, production meetings are one of most critical tools that a producer can use to promote collaboration on viral production projects. The basic purpose of production meetings is to help your team prepare for the upcoming shoot by addressing any unresolved issues or lingering concerns related to the production. Production meetings, especially those that take place during the production phase of the process are used to confirm that all of the production crew members—not just the talent—have been updated and read the most up-to-date version of the script available. The director can also use this opportunity to conduct short table reads or rehearsals with the talent to confirm that everyone is mentally and physically prepared for the rigors of the production to come.

Unfortunately, because of demanding workloads and sometimes conflicting schedules, the time that needs to be set aside for production meetings is often discounted or considered to be less than a necessity. This is especially true of students and other first-time professionals who tend to minimize the importance of production meetings, which can be a fatal mistake. Successful productions require a considerable investment of time, energy, and preparation, so while it is understandable that an individual might be apprehensive about putting so much effort into a project that might yield uncertain returns, it is a requirement that cannot be avoided Without enough preparation time, your project is already destined to fail! That is why ongoing collaboration is so vital to the project, and why each member

FIGURE 4.1 Planning meetings allow the production team to prepare for the shoot by addressing any final technical issues or creative concerns.

of the team must be committed to viewing production meetings as a creative opportunity, not an onerous burden.

Another essential part of production process is the creation of **storyboards,** which help guide the production team previsualize all of the anticipated camera shots and set-ups required for the production. Storyboards come in a variety of combinations. the most well-known are illustrated storyboards. These are fairly detailed frames or squares that can be hand- or computer-generated, and they are used to illustrate the framing, action, and positioning of each camera shot within a scene. On a small-budget production, a director may take on the responsibility of creating the storyboards because of their intimate connection to the material that will be filmed. In turn, the director, director of photography (DP), and/or camera operator will use these drawings to help block out the camera shots on the day of the scene's production.

However, there are some simple alternatives that don't require you to become a storyboard artist. *Shot lists* are a way to implement the same functionality of a storyboard, but rather than drawing out an image a written description of the scene, including the actor's accompanying lines, are plotted out in an Excel spreadsheet, using the film's script to create five descriptive columns, each broken down by scene. The columns include the shot number, location, shot type, camera movement, and shot description.

The first column contains the **shot number**, which includes information such as *Scene #1, Shot#3.* The **location** column specifies whether the scene is an interior (INT) or exterior (EXT) shot. (Hint: It is always best to save your interior shoots for last. that way, if inclement weather or other unanticipated disruptions affect your outdoor shoot, you can always keep the team occupied by moving on to your interiors as you ride out the storm.) The **shot type** column indicates the camera framing: EST (establishing shot), WS (wide shot), or LS (long shot). The **camera movement** column contains directions such as *tilt down, frame sky, tilt up,* or *center house.* The **shot description** column holds detailed information related to specific lenses or cinematic goals.

These are merely examples; Anyone can create a shot list to meet individual specifications. The point is that this type of document is indispensable as a tool for providing framing, story context, and the director's vision to the camera operator. It cuts down on confusion and provides a checklist of exactly which shots have been filmed and which still remain. Throughout

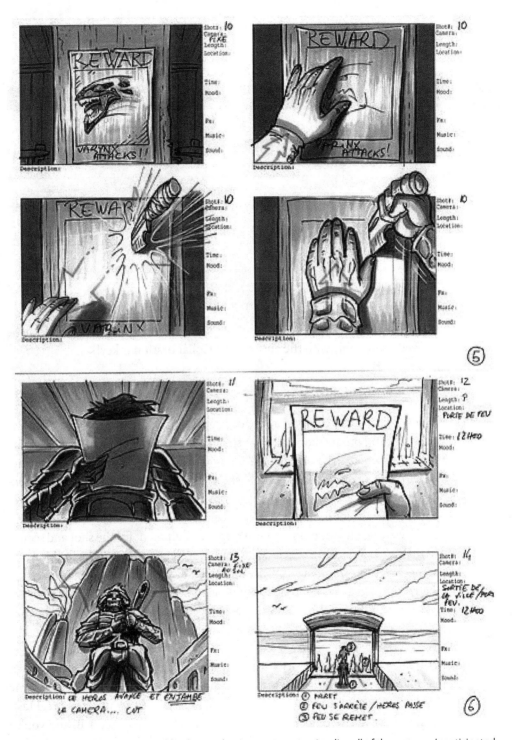

FIGURE 4.2 Storyboards are used by the production team to previsualize all of the program's anticipated camera shots and set-ups.

The spreadsheet shows:

Formula bar: C7 | Establishing shot of CEO Jones Office

SHOT LISTS

Shot No.	Location	Shot Type	Camera Movement	Shot Description
1	Ext-Night	Establishing shot - Downtown L.A. Evening	Drone or helicopter shot of the city at dusk	- Wide angle (18mm).
1a	Ext-Night	Medium Shot - Hancock Building, 25th Floor	Drone or helicopter shot of the city at dusk	Track across downstown skyscrapers; zoom into 25th floor window
2	Ext-Night	CU - Hancock Logo	Drone or helicopter shot of the city at dusk	CU - (250MM)
3	Int-Night	Establishing shot of CEO Jones Office	Camera pans to left, finds CEO Jones seated at his large, oak desk.	Slow pan as we take in a chic, well-panelled office adorned with various works of modern art, business awards and dertificates of honor

FIGURE 4.3 Shot lists work similarly to storyboards and are indispensable to the director in sharing a desired camera framing with the DP.

the production process, any revised or updated scripts, storyboards, or shot lists should all be shared and reviewed thoroughly with the entire crew. Collaboration is key!

START OF PRODUCTION DAY

On a production day, there's a lot going on and a lot to get done before the final take. There is a logical order of events on production sets, even smaller, low-budget productions. First, the director and producer should arrive ahead of the crew to settle any discrepancies about the location itself. Have plenty of printed scripts, shot lists, and storyboards available so that, if necessary, all primary crew and cast can have a personal copy. Second, the production crew arrives on set and begins to assess the location. The camera operator, audio recordist/boom mic operator, lighting/grip crew, and any additional crew set up the equipment for the shot and scene.

Crew time, as the name implies, is a scheduled time for all crew to arrive at the location and set up for the scene. You want the scene to be set up and ready go when the talent arrives. It's a sign of good faith, simultaneously building a confident and responsive crew who is ready for production. Once the crew has finished setting up camera, lights, audio and any miscellaneous requirements, have a test run, using off-duty crew members as stand-ins to test the lights, camera, and audio. If there's going to be a technical breakdown, you want to find it early.

Cast time is the scheduled arrival time for cast members. As producer or director, keep in mind that you want to schedule the cast to arrive in time for the scene. For example, assume the first cast call is at 8:00 a.m. the crew should arrive at 6:00 a.m. to set up, have breakfast, and be willing and ready. Scene #1 at 8:00 a.m. requires Actor A and Actor B, and you've budgeted two hours to complete the scene. Schedule Actor C to show up at 9:00 a.m. to prepare hair and makeup.

Large sets usually include trailers for talent to relax in until they're needed. On small, low-budget productions, this might be a room with refreshments on interior shots or a tented area on exterior shots. The longer talent waits, the edgier they become. Having an actor arrive four hours before a scene with nothing to do lowers morale; actors become restless or get distracted by off-duty crew and talent. Also, instruct your cast and crew to turn their phones off and store them off set. There's nothing more demoralizing than turning your back, only to find crew on their phones during down time.

Access to food is important, as well. If your shoot goes longer than two or three hours, some light refreshments are needed. For an all-day shoot, craft services must be provided, because cast and crew need to eat. Even if restaurants are near the shoot, you don't want your team dispersing to go eat. After they've arrived at your production location, keep your production team and the talent confined to the set as much as possible.

Production assistants (PAs), also known as runners, organize the chaos of a set; if you can afford a PA, get one, because he or she will relieve a ton of stress. On small-budget productions, you may be able to arrange having a volunteer PA. On graduate-level productions, an undergraduate can serve as a PA. For senior productions, juniors can be PAs. On indie or viral productions, be sure the PA is a person you trust; someone who knows a little bit about production and wants to learn from an apprenticeship perspective.

ESSENTIAL CREW

Speaking of the production crew, as we discussed in our earlier chapters, production crew team members come in all sizes and skill sets. Even at the skeleton-crew level, there is debate over the minimum number of crew members required. Decisions such as these are really dependent on the type of content you're producing and the size of your production budget. For a short video, a skeleton crew would need at least four people to serve as **producer/director, camera operator, lighting tech** (commonly known as a gaffer), and **audio recordist/boom operator**. A script supervisor can be a handy addition as well, to help oversee the shooting timetable and help to ensure script continuity. For a documentary-style interview, at least two crew members are needed, doing double-duty (which reduces the distinction between above-the-line and below-the-line crew down to its bare minimum). Nevertheless, a two-person crew can still accomplish a great deal. Once the lights are set up and the interviewer and interviewee have microphones in place, a two-person team can act as camera operator and director, allowing their primary focus to remain centered on recording the talent at optimum levels.

PRODUCER/DIRECTOR

On a viral video project there's a good chance that as a producer or director (or both) you'll end up having to wear many different hats throughout the course of a production day.

In addition to juggling production expenses and making the crucial creative decisions, you may also find yourself serving in the role of strategic advisor, on-set therapist, and general team motivator. so, make sure that you are fully prepared when you begin the shoot. Ensure you have access to the most current **call sheet** and contact list, the documents that contain the crew's contact information and the day's production schedule. It's now quite common to see these forms distributed in a digital format. The popular choice involves creating a universally accessible file with a program such as Google Docs, and then making that file available to the entire team via their personal digital devices. Typically, it is the duty of the **production assistant (PA), associate producer (AP), or assistant producer (AP)** to make the necessary crew calls, text production times, revise schedules, and update the cast and crew on these production times, while also confirming their attendance a day in advance.

On a small-scale production, the producer/director usually assumes the responsibility of completing much of this paperwork in order to assure confidence within the production team. In many contemporary organizations, both professional and academic, a variety of software applications or intranet sites have been designed to allow for group collaboration, planning, and file-sharing, so check with your facility's IT supervisor or your academic resource coordinator for access.

Finally, in your role as the director, you must provide detailed shot lists to all of the camera, lighting, and audio crew members. The shot list informs the camera operator about what shots are to be recorded first, tells the lighting crew which locations to set up, and lets the sound team know how to "mic" the shots. However, it is sometimes best to spare the talent from having to deal with this additional information because it can be a distraction for them.

As the head of the production team, when shooting on location you should arrive on site at least an hour before the rest of the cast and crew show up. Because last-minute changes to previously agreed-upon arrangements are often required, it's always best to have a head start on the problem and allow yourself time to place the production first, and your ego second. Politeness and gratitude will go a lot further

FIGURE 4.4 Behind the scenes on the set of the feature film *Nowhere/ and,* featuring writer and director Robin Bane.

with your crew than unbridled pride and insistence. There's a fine art to negotiating under pressure, so do your best to not lose your temper. Things never go according to plan during production, so be flexible; however, always try to avoid deviating from the script. Be creative, be innovative, and take advantage of new shot angles at the last moment, but always cover yourself. If it's written in the script, make sure that you get the shot in one form or another, preferably from multiple perspectives. Your editor will thank you.

DIRECTOR OF PHOTOGRAPHY/CAMERA OPERATOR

Next to the director, the camera operator has perhaps the most demanding job on the production team. The camera operator must capture the most aesthetically pleasing shots possible for the editor to assemble in postproduction. Before the production day even starts, the camera operator must review the storyboards to determine what equipment is necessary for the shooting location and factor in considerations such as wet or rainy environments, extreme heat or cold, or shooting within tight confined spaces. Due to such responsibilities, the senior camera operator is often referred to as the Director of Photography, or simply the DP. Even on a small-scale production, a DP will need to evaluate all of the production's equipment needs, in addition to choosing a variety of lenses and filters for that day's shoot.

Another important responsibility of the DP is to provide the editor with enough *camera coverage*, which involves shooting sufficient footage of the scene, including the use of multiple camera angles and takes, that will enable the editor to assemble the raw footage into a finished sequence. At its most basic, editing consists of selecting clips of the best available *footage* (raw, unedited material), and then cutting those chosen *shots* (clips containing a single action or uninterrupted "take" by the camera) into a coherent *scene*. A scene typically consists of either single or multiple shots edited together to present a distinguishable component of the production's overall narrative; a scene usually occurs within a particular location, setting or time frame. Individual scenes are then edited together into a *sequence,* which is a series of connected scenes, strung together in such a way as to present a succession of related events, which are crucial to plot line developments.

The DP must also ensure consistent screen directionality by using the *180° rule,* which keeps an imaginary axis between the performers, who are confined to one-half of a 360° arc, from the DP and the camera, which are positioned across from the talent, in the adjoining hemisphere. The purpose of the 180° rule is to help establish on-screen positioning, and to preserve the existing spatial relationships between characters. By adhering to the 180° rule, the DP helps to maintain the continuity of time, space and character movement. Characters to screen left remain on the audience's left, while characters to screen right remain on their right. Preserving this on-screen directionality is very important to continuity, as it allows characters engaged in an on-screen discussion appear to be talking to one another, via an eyeline match, rather than holding a conversation with some unseen entity occupying some off-screen position. This continuity-styled approach to shooting & editing is one of the key principles to modern storytelling. Continuity shooting allows for dialog scenes built together using shot-reverse shot sequences, the inclusion of synchronous audio, and the ability to cut scenes together on matching action, all while optimizing the rhythm and flow of the overall production.

Once the object of the shot has been identified, the camera operator zooms in as far as possible to set a ***critical focus,*** which ensures that the subject is in a crisp, tight focus, before resetting the shot to the desired framing. A determination must also be made as to whether or not the shot will work best as a *simple shot* (a fixed stationary shot with minimal-to-no lens or camera movement) or as a *complex shot* (a shot that includes some degree of lens and camera movement). The decision to move the camera should be motivated by the action taking place within the scene, to either reveal conceal or add some time of dramatic counterpoint to the subject's on-screen performance.

Pivot moves involve adjusting the camera in relation to its support base (usually a tripod). A horizontal, left-to-right movement of the camera in relation to its support is known as a **pan,** while a vertical movement of the camera is called a **tilt.** *Dynamic moves* are those in which both the camera and its support move in relation to the subject being recorded. If the camera and its base move toward or away from the subject, it is referred to as a ***dolly shot.*** A shot that moves parallel to its subject, either to the right or left, is known as a **truck shot.** If the camera is raised or lowered in height, that is known as a **boom** or **pedestal shot.** On shots that require a great deal of extension, a **jib arm** is used, while shots that require the camera to achieve a great deal of height, rely on a **crane.**

Whether using a static or moving camera, DP's are trained to capture an image based on the use of the **rule of thirds**, which attempts to break a larger image down into grids, with three horizontal rows and three vertical columns. For ideal framing, subjects should be aligned at the intersection points of the gridlines, allowing for plenty of **headroom** (the space between the subject and the top of the frame, and **nose room** (the space between the subject and the opposite edge of the frame). Framing is the art of positioning the camera in order to create a composition consisting of an intended subject, incorporating both its lighting and its external environment.

There are actually two aspects related to the concept of a frame.

FIGURE 4.5A The rule of thirds helps camera operators properly frame and compose their subjects.

One concerns the actual **physical frame**, a solitary still image taken from a film or video which is but one of many images used to construct the complete motion picture. The other aspect involves the concept of the **compositional frame**, which is two dimensional in nature, with only height (x-axis) and width (y-axis), but no depth. The exact height-to-width proportions of a particular frame are known as its *aspect ratio*. The exact size and shape of the film frame have changed over time, with early historical cinema and television programs reproduced mostly in a square, 4 × 3 shape, known as a 1.33 aspect ratio. Wide-screen aspect ratios tend to me more rectangular in shape, with a ratio perspective of 1.85 or the even wider 2.35 standard. Regardless of the aspect ratio used, the image presented within the frame remains a two-dimensional reproduction of the image, despite advances in 3D viewing applications.

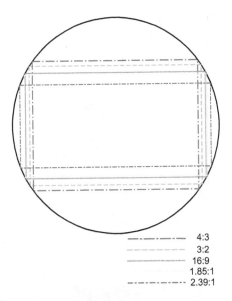

4:3
3:2
16:9
1.85:1
2.39:1

FIGURE 4.5B   The exact height-to-width proportions of a particular frame are known as its *aspect ratio*. https://commons .wikimedia.org/wiki/File:Aspect_ratio.svg

Consequently, it is up to the DP to create the illusion of depth artificially, through the use of creative lighting designs and the precise positioning of characters and objects in relation to one another. In more direct terms, creating this illusion of depth within the composition means planning out character movements across three planes of action: the foreground, midground and background. Controlling action and movement across these three planes helps to create the perception of depth and the existence of a z-axis within an otherwise flat, 2D medium, a photographic term known as **depth of field**, the area in which all objects are in focus. Maintaining a sharp focus across all three focal planes is known as maintaining a *deep focus*, while limiting focus to just one plane is known as a *shallow focus*.

From a technical point of view, essential camera framing is just a technique used to seamlessly move from a wide-angle perspective to a narrower perspective, as a way of symbolically illustrating the movement from a general position to a more specific one. As the camera framing gets tighter on your subject, the enhanced details and emotion inherent within the shot evoke a psychological response from the viewer, as they interpret the meaning of the image. They are literally being drawn into the onscreen action. Thus, properly framing your shot will help you to provide a visually impressive, emotionally satisfying and memorable experience to your viewers. That being said, there are basic framing styles, or shot framings, that every director, camera operator, and editor should understand aesthetically, psychologically, and emotionally. Normally, a scene will open with the widest possible camera framing, known interchangeably as a wide shot (WS), an establishing shot (ES), or a master shot. Such framing

FIGURE 4.6   An establishing shot helps an audience identify the arena or setting in which the action is taking place.

helps the audience identify the arena or setting in which the action takes place, be it a big city, a foreign land, an alien planet, or just a neighborhood bar where everyone knows your name.

In terms of framing an individual subject, the following descriptions are used:

- Full shot (FS): Captures a subject from top to bottom or head to toe
- Medium shot (MS): Captures a subject from midpoint, such as waist to head
- Medium close-up (MCU): Captures a subject from a tighter perspective, such as chest to head
- Close-up (CU): Tightly frames a subject's most important aspect; for a person, it would be from the tops of shoulders to head
- Extreme close-up (ECU): Captures subpart of the subject in detail, such as lips, eyes, etc.

FIGURE 4.7   Shots can be framed as full shots, medium shots (MS), close-ups (CU), or even extreme close-ups (ECU).

For more subjective shots that add meaning to a scene, camera operators often employ specialized camera angles, such as the following:

- Point-of-view (POV): Places the audience directly in the character's shoes, reveals what the main character sees
- A Cutaway or Reaction shot: A shot that "cuts away" from the main scene action scene in order to show a secondary or ancillary activity, such as the reaction of one character to another character's words or deeds.
- Over-the-shoulder (OTS): Shot taken of one character, while literally looking over the shoulder of another; creates the perception of eavesdropping on a conversation
- High or low angle: In a high-angle shot, the camera looks down on a subject from a high vantage point and seems to diminish the individual pictured in the shot. A low-angle shot works in an opposite manner; the camera is placed at a low vantage point, making the subject of the shot seem immense and powerful.
- Bird's-eye vs. bug's-eye view: This takes the high angle/low angle dichotomy to an extreme. A bird's-eye view is when the camera is placed directly above the subject facing straight down, while a bug's-eye view places the camera below ground, shooting directly upwards.

Mastering framing styles and image composition takes time. In very advanced cinematography, a shot may start off as a close-up and transition to a wide shot over the course of a scene. Depending on the size of the lens used, a camera captures images at different *focal lengths.* Some cameras are able to accept *prime lenses,* which have a predefined focal length; a small focal length produces a wide-angle image perspective, whereas a long focal-length lens provides a telescopic image. A *zoom lens* (also called a variable-length lens) allows the camera operator to vary the focal length from a wide angle to telephoto perspective. There's no limitation on how to combine shots in order to create a dynamic and compelling viewing experience.

FIGURE 4.8A&B   In a high-angle shot, the camera diminishes the individual pictured in the shot. In a low-angle shot, the subject seems immense and powerful.

FIGURE 4.8C Professional cameras are able to accept different sized prime lenses which allow images to be captured at varying focal lengths.

Some directors and DPs prefer to combine shots together in montage fashion. Montage is a technique in which a series of short shots are edited into a longer sequence for the purposes of condensing space, time & information. Montage sequences are often used to suggest either the passage of time (in most Hollywood-styled films), or to create symbolic meaning through the collision and juxtaposition of images (as favored by Soviet montage theory). Another visual composition approach involves the use of mise-en-scene, which is a French term that means "placing on stage." Mise-en-scène is used to evoke lasting feelings through the prioritization of long takes, uninterrupted by excessive cuts or editing. In a mise-en-scene styled production, emphasis is placed on the environment, as shots linger on a room or landscape even after characters depart the scene. As a quick exercise, watch one of your favorite films, but take time to pause and identify each type of shot and its intended emotional significance. If necessary, turn the volume down and take note of how the visuals are featured within the production.

DIGITAL CAMERA CONTROLS

As for the operation of the camera itself, there are certain basic functions that everyone should be aware of before hitting the record button. Motion cameras, whether film- or video-based, are a type of image acquisition device that allows the user to capture a series of continuous images at the consistent rate of speed. Film cameras record objects at 24 frames per second (fps), while most U.S. video cameras record images at 30 fps or 60 fps. A camera uses a lens to capture, focus, and redirect light into the camera's internal mechanics. Light passes from the lens through the opening on the camera body known as an **aperture.** The size of the aperture can be modified by using the **iris control** to adjust the length of the **shutter blades**; a small aperture allows less light into the camera but provides for a greater depth of field; a large aperture permits more light to enter into the camera but greatly reduces depth of field. **F-stops** are preset, standardized aperture settings. The shutter speed, the rate at which the shutter blades open and close, can also be adjusted. A quick shutter speed will help to reduce the motion blur of fast-moving objects, but it will also require additional light to be available, in order to offset the rapid rate at which the shutters will be moving.

When light finally passes through the aperture it encounters a prism, which splits the beam of visible light into three primary colors: red, green, and blue. In a digital video camera, each of these colors is than recorded and digitized by a high capacity charge-coupled device (CCD) or complementary metal-oxide semiconductor (CMOS) computer chip. These chips serve as an imaging device, and the quality of the digital image will be impacted by the number, size and pixel-count of the computer chip used. This digitized information carries the data needed to reassemble and reconstitute the image for later playback through the camera viewfinder, output to a recorder unit or transport into a production switcher.

To maximize the quality of the image being recorded, it will often be necessary to use some of the camera functions and control switches located on the side of the camera body. These camera control settings help the DP fine tune the look and detail of the footage being recorded. As noted above, the iris control will allow the operator to increase or decrease the amount of light coming into the camera, to help adjust the image and avoid either over or under exposure. For a novice camera operator who is unsure of how to read and evaluate exposure levels, a zebra switch is provided. When activated, the zebra control will overlay a series of diagonal lines over any part of the image that is over-exposed and receiving too much light. Once proper light levels are achieved by adjusting the iris control, the lines will disappear, confirming that your shot is properly lit.

For extreme circumstances where the image is insufficiently lit, leading to underexposure, the gain control can be used to electronically boost the amount of light being received. However, increasing the gain can also negatively impact your image by adding unwanted graininess, so use this setting only when necessary. To ensure that the color temperature of the light being recorded is ideal, video cameras have a ***white balance*** setting, which adjusts the camera settings to reflect whether or not the shoot is taking place within an indoor or an outdoor environment. Simply set the switch to reflect the proper environmental conditions under which you are shooting, then point your camera at a solid white object and then simply press the white balance switch on the camera.

AUDIO FUNDAMENTALS

As important as camera visuals may be to your production, do not discount the importance of proper sound reproduction. *Acoustics* is the scientific study of sound, especially of its generation, reproduction, and reception. The volume level of a sound source is described as its *loudness,* or amplitude, while the width of the audio signal—from its quietest passage to its loudest—is known as *dynamic range.* The *pitch* of an audio signal refers to the frequency of its sound vibration: A high-frequency sound has a high pitch, and a low-frequency sound has a much lower pitch.

An audio signal recorded at too high a level results in *distortion*, which is an undesirable change in the audio signal usually caused by overamplification. Unlike distortion, *noise* is any unwanted addition to your primary audio signal. This can be acoustic noise, such as picking up the sound of an airplane flying overhead, or contact noise, when an object actually strikes the microphone itself.

Speaking of microphones, it is important to have a basic understanding of the main mics that are used in digital media production. All microphones are a type of electrical generator; they convert sound waves into an electronic signal, in much the same way that your ear converts acoustic energy into an electronic pulse that can be decoded by your brain. The signal that a microphone generates is very weak and must be amplified in order for the signal to be usable. When plugging a microphone into a recording device, always make sure that the input is set to mic level, rather than line level, in order to get the proper signal boost. A microphone uses a type of transducer to convert acoustic energy into a usable electrical signal.

There are three principle types of transducer elements that are used in production microphones: *dynamics, condensers,* and *ribbons.* Dynamic microphones are the most rugged and durable. Dynamic mics do not require an external power source and can handle extremely loud or percussive sounds without incurring damage. A dynamic mic consists of a small diaphragm that moves in relation to the intensity of the sound waves encountered. Suspended from the diaphragm is a coiled wire wrapped around a magnet. The movement of this wire within the magnetic field converts the sound waves into an electronic signal.

On the other hand, condenser microphones use an electrically charged diaphragm assembly, which requires external power via battery or phantom power, which is provided by the recording device itself. Condenser mics operate using two different metal plates. the movement of one plate in relation to the other plate helps to generate the electronic signal. Because condenser mics are powered by electricity, they do not

FIGURE 4.9   A handheld mic with a dynamic-style transducer.

require an actual magnet to be physically present in the mechanics, allowing for a more sleek and compact size. Condenser mics also tend to be more sensitive than dynamic mics, making condensers better suited to capturing sounds from greater distances.

Lastly, ribbon microphones are not only one of the most sensitive of all of production mics, but they also have the longest history: These microphones were the standard during the golden age of radio—from the 1920s through the 1950s. Like dynamic mics, ribbon mics rely on a flexible diaphragm, much like a drumhead, which holds a thin, suspended strip of a grooved metal ribbon. This ribbon is positioned within a very large magnet assembly, and the movement of this corrugated strip of metal within the magnet converts the sound waves into an electronic signal. The drawback to ribbon mics is their acute sensitivity. As such, ribbon mics are used primarily in a controlled studio environment, rather than for on-location shooting.

Another common way to evaluate mics is based on the nature of their sound *pickup patterns*, also commonly referred to as their *polar patterns*. Choosing the right microphone means understanding how microphones pick up sound. Adjusting a microphone's position or aiming can an affect the quality of the recording. The patterns define how the microphone responds to sounds coming from different angles. There are four basic types of polar patterns: omnidirectional, unidirectional, bidirectional, and cardioid, with various subpatterns. Omnidirectional microphones respond to sound 360 degrees equally, which is great for ambience, group conversations, or general environments. Unidirectional microphones are most sensitive to sound coming from one direction and can be aimed at the sound source. bidirectional microphones record in front and in back of the microphone and are commonly used in radio broadcasts and seated interviews. Cardioid microphones' pickup patterns roll off some of the off-mic directionality of an omnidirectional mic, creating a somewhat heart-shaped recording zone.

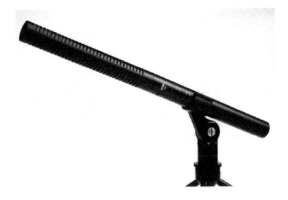

FIGURE 4.10   A shotgun mic with a condenser-style transducer.

FIGURE 4.11   A microphone with a ribbon-style transducer.

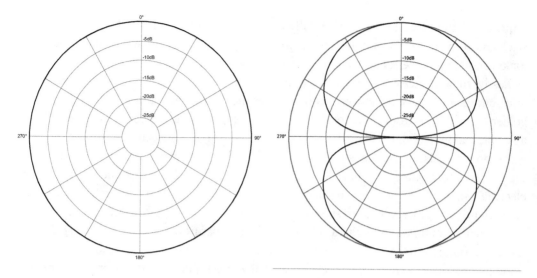

FIGURE 4.12A   An onmidirectional microphone picks up sound from 360°.

FIGURE 4.12B   A bidirectional microphone picks up sound from a figure 8 pattern.

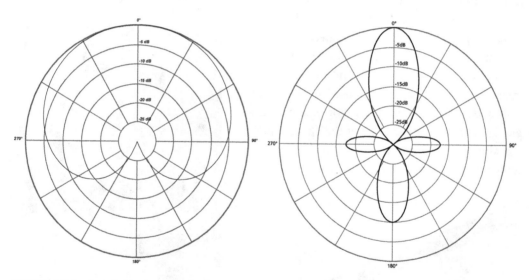

FIGURE 4.12C   A cardioid microphone picks up sound from a somewhat heart-shaped pattern.

FIGURE 4.12D   A unidirectional or shotgun type of microphone can pick up sound from a specific direction, over a good distance.

PRODUCTION SOUND RECORDIST

Audio is often not a priority of novice directors simply because they're focused on the actors; however, it should be. Have you ever found yourself thinking, "I can't hear anything because of all the background noise in this scene?" Poor production audio can result in dialogue that is recorded at too low a level, that is muffled, or that contains a faint echo. Bad audio will ruin your production no matter how well the video is composed. Just consider a shot where the camera mic is positioned several feet away from the actor who is speaking: the sound

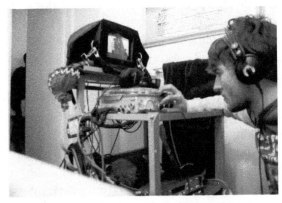

FIGURE 4.13A   Production sound mixer Jonathan Moran is hard at work recording audio.

will have a considerable amount of background noise. How can you hope to record clean audio when it is taken from so far away from the subject?

The answer to this problem is to have a dedicated crew member whose only task is to record quality sound—without accidentally getting caught in the frame. That person is called a production sound recordist. On a large production, this is a team of several people, but on a small production it's one or two individuals. After the sound recordist delivers production audio files to the postproduction editor, the editor begins by syncing audio and replaces the poor audio with the quality audio. The result is having an edit with high-quality sound design the audience will appreciate.

Having a sound recordist takes your team one step closer to eliminating those technical issues. Where can you find one? Well, if you're a student, find the music or audio recording engineering program or department; usually they'll be able to point you in the right direction. Otherwise, for a professional production there are plenty of industry magazines, websites, and social media circles that showcase talented individuals who are agreeable to work-for-hire arrangements.

FIGURE 4.13B   A handheld mic with a dynamic-style transducer.

Be aware of the fact that, with the emergence of podcasts as a popular, online viral media format, sound recordists are in more demand than ever before. Podcasts are online audio webisodes of ongoing programs that users are able to download and listen to at their convenience. The term *podcast* is derived from the blending of the words *pod* (referring to an iPod or similar portable playback device) and *broadcast* (acknowledging this format's historical antecedent in broadcast radio). Even newer recording devices like Zoom units, with their all-in-one mic and recorders, and USB-connected mics, aid in podcast production because they create a seamless interface between digital audio recorders and computers.

However, you manage your production set, always carve out time for the audio team to confirm that they're getting the best on-location audio recording. Most professional microphones typically use an interface format called **external line return (XLR)** designed for providing excellent sound quality. An XLR is a professional-grade audio cable that provides a balanced audio connection, unlike other audio connector types, which are prone to picking up external noise or other electromagnetic interference.

Unfortunately, not all video cameras are equipped with XLR audio inputs. In fact, most DSLR cameras do not come standard with an XLR connector, so if you're using a DSLR camera or variant, you'll want to purchase an adapter in order to run the XLR connector from a professional-grade mic into the smaller format audio adapter that your DSLR camera uses. A common adapter cable is an XLR-to-headphone jack (technically known as XLR-to-3.5 mm). Another option is to purchase a Tascam digital audio recorder that can record directly from an XLR source and sync to the camera. Also, keep in mind that some cheaper consumer video cameras do not even have an interface for an external audio jack, severely limiting one's ability to capture pristine audio.

One additional production option involves the use of wireless or wired lavaliers (lavs), which are very small, inconspicuous microphones that are usually clipped on a shirt collar or hidden in clothing of the talent. Wired lav mics are typically used during on-set interviews

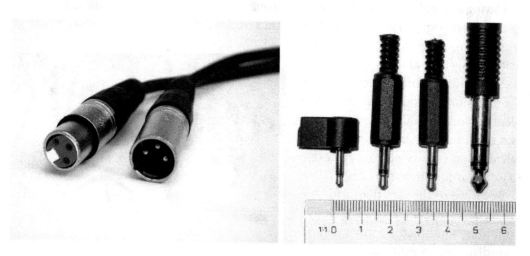

FIGURE 4.14A&B XLRs are a balanced, professional grade audio connector. Most DSLR cameras provide only a consumer-grade, miniplug input.

conducted over relatively short distances, because the microphone is directly attached to the camera. Wireless lav mics, which do not require a hard-wired connection, are typically used in reality TV programs, stage performances, and news programs, where the wireless mics can be concealed in clothing yet are still powerful enough to pick up strong audio signals. A transmitter is attached on the talent and a receiver on the camera or designated audio recorder. However, the drawbacks to wireless mics are that they require batteries to operate, have a limited range, and are susceptible to signal interruptions. A lav microphone normally has an omnidirectional polar pattern with a short range. The advantage is that they are great for recording conversations by picking up the voices of the talent and anyone else near to them. Lavs are very flexible in terms of usage, but they can result in the noisiest recordings.

Another popular microphone for recording dialogue scenes is the shotgun microphone. A typical shotgun microphone has a unidirectional super-cardioid polar pattern, is usually mounted on a boom pole or on top of the camera, and can be aimed directly at the talent to pick up their voices.

The bottom line is to treat audio just as importantly as video. The audience doesn't want to be distracted by poor editing or audio quality. Invest in the audio side of your production, and it will elevate the final product.

LIGHTING FUNDAMENTALS

Lighting can set the mood of the scene, shine a spotlight on an actor, or simply light a scene that is too dark. Lighting is another art form that, if possible, should be handled by a dedicated crew member. The director works with the lighting tech/grip, who lights the scene by physically placing, aiming, and adjusting lights in different locations on the set.

Lighting is another core ingredient of digital media production. If the picture is too dark or underexposed, the audience can't see; if it's too bright, overexposed, the audience can't see. The camera operator needs perfect lighting, and the editor needs a perfect shot to edit; Each complements the other.

Three-point lighting is the standard approach to illuminating a subject and requires a ***key, fill,*** and ***back light.*** The *key light* is typically aimed at the face of the subject; depending on the light mechanics, it can then be adjusted for diffused lighting, giving the subject a soft glow, or sharpened for a more dramatic look. The *fill light* balances out the key light. It is aimed at the side of the subject's face, away from the camera. This creates an image with one side fully exposed and the other slightly darker. The *back light, rim,* or *hair light* is placed above the

STANDARD THREE-POINT LIGHTING

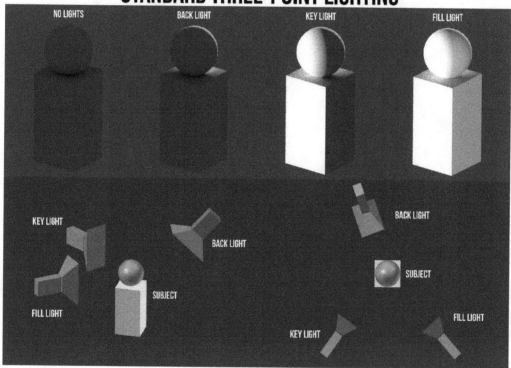

FIGURE 4.15   Three-point lighting is the standard approach to illuminating a subject and requires key, fill, and back lights.

subject, aimed at the talent's back, creating a shine around the head and shoulders. When possible, a fourth *background light* can be used in conjunction with a colored **gel** to add a splash of color.

BASIC LIGHTING PRINCIPLES

When dealing with light, it's important to understand the difference between artificial light sources and natural daylight. These two different light sources have different **color temperatures**. Human-made light fixtures tend to burn at an average value of 3200 °K (the *K* is for the Kelvin temperature scale). Conversely, the color temperature for natural light averages 5600 °K, while being capable of reaching over 10,000 °K on an extremely bright and cloudless day. The result of this color temperature discrepancy is that most artificial lights tend to have a reddish-orange tone, as opposed to natural light, which has a bluish cast. In order to correct for this color difference, video cameras have a **white balance** setting, which requires the camera operator to adjust the camera to either an indoor or an outdoor shooting environment. For more information on the color principles of light, please see the discussion of the electromagnetic spectrum in Chapter 5.

When describing proper lighting techniques, it's also important to distinguish between **directional lighting vs. reflected lighting**. Directional lights are often referred to as *hard lights* because they are designed to be pointed directly at their subject, sometimes resulting in a harsh, over lit effect. Directional lights, by their very nature, are also notorious for creating very noticeable shadows. When directional lights provide a very wide field of lighting, they are referred to as *floodlights,* when the directional light is more focused and concentrated, it's known as a *spotlight.*

On the other hand, reflected lights (also called *soft lights*) are specifically designed to bounce light off of a reflective surface, rather than straight onto the subject. As a result, the light has a much more diffused quality that greatly reduces the opaqueness of any shadows created. Depending on how the combinations of hard and soft lights are used, lighting directors can work toward specialized lighting effects, such as **high key** (scenes with broad, even lighting) or **low key** (scenes with pools of light and dark, with emphasis on shadows). A variety of devices, ranging from barn doors and scrims to gels and diffusion, can be used to control the overall spill of the light, its color, or its intensity.

LOCATIONS

"Location, location, location," a cliché from the real estate industry, is relevant whether you're buying a home or producing a film. Consider locations as additional characters in the story. The location provides a geographical context for the production. Locations are essentially the stage for your actors to play on. Locations can play an interactive or a non-interactive role in your production. They provide physical feedback to the actors without saying a word, while speaking emotionally to the audience. Yet, shooting on location also adds a level of uncertainty into your production. Will the location involve shooting an exterior or an interior? Will it be shot at night or during the day? Outdoor lighting situations can be just as difficult as interior shoots, even with the availability of natural sunlight with which to light your scene. The intensity and quality of that sunlight will also vary throughout the course of the day. That's why it is important to pre-scout a location well before production begins to determine available light for different parts of the day, access to electricity to power equipment, and whether there are any noise or environmental factors that could be a concern.

END OF PRODUCTION DAY

After the last shot, the producer and director should thank the talent, and what's left of the cast should be politely escorted to their vehicles. The crew starts to break down equipment to load into their vehicles. Production lights must be allowed to cool down before they are packed away, and batteries should be recharged in preparation for the next day's shoot.

However, there are two crew teams that can't leave just yet. The camera operator and audio recordist teams need to offload the dailies. Copies of the digital files from the camera and the audio recording device are transferred to a hard drive for detailed review and final organization. The director or editor evaluates the footage for any aesthetic or technical issues, such as shots being out of focus, frame drops, or file corruption. Under no circumstances should the crew be allowed to leave a set without making a backup copy of the footage.

END OF PRODUCTION

"That's a wrap" is an old expression coined in the 1920s, signifying the end of production and the start of postproduction. It's been a stressful but rewarding experience shooting all the pieces of a script. All digital files have been backed up, organized by scene and line. The cast and crew have performed exceptionally, and, if it's in the budget, traditionally production finishes with a wrap party.

Now begins the first step of the postproduction journey: The production footage is handed over to the editor, who starts to create a final production edit assembled from all of the raw footage clips. But before we actually transfer those assets to the editor, let's take some time to discuss exactly what this production footage comprises. We'll do that in **Chapter 5, Digital vs. Analog Media: A Format Comparison**.

CREDITS

- Fig. 4.1: Copyright © Open Knowledge Foundation Deutschland (CC by 2.0) at https://commons.wikimedia.org/wiki/File:June;_Planning_Meeting-fd0000_(9504178076).jpg.
- Fig 4.2: Copyright © Ryzom (CC BY-SA 2.0) at https://commons.wikimedia.org/wiki/File:Storyboard_ryzom.jpg.
- Fig. 4.4: Copyright © Jhillx01 (CC BY-SA 4.0) at https://commons.wikimedia.org/wiki/File:Robin_Bain_director_image.jpg.
- Fig. 4.5: Source: https://commons.wikimedia.org/wiki/File:Rule_of_thirds_applied_on_M%C3%A4dchen_am_Strand.jpg.
- Fig. 4.6: Copyright © Anthony Quintano (CC by 2.0) at https://en.wikipedia.org/wiki/File:Above_Gotham.jpg.
- Fig. 4.7: Source: https://en.wikipedia.org/wiki/File:24-72mm_zoom_demo_horizontal.jpg.
- Fig. 4.8a: Source: https://peach.blender.org/download.
- Fig. 4.8b: Source: https://peach.blender.org/download.
- Fig 4.9: Copyright © ChrisEngelsma (CC BY-SA 3.0) at https://en.wikipedia.org/wiki/File:SennMicrophone.jpg.
- Fig. 4.10: Copyright © Harumphy (CC BY-SA 3.0) at https://en.wikipedia.org/wiki/File:AKG_C451B.jpg.
- Fig, 4.11: Copyright © LuckyLouie (CC BY-SA 3.0) at https://en.wikipedia.org/wiki/File:Rca44.png.
- Fig, 4.12a: Copyright © Galak76 (CC BY-SA 3.0) at https://en.wikipedia.org/wiki/File:Polar_pattern_omnidirectional.svg.
- Fig, 4.12b: Copyright © Galak76 (CC BY-SA 3.0) at https://en.wikipedia.org/wiki/File:Polar_pattern_figure_eight.svg.
- Fig, 4.12c: Copyright © Galak76 (CC BY-SA 4.0) at https://en.wikipedia.org/wiki/File:Polar_pattern_cardioid.svg.
- Fig, 4.12d: Copyright © Galak76 (CC BY-SA 3.0) at https://en.wikipedia.org/wiki/File:Polar_pattern_directional.svg.
- Fig.4.13: Copyright © Jon Moran (CC BY-SA 3.0) at https://commons.wikimedia.org/wiki/File:Jon_Moran_-_Production_Sound_Mixer.jpg.
- Fig, 4.14a: Copyright © Michael Piotrowski (CC BY-SA 3.0) at https://en.wikipedia.org/wiki/File:Xlr-connectors.jpg.
- Fig, 4.14b: Source: https://en.wikipedia.org/wiki/File:Photo-audiojacks.jpg.
- Fig 4.15: Source: https://commons.wikimedia.org/wiki/File:3_point_lighting.svg.

CHAPTER 5

Digital vs. Analog Media
A Format Comparison

Paul Fornelli

As you prepare to begin the postproduction phase of your undertaking, perhaps you've begun to ask yourself, "What exactly does media footage consist of?" Truth is, there was a time when that would have been a pretty straightforward question to answer, because each unique media format used a different type of recording medium: Movies were shot on film, television productions and broadcast news were shot primarily on videotape, and audio recordings were recorded on magnetic tape for later distribution on vinyl LPs or cassette tapes. Each of these recording media was incompatible with the others because each required specialized equipment (phonographs, telecines, VCRs, cassette players, projectors, etc.) in order to access the final content.

All of these various media also happened to be *analog* recording formats. An analog signal exists as a waveform, which is an undulating series of peaks (crests) and valleys (troughs). Analog waveforms are naturally occurring and can take the form of either *mechanical waves* or *electromagnetic waves*. Sound waves and ocean waves are examples of mechanical waves, because they require a medium in order to propagate. Sound requires an atmosphere to travel, just as an ocean wave needs water in order to spread. Mechanical waves are the result of any type of vibration through matter, from a faint ripple in a pond to full-fledged seismic activity.

Light waves, on the other hand, are an example of an electromagnetic waveform, Light waves do not require a material medium in which to spread, which is why light from distant stars is able to reach us despite the vacuum of space. Electromagnetic waves also have other specialized properties that we will discuss later in this chapter in the section covering the electromagnetic spectrum.

At their most basic, waves are merely a disruption or instability within a material medium (mechanical waves) or a magnetic field (electromagnetic waves), that generates a tremor or oscillation. The waves generated by this oscillation spread outward from their source, without the need of electricity to propagate. Waves are measured based on their *frequency*, the rate at which the oscillation or vibration occurs. This vibration, measured in hertz (Hz), represents the number of times the signal's waveform crest passes a fixed reference point within a given length of time (usually a one-second interval). Frequencies represent a significant property of waveforms. With sound waves, frequency determines the pitch of the

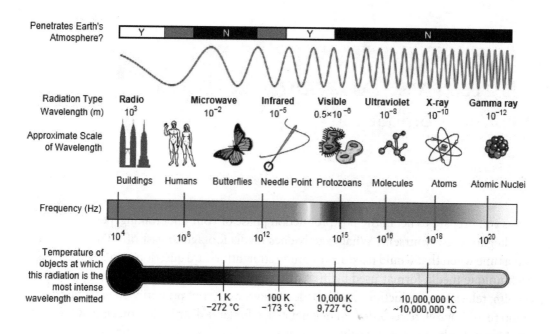

FIGURE 5.1 A diagram of the EM spectrum, showing the type, wavelength, frequency, & the black body emission temperature.

sound: High frequencies generate high-pitched tones, and low frequencies produce low-pitched audio. With electromagnetic radiation, the wave's frequency becomes a measure of safety, given that high-frequency radiation, such as X-rays or gamma rays, poses a danger to human life.

Another meaningful property of a waveform is its ***wavelength:*** the measure of the distance from one crest of the wave to the next crest. The signal's wavelength is inversely proportional to its frequency, meaning that the longer the wavelength, the lower the frequency, and vice versa. A signal's wavelength can vary from hundreds of yards to distances measured at the subatomic level. When judging the waveform's height, referred to as the signal's ***amplitude***, a calculation is made of the distance from the waves' midpoint to the top of its crest. Depending on the source of the wave being recoded, amplitude can be used to indicate the signal's overall intensity, volume level, or voltage strength.

DIGITAL MEDIA FORMATS

Although analog-based media were standard throughout most of the 20th century, the advent of computers and the Internet led to those formats' obsolescence; they now have been largely replaced by digital recording methods. These newer, ***digital-based formats*** allow for more flexibility in the recording, storage, and playback of media files. Unlike analog files, digital media files are made up of combinations of two ***binary digits***: 0 and 1. From these two

TABLE 5.1   Analog vs. Digital Signal Comparison

ANALOG SIGNAL	DIGITAL SIGNAL
Waveform based	Binary number based (1 on/0 off)
Handles fluctuating values	Defined by concrete values
Waveform resembles a ramp	Waveform resembles stair steps
Analog copies result in generational loss	Digital files are clones; no loss of quality
Signal subject to dropout or ghosting	Signal subject to tiling or pixelization

simple digits, entire sequences can be formatted to construct and store complex media files. This sequencing of 0's and 1's creates a coded language in much the same way that Morse code allowed an earlier form of electronic technology, the telegraph, to use two simple characters, a dot and a dash, to build up an entire alphabet's worth of characters.

These digital-based recording formats also help to provide the user with improved image and audio reproduction. Before we delve into the topic of a digital image file quality, though, let's first take a look at some of the main distinctions between analog and digital files.

Another distinction between the rival file formats concerns the fact that digital signals are not waveform-based like analog signals. Digital files require electricity to propagate, so we can discuss them in terms of their *voltage*, with the binary digit 1 representing the positive electrical charge, and the 0 digit representing the absence of such a charge. Given that these binary digits have a concrete value—either 1 or 0—digital recordings do not handle intermediary or rapidly fluctuating values as well as analog systems do. This results in digital signals having a blockier, less-fluid look about them, one that is less curved and well-rounded than a similar analog waveform.

One simple way to distinguish between digital and analog files is to consider the distinctions between a basic light switch and a dimmer control, like the one pictured in Figure 5.3. On the left-hand side of the image is the light switch, which has two possible states of being: an on state and an off state. In its on state, the switch

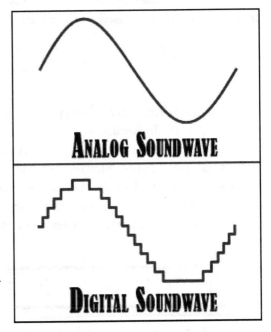

FIGURE 5.2   Analog vs. Digital Waveform Comparison

permits the flow of electricity to a bulb, allowing electric light to shine; in its off state, the switch prevents the flow of electricity to the light. This is exactly how a digital system works: It uses binary code to reflect either a positive electrical state of being (a 1) or the lack of an electrical charge (a 0). No intermediate states or values are possible. The switch is either on or it is off; there is no in-between.

The dimmer switch, in comparison, can handle a number of in-between states, not just on or off. Depending on the level to which it is set, the dimmer permits a number of fluctuating values, displaying varying amounts of light. The dimmer switch is the equivalent of an analog signal, not bound to just an either/or set of values. This distinction is significant because, in terms of final quality, digital files are often considered to be inherently superior to analog files, but that is not always the case. The true quality of a digital file can only be determined based on the **bit depth** and **sample rate** at which a digital signal is recorded.

BIT DEPTH

To understand the role that **bit depth** plays in the final quality of a media file, it is important to understand that the word *bit* is a made-up term, an amalgam coined by joining the words *binary* and *digit* together (*binary* + digi*t* = **bit**). As noted earlier, the binary digits referenced are the 1 and 0 used as the foundational building blocks of digital files. When it's necessary to deal with more complex information or to accommodate a value greater than 1 (given the fact that the number 2 does not exist in the digital world), strings of 0's and 1's must be built up into larger number arrays. A sequence of eight binary digits strung together is termed a

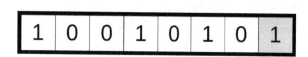

byte, which can contain up to 256 possible values, running from 00000000 to 11111111, inclusive of all of the intermediary values.

The more bytes of data a file contains, the higher its bit depth; by extension, the higher the bit depth, the greater the media file's resolution and detail. Additionally, the higher the resolution of the digital signal, the more that signal will come to approximate the smooth contours of an analog signal.

Furthermore, as Table 5.2 shows, bit depth also has a great deal of impact on determining the final picture quality and color resolution of a digital media file.

In fact, the only real drawback to digital files is the amount of space they take up: Just 10 minutes of 8-bit, uncompressed, 1080-high definition video footage can eat up more than 70 gigabytes (GB) of memory. Fortunately, a feature of digital media files is that they can be **compressed** to reduce their overall size and memory allocation requirements. Although there are scores of different digital media file types, there are three broad categories of digital file compression: **raw, lossless,** and **lossy** formats. Given that the raw format is an uncompressed form of digital file recording and reproduction, we will focus, for a moment, on the lossless and lossy compression formats.

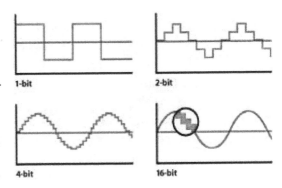

FIGURE 5.5 The more bytes of data a file contains, the higher its bit depth; by extension, the higher the bit depth, the greater the digital signal's resolution and detail.

TABLE 5.2 **Bit Depth Impact on Color Quality**

IMAGE TYPE	BIT DEPTH	TONES/COLORS
Binary image	1 bit	2
Grayscale image	1 byte	256
RGB color	3 bytes	16,777,216
CMYK color	4 bytes	4,294,967,296

FIGURE 5.6A,B,C Bit depth has a profound impact on the final quality and color resolution of a digital image.

The **lossless compression** formats come exactly as they are advertised. These formats can compress a digital file down into a more usable size in order to make that file easier to transport and share across digital media such as email, online dropboxes, or portable hard drives, which often have file size restrictions. Anyone who has ever used a .zip program to shrink a file for emailing has already used a lossless compression system. The main attribute of lossless compression is that it preserves all of the original file's core data and coding, which takes precedence for digital programs that contain complex computer operating systems, or advanced software applications, where even a single line of missing or deleted code could disable a program's functionality. Because preservation of the original source code is the priority with a lossless compression system, the main drawback to this method is the limitations on exactly how small the resulting file can be minimized.

On the other hand, **lossy compression** systems offer a clear trade-off: Some file quality is lost in favor of maximizing compression size. In this type of system, the algorithm at the heart of the compression program deletes redundant bits of data from the original media file in order to shrink the file down to its smallest usable size. As an illustration of lossy compression in action, look no further than your cell phone, which typically comes equipped with an MP3 music player. MP3 files are just a type of heavily compressed digital audio format. By and large, MP3 files offer much less sound quality than a similar .WAV music file does—but that .WAV file comes with a cost of its own, because it is takes up about 10 times the space that the MP3 file does. So why the favoritism for quantity (MP3s) over quality (WAVs)? Ultimately, American consumers have decided, via their online music purchases, that they'd rather store 100 songs of good-but-not-great quality audio on their cell phones than limit themselves to 9 or 10 songs of high-quality music.

How does lossy compression affect visual files? Imagine a video of a lush, green hillside, set against a bright blue sky. In terms of this image's color information, most of the data is redundant; the image consists primarily of minute variations in the colors blue and green as it moves from one frame to the next. Instead of trying to recreate and store every individual pixel's worth of color data, a lossy compression system simply samples color values at various points along the image and then, using an advanced algorithm, interpolates the color values that fall in between the samples' reference points.

SAMPLE RATES

This is where the **sample rate** aspect of a digital file can affect overall file quality. A compression program standardizes how rapidly a measurement, or sample, of the image or audio file is taken. This digital sample is often described as being a snapshot in time that records the appropriate data and information needed to mirror the original analog source. These digital file snapshots are taken thousands of times per second, and the sample rates, accordingly, are measured in kilohertz (kHz). For a digital audio compact disc, the usual sample rate is 44.1 kHz, or 44,100 times a second, whereas the standard rate for DVDs is set even higher,

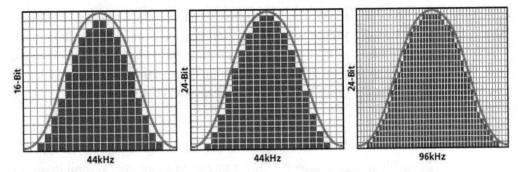

As bit depth and sample rate increase, more information is captured—
resulting in higher-quality audio

FIGURE 5.7   As bit depth and sample rate increase, additional data is able to be captured, allowing for a higher-quality digital file.

at 48 kHz. Signals recorded at a low sample rate often result in a loss of quality due to **sampling errors**, whereas higher sample rates lead to greater accuracy in both signal capture and playback.

CODECS

One final note concerning digital file compression systems: Regardless of how much or how little one may compress a file, at some point that file needs to be decompressed in order to access the media held inside. It does a producer little good to compress a media file for transport to an editor if that file cannot be reopened to extract or download the contents when needed. As a result, most compression systems involve two distinct steps: compression and decompression. As a shorthand, these formats are known as a codecs, which, much like the phrase **bits**, is a term derived by combining two different phrases. When the codec is hardware-based, the phrase is a portmanteau for *coder/decoder*. When the codec is a software-based media converter, the term is short for *compression/decompression* system.

In addition to lossy and lossless codecs, there are also specialized applications such as *transformative codecs* and *predictive codecs*. Regardless of the specific type of codec used, they all share one common purpose: They are specifically designed to convert data from one format to another while compressing that same file for easier broadcast or online distribution. When it comes to high-resolution media files, the conversion from one data type to another most often involves an analog-to-digital file transformation, or vice versa.

One way to think of codecs is to treat them as a type of container, something akin to a piece of luggage. When humans travel over long distances, we use suitcases to safely hold our belongings as we move from one location to another. Codecs provide this same type of convenience, except they serve as containers for our compressed media files rather than for our clothes and personal effects. With codecs, video download times are greatly enhanced, allowing for services such as YouTube or Netflix to offer near-instantaneous media delivery. Without the file compression afforded by codecs, streaming an online video file would take hours, if not days, to complete, simply because of the huge size of the media files.

For additional information on codecs, please see **Chapter 6, Postproduction.**

DIGITAL VIDEO STANDARDS

Productions shot on film run at a universal frame rate of 24 frames per second (fps), but there are two completely different standards when it comes to video playback rates. The United States uses the NTSC standard of approximately 30 fps (actually 29.97 fps), whereas the international video playback standard is 25 fps. However, newer-model digital cameras are beginning to offer an enhanced 60 fps recording rate, which offers the smoother playback and sharper image preferred by online video gamers.

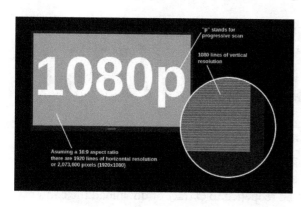

FIGURE 5.8   A diagram of a 1080p, high-definition, progressive scan TV.

Most modern professional digital cameras already permit images to be recorded in one of two different playback formats: *interlaced* or *progressive scan.* The interlaced recording format captures images as alternating sets of lines, known as fields. Together, these two distinct fields are combined into a single frame of video. The interlaced video format is normally selected by an editor when the final production is intended for playback over broadcast TV; especially if the production is likely to be viewed on older model television sets. Interlaced formats are usually designated by a lower-case *i* placed next to the video's lines of resolution number.

Progressive scan formats function in a different manner: They record an image as a continuous stream of pixels in a series of sequential lines, starting at the top of the image and then working their way down, from left to right. Progressive scan displays are associated with computer monitor-based playback, or streaming content. Progressive scan videos are identified by a lower-case *p* placed next to the video's lines of resolution number.

Progressive scan displays are superior to interlaced displays for two important reasons:

- Progressive scan is less susceptible to motion blur, so it retains a sharper image of an object moving at a high rate of speed, such as a pitched baseball or even a high-speed car chase in an action film.

- Interlaced scanning is unable to exceed the 30 fps threshold, whereas the progressive scan-based format is able to function at the higher 60 fps frame rate, mentioned above.

In truth, the distinction between these two formats, at least for the end user, is beginning to dissipate as progressive scanning becomes more customary and newer multimedia display screens, be they smart TVs or computer monitors, can now play back either recording format.

SD VS. HD

When it comes time to finally view the video, your playback monitor will display the finished images via the use of pixels. The word *pixel*, just like the terms bit and codec, is another jury-rigged construct, derived by combining the words *picture* and *element* together. Pixels are the tiny dots or squares that serve as the smallest unit of image reproduction. Pixels are a little like mosaic tiles; individually they don't reveal much, but collectively they add up to form a larger, coherent image. The term **resolution** describes the total number of **horizontal** and **vertical pixels** that are contained in a digital photo or video. The more pixels an image contains, the better the image's clarity and resolution.

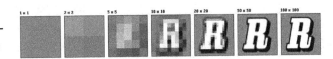

FIGURE 5.9   The term **resolution** describes the total number of horizontal and vertical pixels that are contained in a digital photo or video.

FIGURE 5.10A&B   The more pixels an image contains, the better the image's clarity and resolution.

TABLE 5.3 Video Resolution Display Overview

VIDEO RESOLUTION DISPLAY OVERVIEW		
VIDEO FORMAT	**DISPLAY RESOLUTION**	**PIXEL COUNT**
480 lines: Standard definition	640 × 480	307,200
720 lines: High definition	1280 × 720	921,600
1080 lines: Full HD	1920 × 1080	2,073,600
2K: Enhanced HD	2048 × 1080	2,211,840
4K: Ultra HD	3840 × 2160	8,294,000

In defining acceptable resolution levels, the baseline that was used during the analog TV era was called SD, for standard definition. Standard definition monitors displayed images that contained between 240 and 480 horizontal lines of detail. In the modern digital era, most contemporary video production is now shot in HD, which stands for high definition. To qualify as HD, a video signal must have a least 720 lines of resolution; 1080 lines are considered to be full HD. Anything above 1080 lines of resolution, such as future standards like 4K TV, are referred to as ultra HD.

THE ELECTROMAGNETIC SPECTRUM

Before we conclude this chapter, let us briefly revisit our discussion of waveform types to address specific properties of electromagnetic waves in more detail. The entire gamut of known electromagnetic waves has been arranged according to waves' unique frequencies and wavelengths. This grouping is known as the **electromagnetic spectrum**. From radio waves on the low frequency end of the continuum to gamma rays on the far end, all of the various types of electromagnetic waves contained within the spectrum travel at the speed of light and are therefore considered to be a form of light-based radiation, even though most of these waveforms are, in fact, invisible to the human eye.

The exception to this invisibility rule is a small part of the frequency band, in the middle of the spectrum, between 400 and 790 terahertz (THz), known as **visible light** or **white light**. This band of visible light contains all six major color hues: red, orange, yellow, green, blue, and violet. The specific color of the light is determined by its wavelength, frequency, and how those particular wavelengths interact and refract with the lenses of our eyes. This same process can be observed whenever a rainbow appears after a midday rain. The sun's rays pass through the residual water molecules, which act like a multitude of mini-prisms, refracting the different color wavelengths of the lights at varying angles and degrees.

Since the discovery of the electromagnetic spectrum in the late 19th century, scientists and engineers have found a number of ways to exploit the properties of electromagnetic waves. On the high-frequency end of the spectrum, X-rays and gamma rays are used for

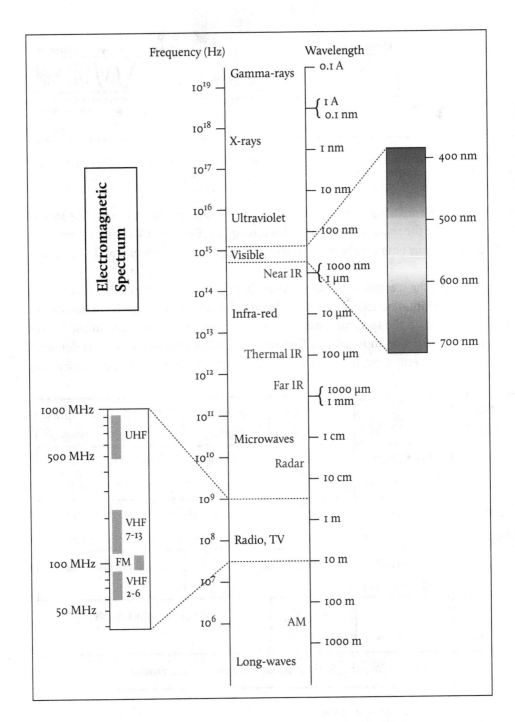

FIGURE 5.11 Electromagnetic waves contained within the spectrum travel at the speed of light, although most of these waveforms are invisible to the human eye.

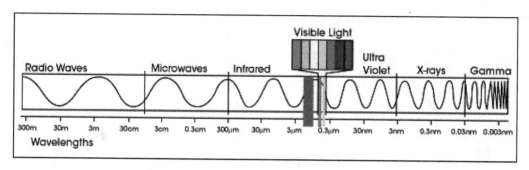

FIGURE 5.12 A small section of the electromagnetic frequency band, between 400 and 790 terahertz (THz), is the part of the spectrum that humans perceive as visible light and color.

medical X-rays, PET imaging, baggage screening, and cosmic ray observations. The low- to midrange bands of the spectrum include radio waves; AM, FM, and TV broadcasting; ultrasound devices; mobile phone technology; radar tracking; microwave ovens; and night vision goggles.

Unfortunately, the electromagnetic spectrum has only so much capacity, since it comprises a finite amount of space. Due to these bandwidth limitations and the demands that continue to be put on the spectrum, use of this public resource is overseen in the United States by the Federal Communications Commission (FCC). One of the biggest demands on the electromagnetic spectrum comes from broadcasting and other communications

54MHz – 218 MHz		470MHz- 578MHz	580 MHz – 698MHz	700MHz- 806 MHz	807MHz - 890MHz
12 VHF Channels	Post-WWII FCC Allotment	70 UHF Channels			
12 VHF Channels	Post-1983 FCC Allotment	56 UHF Channels			Cell Towers
12 VHF Channels	Post-2009 FCC Allotment	37 UHF Channels		Cell & Wireless Tech	
12 VHF Channels	Post-2016 FCC Allotment	17 UHF Channels	Cell & Wireless Tech		
Reallocation of U.S. Broadcast Frequency Bandwidth					

FIGURE 5.13 The FCC is gradually shifting former broadcast-only frequencies, especially those from the old UHF-TV band, to wireless providers and the cell-phone industry.

companies, which rely on the public airwaves to transmit their signals. In order to regulate this part of the spectrum, the FCC must sort through and add various broadcast or radio frequencies to a host of different users, including two-way radio enthusiasts, the airline and maritime industries, local and state emergency services, as well as the U.S. military. To accommodate these ever-growing demands, the FCC is gradually shifting former broadcast-only frequencies, especially from the old UHF-TV band, to wireless providers and the cell-phone industry.

As these broadcast stations are pushed out of the electromagnetic spectrum, a great deal of original video content has now moved to cable TV, satellite, and online streaming sites with fewer bandwidth concerns. This brings us back to our original question: What exactly does media footage consist of? In the digital era, that amazing color cinematography and vivid surround sound that you've managed to capture turns out to be little more than a detailed compression algorithm built on a foundation of long *1* and *0* sequences. With that footage now in hand, it is time to begin editing those 1's and 0's together.

CREDITS

- Fig 5.1: Copyright © NASA (CC BY-SA 3.0) at https://commons.wikimedia.org/wiki/File:EM_Spectrum_Properties.svg.
- Fig 5.3: Source: http://www.electrical101.com/dimmer-switches.html.
- Fig 5.4: Source: https://commons.wikimedia.org/wiki/File:Least_significant_bit.svg.
- Fig 5.6a: Copyright © The Green J (CC BY-SA 3.0) at https://commons.wikimedia.org/wiki/File:2_bit.png.
- Fig 5.6b: Copyright © The Green J (CC BY-SA 3.0) at https://commons.wikimedia.org/wiki/File:8_bit.png.
- Fig 5.6c: Copyright © The Green J (CC BY-SA 3.0) at https://commons.wikimedia.org/wiki/File:32_bit.png.
- Fig 5.8: Copyright © Michael Gauthier (CC BY-SA 3.0) at https://commons.wikimedia.org/wiki/File:Progressive_scan_hdtv.svg.
- Fig 5.9: Source: https://en.wikipedia.org/wiki/File:Resolution_illustration.png.
- Fig. 5.10a: Source: https://en.wikipedia.org/wiki/File:Matakis_-_blurred.jpg.
- Fig. 5.10b: Source: https://en.wikipedia.org/wiki/File:MARTAKIS1.jpg.
- Fig. 5.11: Source: https://commons.wikimedia.org/wiki/File:ElectromagneticSpectrum.png.
- Fig. 5.12: Source: https://earthobservatory.nasa.gov/Experiments/ICE/panama/panama_ex1.php.

CHAPTER 6

Postproduction
Getting Started with Nonlinear Video Editing (NLE)

Jody Mahler

INTRODUCTION

We now turn our attention to the third and final production stage, *postproduction*. This step covers all of the work that is done on your video after the principle photography has concluded including tasks such as editing, dubbing, and the addition of visual effects. *Editing* is the primary focus of this particular step in the production model, as an editor and their assistants begin to sort through all of the raw footage from the production stage and start to assemble the program into its final form. In the not so distant past, postproduction was a step subject to numerous delays, as the editor had to wait for the raw film footage to be sent out to a lab for development and color processing before work could begin. Even as film productions transitioned to videotape, and the earliest digital formats began to appear, postproduction could still be a frustratingly slow experience given that the first digital editing units, known as nonlinear editing systems (NLE), were large, washing machine-sized computers with a control dashboard that contained so many knobs and dials that it looked like it was designed by NASA.

However, now that we've entered the digital era, postproduction can begin as soon as the first day of production. Those earlier digital formats like CDs and DVDs have now been replaced by smaller digital storage cards and memory chips. Modern NLE's are much smaller in size, being primarily software-based, and can now run on most tablets or smartphones. As NLEs have shrunk in size, they have also dropped drastically in cost, as those early protype systems cost as much as $750,000 to purchase, whereas professional NLE software now requires only a modest entry-level investment of $2500 or so. In fact, given the range of NLE options currently available to producers, the question is no longer one of, "should I make the investment in an NLE?" but becomes more about "what specific NLE software should I get?

First, let's begin by defining exactly what nonlinear editing is. The short answer is that NLEs have the ability to edit information out of sequence, to assemble video clips in any random order that an editor chooses That may sound like a reasonable expectation, however, in the past, editing film and video footage had to occur in linear fashion, with one clip placed after the other, sequentially, because the technology could only play the footage back in that way. On a modern **NLE, though,** one also has the benefit of using

FIGURE 6.1 Some of the earliest forms of digital media storage included CDs (compact discs) and DVDs (digital video discs).

a nondestructive editing platform where film does not have to be cut and spliced, or videotape transferred to a submaster. These new digital NLEs give editors complete discretion as to where digital media clips (which are initially stored in the program's bin window) will eventually be placed on the timeline. The clips are then viewed through the program's playback monitor. In order to take advantage of an advanced NLE system, download the appropriate software onto a tablet or computer robust enough to handle the program installation.

SOFTWARE REQUIREMENTS

As to which type of NLE to select, there are many video editing applications available, ranging in cost from zero dollars up to tens of thousands of dollars. Freebies are always attractive; for both students and professional viral video producers alike, it's in your best interest to utilize an established, industry recognized software application, of which Avid Media Composer, Adobe Premiere Pro, Apple Final Cut are the most widely used.

For students, your educational institution likely has licensing arrangements with at least one of these top three NLE developers. Check with your campus IT department to see if you

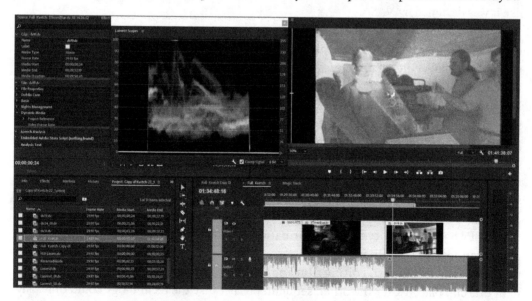

FIGURE 6.2 Digital footage is now edited on NLE software like Adobe Premiere Pro or Avid Media Composer.

are eligible to receive free academic versions of the software; if the software isn't free, most likely it is heavily discounted. For professional viral video producers seeking a NLE upgrade, Adobe offers affordable membership-based access to its video applications such as Adobe Premiere or to its entire library of production software for a small monthly fee.

COMPUTER REQUIREMENTS

Editing digital video seems like a task any computer should be capable of; however, that is far from accurate. A number of important factors must be considered. Most college students and independent filmmakers tend to work on a laptop. There's no denying the advantages: Laptops are portable, compact, and convenient. This is a common denominator for the beginning student and the independent filmmaker.

What type of laptop do you need for editing digital video? The debate over Windows or Apple doesn't really matter; it's more about what system you're comfortable with. In terms of a laptop, four factors must be considered:

- Laptop screen size
- Amount of random access memory (RAM)
- Hard drive type, speed, and size
- Central processing unit (CPU)

Let's break down how each of these factors affects digital video editing.

Screen size is important when it comes to editing. Trying to edit video on a small 12-inch screen can become exhausting over time, squinting and adjusting eye focus to keep up with the screen movement. Consider a 15- to 17-inch screen size. If you decide on 13 inches, a common solution for long editing sessions is to plug the laptop into an external monitor. You can use an HDTV via HDMI connection as a monitor. It is not unusual for a professional video editing suite to have at least two or three playback monitors connected together for video editing.

Random access memory (RAM) is directly related to how many calculations, applications, and processes can happen at the same time. Think of RAM as brain power, giving you the ability to pull up more information faster. When there's not enough RAM available, you'll experience lag and performance issues. Keep in mind, many of today's laptops have permanent RAM that can't be upgraded, so max out when possible.

Hard drives are vital in terms of how much room you have to store data. Video files can become huge. For example, if you have a 256 GB hard drive and have a video session that's 200 GB, it won't take long before your computer starts showing alerts about not having enough space to continue. The larger the hard drive, the more information you can store. It's common for video editors to purchase external hard drives for a specific project to save space.

Hard drives come in different types and speeds. The faster the model, the more expensive it is. Today's mid-level to high-end laptops are going to have solid state drives (SSD), and these drives provide superior speeds compared to the older, cheaper, 7200 rpm hard drives.

Having a faster drive increases the read and write speeds during editing. The minimum recommended size is 256 GB.

The central processing unit (CPU) is probably the most critical component. A more powerful processor is better; however, these come at a high cost. Today (2018), the recommended processor is the mobile Intel® Core i7 or at minimum Core i5. Alongside the CPU is the graphics processing unit (GPU), which is very popular in PC gaming but also has an effect on processing performance. GPUs for laptops are very limited compared to desktop computers, but when possible consider an upgrade. Depending on the software, the GPU can be utilized for faster rendering and editing.

Peripheral devices depend on which operating system you purchased: Windows or Apple. You'll probably need to purchase additional devices and cables. For example, many of today's laptops do not have optical drives, so if you intend to play or burn CDs, DVDs, or Blu-ray discs, you'll need to purchase an external burner. However, it may not be that simple. If you buy a new MacBook Pro, you'll have to purchase a special USB C-to-USB Mini adapter. Making sure your camera, hard drives, etc. can connect with your laptop may require additional adapter devices and cables.

DIGITAL CAMERAS

INTRODUCTION

There's no better moment to become a student or viral video producer. The transition from analog to digital cameras is all but finished. We're not developing film any more for the most part, so you don't need a darkroom and you don't need to know the chemistry. You just need a digital camera and editing software to begin the process. There is a trade-off, though, because now not only do you need to learn how to frame, shoot, and operate a camera, but you also have to become a bit of computer wiz, and deal with all of the intricacies of camera and computer compatibility. Understanding the process of transferring files from the camera to the computer is just another necessary component of the postproduction workflow.

The first step that you'll need to take, is to start to familiarize yourself with the basic digital camera types. Knowing how to deal with digital single lens reflex (DSLR) cameras compared to mirrorless and point and shoot versions, distinguish between a GoPro and an Osmo, and even earn the difference between a VR unit and a smartphone camera. Each of these cameras is markedly different from the other, with features that will vary depending on the brand, lens adaptability, cable connections, and the recording software that are included.

Fortunately, most digital cameras now come equipped with a standard universal serial bus (USB) interface, which allows a device to connect directly to a computer where you can download the files and edit. For older generation devices, there are two typical types of USB connections: USB mini (the most common) and USB micro, an increasingly popular choice for smart and mirrorless cameras. It's important to be aware of the distinction between

FIGURE 6.3   While not a fully professional camera, the GoPro digital video camera has proved to be a popular sports camera with consumers.

connectors. For example, the popular sports camera line GoPro, depending on the model, may use USB mini or USB-C. Identifying the type of interface is step one.

Step two is making sure your computer has a compatible port to interface with your camera. When faced with a compatibility issue between a device and a computer, a trending marketing feature on some new cameras is uploading files to the cloud or to social media sites via Wi-Fi. This is a cool feature for taking short, 30-second selfies, but recording many minutes' (or hours') worth of HD digital video creates huge files that take too long to upload, followed by spending more wasted time in the downloading process.

Device drivers and software are two of the most overlooked hardware aspects. It's great when technology works immediately out of the box, but that's rarely the case. A device driver is a small piece of software installed on the computer that facilitates communication between the device and the computer. When a device is not recognized by a computer, check the manufacturer's website for additional software to complete the install. Device-specific software or applications may require installation before you can connect the device to the computer. New and widely popular virtual reality (VR) cameras tend to have proprietary software that connects the VR camera to a computer and also have features such as converting video files from the camera into an editable format that a digital editing system can use.

When all else fails, an inexpensive alternative is to purchase a secure digital high-capacity (SDHC) or micro SDHC card reader, take the SDHC or micro SDHC card from the device, place it inside the card reader, and plug it into your computer. Even if you don't have the right cables and or interface ports, you can still transfer your files.

DIGITAL VIDEO EDITING

INTRODUCTION TO EDITING

Editing is an art form unto itself and has both a functional and an aesthetic purpose. At its most basic, the functional aspect of the editing process consists of sorting through the raw, unedited camera *footage* (taken during the production stage), then selecting the best clip or *take* (each unique attempt to obtain the perfect shot) from that available footage to cut into a polished, individual scene. These edited scenes are then strung together to build even longer *sequences*, which reflect a succession of related events or thematic plot line developments. Ideally, editing should add energy and tempo to your production, evoke emotion, expand or contract time and, most significantly, help the audience to connect-the-dots as to the details of the story that they are watching.

By contrast, editing aesthetics concern the underlying principles or judgments that are used to determine when and where to make an edit. An aesthetic approach to editing will emphasize using transitions only when required, such as those that are motivated by an obvious movement or flow of action, as a way to inform the audience as to new developments, or to reinforce the main story themes through the use of color, composition or camera framing. Over time, the aesthetics involved in the editing process have developed their own particular set of operating principles and rules of usage. In some ways, mastering the aesthetics of editing is like mastering a new language, and just like with any language, editing comes with its own distinct vocabulary, syntax, and punctuation that constitute its own unique form of grammar.

THE GRAMMAR OF EDITING

Historically, we can thank all of the pioneers of film and television for their contributions to creating the foundation we have today, known as the grammar of editing. These pioneers did more than create motion-picture-camera technology; they recognized the need to comprehensively express the nature of a story. Artists such as Georges Méliès, an early developer of visual effects or Edwin S. Porter, who used cross-cutting and dissolves in his films; and many other artisans from the past and present contributed to the editing tools we use today.

Early film production was heavily influenced by live theater and thus silent cinema adopted the same approach to audience perspective as the theater had. This meant that the first films all used the exact same camera set up, shooting each scene with only a single camera trained on a

FIGURE 6.4A   Georges Méliès (1861–1938), French filmmaker and cinematographer.

FIGURE 6.4B   Edwin S. Porter (1870–1941), U.S. filmmaker and cinematographer.

wide shot of all of the action, as if one is watching the film from a seat in the arena, with a view of the entire stage. Audiences quickly grew tired of this limited approach to viewing perspective and it didn't take long for them to begin demanding more variety and creativity. Soon, filmmakers such as Porter began to experiment with their films by adding more shot variety, interspersing wide shots with medium shots and even close-ups, which helped add to the visual detail and complexity of the storytelling. Today, by our contemporary cinematic standards, unedited media content on any platform (film, TV or streaming) is often considered unwatchable. Today we are accustomed to watching films and videos that contain an incredible number of rapid shot transitions and varying camera perspectives.

The core feature of editing grammar is the use of *transitions* as a means to switch between different characters, locations and/or camera framings. There are three main transition types: **cuts, dissolves and wipes.** A cut is the most common type of edit transition; it is an instantaneous transition from Shot A to the subsequent Shot B. Cuts are vital to editing as they allow an editor to change camera perspectives or to move from one location to the next, in a nearly invisible and transparent manner, without interrupting the main flow of the action. A cut on action is a way of transitioning from shot to shot while still matching the main action.

*Cutaway*s and *cut-ins* are also used in many ways. The main purpose is to provide context in a scene and the environment of the characters. In terms of a narrative tool, editors will cut to a shot that explains what the characters are referring or reacting to and so on. Picture a scene with a nervous man pacing back and forth, while, in the background, a phone starts to ring. As an editor you may want to cut away to a shot of the phone on a table ringing and then cut back to the man to see his reaction and then cut-in to a shot of a hand hesitantly reaching for the phone. This can help build suspense and the pacing of the scene.

Pacing is significant, since editing needs to have a rhythm to the flow of action, depending on the type of video or film being shot. Some cuts are more structured, and others are interpretative. The *hard cut* or *standard cut* is most basic type of cut. It's the end of one shot going to the beginning of another. For a viral video an editor may

FIGURE 6.5 The hard cut or standard cut is most basic type of cut; it is an instantaneous transition from the end of one shot directly to the beginning of another.

want to do something splashy to attract attention, combining rapid hard cuts and bold visual graphics. For a romantic video, slow, drifting shots reveal the chemistry between the characters. A horror movie can use jarring cuts to add suspense, waiting until the last possible moment before revealing the monster. The point is that, as you edit, try to consciously take into account the pace of the overall scene, the emotional effect it should have, and when the appropriate moment is to make that reveal to the viewer. When done correctly, the audience doesn't even notice any cuts, but when the editing is off, even just a little, the audience can detect it immediately, like hearing an off-note in a piece of music.

Occasionally, an editor will want to use a cut in a way that calls attention to itself in a more visible manner. *Jump cuts* are popular way to achieve this effect as they seem to "jump" from one point of reference, time, position, or scale to another. Typically, the sequence is composed of multiple shots from different angles of the same scene, so the editor can jump from position to position in order to show the magnitude of the event, the beauty of the environment, the number of characters involved, or the passage of time, for example. Jump cuts are popular in today's contemporary cinematography.

In addition to these basics, there are also some highly specialized cuts, such as *audio split edit that involves the use of an L-cut or a J-cut.,* These types of cuts are popular way of using the audio from one shot (Shot A) to overlay onto a different shot (Shot B). An L-cut might start with a shot of a character speaking to a group of people, before the visual then cuts to a reaction shot of an audience member, even though the audio from the original clip continues to run. Picture a football locker room at halftime. The team is losing the game, and the camera frames a close-up shot of the head coach who begins an inspirational speech. The coach begins to speak, and you cut to different players, showing their reactions to the coach's speech, including close-ups of one player's fear, another player's determination, a third player adjusting his gear, and so on, all with the coach's speech continuing as the primary audio source. As the coach finishes, the scene cuts back to the coach to see his reaction to the players.

A *J-cut* is the opposite of the L-cut; here, shot B is using the audio from shot A. Using the locker-room scenario, instead of starting the scene with a close-up of the head coach speaking, you decide to use a POV shot that slowly reveals the players walking onto the field, as in the background we hear the coach's speech, but we don't see him. The scene cuts to the locker room and eventually reveals the coach. These types of cuts provide a narrative exposition of the character's purpose and emotional state to the viewer. Why are they called J-cut and L-cuts? Visualize a timeline in a digital editing application, with video track #1 (V1) and audio track #1 (A1). When performing a J-cut, edited shot A cuts to shot B on V1 but uses all the audio from shot B on A1. Visually, on the timeline, the editing of the clips resembles the letter *J*, while the L-cut resembles the letter *L*. Many cut-editing synonyms names are simply reflective of the cinematic era, technology, or geographic location in which it was first used.

Of the remaining transition types, **dissolves** or mixes are the second most common transition type. Dissolves are a type of gradual transition from Shot A to the subsequent Shot B, as Shot A slowly begins to recede and increase in transparency, while Shot B continues to become more pronounced and opaque, until it completely replaces Shot A completely. Fades are a specialized subset of dissolves, used at beginning or end of program, act or scene. Instead of a gradual transition from Shot A to Shot B, a fade in or fade out transitions between an image and a background color, usually black. Editors use long *fade ins or fade outs* to give the impression of time passing or a change of location.

The final transition type is a *wipe*, which is any type of patterned transition from Shot A to Shot B.. There are an unlimited number of wipe transitions such as flips, page turns, vertical blinds or picture-in-picture. Many of these wipes are very visually complex so they call attention to their presence, which can sometimes prove to be an unwanted distraction to the storytelling. However, wipes can be very effective, especially in a viral video, where the goal is to add energy to the program, or to showcase multiple products, locations and characters simultaneously.

This by no means is an exhaustive list of grammar of the editing techniques, but it should be enough to get you going and help you understand the language of editing.

PSYCHOLOGICAL IMPORTANCE OF EDITING

As humans, we connect psychologically with the outside world through our senses, primarily in what we see and hear. So, when we watch a movie where the characters stranded in a cold environment, we begin to shiver right along with them. Similarly, as an audience, our hearts begin to race in anticipation when we hear the suspenseful music build up, just before the killer jumps out from the blackness of the shadows. That is one of the main reasons that we watch emotionally challenging movies in the first place, because they tell stories that we connect with us, based on our

FIGURE 6.6 A wipe is a patterned transition that is used to add energy to the production, show the passage of time, indicate a change in location, or create a split-screen effect.

own personal experiences, as we fight to hold back the tears or burst out in uncontrollable laughter.

Filmmakers know how to press viewers' buttons. In the 1900s, Lev Kuleshov coined the **Kuleshov effect**, a psychological/emotional reaction to a particular sequence of images. In short, an actor's facial expression could be interpreted in various ways, depending on the subsequently viewed image. As an example of this, Kuleshov used a close-up image of an actor with a blank, neutral expression on his face, then immediately after the actor's image appeared, Kuleshov cut to a shot of a steaming bowl of soup, before cutting back, once again, to the same actor with the same neutral expression on his face. No dialogue was uttered anywhere within the footage. Two other versions of the film were also prepared, with the only difference being that the footage of the soup was replaced in one film by an image of a child in a coffin, and, in the other by footage of an attractive young lady.

When the individual edited clips were shown to different audiences, there was universal praise for the actor's performance. What was unique however, was how each different audience interpreted what they had seen. For those that saw the version of the film that included the actor with a bowl of soup, respondents felt that the actor was portraying someone suffering from severe hinger. On the other hand, those that saw the version of the film with the dead child, were certain that the actor was displaying profound grief. Finally, the audience that viewed the third iteration of the film believed that the actor was displaying an emotion of smoldering lust or passion. Realize that the facial expression of the actor never changed; it was exactly the same clip. What had changed was, the viewer's feelings about the actor based on the juxtaposition of images that they had just witnessed. The audience applied their own meaning to the film's visual content based solely upon the emotional connection that had been triggered. The Kuleshov effect can create a powerful experience when visual editing, sound design, and music score are combined.

CORE VIDEO EDITING APPROACHES

There are two broad philosophical approaches applied to the art to editing: *montage editing* style and *continuity editing* style. The montage editing approach is one that is very foregrounded, with edits that often call attention to themselves due to their stylistic excesses. Montage editing favors a collision of images over the seamless blending of visual content used in the continuity editing style. Montage sequences combine numerous shots together in rapid fashion, usually with the inclusion of unique transitions or special optical effects, music, and even dance. Montage sequence are a convenient way for an editor to suggest either the passage of time, or to help create symbolic meaning between images (as is espoused in Soviet montage theory).

The other core video editing approach is *continuity editing*, shuns the use of excessive transitions or flashy optical effects. Even when transitions are used within the continuity style, they are often presented in a subtle, understated manner. In this editing approach, long uninterrupted takes are used without a reliance on frequent cuts or cutaways. Continuity editing also relies heavily on the use of *mise-en-scene*, which is a French term that means "placing on stage." *Mise-en-scene* refers the arrangement of everything that appears on screen and within the camera frame, including the actors, lighting, décor, props, make-up and costumes. Continuity editing and the mise-en-scene approach place a preeminence on the environment in which the story takes place, and it allows for shots to linger on a room or a landscape even after the characters depart that space. Mise-en-scène is most often used to evoke a lasting mood or feelings through the use of sumptuous visuals, and not just for selected scenes but throughout the entire production.

STAGES OF EDITING

Editing can be broken down into three stages, the ***first cut,*** the ***rough cut,*** and the ***final cut.*** The first cut is a quick assembly of clips on the timeline. The editor is spending time organizing files and making notes on the best shots. Normally, the editor has a script and knows what shots to use and the order. During editing, missing shots can be held in place with temporary title cards, such as "car shot goes here." This makes the spot easy to find and replace in future editing sessions. At this stage, the editor establishes the flow of the editing and begins to develop a style. Color correction and transitions will happen down the road. The first cut is usually shown internally to the production team for feedback because it's not polished enough to show to an audience.

Next is the rough cut. Each stage of editing builds on the previous stage. At this point, the timeline has been completely laid out. All temporary clips have been replaced. The editor begins to nip and tuck, working on the timing. Editing becomes more technical and focuses on the narrative. The director usually joins this stage because there's enough content on the timeline to craft the film. Titles, graphics, and visual effects are temporary placeholders at this stage. The rough cut is ready to be shared and receive feedback.

The final cut is when all of the timing and editing to the narrative are finalized. Nothing is truly final, but it's ready to share. On a large production, the editor agrees that all of the edits are final, referred to as ***picture lock.*** This version of the edit is given to music composers, visual effects artists, motion graphics artists, and a colorist. The focus changes from editing to adding sound design, color correction, and visual effects. The final cut will definitely go through a few more

FIGURE 6.7 A video editor reviews footage during an edit session.

editing sessions, where final decisions are made about removing scenes, adjusting effects, and changing music, sometimes based on feedback from viewers.

Ultimately, the goal is to cut together your best available footage into one continuous stream of purposeful action, rather than the mere assemblage of a random series of shots that lack any coherent order or meaning. For an editor to be successful in this goal, they are reliant on production team and DP to provide them with footage that features multiple camera angles, perspectives, and framings. A wide selection of footage with sufficient coverage provides the editor with additional flexibility and creative options.

MOTION GRAPHICS

INTRODUCTION

Motion graphics, animated graphics uniquely designed for a media project, can include specialized logos, fonts, colors, stylized filters, and other artistic special effects. Each major media software developer now markets a trademark motion graphic application, such as Adobe's After Effects or Apple's Motion. These motion graphics programs can be very simple to use or extremely complex. Used properly, they can create emotional and thought-provoking content that helps to establish the tone for the entire production.

Saul Bass, one of the greatest graphic designers and filmmakers of the 20th century, created many of the world's most popular logos for companies including AT&T, Continental Airlines, Quaker, and Lawry's. Bass, who also created animated opening-title sequences for films such as *The Man with the Golden Arm, Vertigo, Psycho, Spartacus, Goodfellas,* and *Casino,* said, "Style is substance." Today, opening titles are typically created by a team of designers, animators, compositors, etc. However, any editor can create simple motion graphics using a digital video editing application.

TITLE SAFE AND ACTION SAFE

Title safe and ***action safe*** are visible margins in a video-editing application, designating safe areas to place graphics, text, and lower thirds without cutting them off because of inconsistent overscan on computer monitors and television sets. Today, most multimedia monitors can control this using their remote control. Even if you don't plan to show your film on broadcast TV, it's still wise to work within the title-safe and action-safe areas. Title-safe and action-safe areas are also necessary for social media sites such as YouTube and streaming sites such as Netflix, which enforce title-safe and action-safe rules for viewers watching on smart TVs or cell phones. That's why it is so important to know the size and shape of the output media's ***aspect ratio***, the mathematical relationship of the image's total height to its overall width, determining how wide or how narrow an image is.

FIGURE 6.8 Motion graphics, animated graphics designed for a media project, can include specialized logos, fonts, colors, stylized filters, and other artistic special effects.

FIGURE 6.9 Title safe and action safe are visible margins in a video-editing application, designating safe areas to place graphics, text, and lower thirds content.

TITLES

Film titles today do more than showcase the name of film. Graphic design and filmmaking combine to create motion graphics. Titles can be simply white text over a black background or can grow into an aesthetic presence just as powerful as the film. Every film, television program, documentary, etc. should have an opening title or more advanced animated opening credits. Early films used a title card, a static frame with text information that took up the full screen. The name of the film, its director, producer, distributor, etc. were all written in a serif-style font created by hand. Today we use digital video editors or specialized software to accomplish this task. Today's titles are not limited to one card, and it's very common to see a title card cross dissolve into additional cards with actor and producer credits, eventually fading to black before opening on the first shot. It's always a good idea to have some sort of opening credits for your film; these can be either static (nonmoving) or animated. For now, as student/viral video producers, let's keep things fairly simple.

LOWER THIRDS

Lower thirds are common in documentaries and television programs, especially news-related programs. However, no rule says that lower thirds can't be used in films, and often they are but in a more advanced form. In its simplest form, lower thirds are a text graphic usually placed in the title safe area on the right or left side of the frame. When animated, moving from right to left, they are known as a *crawl.* The text information can be designed

FIGURE 6.10   Alexia Williams and Morgan Williams hosting CSUDH's Bulletin TV, identified with graphics in the lower third of the frame.

with additional artwork, such as background elements, contrasting colors, icons, animations, etc. The text information can have different font styles, drop shadows, font sizes, etc.

Usually lower thirds are arranged in tiers, and each tier is a line of new information. Visualize a TV news interview; at the bottom of the screen is a lower third with three tiers. Tier #1 contains the most important information; it has the largest font and most prominent position, and it features the interviewee's name. Tier #2, often referred to as a locator, is set in a smaller font, with a font color less contrasting to tier #1, and it contains the interviewee's general location. Tier #3 has the smallest font but the most text, is the same color as tier #2, and is a short, written recap of what the interviewee witnessed. Lower thirds are not always in the lower third of the screen. There are many variations such as news tickers, time and date pop-ups, stock quotes, sports scores, etc.

SUBTITLES AND CLOSED CAPTIONING

Subtitles and closed captioning provide written dialogue of the characters in sync with the actors' speech and gestures, along with additional information to the viewer that can be translated into multiple languages to make content available for audiences with hearing impairments. In the early days of silent film, the predecessor of modern subtitles was intertitles, hand-drafted title cards that were shown between scenes in lieu of dialogue. Subtitles are typically centered and positioned in the lower third portion of the screen. Although there is no official standard for subtitles, most editors use a sans serif font (which is easier to read), white or off-white font color, a drop shadow, and at least a 12- to 14-point font size. Subtitles can be generated in a digital video-editing application. Closed captioning is similar to subtitles in terms of visually displaying text information but isn't limited to films. Congress requires all video programming distributors, cable companies, and broadcasters to provide closed captions for TV programs to make them as inclusive as possible.

ENDING CREDITS

Ending credits, or closing credits, are presented at the end of a film, TV show, documentary, etc. Ending credits are basically a list of everyone who was involved in the project's creation. A common set of credits includes producers, directors, writers, actors, musicians, crew, sponsors, distributors, legal and copyright information,

FIGURE 6.11   Still frame from a closed captioning demonstration utilizing the Felix the Cat cartoon "The Goose that Laid the Golden Egg."

etc. Ending credits can be static title cards or presented in a list format for medium-to-large productions where you need to credit more than 25 people. The most common form of ending credits is a formatted list of names accompanied by job titles. The list is animated, scrolling from the bottom of the screen to the top at a speed that can be read while moving; these are called rolling credits or simply as a *credit roll*. In a simple form, a credit rolls is white text over a black background with music. Ending credits are not limited to black and white. Many films have enhanced ending credits with animation, creative fonts, color, size, position choices, video clips, out- takes/bloopers, and additional short scenes announcing a sequel or spin-off film after the credits, referred to by many names such as post-credit scene, stingers, credit extras, and after-credits scene.

VISUAL EFFECTS

INTRODUCTION

Visual effects (VFX) manipulate or enhance live-action footage in ways that can't be accomplished during the live-action shoot. In short, the effects are applied during the post-production stage, typically in conjunction with or after picture lock. VFX is a huge umbrella that includes disciplines in special effects, motion graphics, compositing, 3D animation, motion capture, and much more. As a student/viral video producer, this isn't something to worry about just yet.

FIGURE 6.12 Video of Obama-impersonator Iman Crosson (YouTube channel Alphacat). Top panel: in front of a green screen (chroma key). Bottom panel: in the composited version.

COMPOSITING

A common and affordable technique for student/viral video producers is shooting video on a green screen. This can lead to simple but effective visual effects. Actors perform in front of a consumer-grade green screen background, or *chroma key,* made from cloth, paper or plastic. Chroma key green paint and green body suits can also be used. After lighting and shooting the subjects, a video-editing application such as Premiere Pro or a visual-effects application such as After Effects can be used to key out the green color and substitute a background plate, a separate video or image of another location. Put them both together, and you've created a composite.

COLOR GRADING

Color grading allows a video editor to visually adjust the color properties of a clip. There's a technical side and an artistic side to color grading. On the technical side, clips that are over- or underexposed can be adjusted to match more closely. For example, if the color doesn't match when cutting from shot A to shot B, that can be distracting to the viewer. On the artistic side, color has an emotional value to humans, and it can be used to direct the mood of the storyline. To give the impression of physically being cold, a blue tint can be added to the video. An overcast day at the beach can be given a warm impression with an orange tint. With the right combination of techniques, a day scene can become a night scene.

AUDIO POSTPRODUCTION

INTRODUCTION TO SOUND DESIGN

Sound design is absolutely necessary and shouldn't be an afterthought. Sound design includes sound effects, spoken dialogue, ambience, music, etc. Take all of these sound elements and combine them to elevate your film. Consider sound design as another character in the story. In audio postproduction, in the editing stage, dialogue is usually the first concern. It needs to be the loudest and cleanest audibly. Second are sound effects, including Foley and ambience sounds. Finally, music is added, using popular music or original music scored by a composer. Great sound design can take an average motion picture and give it life by creating an atmosphere that emotionally grabs the audience's attention. However, poor sound design can take the most beautiful shot edit and make it painful to watch.

SOFTWARE

Like digital video-editing applications, there are many digital audio-editing applications. Programs such as Audacity, Avid's Protools, and Adobe's Audition are popular choices. Buying separate audio software isn't necessary. All modern digital video-editing systems offer limited audio-editing tools, plug-ins, and overall functionality, offering more than enough for a student/indie filmmaker to use proficiently. More important than software are basic audio-editing techniques. Many of these audio-editing programs mirror those for editing video, reducing the technical learning curve. Viewers are very good at hearing distinguishable changes in audio, the background-noise ratio, pops between cuts, and sync issues that immediately divert their attention from the film. On a major production with a large budget, a team of editors works on sound design. You won't have that luxury on a small-scale viral video, but that's not a valid excuse for your projects to not have clean-sounding audio.

CORE AUDIO EDITING TECHNIQUES

Audio can be mixed in mono, stereo, and surround-sound formats. Cuts work the same in audio as they do in video in a standard digital video-editing application. Video and audio are separated into tracks: one track for video and one track for audio. By default, when you cut a video clip, the audio clip is automatically cut in the same location. As your editing experience grows, you will need to have control directly over the audio clip length without affecting the video length. In the core video-editing techniques section, we discussed J-cuts and L-cuts, which are a form of split audio editing, having audio from shot A also on shot B and vice versa.

Synchronization, or sync for short, comes into play for dialogue, music, or sound effects in your project. In terms of dialogue, when audio is out of sync with the picture, the characters' mouths move but the audio is noticeably off or out of sync, and you must make adjustments. **Offset** is nudging the audio to the left or right until the voice matches the mouth movement. Another concern is background noise, also referred to as **ambience** or **room tone.** It's not uncommon to be on a noisy location, making it hard to understand the dialogue, but you can apply a noise-reduction effect such as DeNoiser in Premiere Pro, Background Noise Removal in Final Cut, or Audio Noise Reduction in Avid to reduce noise and clean up the dialogue.

In extreme cases where the audio is completely unusable, you'll need to replace the dialogue. **Automatic dialogue replacement** (ADR) is a technique of recording replacement dialogue. The actors repeat the same lines from the scene in the same exact way as first performed. ADR can also be used to fix mistakes during production. This is really a last resort because ADR is time consuming and difficult to match with other production audio. Another option is **voice over** (VO), recorded separately as a new narration dialogue track and used over a shot that doesn't have any speaking parts.

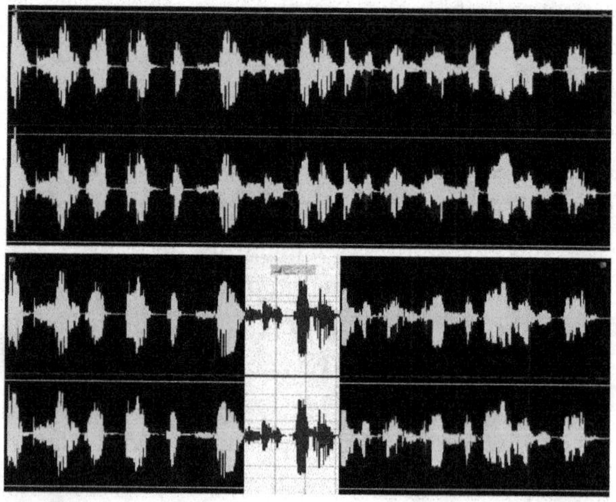

Popping occurs when the background noise level is noticeably different from shot A to shot B, cutting on a spoken dialogue or a sound from shot A that should be heard in shot B. It's a balancing act, trying to match the noise levels. Filters and effects can be used to achieve that balance, but another option is to crossfade audio on the cut between shot A and shot B using an audio transition. Begin by finding the shot with loudest ambient noise first and make adjustments to reduce noise

FIGURE 6.13   A digital audio file waveform display.

levels. Use that clip to determine and compare levels on the other shots in the scene. The ambient noise level should be consistent throughout the entire film.

When it comes to mixing audio, there are a variety of workflows, techniques, and philosophies. To keep things simple, let's assume you're creating a stereo mix, meaning that audio can be heard on the left and right sides. Your camera most likely is recording in stereo by default, as well. Every digital editing application has a **volume unit meter** (VU meter). This meter has a scale, typically from -∞ dB at the bottom to 0 dB at the top, split into two columns that represent the left channel and the right channel in a stereo mix. When you play back the timeline, the audio signal is shown bouncing up and down on the VU meter, in Adobe Premiere from green to red. Green audio levels are low, and as the level increases, green turns into yellow, and when audio exceeds 0 dB or *peak,* it turns red. You never want audio to hit peak levels, which will probably result in audible distortion.

A quick explanation about decibels (*dB*): Invented by Bell Telephone Labs, named after Alexander Graham Bell, a **decibel** is a unit of measurement used to measure the intensity of a sound. The digital VU meter uses a logarithmic scale, starting with -∞ dB meaning no detectable sound or negative sound. As sound levels increase, they are reflected on the meter, with 0 dB representing the loudest sound. Exceeding 0 dB, audio will have distortion. Using the VU meter as guide can help you visually adjust the audio levels of dialogue, sound effects, music, etc. Here's a formula to get you started: Dialogue or spoken words should be adjusted to land between -12 dB and -6 dB, the latter being louder as the level gets closer to 0 dB. Adjust sound effects to land between -24 dB and -18 dB. In scenes where there's dialogue, place music at -36 dB to -30 dB to prevent the music from fighting with dialogue. For scenes where there isn't any dialogue, music takes over the scene at levels set between -12 dB and -6 dB. No matter what combination of levels, effects, or edits are made on the timeline, the best tool for mixing audio is your ears.

EXPORTING FILES FOR DISTRIBUTION

INTRODUCTION

Digital technology has changed every aspect of the film industry. The accessibility and compatibility of digital media files makes them easy to distribute across multiple platforms and devices. You can export your digital content or quickly upload it to social networks, making it instantly available to watch and enjoy practically anywhere within the known universe. The most important part of this process is learning how to export your content in the most applicable file format. Exporting files is a function that every NLE offers, but before you export, you need understand the difference between video and audio file types, lossy and lossless compression, and final image size.

FILE TYPES

Another technical aspect of digital video editing is understanding file types. Most digital editing systems import a wide range of file types, including .jpg, .png, .psd, .mp4, .mov, .avi, .mp3, .wav, .aiff, .m4a, and many more. The typical three-letter file extension tells the computer's operating system the type of file. For example, a .jpg file (/jay peg/), an acronym for Joint Photographic Experts Group, is an image file. An .mp4 (/m p four/), an acronym for Moving Picture Expert Group-4, is a file format that can store video and audio data, made most popular by its ability to be streamed over the Internet. An .mp3 (/m p three/) is an audio file format with optional metadata information such as the name of the song, the artist, a thumbnail image, etc. It's not uncommon for manufacturing and technology companies to use completely different file formats, or even proprietary or modified formats for their products. Knowing the difference between an image, audio, and video file is imperative to determining the types of files that can be imported into a digital video-editing application for editing.

COMPRESSION

Media compression comes in three forms: lossy, lossless, and uncompressed (also referred to as "raw"). All media, whether video, audio, or image files, can be compressed. Lossy compression encodes a file by permanently removing data based on an algorithm called a codec. These codecs affect file resolution, image size, and bit depth, creating a smaller file with less quality. Lossless compression reduces file size and uses a codec, but the quality stays the same. Raw media is not compressed and offers the highest quality; however; it also has the largest file sizes, taking up more hard-drive space and requiring more processing power from the editing computer. Video and audio files specifically have two parts: a container or format and a codec or compression algorithm.

Choosing the format depends on the requirements of the distribution platform. YouTube, for example, recommends using an .MP4 container and H.264 codec for maximum quality. The .MP4 format is designed to play on computers, tablets, smart phones, etc. The H.264 codec creates a small file size that downloads faster. Compressing media is extremely technical but is also a common and necessary process; it's a balance between file size and quality. All professional video editing applications have export presets, making the process simple. Just find the preset and the application does the rest.

IMAGE SIZE

SD, HD, AND UHD (4K)

As discussed in **Chapter 5—Digital vs. Analog Media**, digital image size is composed of width and height in a unit of measurement called a *pixel*. Broadcast video files have predetermined image sizes. Digital *standard definition* (SD) is 720 × 480, *high definition* (HD) is 1280 × 720, and full HD is

1920 × 1080. (In this instance, the number *1920* refers to 1920 pixels of vertical resolution, and the *1080* refers to 1080 pixels of vertical resolution. Increasingly, *ultra high definition* (UHD), also referred to as 4k, which is 3840 x 2160 in size, is gaining traction as the de facto, digital video standard.

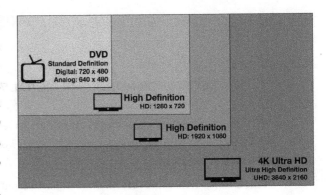

FIGURE 6.14 A graph of standard video resolutions as encountered in different media.

When editing the video sequence, you should always strive to match the project's frame size to that of the source files. If you shoot in 1080p, for example, then your sequence should also be in 1080p. Mixing formats can cause timing issues. In cases where you want to shrink the image size and optimize it for online distribution, choosing the right export settings will do this for you. The point is to edit the project just once and then allow the software's editing application to create all of the various export sizes that are needed.

With a review of all of the three main production stages behind us, it's now time for our viral production to be released to its intended audience. What is the best way to drum up publicity for our video and help it to reach its target audience? We'll explore exactly what steps to take in order to maximize the popularity of your viral video in Section III, **Digital Distribution in the Viral Age.**

SECTION II: WRAP UP AND REVIEW

KEY TIPS FOR NONLINEAR DIGITAL VIDEO EDITING

- Confirm that your computer meets the minimum requirements for editing high-definition 1080 digital video, i.e., CPU i7, 1 GB or higher GPU, 12–16 GB RAM, 1 TB hard drive space.

- Create a workflow or process for shooting on a digital camera and transferring the data to the editing computer.

- External hard drives are recommended. For example, shooting digital video at 1920 × 1080 HD resolution at 24 frames per second (fps) is approximately 500 MB per minute, roughly 30 GB for an hour.

- Avoid cloud-based storage as an alternative to internal or external hard drives.

- Using professional-grade NLE software is highly recommended. Buying cheaper software can save you money, but often times they fail to offer specific editing features or easy compatibility with your existing hardware.

- Use online video services such as Google Drive, iCloud, YouTube, and Vimeo to share video edits with production members, clients, etc.

- When it comes to both your raw footage and your edits in postproduction, always create backup copies—even backups of backups!

QUESTIONS

1. Have you identified the basic members essential to a viral media production crew and the responsibilities of each of those crew members? Imagine a scenario in which that production crew must choose a location at random, e.g., an isolated desert oasis, a busy downtown street corner, a large sporting event, or a seedy, after-hours cabaret, that poses some level of shooting complexity. Assign your student teams the responsibility to detail exactly what production hardware, practical shooting skills, postproduction expertise, and/or additional resources will be required to complete this hypothetical production, and how long it will take to complete.

2. What is a *codec*? How is a codec related to digital file compression, file type, and file distribution? What are the primary differences between an *analog signal* and *digital waveforms*? How do pixel size and image resolutions such as SD, HD 720, Full HD, 2K HD, and 4K UHD factor into the selection of codec for final export?

3. According to the readings, what are three main editing components or techniques? What purpose do these techniques serve in advancing the overall storytelling? What helps a video editor determine when to choose one specific editing technique over another as they try to create a meaningful visual narrative? How does the overall edit evolve as it progresses from first cut to final cut?

4. According to the readings, how has the *Grammar of Editing* changed over the history of filmmaking? How does editing heighten a production's psychological importance by increasing the audience's emotional tension and level of engagement? How does the Kuleshov effect contribute to the perceived emotional impact that a film or video has on an audience?

PROJECTS AND EXERCISES

- **Storyboard exercise:**
  In order to gain a better understanding of the previsualization process, have students create a traditional hand-drawn storyboard of at least 10–15 individual frames that will then be scanned and uploaded as separate digital image files. The frames will be imported and laid out for a final presentation using a program such as Power-Point, Photoshop, Premiere Pro, Final Cut, Illustrator, etc. Have students rearrange the order and sequence of the storyboard to help visualize the story in different ways. To master video editing, a student will first need to develop their own sense of visual logic and layout in order to tell a story that can hold an audience's attention. Students should be able to explain their final layout decisions based on the logical sequencing of their storyboards.

- **Camera framing/scavenger hunt challenge:**
  To help students gain a better perspective on the importance of visual composition and layout, create a list of locations and camera-framing challenges. The list should progressively become more difficult to find the subject and frame the shot. Encourage creativity over technicality so students can focus on understanding composition individually rather than simply aiming and taking the shot. Students submit their work for class feedback; allow time for each student to describe how the shot was composed.

- **Individual hardware and software evaluations:**
  Have each student bring their camera and laptop to class. Escort the students to a location where there is enough space for each student to pair up and shoot a small a clip. The clip will be approximately ten seconds long, beginning with a slate and countdown then the student saying "Hello, my name is (their name) " Bring the entire class back into the classroom. The students will connect their camera to their personal or instructional computer and transfer the file to the desktop. Students should be able identify the file type, file size, and resolution of the digital video file.

- **Demystifying the digital media export process:**
  Exporting video can be complex and confusing, as there's a lot of technical requirements that require consideration. To accommodate for all of these possible media configurations, most video editing applications provide some type of user interface filled with menu options and user presets to choose from. For this exercise, have students export a video or audio file in at least three different configuration settings, by having them vary the basic property settings for: image resolution, compression and file type.

- **Complete your own viral video production:**
  For advanced classes, have your student groups create a narrative video that contains original HD video footage, employs proper lighting and digital audio recording standards, includes a polished soundtrack mix, and features advanced video edit transitions along with appropriate text, motion graphics, and/or special effects. The content and length of the completed video will be decided by the instructor based on the scope of the production. All preproduction and production assets, including scripts, storyboards, research materials, equipment checkout sheets, character descriptions, edit logs, etc., must also be submitted.

CREDITS

- Fig. 6.1: Copyright © Multimediadiscount (CC BY-SA 3.0) at https://commons.wikimedia.org/wiki/File:CD_DVD_Collections.jpg.
- Fig. 6.2: Copyright © 2018 by Adobe Systems Incorporated.
- Fig. 6.3: Copyright © Resolution hire (CC BY-SA 4.0) at https://commons.wikimedia.org/wiki/File:GoPro_Hero_4_Black.jpg.
- Fig. 6.4: Copyright © Klaus Eichler (CC BY-SA 3.0) at https://commons.wikimedia.org/wiki/File:Max_Mittelbach_digital_editing_suite.jpg.
- Fig. 6.5a: Source: https://commons.wikimedia.org/wiki/File:George_Melies.jpg.
- Fig. 6.5b: Source: https://commons.wikimedia.org/wiki/File:Edwin_S_Porter.jpg.
- Fig. 6.6: Copyright © Thetawave~commonswiki (CC BY-SA 3.0) at https://commons.wikimedia.org/wiki/File:Hard_cut.jpg.
- Fig. 6.7: Copyright © Thetawave~commonswiki (CC BY-SA 3.0) at https://commons.wikimedia.org/wiki/File:Soft_cut_trick.jpg.
- Fig 6.11: Source: https://commons.wikimedia.org/wiki/File:Closed_Caption_Demonstration_Still-Felix.png.
- Fig 6.12: Copyright © Iman Crosson (CC BY-SA 3.0) at https://commons.wikimedia.org/wiki/File:Greenscreen-Compare.png.
- Fig. 6.13: Copyright © Jordy R. (CC by 3.0) at https://commons.wikimedia.org/wiki/File:Arxiu_audio.PNG.

SECTION III

Digital Distribution in the Viral Age

INTRODUCTION

One hallmark of living in the viral media age is that we find ourselves bombarded with an onslaught of information content, much of it coming in the form of marketing pitches and advertising. The reality is that digital marketing has already become an inseparable cornerstone of modern life, both financially and culturally. Section III will examine how digital media producers are relying more and more on *word-of-mouth communication* as a way to make their product, brand, or organization stand out from all of the *dense content* and media clutter that envelops us each and every day. The ironic aspect of this is that word-of-mouth communication has been a tried-and-true marketing strategy for decades. The problem has always been that this communication methodology is quite limited in terms of its applications since it requires setting up face-to-face meetings with clients, over-the-phone conference calls, or, at its nadir, the use of direct mailings.

The exponential growth of the Internet that has added a new wrinkle to word-of-mouth communications, as interactive banner ads, visual memes, RSS (Rich Site Summary; often called Really Simple Syndication) streams, user groups, e-mail, e-commerce, and social media sites are proving, in many ways, to be modern digital variants of this more traditional communication form. These new digital iterations provide the perfect conduit for the spread of *consumer-initiated viral marketing* campaigns; a promotions strategy that relies on the unsolicited testimonials of individual, online consumers as the main sales tactic driving brand popularity. Now, when online content becomes hugely popular, especially if it does so at an extremely rapid pace, that information is said to have gone *viral*. When it comes right

KEY TERMS

- blogs
- business-initiated viral marketing
- buzz marketing
- consumer-initiated viral marketing
- customer engagement
- dense content
- guerilla marketing
- online influencers
- ROI (return on investment)
- visual memes
- word-of-mouth communication

down to it, viral marketing is nothing more than the leveraging of digital, word-of mouth communication techniques as a means of generating an interest or *buzz* about a particular person, product, brand, or organization. Consequently, consumer-to-consumer-oriented marketing campaigns are an example of viral marketing at its purest.

Section III reveals the best techniques used to stir up word-of-mouth interest, and the type of content needed to actively engage your target audience. To that end, the text will help to dispel a number of lingering myths concerning the types of viral content that generate the largest number of views, web clicks and online "shares." To help separate fact from fiction, research data will help guide viral media providers develop content that engages viewers in ever more novel and surprising ways. Special attention is paid to a pair of case studies about the successful viral marketing campaigns developed by the Unilever company to revitalize their Dove and Axe personal body care brands.

The data contained in Section III show that consumer-initiated viral marketing campaigns offer many advantages to traditional business-controlled information sources. For one, consumer-initiated viral marketing recommendations are considered to be more reliable by the public since the feedback comes from friends, family members, or other trusted figures and not directly from advertisers or other corporate spin-control specialists. Consumer-to-consumer-based outreach efforts also prove to be equally effective for brands both large and small, and they offer just as much value to business startups as to long-established organizations. Significantly, these campaigns require relatively low financial investment costs. As a final benefit, all of the positive consumer feedback received acts as a de facto brand endorsement for the featured product or organization; one that is supplied free of charge by loyal, online users who act as surrogate brand ambassadors.

CHAPTER 7

Viral Marketing
Techniques and Implementation

Brandon Rollins, Ismet Anitsal, and M. Meral Anitsal

INTRODUCTION

Marketing messages have become a pivotal and inseparable part of society. Decades of listening to similar business-to-consumer messages have made consumers inattentive and skeptical about advertisements. The advent of new media via the Internet has allowed businesses to change their advertising methods to be more suitable for emerging trends in consumer behavior such as sharing through social media. Instant communication has provided consumers with a way to communicate directly with businesses, therefore allowing for two-way communication. Many corporations, including large ones such as Old Spice, Levi Strauss, Nike, Chevrolet, and Burger King have taken advantage of viral marketing by providing unusual, mold-breaking advertisements that have generated buzz by interacting with or entertaining consumers.

An effective way to raise interest in a company's products and services is to stimulate word-of-mouth communication among the company's prospective target market (Palka 2009). As friends and acquaintances exchange product recommendations, word-of-mouth becomes a powerful vehicle for generating buzz, boosting sales revenues, increasing market share, and building a commendable reputation (Emakina 2007). Word-of-mouth can also stifle the progress of a company, if the goods or services provided consistently disappoint consumers (Dufour 2011). This places additional importance on the customer's perception of quality and value in a company's products and services in terms of customer satisfaction since both bad and good reviews spread quickly through recommendation networks (Leskovec 2007).

The popularity of the Internet, social media, and mobile computing has provided a new conduit for word-of-mouth. The Internet removes many of the communication barriers that lie between people such as distance, time of day, and culture. As a consequence, sharing information is more open than ever before (Leskovec 2007). This unhindered form of online word-of-mouth that has arisen with the advent of the Internet, is often termed viral marketing (Palka 2009). Viral marketing can promote the exponential spread of marketing messages to niche segments on a scale unparalleled by even multimillion dollar traditional marketing campaigns (Leskovec 2007).

Brandon Rollins, Ismet Anitsal, and M. Meral Anitsal, "Viral Marketing: Techniques and Implementation," *The Entrepreneurial Executive*, no. 19, pp. 1-17. Copyright © 2014 by Allied Business Academies (https://www.abacademies.org/). Reprinted with permission.

Viral marketing campaigns can be unpredictable because it relies on the reception and interpretation of marketing messages by consumers (Dufour 2011). Viral marketing, unlike television marketing, radio marketing, billboards, or fliers, requires on direct consumer input (Phelps 2004). Traditional marketing allows consumers to passively consume messages, whereas viral marketing relies on consumers who are willing to take an active part in spreading a message (Stonedahl 2010). When videos, images, and phrases become popular on the Internet, they are said to go "viral" (Sexton 2011). The same semantic principle applies to viral marketing campaigns. The word "viral" in viral marketing refers to popularity and exponential spread of ideas. When a marketing campaign becomes popular online at a very rapid pace, then it is considered viral marketing (Sexton 2011).

There are two broad ways to classify how corporate messages go viral: consumer-initiated viral marketing and business-initiated viral marketing. First, some companies receive viral promotion without investing any time at all. Through recommendation networks such as the iTunes Store and Amazon.com, well-received products begin to stand out, perhaps even ranking higher in popularity (Leskovec 2007). Second, some corporate messages become popular because consumers mention them through social media networks such as Facebook, Twitter, Tumblr, Pintrest, or YouTube (Chen 2010). We will refer to this kind of hands-off viral marketing as consumer-initiated viral marketing.

Companies do not have to be completely passive, and can indeed attempt to make their own messages go "viral." Hotmail.com successfully marketed their email service through viral means, by putting a signature at the bottom of user's emails linking to Hotmail, offering a free email address (Leskovec 2007). Old Spice made humorous videos on YouTube, which soon became very popular (Sexton 2011). In both cases, companies created the messages, which users disseminated and popularized. We will refer to this kind of hands-on viral marketing as business-initiated viral marketing.

The purpose of this paper is to provide managers, entrepreneurs, and marketers with the knowledge necessary to seed a successful business-initiated viral marketing campaign. First, there will be a discussion of the underlying mechanics of viral marketing campaigns. This will allow for an informed overview of the advantages and disadvantages of viral marketing. Knowledge of these advantages and disadvantages will be used to suggest a model for marketers to use, which will maximize the chance of success in viral marketing.

LITERATURE REVIEW

Viral marketing, in the most literal sense, encompasses all marketing messages which are spread by consumer-to-consumer communication (AMA 2012). As such, it is one of the most basic marketing phenomena and it has existed long before present-day media. Viral marketing has become more powerful with the rise of the Internet and resulting online media. Today, the term "viral marketing" is used consistently in common vernacular to describe online business-initiated viral marketing campaigns (Summers 2012). Viral marketing, in the sense of its popular connotation, can be described as the relationship between buzz marketing, word-of-mouth marketing, and online marketing as shown in Figure 1.

Buzz marketing, word-of-mouth marketing, and online marketing are enumerated as the three primary antecedents of successful viral marketing campaigns (Figure 1). Section A represents buzz marketing, the practice of creating excitement through noteworthy marketing messages (Emakina 2007). Some examples would be based on event marketing, which uses significant events as opportunities to advertise through methods such as sponsorships (AMA 2012). Another example would be guerilla marketing, which hinges on unusual and eye-catching marketing methods such as sidewalk chalk arts that appear to be three-dimensional. Guerilla marketing is often used in an attempt to reduce costs (AMA 2012).

Section B represents word-of-mouth marketing. Word-of-mouth marketing occurs when consumers spread marketing messages to other consumers (AMA 2012). Before the Internet, word-of-mouth marketing was done in person, on the phone, or through mail. Word-of-mouth marketing is a broad spectrum of marketing phenomena that include consumers talking about notable marketing campaigns and product or service recommendations (Wiedemann 2010). Word-of-mouth can be facilitated by person marketing and social marketing. Both of these types of marketing attempt to influence consumer behavior. Person marketing influences individuals where as social marketing influences groups of individuals, or society at large (AMA 2012).

Section C represents online marketing, which covers all marketing messages facilitated by the Internet. One readily visible subset of online marketing would be banner advertisements on websites, a form of digital marketing. Email newsletters from companies would be an example of email marketing. E-commerce shopping experiences are also affiliated with online marketing, as well as global marketing (AMA 2012). This also includes consumer and business interactions on social media websites such as Facebook, Twitter, and YouTube.

Section AB is the overlap of Section A (buzz marketing) and Section B (word-of-mouth). Before the Internet, this was the

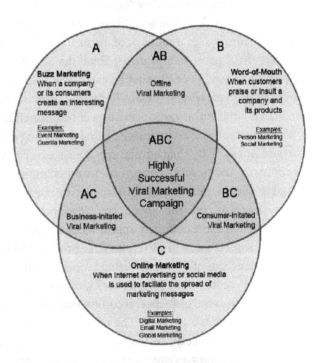

FIGURE 7.1 Key Relationships in Viral Marketing

primary definition of viral marketing (AMA 2012). When some marketing message generated buzz and people talked about it frequently, it became offline viral marketing. This still happens today, and is often a byproduct of successful online viral marketing (Sexton 2011).

Section AC is the overlap of Section A (buzz marketing) and Section C (online marketing). When companies successfully generate buzz on the internet, this is considered business-initiated viral marketing. Marketing messages that fall in this category are made by intentional efforts by businesses.

Section BC is the overlap of Section B (word-of-mouth) and Section C (online marketing). This is referred to as consumer-initiated viral marketing, and businesses have no direct impact on the spread of these marketing messages. This encompasses all of the communications that consumers have about businesses and their products and services that are facilitated by the Internet. This can also be referred to as "word-of-mouse" (Bampo 2008).

Section ABC is where buzz marketing, word-of-mouth, and online marketing meet. Companies that make strong marketing messages, or buzz, often succeed in indirectly creating word-of-mouth. Word-of-mouth, facilitated by the Internet, quickly becomes a rapid and exponential force of marketing, referred to as word-of-mouse marketing. In simpler terms, when companies create buzz on the Internet and consumers share it, a highly successful viral marketing campaign just occurs (Emakina 2007).

Audience participation is the foundation of viral marketing (Phelps 2004). Viral marketing messages cannot spread or "go viral" without meeting the viewer's sharing threshold (Phelps 2004). Once this sharing threshold is met, the viewers of marketing messages will spread the message at a rapid pace, or in the most successful cases of viral marketing, at an exponential pace (Bampa 2008; Emakina 2007). In order for a marketing message to be spread at a viral pace, it must be especially relevant. Messages can achieve marketable relevancy through several means, including humor, visual impact or interesting content, interactivity, and enthusiastic peer-to-peer recommendations (Bampa 2008; Emakina 2007).

Many successful business-initiated viral marketing campaigns focus more on humor, content, and interactivity than advertising. These advertisements downplay the importance of the company, and clear the consumer's impression that the companies have ulterior motives related to sales figures. The advertisements are made more for the consumer's pleasure than the company's success (Emakina 2007). Consumers see the company as a friendly organization, which makes the company appear more trustworthy (Emakina 2007). Trustworthiness makes consumers more likely to purchase products from the company (Emakina 2007).

The other form of viral marketing, consumer-initiated viral marketing, encompasses peer-to-peer recommendation networks, online and offline (Leskovec 2007). Because there is no direct corporate influence, recommendations from one consumer to another are perceived as pure and trustworthy. The nature of consumer-initiated viral marketing excludes businesses from directly setting consumer-initiated viral marketing trends. The only influence that businesses can exert upon this form of viral marketing starts from the beginning—production. Consumer-initiated viral marketing is honest and will reveal the flaws in low-quality products. Businesses are held accountable for their products, and must create better products to survive. The source of peer-to-peer reviews, or consumer-initiated viral marketing, makes it a trustworthy and powerful force in the business world (Leskovec 2007).

Consumer-initiated and business-initiated viral marketing both give power to the consumers. There is some social risk associated with giving power to consumers, but allowing consumers to discriminate the low-quality from the high-quality, whether advertisements or products, means only the consumer's best wishes are fulfilled. A company known for high-quality products and messages will succeed, because consumers trust other consumers more than companies (Chen 2010). Marketing messages only "go viral" or spread by "word-of-mouse" when consumers trust and like a company. Because viral marketing gives consumers power over marketing messages, we can arrive at the following conclusion.

> P1: *Consumers will perceive viral marketing as more trustworthy*
> *than traditional marketing-controlled information sources,*
> *since it is communicated via friends and trusted figures by*
> *"word-of-mouse."*

The advent of the Internet and online commerce has removed many of the barriers to entry that small businesses often face, such as distribution channels, customer service, and corporate promotion. Financial assets tend to be quite limited for small firms, and consequently, marketing departments need inexpensive means of product and service promotion. The Internet provides a host of economically efficient alternatives to expensive marketing campaigns, such as mass media campaigns. Attempting to seed a viral marketing campaign is one such alternative (Bampo 2008). If it succeeds, consumers will do the majority of the talking regarding marketing messages, leading to smaller marketing expenses for the company (Emakina 2007).

New firms, small firms, and obscure firms frequently struggle from underdeveloped brand loyalty. Firms like this often operate by targeting niche markets. It is inefficient to attempt to generate buzz in niche markets by traditional mass media marketing. Below-the-line viral marketing techniques can be used to generate marketing buzz in a more focused manner by appealing to the unique aspects of the targeted consumers (Leskovec 2007).

After an initial buzz is started, either by consumer-initiated or business-initiated means, marketing messages spread by word-of-mouse (Emakina 2007). Eventually, successful viral marketing will cause the word-of-mouse to culminate into a well-established reputation. Reputations can be built from good reviews on recommendation networks (Leskovec 2007). For example, the reputation of Sennheiser, a high-end headphone and microphone manufacturer, has arisen predominantly from "audiophile" communities (Head Room). Blendtec, a firm that produces blenders, became famous by a business-initiated viral marketing campaign that involved blending strange items such as golf balls, marbles, consumer electronics, and a garden rake (YouTube 2007). The amusing nature of the videos and the clear demonstration of durability and utility have led the small startup firm to have a large and prominent online persona. Viral marketing helps remove obstacles that small and new firms face, therefore:

> P2a: *Small and new firms are capable of using viral marketing to generate buzz and establish a reputation, similar to large and well-established firms.*

Reputation and buzz bring financial benefits such as market share and revenues. In the case of Blendtec, sales revenues increased by 500 percent between the first episode of *Will it Blend* in October 2006 and September 2007 (Nicole 2007). Blendtec claims to have created these original commercials with a budget of only $50 (Blendtec Media Kit). Their blender products are all upwards of $400 (Blendtec). Therefore, the revenue from selling a single blender covers the cost of the original commercials eight times.

Blendtec became extraordinarily popular within a remarkably brief time period. Blendtec annual sales after the video series on YouTube are "around 40 million dollars" (Blendtec Media Kit). Since the firm's sales increased by 500 percent after the video series, it is safe to assume that sales revenues before the video series was closer to $8 million (Blendtec Media Kit; Nicole 2007). Small firms can take advantage of this form of viral marketing to capitalize on buzz and reputation. Once excitement and trust are instilled in prospective consumers, revenues and market share often follow (Emakina 2007). This data suggests that

> P2b: *Small and new firms are also capable of using viral marketing to secure significant portion of the market share and bring in revenues, since viral marketing buzz eases barriers to market entry.*

Viral marketing campaigns are not limited to small businesses with limited budgets. More established companies, such as Old Spice and Nike, can benefit from carefully planned viral marketing campaigns. Utilizing viral marketing can bring old brand or product line back to the forefront. In Old Spice's 2010 campaign "The Man Your Man Could Smell Like," the company did not promote anything particularly innovative. It merely gave people a reason to remember and discuss an old brand through sharing videos, and in many cases, quoting lines from them such as "look at your man, now back to me" (Sexton 2011). As of February 26, 2012, the original video of this marketing campaign has had nearly 40 million views (YouTube 2010).

Sometimes viral marketing can take a currently established and well-known brand, and bring it to a younger or different audience. Because viral marketing is perceived as organic, using viral marketing to promote an already established product line can make positive changes to brand perception. Chevrolet did something like this with their existing line of cars, Chevrolet Aveo. In 2012, Chevrolet released the car under the catchier brand name, Chevy Sonic (Healey 2010). They gave a free Chevy Sonic to a band named OK Go, for use in their music video for the song "Needing/Getting" (YouTube 2012a). This music video, like other OK Go music videos, is very elaborate and unusual (Bowie-Sell 2012). It shows the band riding in a Chevy Sonic, with poles attached to the side, which hit instruments as they drive. A short clip of this video was shown in one of the commercial breaks during Super Bowl XLVI (YouTube 2012a). The music video shows the car's ability to handle well, even off-road. It also shows the logo of the car. However, it is still not an outright advertisement. This video has generated a buzz on the Internet, giving new life to a previously established brand. As of March 15, 2012, the "Needing/Getting" music video has been viewed nearly 17.5 million times (YouTube 2012a).

As target markets age, companies are often saddled with an unfortunate realization: an older target market cannot be sustained forever. Companies with aging target markets are forced to rebrand their products and services and essentially alter their company's modus operandi to better suit a younger audience. Corporate attitudes have to change to reflect the younger audience. Launching a viral marketing campaign requires some background knowledge of popular culture. Ergo, a successful viral marketing campaign demonstrates to the audience that the company is trendy and fresh. Levi Strauss, for example, rebranded their clothing line after finding out it did not appeal to a younger audience. After changing the product, they released a video on YouTube called "Guys backflip into jeans" which soon became viral (YouTube 2008a). This video had nearly 8 million views by March 15, 2012. Levi Strauss changed their jeans, made videos of young men jumping from objects like swing sets and seesaws into jeans, and effectively rebranded the company from the bottom-up using viral marketing in conjunction with product differentiation (YouTube 2008a).

Chevrolet, Old Spice, and Levi Strauss are all at least seventy-five years old. They are not considered to be young organizations. Yet, despite age, these companies have still benefited from viral marketing. This proves that viral marketing is not strictly the territory of the young and yet-to-be established corporations. Viral marketing can work for corporations of any size and age. Therefore,

> P3: *Viral marketing campaigns can benefit older businesses by repositioning their overall marketing strategy, which can improve their reputation, generate buzz, improve market share, and increase sales.*

Many of the most successful business-initiated viral marketing campaigns are based on humor, interesting content, and interactivity (Emakina 2007, Phelps 2004). For example, a recent campaign by Old Spice called "The Man Your Man Could Smell Like" has become a textbook example of highly successful viral marketing. This campaign involved a series of entertaining dialogues delivered by former National Football League player Isaiah Mustafa

(Sexton 2011). The first video in the series had nearly 40 million views on YouTube in its first two years and quotes from the commercials have found their way into popular culture (You-Tube 2010). It succeeded because Mustafa's monologues revolve around an amusingly smug character delivering ridiculous, surrealistic, and breathless claims of purported benefits that come from using Old Spice products (Sexton 2011). The description below the video on YouTube captures the spirit of the commercial series: "[we're] not saying this body wash will make your man smell into a romantic millionaire jet fighter pilot, but we are insinuating it" (YouTube 2010). This series of commercials has benefited consumers by entertaining them.

Another successful viral marketing campaign was done by Burger King in 2004. This campaign is called "The Subservient Chicken." It was a Flash-based game where users could enter one of hundreds of phrases in a text box, which would result in video clips of a man in a chicken suit acting them out (Snopes 2011). Some of the commands included "sleep," "rage," "fight," "air guitar," "the robot," and several Michael Jackson dance moves. There are more than three hundred known commands for this campaign. The chicken responds to the names of some rock bands by doing the hand gesture for "I love you." Even more amusing, the chicken responds to offensive suggestions by wagging his finger back and forth at the user (Wikipedia 2004). This campaign is remarkable because of its amusing nature and its interactivity which surpassed the expectations of online consumers in 2004.

Nike also has adopted similar techniques by recruiting Kobe Bryant, a famous basketball player known for jumping ability for commercials. For these online videos, he performed stunts in Nike shoes that involved jumping over a speeding Aston Martin car and a pool of snakes (YouTube 2008b). These videos have shocked and confused consumers into wondering about the legitimacy of the videos. Whether they are real or not is debatable; but either way, consumers have enjoyed watching the crazy videos and discussing them (YouTube 2008b).

Nike seems to have met success with the "Kobe Bryant Jumps" videos, and they recently launched another video campaign named "the Kobe System." This series has featured dozens of celebrities, all attending a self-help seminar hosted by Kobe Bryant, who gives them nonsensical advice such as "achieve success at success at success at success" (YouTube 2012). Seeing famous personalities such as Serena Williams and Richard Branson seeking Kobe Bryant's advice at a self-help seminar is amusing, and consumers have shared these videos. Consumers seem to genuinely enjoy well-executed viral marketing campaigns, which suggests

> P4: *Viral marketing campaigns can benefit consumers by promoting sharing, social connections, interactivity, and entertainment.*

Win-win conditions for businesses and consumers are frequently a result of viral marketing campaigns. Businesses generate buzz and build a reputation for themselves, while entertaining and facilitating social connections for consumers. There is a more concrete benefit of viral marketing campaigns that insofar has not been discussed. Viral marketing campaigns have the potential to be significantly less expensive than traditional mass media campaigns.

Using the Internet to disseminate a viral marketing campaign is not expensive. Many web hosting services provide acceptable web hosting service for less than $100 per year (FindWebHosting.com). However, the price of a 30-second national television commercial is much higher, where production costs are typically closer to $500,000 (Davis 2011). Websites also have the advantage of being global, customizable, and not limited by air time. Even when considering the cost of high-end graphic and web designers, creating a website for potential viral marketing is not nearly as expensive as traditional media. Websites such as Burger King's Subservient Chicken were made for no other reason than to be viral marketing campaigns. Other companies can take advantage of this website-only approach to viral marketing.

YouTube provides a way for users to post videos online for free, with no limit to potential growth. There are still costs incurred in the production of a YouTube video, however, these are significantly lower than traditional campaigns as well. Many popular viral campaigns such as the aforementioned Blendtec and Old Spice campaigns, succeeded mainly through this website. In addition to YouTube, other social media sites such as Facebook, Twitter, Tumblr, and Pintrest show promising opportunities for viral marketing campaigns as well. Being able to directly communicate with consumers at no explicit cost facilitates business-initiated viral campaigns with as little financial risk as possible. This is because

> P5: *Viral marketing campaigns will have a significantly lower*
> *financial cost, compared to traditional marketing campaigns*
> *through mass media.*

There are commonalities among most of the business-initiated viral marketing campaigns mentioned in this paper so far. Levi Strauss, Old Spice, Blendtec, Nike, Chevrolet, Burger King, and Hotmail all started by creating what customers see as a valuable product. Levi Strauss rebranded their jeans to be trendier. Old Spice worked hard to create a satisfactory scent for their body washes and deodorants. Blendtec made a blender so powerful it could blend marbles. Nike strived to create comfortable, durable, and stylish shoes. Chevrolet made a car customers want to drive. Burger King emphasized customizability and customer-oriented food service. Hotmail created the first major email service for free, without any limiting conditions to inconvenience consumers.

Backed by a good product, all of these companies capitalized on creative thoughts, which in many cases, were limited to a small budget. All of these companies made something interesting, humorous, interactive, and/or shareable. Levi Strauss made videos of young men jumping into pairs of pants. Old Spice created bizarre and humorous commercials that switch rapidly from scene to scene. Blendtec destroyed garden tools and consumer electronics with their blender (Blendtec Media Kit). Nike worked with celebrities to create unbelievable videos, with the shoes being a minor point instead of a major attraction (YouTube 2008b). Chevrolet teamed up with the popular and stylized band Ok Go (YouTube 2012a). Burger King made a strange and amusing video game (Snopes 2011). Hotmail provided free email accounts.

If good products are advertised with humor, style, visual impact, free giveaways, or other interesting content, marketing messages will acquire viral potential. As long as the company seems genuine and friendly, interesting messages should be able to hold their viral potential (Emakina 2007). After viral potential is achieved, popularizing a marketing message should be as simple as using the right social networks as conduits. Whatever networks are popular on the Internet for a target market at the time should be used. As of today, Facebook, YouTube, and Twitter hold the most potential. Tomorrow, Tumblr and Pintrest may become better conduits. Marketers must keep an eye on emerging trends in social media in order to determine the right social networks for spreading potentially viral content. So far, it seems that

P6:   Successful viral marketing campaigns are more likely to succeed when marketers appeal to highly-connected individuals and opinion leaders with interesting, humorous, or interactive content.

MANAGERIAL IMPLICATIONS

Business-initiated viral marketing campaigns benefit from several advantages which make them worthwhile to consider in a practical managerial setting. The most easily quantifiable benefit of seeding a viral marketing campaign is the potentially low financial risk, such as Blendtec's $50 budget for the first videos in the series *Will it Blend* (Blendtec Media Kit). Viral marketing messages thrive online, most likely as a result of the manageable expenses. Social media websites such as Facebook, Twitter, and YouTube, offer businesses viral marketing conduits completely free of charge. The only financial expense of using these social media channels is the implicit time value of the social media manager. Furthermore, the price of web hosting is often quite reasonable, at a price of less than $ 100 per year for small business websites (FindWebHosting.com). The inexpensiveness of viral marketing allows small businesses to completely rely on it. Likewise, large businesses can choose to supplement their traditional marketing campaigns with inexpensive viral marketing campaigns (Emakina 2007).

An online presence is expected of businesses, regardless of size. Being online, in and of itself, does not provide businesses with a major advantage. Creating an interesting online experience that goes above and beyond consumers' expectations (Emakina 2007), however, can make significant improvements to a company's reputation. For example, when Old Spice introduced their viral marketing campaign "The Man Your Man Could Smell Like" and its associated website, body wash sales increased by 27 percent in six months and Old Spice became a trendier brand among younger males (Anderson 2012). This video series has had profound and almost unilaterally positive effects on consumers' perception of the company, as evidence by the 49:1 ratio of "likes" to "dislikes" on YouTube (YouTube 2010).

Viral marketing campaigns are unique, in that they often actively attempt to please and entertain consumers by appealing to basic consumer interests (Emakina 2007). Traditional mass media marketing, at best, can be humorous and quotable. Viral marketing, on the other hand, must almost always be humorous, entertaining, or interesting to succeed because consumers facilitate the message (Sexton 2011). Often, viral marketing will go above and beyond this by being interactive and social, as well. Fun marketing messages spread throughout the Internet like none other, benefiting businesses and consumers simultaneously.

Another significant factor in viral marketing is the sheer rate at which marketing messages are capable of spreading (Wilson 2005). A single status update by one Facebook user is theoretically capable of reaching thousands of people. Realistically, not all of a single person's Facebook friends will read and react to a single status update. Even still, if a person with 500 Facebook friends is capable of making 5 people react to a viral message, this message can disseminate at an exponential rate. Perhaps 5 of these 500 individuals will repost the status update, each causing 5 more people to repost (Wilson 2005; Emakina 2007). This example does not even include other social media sites such as Twitter, YouTube, Tumblr, and Pintrest.

Though there are many benefits to viral marketing, there is one major caveat to viral marketing of which managers need to be fully aware. Viral marketing relies on consumers, who add their own biases when spreading marketing messages (Emakina 2007). Word-of-mouth and word-of-mouse are affected both by the subjectivity of the message distributor and the message recipient. Marketing messages can take on a life of their own. There is a limit to which marketers can control viral marketing. This lack of control over marketing messages and their distribution should be a foremost concern in the mind of marketers who are considering seeding a viral marketing campaign.

Poorly conceived marketing messages can be misconstrued by consumers. In 2008, Cartoon Network attempted a viral marketing campaign for their show "Aqua Teen Hunger Force" in Boston. The end result of this was a bomb scare caused by poorly placed LCD light panels in the city. Cartoon Network, as expected, suffered from negative publicity and harsh criticism after this gaffe (CBS News 2009).

Even good marketing messages can attract the wrong consumers. Being supported by the wrong audience can turn a brand into a stigma. For example, if the Levi Strauss "Guys backflip into jeans" campaign had appealed to men older than 60 instead of the 18–25 demographic, Levi Strauss would have had a hard time maintaining their target audience. The company sales would increase in the short-run, but long-run concerns like an aging consumer base can cost a company dearly.

By attempting to seed a viral marketing campaign, companies are assuming a high degree of social risk. This is one unfortunate counterbalance to the low financial risk. Negative reviews and publicity spread even more rapidly on the Internet than good publicity. Consumers are empowered through viral marketing. Consumers can use their power altruistically by to informing other consumers about good products and services. Unfortunately for marketing managers, empowered consumers can also exact revenge on companies through negative publicity or even outright manipulation of information. Angry Internet users have exercised this ability against banks who tried to introduce monthly debit card usage fees. Even government bills are subject to empowered Internet users, (i.e. Stop Online Piracy Act and Protect IP Act). Consumers who feel offended or cheated by companies will strike back, sometimes with devastating social force.

Successful business-initiated viral marketing campaigns on the internet occur when buzz marketing generates word-of-mouse communication. Seeding a viral marketing campaign is, to some degree, predictable in nature. As stated in Proposition 6, "[s]uccessful viral marketing campaigns can be established consistently, if the marketers use current information distribution channels to appeal to highly-connected individuals with interesting or humorous content." Adept managers with responsibility over viral marketing messages can use these commonalities to craft a successful campaign.

As with traditional mass media marketing or offline marketing, creating a buzz online relies heavily on the nature of marketing message to be spread. Marketers will need to carefully analyze the target audience. Marketers need to know and understand the interests, motivations, likes, dislikes, and sharing habits of their audience. Viral marketing tends to target the trendsetting market demographic of 18–25 year-old men and women, since they actively use the Internet and social media for personal and practical reasons. Persons of this marketing demographic tend to respond to marketing messages centric around entertainment and interactivity. The way this demographic perceives the company will be especially positive if the company seems friendly, unique, and genuine.

Marketers then need to come up with an unusual and entertaining or interesting content to spread as a marketing message. The specifics of this content are reliant on the nature of the company's products or services and the company's corporate culture. Marketers in charge of making these messages need to be especially competent. The initial content in a business-initiated viral marketing campaign is where the greatest risk must be taken. The initial marketing message can propel a company to financial and social success or endanger the company's longevity.

After creating a great viral marketing message, finding the right online distribution channel should prove to considerably less difficult. Before choosing a social conduit for the marketing messages, marketers should consider three aspects: popularity, associated culture, and methods of sharing. Naturally, social conduits with a weak following do not make good locations for marketing message dissemination. Although, overpopulated social conduits may be difficult to use as well, due to all the social white noise of constant sharing.

The culture associated with the social conduits is also a point of consideration. Facebook and Twitter have different cultures, especially regarding message length. YouTube commenters are notorious among video sharing sites, regarding the often shocking candor of the commentary. Pintrest seems to appeal mostly to women. Initiating a campaign on any one site may require marketers to alter the message slightly.

Lastly, each site has different methods of sharing. Facebook revolves around brief status updates about the length of sentences, liking other pages, and sharing links. Twitter "tweets" are shorter than text messages in length. YouTube easily integrates itself into other popular social media. Tumblr tends to be more humorous and many of the users share videos and animated GIFs with each other. Until April 2012, Pintrest users were not capable of "pinning" videos. Every social conduit has its own social norms and folkways, which must be taken into consideration by marketers. Preferably, marketers should delegate social media power to employees who are enjoyably immersed in the culture of the websites on their own personal time.

RESEARCH IMPLICATIONS

One commonly accepted assertion about viral marketing is that consumers see it as an inherently honest and trustworthy form of communication. Though little information has come about to challenge this assertion, there is a lack of academic research proving that consumers consistently perceive viral marketing as honest. Even under the assumption that consumers did at some point perceive viral marketing as trustworthy, consumer sentiments toward viral marketing may have changed in a manner that the existent literature has not observed or predicted. Quantitative research in the form of well-designed opinion surveys could be used as a barometer to measure consumer perceptions toward viral marketing. This consumer perception research should be refreshed frequently, to account for the rapidly changing nature of the Internet, online social conduits, and viral marketing methods.

This paper establishes the theoretical possibility of small firms growing exponentially through viral marketing. Only Blendtec, however, was used pervasively as an example of small firm viral marketing success. There should be a closer examination of small firm viral marketing campaigns. Qualitative research could be used to provide detailed insights about the notion that small firms are consistently capable of marketing virally.

It seems that older and larger firms can use viral marketing to improve their reputation, generate buzz, and increase sales. Future research could compile a list of several large publicly-owned businesses that succeeded in seeding viral marketing campaigns. Each of these twenty-five businesses would be examined financially based on their annual reports to see if viral marketing increased sales revenues and profit margins. More sophisticated metrics could be developed to measure level of buzz and quality of reputation before and after the viral marketing campaign success.

Viral marketing campaigns are said to benefit consumers by being entertaining. This statement hinges upon an under-researched opinion of consumer perception. Opinion surveys could be used to compile and analyze consumer perceptions of viral marketing campaigns in terms of enjoyment and how willing they are to share the campaign. We need to investigate the possibility that consumers could be uninterested in or annoyed by viral marketing campaigns.

The notion that viral marketing campaigns cost less money than traditional mass media campaigns should be investigated in future research. Without the expenses incurred in buying television or radio airtime or physical advertising space, it seems that viral marketing campaigns would cost less than traditional mass media. A close analysis of the financial cost of seeding viral marketing campaigns would be immensely useful in the validation of the claim that viral marketing is relatively inexpensive. However, be aware that finding access to detailed financial documents may prove difficult for this sort of research.

Finally, there is the assumption that business-initiated viral marketing campaigns can succeed on a regular basis as long as two conditions are fulfilled. The marketing message must appeal to the target audience and the message distribution channel must be adequate for reaching the target audience. This assumption is the basis for much of the Managerial Implications section of the paper, where a marketing model is suggested for viral marketing. This idea needs heavy research in order to stand as a respectable theory.

Investigating this assumption will require very in-depth qualitative research, in the form of a case study. Small and new businesses interested in viral marketing would be researched in their efforts to establish viral marketing campaigns. The small businesses would follow the marketing model laid out in this paper as closely as possible. The businesses would develop content, which would be examined by a focus group comprised by their target audience. The focus group members would evaluate the content on two metrics. The first metric would measure whether the focus group members find the content entertaining or interesting. The second metric would measure whether the focus group members feel that the content is made with consideration of their interests, motivations, likes, dislikes, and sharing habits. Content would be revised until it passes evaluation for both of these metrics within the focus group.

After creating adequate content, small businesses would find the right distribution channel or social conduit to spread their marketing messages. To determine the right distribution channel, the target audience would be surveyed on their opinion of popular social media sites and viral marketing distribution methods. The results would be aggregated and the businesses would focus the majority of their viral marketing efforts on the social conduits that the survey respondents use and like the most.

The small businesses would all regularly follow up on their viral marketing successes. They would disclose relevant financial statements for analysis. Changes in sales revenue and profit margin would be used as measures of viral marketing financial success. Return on investment with respect to expenses incurred by viral marketing would also be used as an important metric of success. If attainable, data about changes in market share would make an excellent yardstick for viral marketing financial success.

These small businesses would also be evaluated on changes in marketing buzz and reputation. Google, Yahoo!, and Bing searches, website statistics such as page views, and level of social media activity could be used as measures of buzz. Target audience surveys could be used to measure reputation on a numeric scale after the viral marketing campaign. Again, search engine searches can also be used as measure of reputation, depending on the quantity of negative and positive searches.

Viral marketing on the Internet is still a fairly recent development in marketing. This paper has provided a framework for managers interested in viral marketing. However, this framework is untested and theoretical, so future research could provide beneficial insights on its relevancy.

CONCLUSION

Business-initiated viral marketing campaigns have potential to spread marketing messages quickly and effectively. Viral marketing empowers consumers, meaning that businesses that satisfy consumers will reap benefits from consumer-to-consumer communication. Small firms and large firms are both capable of using viral marketing to their advantage. Smaller firms can use it to establish a reputation and market share. Large businesses can use it to generate buzz, increase sales, or reposition their marketing strategy. Businesses and consumers both benefit from viral marketing: businesses can benefit financially and consumers can benefit socially. Viral marketing campaigns circumvent many of the costs associated with mass media campaigns, making them a logical choice for small firms trying to become popular and large firms looking to supplement their current marketing strategy. Finally, viral marketing campaigns can be implemented by astute managers who are familiar with the underlying mechanics of viral marketing. Creating consumer-pleasing content and disseminating it on topical online social conduits can consistently launch successful viral marketing campaigns.

REFERENCES

AMA (American Marketing Association), Dictionary, Retrieved March 25, 2011, from http://www.marketingpower.com/layouts/Dictionary.aspx.

Anderson, Mae (2012). USA Today. Some old brands enjoy a revival, Retrieved April 18, 2011, from http://www.usatoday.com/USCP/PNI/MONEY/2012-01-13-PNIO113biz-comeback-brandsPNIBrd_ST_U.htm.

Bampo, Mauro (2008). The Effects of the Social Structure of Digital Networks on Viral Marketing Performance. *Information Systems Research*, Vol. 19, No. 3, 273–290.

Blendtec. Retrieved March 13, 2012, from http://www.blendtec.com/.

Blendtec Media Kit. Retrieved March 18, 2012, from http://commercial.blendtec.com/media/pdf/commercial/BlendtecMediaKit.pdf.

Bowie-Sell, Daisy (2012). OK Go premiere elaborate new music video during Super Bowl. Retrieved March 15, 2012 from, http://www.telegraph.co.uk/culture/music/music-news/9064293/OK-Go-premiere-elaborate-new-music-video-during-Super-Bowl.html.

CBS News (2009). 2 Arrested in Boston Bomb Scare. *CBS Interactive Inc.* Retrieved March 30, 2012, from http://www.cbsnews.com/2100-201_162-2421734.html.

Chen, Wei (2010). Scalable Influence Maximization of Prevalent Viral Marketing in Large-Scale Social Networks. *KDD*, July 25–28, 1029–1038.

Davis, Gary (2011). Frequently Asked Questions About Television Advertising. Retrieved April 7, 2012, from http://television-nadvertising.com/faq.htm.

Dufour, Carole (2011). An Investigation into the Use of Viral Marketing for the Companies and the Key Success Factors of a Good Viral Campaign. *Dublin Business School,* 1–50.

Emakina (2007). Viral Strategies and Buzz Marketing. Retrieved January 30, 2012, from http://www.slideshare.net/emakina/viral-marketing-theory

FindWebHosting.com. Best 10 Web Hosting Companies. Retrieved April 7, 2012, from, http://fmdwebhosting.com/

Head Room, Selection Guide: Full Size, Retrieved March 13, 2012 from http://www.headphone.com/selection-guide/full-size-headphones.php.

Healey, James (2010). GM's Chevrolet Aveo renamed Sonic. USA Today. Retrieved March 15, 2012, from http://content.usatoday.com/communities/driveon/post/2010/12/gms-chevy-aveo-renamed-sonic/1#.T2l2HBEgcTY.

Leskovec, Jure (2007). The Dynamics of Viral Marketing. *ACM Transactions on the Web,* Vol. 1, No. 1, Article 5, 1–39.

Nicole, Kristen (2007). "Will it Blend" Videos Boost Sales 5x. Mashable, Inc. Retrieved March 13, 2012, from http://mashable.com/2007/09/27/blendtec-sales/.

Palka, Wolfgang (2009). Mobile word-of-mouth—A grounded theory of mobile viral marketing. *Journal of Information Technology,* Vol. 24, 172–185

Phelps, Joseph (2004). Viral Marketing or Electronic Word-of-Mouth Advertising:Examining Consumer Responses and Motivations to Pass Along Email. *Journal of Advertising Research,* Vol. 44, 4, 333–348.

Sexton, Jarrett (2011). Viral Marketing. *SPORT Business Review,* Spring 2011.

Snopes (2011). Burger King Subservient Chicken. Retrieved February 25, 2012, from http://www.snopes.com/business/viral/chicken.asp.

Summers, Nick (2012) Click This Ad Already! *Newsweek.* March 18, 2012.

Wiedemann, Dietmar (2010). Analyzing the Forwarding Behavior in Mobile Viral Marketing: An Empirical Study. *IGI Global,* 381–382.

Wilson, Ralph (2005). The Six Simple Principles of Viral Marketing. *Web Marketing Today.* February 1, 2005. Wikipedia. The Subservient Chicken. Retrieved March 15, 2012, from http://en.wikipedia.org/wiki/The_Subservient_Chicken..

YouTube (2007). Will It Blend?—iPhone, Retrieved March 13, 2012, from http://www.youtube.com/watch?v=qg1ckCkm8Yl.

YouTube (2008a). Guys backflip into jeans, Retrieved March 15, 2012, from http://www.youtube.com/watch?v=pShf2VuAu_Q.

YouTube (2008b). Kobe Bryant Jumps Over A Moving Car And A Pool Of Snakes, Retrieved April 7, 2012, from http://www.youtube.com/watch?v=_Dcv9qzWrps.

YouTube (2010). Old Spice | The Man Your Man Could Smell Like, Retrieved February 26, 2012, from http://www.youtube.com/watch?v=owGykVbfgUE,.

YouTube (2012a). OK Go—Needing/Getting—Official Video, Retrieved March 15 2012, from http://www.youtube.com/watch?v=MejbOFk7H6c.

YouTube (2012b). Nike: #Kobesystem—Level 7 Success at Success, Retrieved February 25, 2012, from http://www.youtube.com/watch?v=CtlXGip_700.

CHAPTER 8

Creating Online Videos That Engage Viewers

Dante M. Pirouz, Allison R. Johnson, Matthew Thomson, and Raymond Pirouz

Many companies seek to create online video content that will become popular with consumers. But what are the characteristics of videos that engage consumers?

The Holy Grail of modern online marketing is video content that "goes viral," meaning that it captures an enormous number of views and leads audiences to share, comment or click that they "like" a video. Advertisers, marketing consultants and filmmakers have all ventured theories about what kind of content makes for a hit. The trouble is that the advice varies widely and is even contradictory. Depending on the expert, success is thought more likely if a video is humorous, shocking, dramatic, topical, warm, arousing, angry, scary, socially beneficial, cute, violent, sexy, uplifting, intriguing, quirky, interesting, authoritative, tear-jerking, educational, controversial or baby- and animal-filled.

THE LEADING QUESTION

What characteristics make an online video popular?

FINDINGS

- Emotionally surprising videos generate more likes and views.
- Consider showing viewers something they have never seen—or familiar things juxtaposed in a new way.

One of the reasons for the wide range of recommendations is that researchers have often looked at only popular videos. For example, one study that tracked the distribution of videos on Facebook focused only on those that were shared most often, which meant that the researchers did not compare the most popular clips with the content almost no one saw. Nor have marketing scholars reached conclusions about the characteristics of other kinds of popular shared content, despite the vast amount of data now available. One of the more successful papers on viral messages,[1] which looked at forwarding behavior in viral email marketing campaigns, suggested that many emotions can play a role, including surprise, joy, sadness and fear. Another study looked at the sharing of *New York Times* articles and found that still other emotional responses, such as awe and anxiety, also predicted sharing.[2]

To see if we could clarify some of the contradictions, we decided to take a different approach. Rather than catalog a hodgepodge of content elements found in popular videos, we examined a mix of popular and unpopular videos, then systematically coded and empirically tested the effect of each element on some relatively objective and observational measures of viewer engagement.

First, we gathered a data set of 750 YouTube videos that varied across a wide range of topic categories (including automotive, comedy, gaming and politics) and a wide range of success in gaining viewership. (See "About the Research.") We excluded music videos because they were associated with an exceptional number of views (in fact, 29 of the top 30 YouTube videos of all time are music videos) and would therefore skew our analysis. We also excluded videos longer than 10 minutes because these were a specialized type of content likely to be governed by different rules than the majority of YouTube content. (Think a 15-minute-long instructional video on using a pressure cooker, compared to a video of a digitized cat with wings on a rainbow.)

We assigned a team of research assistants as blind coders to watch the videos and to independently score each on a range of attributes. Did the video feature babies, attempt to be funny or use sexually suggestive content? How would watching the video make the typical viewer feel (for example, sad or surprised)? We collected information on dozens of different video elements and correlated these with three measures of engagement: the number of times people left comments on the video, the overall "liking" index for each video (calculated by subtracting the number of "dislikes" from "likes") and the number of views.

We also coded for three content themes that we hypothesized might be particularly powerful in creating engagement because they are likely to induce a strong emotional reaction: novelty, incongruity and hyperbole. The first, novelty, was chosen because we know that people enjoy experiences that are new and original. For example, research suggests consumers pay more attention to novel advertisements and public service announcements.[3] New or "fresh" content creates feelings of surprise, pleasure, entertainment and interest.[4] We thought this might also be true online, so we coded for video novelty.

Second, we assessed incongruity, which is the presentation together of two contradictory or unrelated things.[5] Incongruity forms the basis of much humor, but serious videos with incongruous content may also be more engaging than those without it. For example, the famous "Kony 2012" video[6] discussed crimes against humanity, and that topic was juxtaposed against the youth and hopefulness of the protagonist. It was not remotely funny, yet received almost 100 million views. We thought the concept of incongruity might help to explain this type of engagement.

Third, we looked at hyperbole, which essentially boils down to the use of excess or exaggeration.[7] This included content that was very dramatic, extravagant or even ridiculous. Video creators hope that, by making an over-the-top claim or elaborating effusively, they can more easily get and hold the viewer's attention. We believed hyperbolic content might be an effective way to create a strong emotional reaction and engage audiences.

We initially collected a data set of 750 English-language videos hosted by YouTube across 15 categories in May 2011. We culled the set by omitting music videos and videos that were more than 10 minutes long. We base our conclusions on a final sample of 622 videos.

First, one independent coder (in other words, not one of the researchers and therefore blind to the hypotheses) compiled a database of viewer engagement statistics for each video. Given our definition (see "What is Engagement?"), we used three proxies in the YouTube context: (1) the number of "likes" minus the number of "dislikes" (for an overall "liking" measure, something that probably approximates how positive or negative consumer attitudes are), (2) the number of comments, and (3) the number of views.[i]

On these measures of engagement, the database was diverse: The number of likes ranged from 0 to 77,152; the number of dislikes ranged from 0 to 31,064; the number of comments varied between 0 and 68,254; and the number of views ranged from 39 to 8,094,236, with a median of approximately 58,000. These engagement metrics were strongly correlated ($r =.66$ to $.83$, $p <.01$), but we examined them separately. None was normally distributed.

Three experienced research assistants, also blind to the hypotheses, classified the features of the videos. Each of these coders viewed every video at least once and rated it on many dimensions according to a classification scheme that we provided, as described herein. The coders did not interact with one another or consult to arrive at a consensus, preserving individual variation as an approximation of diverse viewer response. After watching each video, the coders indicated the strength of various emotional responses likely to be inspired by the content. We focused on six basic emotions: joy, love, sadness, fear, anger and surprise.

We also assessed a series of control variables. Based on information provided by YouTube about the source of each video, the coders judged whether it was likely a private or commercial undertaking. They also coded whether the video contained a specific call to action (for example, a URL within the video inviting a user to click for more information) or a specific behavior requested (such as a petition to sign) and whether there was an interactive component (for instance, viewers were given a choice to click "yes" or "no" within the video).

Finally, we coded for other elements. We identified the extent to which a video could be described as containing (1) people (absent or present); (2) attractive people; (3) animals; (4) babies; (5) anthropomorphized content (for instance, a pony playing the trumpet); (6) stunts and amazing feats (such as a monster truck doing a back flip); (7) music; (8) sexually suggestive imagery; (9) humor; (10) disgusting imagery (for instance, rats in a coffee shop or a mysterious object in a juice box); (11) satire (such as a spoof of a political debate or a spoof of an ad campaign); (12) a serious tone (for instance, a landslide occurring on a railway line); or (13) references to an underdog (for example, a storyline about bullying).

WHAT IS ENGAGEMENT?

One reason so little is understood about video engagement is that the phenomenon is less than 20 years old. The first real example of the power of engaging online content was the "Dancing Baby" video, created as a product demonstration by a 3-D character animation software development team. Released in 1996, the Dancing Baby "oogachuckah'd" its way across Internet forums, websites and email inboxes.[8] Though a relatively low-budget animation, the Dancing Baby video captivated viewers' attention and became a cultural phenomenon noted around the water cooler and even on the evening news. In 1998, the Dancing Baby landed on the hit TV comedy "Ally McBeal," cementing the video's status as a cultural icon.

Perhaps because the phenomenon is relatively young, scholars have not yet even reached a consensus about what engagement is,[9] and we won't try to settle that debate here. We take a broad view, and define engagement as behavior that includes sharing but also extends to other forms of measurable user involvement. This view is in line with TV advertising norms, which link engagement loosely to attention and viewer interaction.[10] Ultimately, it seems likely that different engagement-related behaviors—commenting, sharing, "favoriting," "liking" and so on—are highly correlated.[11] For this study, we measured engagement using YouTube commenting, liking and viewing behaviors. These measures of engagement were readily available for the full range of videos we studied (both successful and unsuccessful), which allowed us to perform a representative content analysis.

MYTHS DISPELLED

Our study allowed us to dispel a number of myths about online videos. For one thing, when it comes to garnering views, professionals seem no better than amateurs at creating compelling content. We found no difference in the aggregate number of comments between homemade and commercially created videos. While branded videos tend to be liked more, they are also disliked more.

The presence of babies also did not have any impact on views or comments. Sure, babies are cute and give people warm feelings, but they don't seem to increase viewer engagement. Safe creative choices are less risky, but because they don't generate much emotion, they are also less likely to engage.

Likewise, videos of animals do go viral sometimes, but probably not *because* they contain animals. Rather, we think engagement with animal videos happens because many of these videos contain animals doing something surprising. In other words, it's not about the animal per se but about the feeling of surprise inspired by using novel or incongruous content such as Grumpy Cat,[12] an apparently frowning cat whose owners signed an endorsement deal with Nestlé Purina PetCare. One might think that anthropomorphized animals such as dancing dogs, trumpet-playing ponies or talking mice would be old hat by now, but it seems not. Among Internet viewers, all those talented animals are apparently still novel and incongruous enough to inspire engagement. Our findings that babies and animals in general are not particularly effective are consistent with other research.[13]

We also found that attractive people don't engage viewers particularly well. Videos with attractive actors were linked to lower levels of surprise, which in the context of online videos is not a good thing. Maybe this is because it's hardly unusual to see beautiful people in front of the camera. In fact, it's perhaps entirely too expected, which makes it an ineffective way to get people's attention. Even sexually suggestive content doesn't seem to especially interest people.

Nor are people especially interested in seeing stories about the triumph of underdogs. We looked at a lot of videos that contained the idea of the underdog and found evidence that they don't engage viewers. Perhaps they have become a cliché.

Other kinds of content did drive more comments and views but could be problematic for advertisers. Satire was associated with hyperbole and feelings of anger and with high levels of both comments and views. If the goal is to engage viewers by creating anger-inducing content, satire seems to be a good way to stir up a hornet's nest.

People also liked what we called "stunts and amazing feats." Watching other people do remarkable things gave viewers feelings of surprise and sometimes fear, which didn't seem to hurt engagement and led to increased views. This finding probably explains why the video of Felix Baumgartner performing the world's highest skydive was one of the top 10 videos of 2012.[14]

Disgusting content also seems to boost views. If it seemed exaggerated, viewers sometimes felt angry, but other times it was seen as novel, incongruous and surprising—and led to more liking and views. It is likely a polarizing creative choice, repelling certain viewers (such as older consumers) while attracting others (such as teenagers).

Finally, anger- and fear-inducing content seem to trigger more views, but make a sad video and you'll probably cry alone.

THE ELEMENT OF SURPRISE

What matters most? Surprise!

In our study, *emotionally surprising* videos generated liking and views more than any kind of specific content element we studied. Surprise had indirect effects, too. In addition to the direct positive effect surprise had on liking and views, it was linked to fear. Frightening videos got significantly more views. This probably does not reflect a "horror movie" effect (where audiences enjoy being frightened) because the overall liking index of such videos also went down. This suggests that fearful content can increase views but at the risk of generating negative attitudes, whereas content that is surprising but not scary doesn't seem to have a downside, because both liking and views increase.

We started this study with three ideas about how a strong emotional response like surprise might be created: novelty, incongruity and hyperbole. No matter how we looked at it, there was never a connection between hyperbole and surprise. This suggests that in terms of creating unexpected or fresh content, exaggeration is not the way forward. However, hyperbole had effects that we didn't anticipate: We found it correlated with increased anger, which in turn boosted comments and views. This suggests that using exaggerated content may earn views, but at the expense of angering customers. Perhaps some "extreme" brands or certain types of organizations (for example, political campaigns or nongovernmental organizations) can use hyperbolic themes without fear of damage to their reputation, but for most business-content producers, this option will be problematic. The creative choices most strongly linked with hyperbole were satire and disgusting content, whereas nonsatiric humor was not.

> *When it comes to garnering views, professionals seem no better than amateurs at creating compelling content. We found no difference in the aggregate number of comments between homemade and commercially created videos.*

When we looked at novel and incongruous content, we found that both were associated with feelings of surprise, which increased views and liking. This suggests to us that if a marketer's goal is to get viewers' attention by surprising them, they have two good choices: Show them something they have never seen before, or show them two things they are familiar with but in an original, juxtaposed way—to "make it new," as the poet Ezra Pound once advised.

WHY DO PEOPLE SHARE VIDEOS?

A final important question, but one that goes beyond the scope of this study, is *why* people share videos. Recent research has shown that people are more likely to share videos linked to brands they like.[15] This makes sense, because a consumer who feels connected to a particular brand will do all sorts of exceptional things for that brand, such as paying a premium for it and recommending it to friends. We also know that people prefer to share videos that they have received from their own friends and family because it's easy and safe to pass along something that is socially sanctioned.[16] These two factors suggest that if businesses create compelling video content, then pushing this content to brand fans or other key influencers might result in a cascade of sharing.

Other researchers have found that videos with superior creativity are better liked and are both forwarded and viewed more.[17] This research doesn't provide clear definitions of what is meant by creativity,[18] but we speculate that our study might provide clarification: Creativity often is evident in contexts where something is novel or juxtaposed for a dramatic or comic effect, such as a hamster eating a tiny slice of pizza off of a china plate on a picnic blanket.[19] Our results confirm that both approaches are likely to be effective in engaging audiences because of their powerful influence in surprising viewers. What else might make a video seem more creative? Our research suggests some candidates in elements such as humor, stunts and amazing feats, and disgusting content, which all drive higher views.

Much of the academic research on viral videos has tried to contribute a better understanding of the role of emotions in the decision to share a video by focusing on the intensity of the emotion that a person feels watching a video and whether that emotion is positive or negative. For example, the results of several recent papers seem to suggest that more emotionally arousing content is shared more, but being *positively* arousing (for example, hilarity) generates more sharing than being *negatively* arousing (for example, shock).[20] The main conclusion of these studies, as in ours, is that, while it pays to be intense, to be intense in a positive way usually pays off. These results are largely consistent with ours and seem to point in the same direction: If emotionally intense videos prompt more sharing—whether positive or negative—then, generally speaking, those videos are watched more often.[21] For example, we find that anger-inducing videos can lead to high numbers of views, just as joy-inducing ones can. But our research suggests that an element of *surprise*, a highly arousing emotion that can be either positive *or* negative, may produce the strongest viewer reaction of all.

Dante M. Pirouz and *Allison R. Johnson* are assistant professors of marketing at Ivey Business School at Western University in London, Ontario, Canada. *Matthew Thomson* is the R.A. Barford Professor of Marketing and an associate professor of marketing at Ivey Business School. *Raymond Pirouz* is a lecturer in marketing at Ivey Business School. Comment on this article at http://sloanreview.mit.edu/x/56406, or contact the authors at smrfeedback@mit.edu.

REFERENCES

1. While the following paper only considers successful (branded) viral marketing campaigns, it is a serious, systematic effort to understand why sharing occurs; see A. Dobele, A. Lindgreen, M. Beverland, J. Vanhamme and R. van Wijk, "Why Pass on Viral Messages? Because They Connect Emotionally," Business Horizons 50, no. 4 (July-August 2007): 291–304.

2. J. Berger and K.L. Milkman, "What Makes Online Content Viral?," Journal of Marketing Research 49, no. 2 (April 2012): 192–205.

3. See, for example, G. Fennell, "Attention Engagement," Current Issues & Research in Advertising 2, no. 1 (1979): 17–33; and L. Shen and E. Bigsby, "Behavioral Activation/ Inhibition Systems and Emotions: A Test of Valence vs. Action Tendency Hypotheses," Communication Monographs 77, no. 1 (March 2010): 1–26.

4. See P.J. Silvia, "Interest: The Curious Emotion," Current Directions in Psychological Science 17, no. 1 (February 2008): 57–60; and J.L. Sherry, "Flow and Media Enjoyment," Communication Theory 14, no. 4 (November 2004): 328–347.

5. A.P. McGraw and C. Warren, "Benign Violations: Making Immoral Behavior Funny," Psychological Science 21, no. 8 (2010): 1141–1149.

6. Invisible Children, "Kony 2012," March 5, 2012, www.youtube.com.

7. L. Cano Mora, "All or Nothing: A Semantic Analysis of Hyperbole," Revista de Lingüística y Lenguas Aplicadas 4 (October 2010): 25–35.

8. Awesome, "Dancing Baby," 2010, http://knowyourmeme.com.

9. For a good discussion, see B.J. Calder, E.C. Malthouse and U. Schaedel, "An Experimental Study of the Relationship Between Online Engagement and Advertising Effectiveness," Journal of Interactive Marketing 23, no. 4 (November 2009): 321–331.

10. R.G. Heath, "Emotional Engagement: How Television Builds Big Brands at Low Attention," Journal of Advertising Research 49, no. 1 (2009): 62–73.

11. Business scholar A.J. Mills argues that the willingness to consume is highly related to the willingness to distribute—meaning sharing and views are likely to be positively correlated; see A.J. Mills, "Virality in Social Media: The SPIN Framework," Journal of Public Affairs 12, no. 2 (May 2012): 162–169.

12. CNN, "Grumpy Cat Goes From Meme to the Big Screen," May 30, 2013, www.youtube.com.

13. K. Nelson-Field, "Viral Marketing: The Science of Sharing" (Victoria, Australia: Oxford University Press Australia & New Zealand, 2013).

14. D. Hurwitz, "Watch: YouTube's Most Popular Videos of 2012," Dec. 21, 2012, www.usatoday.com.

15. J.L. Hayes and K.W. King, "The Social Exchange of Viral Ads: Referral and Coreferral of Ads Among College Students," Journal of Interactive Advertising 14, no. 2 (2014): 98–109; and J. Huang, S. Su, L. Zhou and X. Liu, "Attitude Toward the Viral Ad: Expanding Traditional Advertising Models to Interactive Advertising," Journal of Interactive Marketing 27, no. 1 (February 2013): 36–46.

16. R.E. Guadagno, D.M. Rempala, S. Murphy and B.M. Okdie, "What Makes a Video Go Viral? An Analysis of Emotional Contagion and Internet Memes," Computers in Human Behavior 29, no. 6 (November 2013): 2312–2319.

17. E. Botha, "A Means to an End: Using Political Satire to Go Viral," Public Relations Review 40, no. 2 (June 2014): 363–374; and D. Southgate, N. Westoby and G. Page, "Creative Determinants of Viral Video Viewing," International Journal of Advertising 29, no. 3 (2010): 349–368.

18. Botha provides no definition of creativity while Southgate, Westoby and Page define creativity in terms of involving and enjoyable (branded) content without explaining what these terms mean and how they differ from, for example, outcome measures of engagement. For example, one might argue watching a video is a measure of involvement, not an indicator of creativity.

19. AprilsAnimals, "Tiny Hamster Eating a Tiny Pizza," May 7, 2014, www.youtube.com.

20. P. Eckler and P. Bolls, "Spreading the Virus: Emotional Tone of Viral Advertising and Its Effect on Forwarding Intentions and Attitudes," Journal of Interactive Advertising 11, no. 2 (spring 2011): 72–83; Guadagno et al., "What Makes a Video Go Viral?"; and K. Nelson-Field, E. Riebe and K. Newstead, "The Emotions that Drive Viral Videos," Australasian Marketing Journal 21, no 4 (November 2013): 205–211.

21. The results do, however, suggest some interesting research questions. For example, Nelson-Field, Riebe and Newstead suggest that sad videos may be shared more, whereas our data suggests sad videos are watched less. Between the two, there is a logical disconnect that bears examination. For example, could it be that if people knowingly receive a link to a sad video, most prefer not to watch it in order to maintain their mood?

i. The number of views does not reflect differences in viewership composition or social transmission (in other words, sharing). For example, it does not distinguish whether one person has viewed a video many times or whether many people have viewed a video only once.

CHAPTER 9

Social Media

Customer Engagement Via Visual Content

Sushree Das

Case Study

This case was written by **Sushree Das** and reviewed by **Dr. A. Saravanan Naidu**, Amity Research Centers Headquarter, Bangalore. It is intended to be used as the basis for class discussion rather than to illustrate either effective or ineffective handling of a management situation. The case was compiled from published sources.

Abstract: For some entrepreneurs, social media marketing was probably the next big thing. According to reports, most of the marketers claimed that social media was important for their businesses in terms of increase in traffic to their websites. While some marketers said, they participated in social media; a few others claimed that they were not sure what social media tools could be the best for them. Analysts mentioned that, social media marketing could help the company enhance its brand visibility and recognition, improve customer-brand relationship, decrease marketing costs, increase inbound traffic, while also improving customer insights and provide a rich customer experience. Likewise, to sustain a social media campaign, it was necessary for marketers to engage customers both emotionally as well as behaviourally, by providing rich visual content. Apart from other customer engagement strategies, experts highlighted that brands had the inclination to use visual contents on social media platforms. This was effective, since social networking was one of the customers' most preferred platforms for engagement and interaction. However, marketers had to be careful as to how long they could keep the visitors on their websites engaged and turn them into customers in the long run. Moreover, whether use of visual content could be sufficient as a customer engagement strategy was also uncertain.

CASE STUDY

Social networking had become a trend among people all over the world. Hectic lifestyles made it difficult for people to catch up with others, while the advancement of technology drove people to stay connected with the outside world, without disturbing their professional commitments. Social networking gradually became indispensable for people. This was again possible through social media platforms such as Facebook, Twitter and LinkedIn, apart from other emerging ones. Marketing practitioners and entrepreneurs had started using social media for marketing their brands, their company as well as themselves. With most of the audience glued to different forms of social media, it became easier for marketers to reach their target customers. It also helped them in enhancing their brand visibility and recognition, generating new leads, cutting marketing costs, apart from a host of other benefits. They used audio content, visual content as well as other forms to make their brands and products visible to the customers. However, utilisation of visual content for marketing on social media received mixed responses. Entrepreneurs and marketers said it was important for their businesses, some said they had no idea which social media tool to use, while others claimed that it required proper planning and strategy making. Keeping these in mind, whether social media marketing with the help of visual content could be profitable and beneficial for marketers remained to be seen.

SOCIAL MEDIA AND BUSINESS: THE NEXUS

The year 2016 was a great year for online marketing, though the industry had never slowed down. Analysts identified a few trends, some of which became noticeable when users turned up to them while some others were innovations that came up as response to other developments. These trends were expected to shape up the existing social media marketing world, and be the forerunners of future developments.[1] (**Exhibit 9.1**).

Further, analysts noted that there were five major issues faced by marketers in social media marketing: tactics, engagement, measurement, audience and tools. According to the results of a survey conducted in January 2016, almost 92% marketers wanted to know which tactics worked best, while constant changes took place across many social networks. 90% marketers looked for the best ways to engage customers. While 86% of marketers wanted to know how to measure their return on investment for social media activities, connecting with the ideal customers and prospects was a concern for 86% marketers. Similarly, 86% marketers sought better tools to simplify their social media tasks, around 90% said social media was important for their businesses.[2]

It was observed that the top two benefits of social media marketing were increasing exposure and increasing traffic. A significant 89% of all marketers claimed that their social media efforts generated more exposure for their businesses. Increasing traffic was the second benefit, with 75% people reporting positive results. Most marketers utilised social media to

---

1   DeMers Jayson, "The Top 7 Social Media Marketing Trends Dominating 2016", http://www.forbes.com/sites/jaysondemers/2016/08/01/the-top-7-social-media-marketing-trends-dominating-2016/#7237f4f35da7, August 1st 2016
2   Stelzner Michael A., "2016 SOCIAL MEDIA MARKETING INDUSTRY REPORT", https://www.socialmediaexaminer.com/wp-content/uploads/2016/05/SocialMediaMarketingIndustryReport2016.pdf, May 2016

EXHIBIT 9.1 The Top Seven Social Media Marketing Trends of 2016

- **Less is more, better is better:** Most platforms' newsfeed algorithms looked for posts based on a degree of perceived relevance, rather than time of publication. Focus on quality continued to prevail over quantity.

- **Shift in platform dynamics:** Apart from Facebook, Twitter and LinkedIn, who served similar functions, Instagram and Snap chat entered the game, thereby changing the positions of all the platforms.

- **Live streaming got bigger:** Combined with the trend of users demanding more 'live' and 'in- the-moment' updates, live streaming video noticed a major upsurge in popularity, especially with the release of Facebook Live.

- **Growing regularity of 'buy' buttons:** Advertising became more akin to a shopping experience. Ads and products available to purchase worked their way into users' newsfeeds and profiles more smoothly and with fewer distinctions from organic content. 'Buy' buttons made it easier for marketers to convert followers into real customers.

- **New applications changing social interaction:** Platforms like Snap chat started allowing more one-sided conversations, Facebook launched new communication channels like Messenger for Business. Brands and consumers found broader ways to interact.

- **Push for more personalization:** There was a greater demand for personalisation and customisation to display different types of content.

- **Broader app functionality:** Functions such as in-app search, embedded content, and a personal digital assistant in Facebook offered peripheral functionality to keep users contented on more fronts.

Source: Compiled by the Author from—"DeMers Jayson, "The Top 7 Social Media Marketing Trends Dominating 2016", http://www.forbes.com/sites/jaysondemers/2016/08/01/the-top-7-social-media-marketing-trends-dominating-2016/ #7237f4f35da7, August 1st 2016

develop a dedicated fan base (68%) and gain market place intelligence (66%). Moreover, while 66% said it helped them generate leads, around 58% marketers agreed social media enhanced their search rankings. For 55% people, social media boosted growth in business relationships, and another 55% marketers could establish thought leadership. While it helped in improving sales for 51% marketers, 50% said social media reduced their marketing expenses.[3] **(Exhibit 9.2)**

Furthermore, while B2C marketers were more focused on Facebook, YouTube, Instagram, and Pinterest, B2Bmarketers focused more on LinkedIn, Twitter, Google+, and Slide Share. When asked to select the most important social platform for their business, the survey indicated that, 55% marketers chose Facebook as their most important platform, whereas 18% chose LinkedIn, 12% selected Twitter, and 4% chose YouTube respectively. The survey also revealed that Facebook was still the main platform for marketers, where in its importance increased from 52% in 2015 to 55% in 2016. LinkedIn's significance decreased from 21% to 18% and importance of Twitter also decreased from 13% in 2015 to 12% in 2016. Besides, around

---

3   "2016 SOCIAL MEDIA MARKETING INDUSTRY REPORT", op.cit.

<EXHIBIT 9.2 Advantages of Social Media Marketing>
EXHIBIT 9.2   Advantages of Social Media Marketing

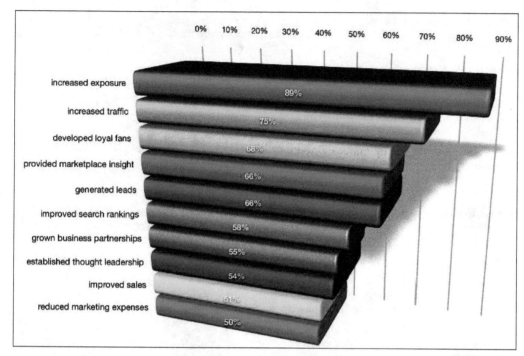

0% 10% 20% 30% 40% 50% 60% 70% 80% 90%

increased exposure — 89%
increased traffic — 75%
developed loyal fans — 68%
provided marketplace insight — 66%
generated leads — 66%
improved search rankings — 58%
grown business partnerships — 55%
established thought leadership — 54%
improved sales — 51%
reduced marketing expenses — 50%

Source: Michael A. Stelzner, "2016 SOCIAL MEDIA MARKETING INDUSTRY REPORT", https://www.socialmediaexaminer.com/wp-content/uploads/2016/05/Social MediaMarketingIndustryReport2016.pdf, May 2016

65% marketers in the B2C segment selected Facebook as their top choice, while LinkedIn was more significant for B2B marketers.[4]

Among the most commonly used social media platforms used by marketers, Facebook, Twitter, LinkedIn, YouTube, Google+, Instagram, and Pinterest topped the list. Usage of all the other platforms such as Forums, Social review sites, Geo-location, Snapchat, Vine and others was negligible. Usage of Instagram jumped from 36% in 2015 to 44%. Among the larger social networks, Twitter dropped from 79% to 76%, LinkedIn declined from 71% to 67%, YouTube went down from 55% to 53%, Google+ fell from 56% to 49%, and Pinterest dropped from 45% to 40%. Similarly, on being asked about their future usage of activities on social media, marketers gave their preferences accordingly.[5] **(Exhibit 9.3).**

Moreover, marketers also identified the paid social media platforms which they used regularly. Nearly 87% marketers used Facebook ads, while 39% and 18% used Google and Twitter ads respectively. While 90% B2C marketers used Facebook ads, 79% B2B

---

4   ibid.
5   "2016 SOCIAL MEDIA MARKETING INDUSTRY REPORT", op.cit.

EXHIBIT 9.3 Future Use of Social Media Activities

PLATFORM	INCREASE	DECREASE	STAY THE SAME	NO PLANS TO UTILISE
Facebook	67	5	25	3
YouTube	63	3	18	16
Twitter	61	4	26	10
LinkedIn	61	2	23	14
Instagram	57	1	13	28
Pinterest	42	2	22	33
Google+	35	6	31	28
Forums	25	3	20	52
SlideShare	22	2	14	62
Social Review Sites	20	2	18	60
Social Bookmarking	16	2	15	68
SnapChat	16	1	9	74
Vine	11	2	12	75
Geo-location	10	2	14	74

Source: Compiled by the Author from—Michael A. Stelzner, "2016 SOCIAL MEDIA MARKETING INDUSTRY REPORT", https://www.socialmediaexaminer.com/wp-content/uploads/2016/05/SocialMediaMarketingIndustryReport2016.pdf, May 2016

marketers used the same. Besides, 28% B2Bmarketers used LinkedIn ads compared to 11% B2C marketers.[6]

Apart from identifying the existing social media marketing trends, analysts also highlighted a few trends that were expected to dominate the industry in 2017.[7] **(Exhibit 9.4)**

As far as the type of content was concerned, marketers identified the ones they used in their social media marketing. At least 74% marketers used visual assets in their social media marketing, compared to 71% of them in 2015. This was followed by blogging at 68% and video at 60%.Analysts mentioned that Live video content such as Facebook Live and Periscope was introduced in 2016 and used by 14% of marketers. Only 10% of them used Podcasting. Likewise, at least 78% of B2B marketers were much more likely to use blogging compared to 6% B2Cmarketers. Further, the report also revealed that the most important form of content for marketers was blogging, which dropped from 45% in 2015 to 38% in 2016. Visual marketing

---

6 ibid.
7 DeMers Jayson, "7 Online Marketing Trends That Will Dominate 2017", http://www.forbes.com/sites/jaysondemers/2016/11/14/7-online-marketing-trends-that-will-dominate-2017/#78698 aa2dec8, November 14th 2016

EXHIBIT 9.4   Social Media Marketing Trends for 2017

- **Rise of augmented reality (AR):** Ushered in by the radical success of Pokemon Go, brands could be expected to launch AR games, AR ads and capitalising on existing AR apps. These could not only give the users an augmented reality experience, but also boost the marketers' earning potential.

- **Live video streaming to pick up pace:** With the availability of faster Internet and mobile devices, live video could continue as a trend, with more and more apps and online platforms giving 'live streaming' functionality, such as the 2016 US Presidential Debate streamed live.

- **Need for data visualization and expansion of such tools:** With more sophisticated technology and greater need for data analysis, businesses could be expected to catch up to the 'interpretation' part of data analysis, with the help of data visualisation tools.

- **Improved forms of native advertising:** As consumers continued to ignore most forms of conventional advertising, native advertising becomes an effective way to get those consumers' attentions.

- **Focus on niche markets based on necessity of brands:** As number of businesses increased in the content and social media marketing space, brands could target a more specific niche, appealing to a narrower range of demographics with a more specific topic. As a result, more companies could opt for more targeted, almost personal-level content and campaigns.

- **Rise of 'immersive experience' content marketing:** Augmented reality, virtual reality, 360 degree videos could be the technologies that might give users a more real and bigger experience.

- **Significance of 'dense content':** The potentially infinite scrolls of social media newsfeeds and endless streams of content from almost every brand or individual usually force us to filter out the majority of messages we see as white noise. More marketers could gradually learn that dense content is key, making every line and every word count.

Source: Compiled by the Author from—DeMers Jayson, "7 Online Marketing Trends That Will Dominate 2017", http://www .forbes.com/sites/jaysondemers/2016/11/14/7-online-marketing-trends-that-will-dominate-2017/#78698aa2dec8, November 14th 2016

rose from 34% in 2015 to 37% in 2016. Moreover, 42% B2C marketers and 27% B2B marketers claimed that visual content was most important for their businesses.[8]

Further, marketers indicated their plan to change their social media content activities in future. They responded in terms of increasing, decreasing, retaining the same or not utilising the various forms of content. Analysts observed that, the use of video was a key part of marketers' plan in 2016. Though live video was a new content option, 39% marketers planned to increase their use of live video in 2016 (**Exhibit 9.5**). Besides, marketers emphasized that they wanted to learn more about creating videos, followed by blogging and creating visuals, while nearly 50% were keen on learning about live videos.[9]

---

8   "2016 SOCIAL MEDIA MARKETING INDUSTRY REPORT", op.cit.
9   "2016 SOCIAL MEDIA MARKETING INDUSTRY REPORT", op.cit.

EXHIBIT 9.5 Marketers' Plans to Change the Future Content Activities (2016, in %)

CONTENT	INCREASE	DECREASE	STAY THE SAME	NO PLANS TO UTILISE
Video	73	1	14	13
Visuals	71	1	20	8
Blogging	66	2	18	13
Live Video	39	1	11	49
Podcasting	26	1	13	60

Source: MICHAEL A. STELZNER, "2016 SOCIAL MEDIA MARKETING INDUSTRY REPORT", https://www.socialmediaexaminer.com/wp-content/uploads/2016/05/SocialMediaMarketingIndustryReport2016.pdf, May 2016

VISUAL MEMES IN SOCIAL MEDIA: A NEW AGE MARKETING TOOL?

According to the annual Marketing Monitor study across the Asia-Pacific by global insights consultancy TNS, social media became the top strategic priority for brands in India as they looked for customer engagement. Marketing professionals across the region ranked social media as the top element that decided their planning process as well as the top parameter to measure performance of campaigns. In the opinion of TNS MD, South India & Sri Lanka and Head of Brand and Communications Practice, S Visvanathan, "businesses are typically overwhelmed by the sheer volume of data generated. India's online environment is developing very fast. As more consumers and customers start connecting to the internet through mobile and start accessing different digital platforms, the amount of data available will explode. It is important that marketers devise effective ways of extracting insight from this data before it is too late."

The study also highlighted that customer relationship management was the top priority for marketing departments in 2016. The findings revealed that marketers' sphere of activity had expanded, as they concentrated on ways to deliver the best customer experience, beyond the traditional aim of increasing brand awareness. To achieve this objective, businesses used social media across many disciplines. The study further revealed that, nearly 50% of the marketers used social media for brand communications, while 43% used it for customer service. According to TNS Digital Director (APAC), Zoe Lawrence, "It's no secret that social has become an intrinsic part of our daily lives—94 per cent of connected consumers in India use social networks, switching between Facebook, Google+, and Twitter as the top three channels. This mass adoption of social provides marketers with an array of sources when it comes to developing strategies and evaluating the effectiveness of their marketing activity. As the digital ecosystem evolves, we will continue to identify new ways to build insights. However, whatever the metric

EXHIBIT 9.6   Steps for Execution of Social Media Optimisation

Community Building: The first step to engage real-time leads for a business was to deliver great content and information and focus on building a community before monetary gains.

Turn Around Time (TAT): For SMO to excel, the TAT had to be quick. A Blog Post, Twitter, LinkedIn or Face book campaign should be operated as per the stipulated time of delivery or leads.

Engagement: Social Media was about community building and the target audience's interested in the brand and its value. Social Proofing was immensely necessary for engagement i.e., a majority of interested audience committed over digital platforms to your business.

Driving sales: To drive sales for business and even for personal promotion of an individual, daily content marketing and advertising over Social Media tools played a major role. Facebook, Twitter, Instagram and LinkedIn campaigning exert influence on the audience and usually drive enormous amount of sales.

Source: Rajsekar Siddharth, "The Power Of Social Media For A Business", https://www.entrepreneur.com/article/284178, October 24th 2016

used, it's important to ensure marketers are monitoring the indicators that contribute to sales."[10]

Analysts further mentioned that earlier in the digital world, marketing was mostly confined to website building and seeking information over Google. However, the most powerful source of marketing in the current times was none other than 'social media', both online and offline. Siddharth Rajsekar, Social Media Expert at Scion Social, highlighted a few points which were essential for every social media follower to execute Social Media Optimization (SMO) for a project. There were four important steps to understand the actual potential of a social media tool: strategies, optimise, socialise and monetise.[11] **(Exhibit 9.6).**

Industry observers noticed that, over the years brands became increasingly more visual savvy. From celebrating special occasions such as birthdays or weddings, and popular festivals to not-so-popular days of the year, 2016 witnessed a significant rise in Indian brands investing in their visual content creation. On the occasion of Gandhi Jayanti, brands from varied sectors offered visual tributes to the 'Father of the Nation' or the Mahatma. Brands relied on the world's most influential thinker of the century for his ideals and beliefs based on peace and non-violence. Inspirational quotes accompanied the visuals with help from many of his minimal attachments in life including his well-known round- rimmed spectacles, his charkha, and his walking stick. Gandhiji's three monkeys were also seen in the visual content.[12] **(Annexure 9.1)**

Although statistics and reports revealed that, an effective social media campaign had a positive impact on brand building, some marketing professionals were unclear about why

---

10   "Social media at the heart of brands' strategy in India: TNS study", http://www.afaqs.com/news/story/48720_Social-media-at-the-heart-of-brands-strategy-in-India-TNS-study, August 17th 2016

11   Rajsekar Siddharth, "The Power Of Social Media For A Business", https://www.entrepreneur.com/article/284178, October 24th 2016

12   Vinaya, "#Gandhi Jayanti: 60 thoughtful brand tributes in cool visuals & gifs", http://lighthouseinsights.in/best-gandhi-jayanti-visuals-and-gifs-of-2016.html/,October 5th 2016

EXHIBIT 9.7 Impacts of a Social Media Campaign

Enhanced brand recognition and thought leadership: The more frequently the brand appeared on social media, the greater could be the brand exposure. This could help in offering more recognition and credibility, not only for the company, but also for the personal brand, product and business. Similarly, if a brand or a person showed up regularly on any search engine, the expert was more likely to treat it/him as a thought leader.

Increase in trust through leveraged credibility: Leveraged credibility was something when a company says, 'We have enough trust in your expertise to put our brand behind yours'. This could help create the kind of trust necessary for brand success.

Competitive advantage in cold conversions: For a brand or business, converting visitors who come through internet search sites instead of referrals, into potential customers was the third benefit of a social media campaign. These visitors usually tend to choose the brand which has a more qualitative social media presence (be it with a blog, Pinterest, LinkedIn or another channel), than its competitor.

Greater percentage of referrals closed: With change in the nature of referral marketing, social media made it easier for employers to shortlist and start a dialogue with a potential candidate.

More cash and customers: Finally, while social media was not a total solution to increase your sales, it was not harmful. Research from social sales expert Jim Keenan showed that in 2012, nearly 79% of salespeople who used social media in their selling process achieved better results than their counterparts who did not use it.

Source: Tiber Leland Karen, "5 Impacts a Social Media Campaign Can Have on Your Brand", https://www.entrepreneur.com/article/277749, August 12th 2016

and how they could use social media for their business. According to a report by Social Media Examiner, 85% of marketers who used social media were not clear which social media tools might work best for their business. To realise the benefits of social media on a brand's success, analysts identified five impacts, a social media campaign could have on a brand.[13] **(Exhibit 9.7).**

Analysts claimed that apart from the above mentioned benefits, social media could act as a signal to inform brands about potential clients as well as a channel to direct the same visitors into the brand's website. Later, it becomes the company's job to convert them into customers.[14] Experts claimed that, in order to achieve higher levels of customer engagement, it was necessary for marketing professionals to build trust and a strong customer-brand relationship, while also reviewing the value of their communication through social channels. In order to understand the effects of engagement, it was also important to engage the customer both emotionally and behaviorally, by facilitating different forms of interaction with the brand. However, it was imperative to remember that customers had limited resources and did not wish to spend significant time and effort on their brands' fan pages. Experts warned that, any strategy that failed to consider this issue might not bring the expected outcome or may even result in a boomerang effect.[15]

---

13 Tiber Leland Karen, "5 Impacts a Social Media Campaign Can Have on Your Brand", https://www.entrepreneur.com/article/277749, August 12th 2016
14 "5 Impacts a Social Media Campaign Can Have onYour Brand", op.cit.
15 "Do brands engage their customers through social media?", http://www.marketcommunity.com/Content/articles/MARKET-68—Brand-Engagement/Do-brands-engage-their-customers-through-social-media

Mumbai Indians: The IPL team presented cricket in a subtle way.

Mumbai Indians @mipaltan
Paltan, let's come together and pay respect to the father of our nation on the occasion of #GandhiJayanti #DilSeIndian

Yes Bank: The bank spins a deep quote in this gif.

YES BANK @YESBANK
The sole way to bring a change is to be the change. This #GandhiJayanti, pledge to be a better version of you. #INDIAboleYES

Penguin Books India: The publisher adhered to his quotes.

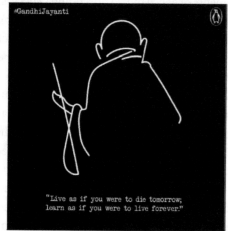

Penguin India@PenguinIndia
Generations that came scarce believed that such a one as this walked the earth in flesh and blood! #GandhiJayanti

Cox & Kings India: The travel brand takes you on a short but interesting virtual tour.

Cox & Kings @coxandkingsIN
This #GandhiJayanti, come explore 14 beautiful memorials of one of the most transcendental leaders of the world, #MahatmaGandhi.

Quikr: Quikr found a cool brand connect with Gandhi's quote on 'change'.

Quikr@Quikr
This Gandhi Jayanti, let's remember his sayings and make a difference to our lives.
KyunkiAasaanHaiBadalna
With #Quikr. #GandhiJayanti

Bajaj Allianz Life: The life insurance brand urged people to act 'now'.

Bajaj Allianz Life @BajajAllianzLIC Saluting the Father of our beautiful Nation.
#HappyGandhiJayanti

Moto India: The smartphone brand emphasised on 'different'.

Moto India@Moto_IND
To the inspiration that moved the entire nation!
#GandhiJayanti#differentisbetter

Dulux India: Splashes of paint in the visual by the paint maker.

@DuluxIndia
Dulux salutes the Father of the Nation on his birthday.
Happy #GandhiJayanti.

CHAPTER 10

Increasing the ROI of Social Media Marketing

V. Kumar and Rohan Mirchandani

By following a seven-step process to identify and recruit potential brand ambassadors in online social networks, an ice cream retailer substantially improved the effectiveness of its social media marketing.

N ow that so many people worldwide participate in online social networks—955 million on Facebook alone[1]—influencing consumer preferences and purchase decisions through these networks and word of mouth (WOM) is an increasingly important part of every marketer's job. Many enterprises are investing in social channels to rapidly create or propagate their brand through viral content, social media contests and other consumer engagement efforts. Their traditional campaigns are changing, too. Companies such as Geico, Dell and eBay are adapting the traditional "one-way" advertising message and using it as a stepping-stone to begin a two-way dialogue with consumers via social media.[2]

Marketers know that theoretically, social media should be a powerful way to generate sustainable, positive WOM. If they can only select the right social media platform, design the right message and engage the right users to spread that message, their campaign should be a success. But until now, that's been a big if.

THE LEADING QUESTION

How can a company improve the ROI of its social media campaigns?

FINDINGS

- Identify social media users who are both influential and particularly interested in the company's product or service category.
- Incentivize those influencers to talk about the company's product or service.
- Use metrics to calculate the value of an individual's influence.

CREATING SUCCESSFUL SOCIAL MEDIA CAMPAIGNS

An effective social media strategy should clearly define the marketing objectives, evaluate the opportunities and select an appropriate form of social media to communicate. Today's

V. Kumar and Rohan Mirchandani, "Increasing the ROI of Social Media Marketing," *MIT Sloan Management Review, vol. 54, no. 1.* Copyright © 2012 by MIT Sloan Management Review. Reprinted with permission.

FIGURE 10.1 Ice-cream retailer Hokey Pokey encouraged influential social media users to tweet about their custom ice-cream creations.

social networking sites are also equipping themselves with analytical capabilities to analyze the reach, spread and impact of a social media message. In light of these goals and tools, we developed a seven-step approach to ensure a successful social media campaign. (See "Seven Steps to Social Media," p. 56.)

Our research suggests that by developing and implementing this seven-step method to first identify the net influence wielded by a user in a social network and then to predict that user's ability to generate the viral spread of information, businesses can identify the "right" individuals to engage in social media conversations to promote WOM. Further, we found that by linking the generated WOM to actual sales, social media can be used to induce positive WOM, spread brand knowledge, generate sales and increase return on investment.

A SEVEN-STEP FRAMEWORK FOR SOCIAL MEDIA MARKETING

Step 1: Monitor the conversations. By monitoring brand-related conversations that are happening in the social media platforms, businesses can gain access to valuable information, influential people and relevant conversations that already show engagement with the brand.

Step 2: Identify influential individuals who can spread messages. Companies can use the data to identify a pool of influential individuals (we refer to them as "influencers"), some of whom might be induced to spread the "right" message, from the company's perspective.

Step 3: Identify the factors shared by influential individuals. Next, companies should find commonalities among the candidates and create profiles of typical influencers. Creating such profiles prepares businesses subsequently to locate all the influencers relevant to their campaign and design ways to encourage those influencers to talk about the company's products or services. Previous researchers[3] have found that influencers on social media exhibit high levels of engagement in three aspects: (1) message spread (the number of times a message is forwarded, with or without modification, by the receivers); (2) influence (the number of times the message is forwarded by recipients to their friends); and (3) social impact (the number of comments and replies received for each message). We developed a metric to capture these three aspects, which we call our Customer Influence Effect (CIE) metric. (See "Calculating the Effect and Value of Social Media Influence," p. 58.)

Step 4: Locate those potential influencers who have interests relevant to the campaign. To find potential influencers for a particular social media campaign, it is not enough to identify social media users with influence; instead, a company needs to identify those influential social media users who are particularly interested in the company's category of goods and services. To do this, we developed a metric we call the Stickiness Index (SI), which measures the degree of WOM generated by a particular user on a given topic—essentially, how much of a user's discussions via social media are about a particular topic. This metric can help businesses locate the individuals who not only have influence but also like to talk about a particular product category. (See "Calculating the Effect and Value of Social Media Influence," p.58.)

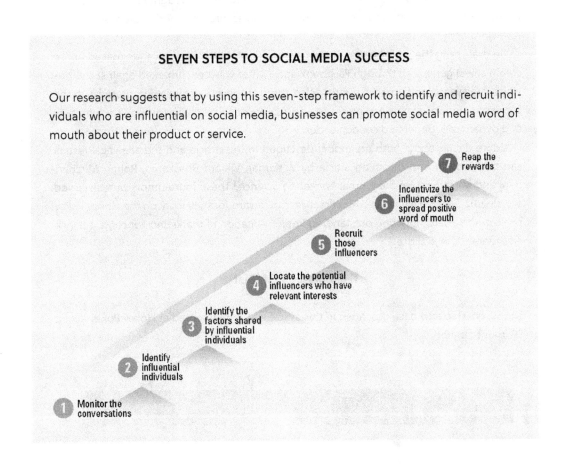

SEVEN STEPS TO SOCIAL MEDIA SUCCESS

Our research suggests that by using this seven-step framework to identify and recruit individuals who are influential on social media, businesses can promote social media word of mouth about their product or service.

7 Reap the rewards

6 Incentivize the influencers to spread positive word of mouth

5 Recruit those influencers

4 Locate the potential influencers who have relevant interests

3 Identify the factors shared by influential individuals

2 Identify influential individuals

1 Monitor the conversations

By identifying influential individuals who are especially interested in their product categories, marketers can go beyond simply "listening" to conversations on social media platforms and actively identify potential brand ambassadors.

Hokey Pokey is a super-premium ice-cream retailer in India offering customized mix-in flavors in more than a dozen outlets. Realizing that most of its existing brand advocates are from the "millennial" demographic cohort, Hokey Pokey executives believed social media platforms might be a good way to connect with the company's target customer base. The retailer wanted to (1) acquire and retain profitable customers and (2) develop a strategy to create a buzz about Hokey Pokey in social media, while ensuring a high return on investment, which was constrained by a limited marketing budget. To help Hokey Pokey with this issue, we implemented the seven-step framework described in this article over a 30-month period. (See "The Project Timeline.") By identifying the "right" message to be spread by the "right" individuals on the "right" social media platforms, we sought to optimize Hokey Pokey's marketing efforts; the result was increased sales, profits, brand awareness and positive word of mouth.

In evaluating the performance of the framework, Hokey Pokey's revenue (based on ice cream sales) generated through Facebook and Twitter was benchmarked against the previous three years' performance metrics. Also, the store-level sales were integrated with the corresponding social network, message and influencer social graph through tracking tags and dynamically generated coupon codes.

More details about both the model described in this article and the analytical results can be found in a forthcoming article by V. Kumar, Vikram Bhaskaran, Rohan Mirchandani and Milap Shah in the journal *Marketing Science*.[i] These four authors were awarded a 2011–2012 Gary L. Lilien ISMS-MSI Practice Prize award for their work on the Hokey Pokey project—an award honoring outstanding implementation of marketing concepts, science and methods in practice.

THE PROJECT TIMELINE

The seven-step approach described in this article was implemented at Hokey Pokey over a 30-month period.

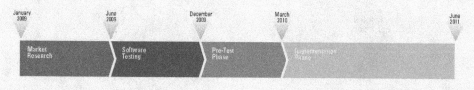

Step 5: Recruit those influencers with interests relevant to the campaign to talk about the company's product or service. Once a company has identified influential users who are particularly interested in the company's product or service category, the next step is to enlist those influencers in the company's social media campaign or campaigns to spread positive

WOM. This can be achieved by developing interactive online content and designing ways in which influencers can promote positive WOM that can be tracked and measured, such as through online games.

Step 6: Incentivize those influencers to spread positive WOM about the product or service. By incentivizing influencers to create buzz about their products or services in a social media campaign, businesses can both retain customers and attract prospects. The incentives offered to influencers can be tangible (such as discounts or freebies), intangible (such as recognition in a social network) or both.

Step 7: Reap the rewards from increasingly effective social media campaigns. By taking the above steps, businesses can more accurately measure the performance of their social media campaigns. By monitoring and tracking positive WOM and linking it to product and brand growth, businesses can develop more effective social media campaigns—and should, as a result, start to see enhanced financial performance, more customer engagement and increased brand awareness.

IMPLEMENTING THE SEVEN STEPS AT HOKEY POKEY

Hokey Pokey Ice Cream Creations is an upscale icecream retailer with more than a dozen outlets across India, offering a unique selection of super-premium ice-cream. Three years ago, Hokey Pokey executives, realizing that most of their consumers were active social media users, decided they needed to engage their customers in social media through a profitable media strategy. Working within a limited marketing budget, the retailer wanted to create positive buzz about Hokey Pokey and acquire and retain profitable customers, while ensuring a high ROI. To help Hokey Pokey with this issue, we implemented the seven-step approach over a 30-month period. (See "About the Research," p. 57.)

For the first step—monitoring the conversations—we spent six months understanding the local social media market in the city where Hokey Pokey has the most outlets and its potential for generating and influencing purchase decisions. We monitored 825,091 conversations involving 1,736 individuals across various social networking sites.

In the second step, we identified the kind of influential individuals in the local social media market who might spread Hokey Pokey's message, based on three parameters: (1) the number of times an individual's messages were forwarded (or modified, then forwarded) by recipients; (2) the number of connections that those messages jumped (for example, if a message from one individual was received by a second individual and then forwarded to a third individual, we considered the message to have jumped two connections); and (3) the number of comments and replies the users received for each message. Based on these characteristics and the ease of data collection, we zeroed in on Facebook and Twitter as suitable platforms for this study.

In the third step, we identified four ideal, generalizable characteristics of key influencers:

1. *Activeness*, which we defined as the number of times the influencer and his or her network of friends "see" and "share" a message.
2. *Clout*, which we defined as the number of connections and followers an influencer has.
3. *Talkativeness of the receiver*, which we defined as how often the influencer's message is being "retweeted," "hashtagged" or shared.
4. *Likemindedness*, which we defined as similarities and common interests shared by the influencer and his or her network friends.

CALCULATING THE EFFECT AND VALUE OF SOCIAL MEDIA INFLUENCE

In our work with Hokey Pokey, we developed three new metrics, which we call the Customer Influence Effect (CIE), the Stickiness Index (SI) and Customer Influence Value (CIV).

The Customer Influence Effect In a group of social media users who like to discuss, for example, ice cream, the CIE measures the influence a user has on other users in the network in regard to conversations relevant to ice cream. To develop the CIE, we used Charles Hubbell's classic network centrality theory, which measures the influence of a user as a function of the influence of the people that he or she is connected with, plus a factor attributable to his or her own decision to spread the message.[ii] This approach departs from the traditional approach to studying social ties by permitting the links to have fractional and/or negative strength and by taking simultaneous account of direct and indirect linkages.

Conceptually, the CIE represents the relative influence of an individual on another user or set of users. Consider the case of C receiving tweets from A and B. If A and B each send 50 tweets to C, and if C does not even respond to B but reciprocates to A and forwards A's tweets to many others, then the relative influence of A on C is close to 1 and the relative influence of B on C is close to 0, since C has seen B's tweets but has not responded to them.

The Stickiness Index To be effective influencers for Hokey Pokey, individuals needed not only to be influential on social networks but also to like to talk about ice cream. Toward this end, we developed a metric known as the Stickiness Index. To calculate the SI, we matched an influential individual to a particular category of words, based on the association of the words with each other and with other words used by all users globally. For instance, a user who extensively discusses desserts, milkshakes and sundaes online is likely to be closely associated with discussions about ice cream. SI measurements helped us identify (1) the number of social media users in the region who actively discussed ice cream, and (2) other types of topics that people who discussed ice cream frequently talked about. These analyses were instrumental in estimating the possible size of the target market and identifying the incentives that were likely to be optimal for these users.

Customer Influence Value To measure the monetary gain or loss realized by a social media campaign, we also developed the Customer Influence Value metric, which accounts for an individual's influence on other customers and prospects. After calculating a user's CIE, we could calculate his or her CIV for this campaign. To compute the CIV of users in this network, we combine the value that each individual influencer brings to the company through his or her own purchases—a metric known as customer lifetime value (CLV)—with the proportion of the CLV of each of his or her influencees that is attributable to the individual's influence. For Hokey Pokey's social media campaign, the CLV is the profit contributed by a customer through purchases of a custom ice-cream creation after a message about it has gone out.

By calculating CIV, we can assign a numeric score to each influencer. These numbers can be used to rank order the potential influencers and recruit the high-scoring influencers to participate in the social media campaign on an ongoing basis.

More details about these metrics can be found in a forthcoming article by V. Kumar, Vikram Bhaskaran, Rohan Mirchandani and Milap Shah.[iii]

FIGURE 10.2   Hokey Pokey's social media campaign increased brand awareness and sales revenue growth.

These ideal characteristics matched well with Hokey Pokey's objectives in this study, which were to create and spread its brand identity, to stimulate and encourage a strong brand association among consumers and proactively identify brand advocates, and to reach potential customers through existing customers. These factors helped us compute the CIE metric that we created. (See "Calculating the Effect and Value of Social Media Influence.")

In the fourth step—locating the potential influencers with interests relevant to the campaign—we helped Hokey Pokey move beyond simply monitoring conversations on social media platforms and begin to actively engage in the identification of brand ambassadors. While the CIE metric enabled Hokey Pokey to identify individuals exhibiting the ideal characteristics to be influential on the social networks, we wanted to make sure these individuals also liked to talk about ice cream. They needed to have not only a high CIE but a higher-than-average share of WOM about ice cream in social media. Toward this end, we developed the SI metric. (See "Calculating the Effect and Value of Social Media Influence.") The SI metric helped us identify the number of individuals in the region who actively discussed ice cream on social media.

In the fifth step, we recruited those influencers who were already engaged in social media discussions related to the category to participate in a campaign designed to promote Hokey Pokey ice cream. This campaign helped us to track and measure the positive WOM of Hokey Pokey's offerings.

For the sixth step, we implemented the campaign in two stages: "Creations on the Wall" and "Share Your Brownies." These two stages of the campaign encouraged the influencers recruited for the campaign to make custom ice-cream creations at any of the Hokey Pokey parlors, identify themselves with their creations and spread WOM about their creations via the social media platforms. In the "Creations on the Wall" phase of the campaign, Hokey Pokey marketers trained the parlor employees to educate influencers about custom creations and distribute a form into which influencers could enter the recipes for their creations. Influencers could name their creations, identify themselves with their creations and post their recipes on a wall in the parlor dedicated to the purpose. Customers walking into the parlor could browse this wall and purchase these creations or order from the regular menu.

The second, "Share Your Brownies" phase of the campaign was aimed at generating a viral spread of the ice-cream creations by nurturing a sense of personal identity. In this part of the campaign, the influencers from "Creations on the Wall" were motivated to tweet about their creations to compete for both tangible incentives (such as customized T-shirts) and intangible ones (such as a chance to enhance their peer standing by sharing their creations on Facebook and Twitter). Each creation was shared with all the parlors of Hokey Pokey, which increased the buzz about the campaign. We tracked all relevant social media discussions during four time points in the study (May 2010, September 2010, January 2011 and June 2011), and Hokey Pokey incentivized influencers by giving them "Brownie Points" when their followers or friends made a purchase or discussed their ice-cream creations online. These points were redeemable for prizes and product discounts.

Our tracking revealed some interesting business trends for Hokey Pokey. For instance, the "Sahara Surprise" flavor was only mildly popular during the initial phases of the campaign and was seldom discussed between March and September of 2010, but it became one of the most discussed creations after influencing a few high-CIE users around November of 2010. We continuously recalculated the CIE metric and used it to identify sets of consumers who evangelized their own creations at different points in time and kept the buzz alive.

In the final step, we measured the results of the social media campaign by relating the abstract social media measures such as "comments" and "conversations" to the financial metrics in order to demonstrate the increase in buzz and monetary gains. We accomplished this by using the Customer Influence Value (CIV) metric that calculates the influence of an individual's WOM on future sales. (See "Calculating the Effect and Value of Social Media Influence" p. 58.)

The implementation of the above phases enabled us to identify the influencers using the CIE (intangible contributions) and CIV (tangible contributions) metrics for Hokey Pokey's customers.

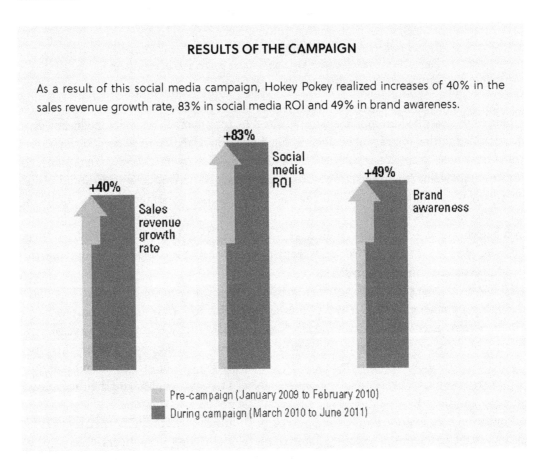

RESULTS OF THE CAMPAIGN

As a result of this social media campaign, Hokey Pokey realized increases of 40% in the sales revenue growth rate, 83% in social media ROI and 49% in brand awareness.

+83%
Social media ROI

+40%
Sales revenue growth rate

+49%
Brand awareness

Pre-campaign (January 2009 to February 2010)
During campaign (March 2010 to June 2011)

THE CAMPAIGN RESULTS AND IMPLICATIONS

This campaign had effects at both the company and the customer level. At the company level, the main impact was in the area of social media accountability. While most companies are still grappling with social media accountability, the use of the CIE and CIV metrics gave Hokey Pokey an important competitive edge. At the customer level, being able to calculate the value of an individual's influence in a network and measure the monetary value of customer influences made it possible for Hokey Pokey marketers to greatly enhance the efficacy of their social media campaign. In evaluating the performance of the framework, we benchmarked Hokey Pokey's revenue (based on ice-cream sales) generated through Facebook and Twitter against the previous three years' performance metrics, including sales growth rate, ROI, number of positive and negative conversations, and number of repeat visits. We found that out of the total revenue generated from the "Share Your Brownies" campaign, about 23% was attributable to conversations on Twitter and about 80% was attributable to Facebook, with a 3% to 8% overlap between the two social networks. Overall, the campaign was a huge success: Hokey Pokey realized increases of 49% in brand awareness, 83% in ROI and 40% in the sales revenue growth rate. (See "Results of the Campaign.")

Hokey Pokey incentivized influencers by giving them "Brownie Points" when their followers or friends made a purchase or discussed their ice-cream creations online.

Our study described the application of our seven-step approach to social media analysis in a localized setting for a small business chain, but it could be directly extended to a larger global enterprise. Companies such as Dell and Zappos already have strong customer relationship management and ticketing systems tied to social networks, which should make measuring the impact of influence at the point of sale relatively straightforward for them. This study focused on a brick-and-mortar retailer, but the same methodology should work even better online. For instance, online retailers could allow their customers to sign in at their sites with their social network IDs from Twitter, Facebook, Google+, etc. and directly tie online customer influence to sales.

However, changes in social network privacy policies may make collecting this data increasingly challenging. The privacy rules at Facebook and Twitter, for example, have grown more stringent since we collected the data for this study; at that time, it was easier to track influencers' conversations. Analysts may now have to find new ways to gather this type of data, such as encouraging users to give them permission to follow the relevant communications or even creating company-sponsored forums to help people share their messages. However, our three metrics should still function despite these restrictions.

The seven-step approach described here, along with the CIE and CIV metrics, solves an important problem for social media marketers: identifying influencers. Despite the vast amount of individual and relationship data available through these media, most organizations have been unable to directly and efficiently measure the effectiveness of their social media strategy. The lack of robust methodologies to measure the impact of social media efforts is addressed in this study. It provides tangible metrics and a robust methodology to measure the effectiveness of social media marketing spending and to maximize the ROI of social media campaigns.

*V. Kumar is the Richard and Susan Lenny Distinguished Chair in Marketing and the executive director of the Center for Excellence in Brand and Customer Management at the J. Mack Robinson College of Business at Georgia State University in Atlanta, Georgia. **Rohan Mirchandani** is a cofounder of Drums Food International Pvt. Ltd. (owner of Hokey Pokey), based in Mumbai, India. Comment on this article at http://sloanreview.mit.edu/x/54115, or contact the authors at smrfeedback@mit.edu.*

REFERENCES

1. Facebook.com statistics on the number of active users at the end of June 2012.

2. P. Kotler and G. Armstrong, "Principles of Marketing" 12th ed. (Upper Saddle River, New Jersey: Prentice Hall, 2007): 481.

3. P.V. Marsden and N.E. Friedkin, "Network Studies of Social Influence," in "Advances in Social Network Analysis: Research in the Social and Behavioral Sciences," eds. S. Wasserman and J. Galaskiewicz (Thousand Oaks, California: SAGE Publications, 1994); and D.J. Watts and P.S. Dodds, "Influentials, Networks, and Public Opinion Formation," Journal of Consumer Research 34, no. 4 (December 2007): 441–458.

i. V. Kumar, V. Bhaskaran, R. Mirchandani and M. Shah, "Creating a Measurable Social Media Marketing Strategy for Hokey Pokey: Increasing the Value and ROI of Intangibles & Tangibles," Marketing Science, in press.

ii. For more details, see C.H. Hubbell, "An Input-Output Approach to Clique Identification," Sociometry 28 (1965): 377–399.

iii. Kumar et al., "Creating a Measurable Social Media Marketing Strategy for Hokey Pokey."

CHAPTER 11

Unilever Ad Campaigns

FOR WOMEN: Dove's 'Real Beauty Sketches' Campaign

Syeda Maseeha Qumar, Debapratim Purkayastha, and Jayasri Bhimalapuram

> *This case was written by **Jayasri Bhimalapuram**, under the direction of **Syeda Maseeha Qumer** and **Debapratim Purkayastha**, IBS Hyderabad. It was compiled from published sources, and is intended to be used as a basis for class discussion rather than to illustrate either effective or ineffective handling of a management situation.*

In April 2013, UK-based consumer goods giant Unilever, Plc's global personal care brand Dove launched a global ad campaign 'Real Beauty Sketches'. The campaign went on to become one of the most watched online video ad campaigns of the year with over 163 million global views. It was also the most shared video ad in over a year with over 4 million shares across various online platforms *(See Exhibit 11.1)*. Commenting on the success of the campaign, Fernando Machado (Machado), Vice President of Dove Skin, said, *"The moment that the Dove Real Beauty Sketches film was uploaded to the Dove YouTube page, it quickly started to gain traction around the world with men, women, media, and even other brands sharing the film. The campaign evoked an emotional reaction in millions of people that inspired them to share the positive message with others. Beyond just the millions of views and publicity impressions, it is the outpouring of testimonials from around the world that are exciting us."*[1]

Dove was one of the biggest personal care brands of Unilever. The Dove Beauty Bar launched in 1957 was marketed as an alternative to soap. Over the years, Dove expanded its brand franchise in the women's personal care market to include antiperspirants, deodorants, body washes, beauty bars, lotions, moisturizers, hair care, and other related products. According to some industry observers, the Dove brand had changed the way women cared for their skin.

Launched as part of Dove's 'Campaign for Real Beauty',[1] the three-minute ad campaign was meant to ignite a global conversation about the definition of beauty and about how

---

1 In September 2004, Unilever launched a global campaign called "Campaign for Real Beauty" to challenge the stereotypes set by the beauty industry. The campaign featured regular women (non-models) who were beautiful in their own way and did not fit in with the idealized images of models, super-models, and celebrities. This campaign was a huge success as it was appreciated by many consumers and resulted in increased sales of Dove products.

women viewed themselves. The ad featured a forensic sketch artist drawing a woman's portrait from behind a curtain based on a self-description. The artist then created a second sketch of the same woman, this time based on descriptions from strangers who were asked to spend time with the woman earlier in the day. The resulting sketches were displayed side by side. The artist sketched different women and in all the cases, the portraits inspired by strangers were more attractive than the women's own versions of themselves, which drove home the point that women were more beautiful than they thought.

The response for the 'Real Beauty Sketches' campaign was mixed. Some industry consultants lauded the campaign calling it one of the most original and touching experiments to come from the Dove's 'Campaign for Real Beauty'. According to them, it had changed the perceptions of beauty and pushed sales of Dove products globally. However, some analysts dismissed the campaign as cynical, and as depicting a very narrow definition of beauty. They felt using a faux representation of 'real' women might hurt the Dove brand.[2] *"The Dove spots can be critiqued on a number of grounds, particularly their pernicious emphasis on whiteness: not only is minimal attention given to women of color, the traits categorized as aspirational (straight hair, a narrow chin, blue eyes) are hallmarks of racialized beauty norms. Also troubling is Dove's exclusion of male voices from those expressing body image anxiety (to say nothing of the campaign's implicit endorsements of heteronormativity, fat phobia, and binary gender structure). Yet if cosmetic company collusion with cultural hegemony is common practice, Dove's dubious disavowal of its commercial's culpability is especially inventive,"*[3] commented Li Cornfeld, a contributor at* Flow.*[2]

ABOUT UNILEVER AND DOVE

Unilever was one of the world's leading manufacturers of fast moving consumer goods including food, home care, personal care, nutrition, and health products. The company's products were sold in over 180 countries across the globe and used by two billion consumers every day. Some of its well-known personal brands were Dove, Fair and Lovely, Sunsilk, Lifebuoy, Lux, and Rexona. For the year ended 2015, the company's turnover was €53.3 billion.

Unilever developed the formula for the Dove Soap Bar in 1940. During World War II (1939–1945), it was used for cleaning wounds. In the 1950s, the formula was refined and the Dove Beauty Bar was developed and launched in the market in 1957. In the 1970s, Dove's popularity increased as an independent clinical dermatological study proved that the Dove Beauty Bar was milder than other leading soap brands at that time. In the following decade, the Dove Beauty Bar became a leading cleansing bar and was even recommended by physicians. In the early 1990s, Unilever launched Dove Beauty Wash, a body wash product. It was a success though its price was 50% more than that of other body wash brands.[4] In 1995,

---

2 *Flow* is a critical forum on television and media culture published by the Department of Radio, Television, and Film at the University of Texas at Austin.

Unilever extended the Dove range by introducing Dove Moisturizing Body Wash, Dove Sensitive Skin Bar, Dove Facial Care Cleanser, Dove Facial Cleaning Scrub, and Dove Facial Care Daily Moisturizer.

Over the years, Dove was positioned as a feminine brand that enabled women to celebrate their real inner beauty at every age. The Dove ads broadened the definition of beauty through confidence building messages thereby making more women feel beautiful. Moreover, the name and logo of the brand (the image of a Dove signified purity and softness) had a feminine appeal too. Featuring real women in advertising was an integral part of the brand's DNA. By 1999, sales had reached around US$ 1 billion and the brand was growing at a rate of 20% annually.[5] Its main competitors were Olay from Procter & Gamble,[3] Nivea from Beiersdorf AG,[4] and Neutrogena from Johnson & Johnson.[5] In 2001, the Dove Antiperspirant / Deodorant line was launched. In 2003, the company extended the brand further with the Dove Hair Care line. In 2004, it introduced Dove Massage Body Wash and Cool Moisture Body Wash and Bar.

However, though the brand's product range had increased, sales since the early 2000s were not up to the mark as teenagers generally perceived Dove as a brand for mature women. Moreover, increased competition from other brands and the resulting advertising clutter made it difficult for the company to communicate effectively to the customer. Since the brand was more than 50 years old, the brand image too had to evolve so that it became more relevant to modern times and appealed to the younger generation.

CAMPAIGN FOR REAL BEAUTY

In September 2004, Unilever launched a global campaign called "Campaign for Real Beauty" to challenge the stereotypes set by the beauty industry over the years and to broaden the definition of beauty and encourage discussion about its aspects. This campaign featured regular women (non-models) who were beautiful in their own way and did not fit in with the idealized images of models, super-models, and celebrities. The campaign was a huge success as it was appreciated by many consumers and led to increased sales of Dove products. It also generated plenty of buzz and wide media coverage for the Dove brand. In October 2006, Dove launched the 'Evolution' commercial as a key message in its Campaign for Real Beauty. The ad was a one-minute, mute video fast-forwarding the process of turning an average woman into a made-over, photo shopped billboard model.

In 2007, Dove established the Dove Self-Esteem Fund which aimed to contribute to the healthy development of self-esteem in girls and help them grow up feeling happy and

---

3   Based in Cincinnati, Ohio, Procter & Gamble is a global corporation which manufactures a wide range of consumer products in the areas of pharmaceuticals, cleaning supplies, and personal care.

4   Beiersdorf AG is a Germany-based personal care products company.

5   Johnson & Johnson, based in New Jersey, US, is an international pharmaceutical, medical devices, and consumer goods manufacturer.

confident about the way they looked. The fund was created to act as an agent of change to inspire and educate girls and women about a wider definition of beauty.'

Continuing with its commitment to widen the narrow definition of beauty, in February 2007, Dove launched the third phase of the 'Campaign for Real Beauty' called 'Beauty Comes of Age'. The campaign featured a series of ads involving real women aged between 47 and 62 revealing their age spots, grey hair, and curves. In October 2007, as part of the Real Beauty campaign, Dove released a short film called *Onslaught* featuring a young girl being barraged by various beauty related ads that enforced unrealistic and unhealthy standards of beauty. The film exposed the inner ugliness of the beauty industry and urged parents in its tagline, "Talk to your daughter before the beauty industry does."

By 2010, Dove became one of the largest personal care brands in the world with annual sales of €2.5 billion in over 80 countries.[6] However, while Dove had a very extensive product range, not all its products were picked up from the shelf owing to the intense competition in the women's personal care market. Unilever, therefore, decided to target a totally new segment of customers. Building on the strength of its range of products for women, Dove entered the men's grooming market by launching deodorants for men in February 2010. The same year, Dove launched the "Dove Movement for Self Esteem" that provided women with opportunities to mentor the next generation and celebrate real beauty. As part of the movement, Dove developed "The Self-Esteem Toolkit" to encourage girls to embrace their own unique beauty through various workshops, guides, activities, and videos.

In 2012, Dove debuted on the social media with four social lead efforts, three of which were applications that used social networking site Facebook as the platform to engage with its customers. 'The Dove Friends App' triggered conversations about what real beauty was, 'The Wave Goodbye to Dry Hair App' allowed Dove fans to upload pictures and get a chance to feature on the advertising billboard and, 'The Dove Book App' collected quotes about real beauty to be featured in a book. The fourth initiative "The Dove Breast Cancer Campaign" was an activation that utilized vouchers for women to access mammograms at a reduced cost. In just seven months of the release of these initiatives, Dove's fan base grew by 75% to total to 61,255 members. Reportedly, about 545 participants engaged on the 'Dove Friends App' and the 'Wave Goodbye to Dry Hair App' had 1085 uploads. About 2,270 fans were attracted by the 'Dove Book App' and the 'Dove Breast Cancer Campaign'.[7] Experts said that the 'Real Beauty Campaign' came at a crucial time when sales of the Dove brand were dramatically lower and helped in attracting consumers.

THE REAL BEAUTY SKETCHES CAMPAIGN

In 2011, Dove carried out a global study on women's relationship with beauty called "The Real Truth about Beauty: Revisited". According to the study, only 4% of women globally considered themselves beautiful while 11% of girls globally felt comfortable describing themselves as 'beautiful'. About 54% women who participated in the study agreed that when it came to how they looked, they were their own worst beauty critic.[8] The study indicated that women were still under pressure from the narrow beauty standards in society which negatively affected their self-esteem.

In order to make women feel better about themselves and to ignite a global conversation about the need for a wider definition of beauty, Unilever decided to conduct a social experiment. In 2013, Unilever launched the 'Dove Real Beauty Sketches' campaign to explore how women viewed their own beauty in contrast to what others perceived. The aim of the campaign was to turn beauty into a source of confidence, not anxiety, for women.

As part of the campaign, women described their physical appearance to a forensic artist from behind a curtain and he created individual sketches based on their self-descriptions. The artist then created a second sketch of the same women, this time based on descriptions from strangers with whom the women had spent some time earlier in the day. The resulting sketches were then placed side-by-side and compared. What the campaign revealed was that the sketches of the women as described by the stranger looked significantly more attractive, happy, and beautiful than the sketches created based on self-descriptions.

Unilever selected FBI-trained sketch artist Gil Zamora[6] (Zamora) for the job. A group of women who represented a range of ages (20s-40s age group), sizes, and ethnicities were selected through a normal casting session. For the role of strangers, the company picked people who were outspoken and who could quickly befriend someone. The campaign was produced by Ogilvy[7] Brazil and the video was shot for three days in a loft in San Francisco. Reportedly, Zamora created the pictures of about 20 women of which 7 were selected by Dove for the ad campaign.

The video featured Zamora drawing facial portraits of women based on their own self-description. A curtain divided the artist and the subjects. The artist was seen in the video asking the women, "Tell me about your chin," to which the women replied, "It kind of protrudes a little bit, especially when I smile," or "My mom told me I had a big jaw." The artist then created a second sketch of the same women, this time based on descriptions from strangers who were asked to spend some time with the women earlier in the day. The resulting sketches were displayed side by side. In all the cases, the portraits described by the strangers were more attractive and similar to what the subjects actually looked like compared to the women's own versions of themselves *(See Exhibit 11.2)*. Almost all the participants agreed that they looked more beautiful when described by strangers, and were more beautiful than they thought. The video ended with the tagline, "You are more beautiful than you think", driving in Dove's point that women were often overly critical of their appearances and did not realize their true beauty.

---

6   Gil Zamora was trained by the Federal Bureau of Investigation (FBI) to draw the images of suspects based on witnesses' descriptions at San Jose, California, Police Department.
7   Ogilvy & Mather is one of the largest marketing communications companies in the world.

Dove stated that it was committed to a world where beauty was a source of confidence and through the film it aimed to reinforce its commitment to fostering self-esteem in women. Commenting on the campaign, Zamora said, *"When I was asked to be a part of the film for Dove, I never imagined how different the two sketch portrayals would be. What has stayed with me are the emotional reactions the women had when they viewed the composite sketches hung side by side. I think many of these brave women realised that they had a distorted self-perception that had affected parts of their lives in significant ways."*[9]

Initially, the campaign was launched in four key markets –US, Canada, Brazil, and Australia. Later, it was released across 25 countries globally with the support of TrueView in-stream,[8] TrueView in-search,[9] YouTube homepage masthead,[10] and search ads.[11] The video was uploaded in 25 languages across 110 countries on Dove's YouTube channels.

RESULTS

Some industry observers felt that the campaign was successful in its attempt to show women that they were too critical of their own beauty and that their perception of what they looked like was distorted and inaccurate. The campaign struck an emotional chord with millions of women who realized that they were their own worst beauty critics. Experts said that it was one of the most original and touching experiments to come from the 'Campaign for Real Beauty' because, according to them, Dove through this campaign, empowered individual women to appreciate their inherent beauty. Dove's sales in the US shot up by 1% in the four weeks ended May 19, 2013, right after the release of the campaign. That amounted to a 3% rise in sales to US$1.5 billion for the full year.[10]

In a very short period of time, the campaign amassed global reach and buzz. According to officials, when the 'Real Beauty Sketches' video was uploaded to the Dove YouTube page, the video garnered widespread attention across all media channels and received a positive response globally. In the first two weeks of its release, it attracted 3.17 million shares, more than any other ad had managed in the same period *(See Exhibit 11.3).*

The video became the most viewed online ad ever, according to Unilever, with over 163 million global views. It was also the most shared video ad in over a year with over 4 million shares across a variety of platforms, and the third most shared film of all time. By December 2013, the campaign generated 4.6 billion PR and blogger media impressions and reached

---

8   TrueView in-stream ads run on videos served on YouTube watch pages or within Google Display Network videos, games, and apps. These ads may also run on YouTube videos that are embedded on other sites.

9   In-stream ads allow viewers to skip the pre-roll ads after five seconds. Sponsors pay only for ads that are viewed in their entirety or until 30 seconds have elapsed. In-stream ads are suitable for short or long video content.

10   The YouTube Desktop Custom Masthead is a 970x250 pixel in-page unit running the full width of the YouTube homepage below the navigation bar for 24 hours.

11   In-search ads appear in YouTube search results when the viewer's search is related to the ad's keywords. Sponsors pay for ads that the viewer begins to watch.

275,000 followers on Google+[1] (*See Exhibit 11.4*). Anselmo Ramos, vice president and creative director at Ogilvy Brazil, said, *"I think it went viral because it moves you, because it makes you think, because it's based on a true insight. Most ads today don't evoke any clear emotion, they just communicate a particular product or service benefit. We wanted to do something really emotional. Most women cry when they watch it. But not only women; men, too, because they think about their mothers, sisters, and daughters. I myself cried several times. We knew we had something good in our hands, but yes, we are a little surprised by how fast it went viral."*[12]

With comments from women on YouTube about the ad such as "this made me cry" and "I showed this to my high school students the other day. It made a real impact on them," it was evident that the campaign had made a difference in the lives of women. The Dove 'Real Beauty Sketches' campaign was ranked #1 on the Cannes YouTube Ads Leaderboard,[13] based on paid and organic views of all ads uploaded between March 2012 and April 2013. It also won the Titanium Grand Prix at the 2013 Cannes Lions International Festival of Creativity. According to David Waterhouse, global head of content and PR at Unruly Media,[14] *"I think what made this campaign perform particularly strongly is the content, which elicited the intense emotional responses of 'warmth,' 'happiness' and 'knowledge' from its target demographic—one of the key factors behind a video's sharing success. But, more importantly, we are really seeing social motivations behind sharing becoming a lot more important. Brands have to give people a reason to share the video."*[12]

CRITICISM

Some critics felt that the campaign's attempt to define 'real beauty' was ineffective. According to them, the campaign propagated a narrow cultural perception of beauty, as youth, light-colored skin, and being skinny were considered positive attributes. They felt that the portraits of women in the video were distinguished based on characteristics such as a mole, shadows under the eyes, roundness in facial shape, or wrinkles implying that such appearances reflected beauty. Analysts said that while Dove in its earlier ads attempted to combat the stigma that beauty came in only one shape and size, especially with their ads featuring plus-size women, the message it conveyed with this campaign was that women were not valuable without beauty. *"Dove has strategically selected particular women and girls 'real women' to help further their corporate and social agenda. Has Dove engaged critical race feminists, fat activists, disability activists and scholars for example in their pursuit to change the face of beauty and beauty ideals or assumptions? I reckon they haven't because these key stakeholders I suspect would be too quick to see through the mirage,"*[13] remarked columnist Jill Andrew.

---

12   Google+ is a social network owned and operated by tech giant Google, Inc.

13   The YouTube Ads Leaderboard displays the most creative ads that people choose to watch each month.

14   Unruly Media is a UK-based global social video marketing company.

The campaign was criticized for the main participants lacking in diversity of as it featured mostly attractive skinny white women. Reportedly in the video, only two of the seven women featured were colored, making the ad devoid of minority representation of women. The remaining participants were Caucasian, thin, and young. Moreover, the two black women featuring in the video were briefly shown describing themselves in a negative light like one thought that she had a fat, round face while the other said that she was getting freckles as she aged. Reportedly, out of 6:36 minutes of footage, people of color were onscreen for less than 10 seconds in the video.[14]

Some analysts felt that Unilever had launched the campaign as a marketing ploy to manipulate women in order to sell more products. They said the campaign was two-faced because Unilever in its other brand related ads degraded women and promoted physical beauty. *"[Dove's] long-running Real Beauty campaign has shed light on some important truths about the media's unrealistic portrayals of women, but given the fact that Dove is owned by Unilever, which also owns Axe (ugh) and the company that produces Fair & Lovely skin lightening cream (double ugh), the campaign comes across as hypocritical and patronizing—a way for the company to pander to women for sales while practicing the very evil it preaches against,"*[15] remarked Charlotte Hannah, a blogger for Twirl It.

According to some analysts, the campaign positioned beauty as the yardstick by which women measured themselves and portrayed women as their own enemies for having low self-esteem rather than as victims of a sexist society. They felt that behind the Dove's 'Real Beauty Sketches' campaign was the reinforcement of the same old messages about how beauty was the most important asset for a woman to have. However, some analysts defended the campaign saying it was unfairly criticized. *"Everything in Dove's world is centered around beauty because that's the business they are in. Within that market, they have found a truth that connects with women (well, most of them), a truth that, when brought to life in the "Sketches" film, improves the way women look at themselves. To Dove, you are already more beautiful than you think. Before you even use their product. And they proved it through this innovative idea/stunt. If you want to hammer a brand, hammer the cosmetic companies who overtly say you'll be more beautiful with their products. But don't hammer Dove. Not for this idea,"*[16] noted Will Burns founder and CEO of Ideasicle, a virtual ideation company.

LOOKING AHEAD

According to some analysts, not only had the 'Real Beauty Sketches' campaign helped Dove effectively increase its sales but it was also successful in communicating its message and increasing self-appreciation and self-worth among women. The campaign was innovative and ground breaking, setting the bar for future campaigns of Dove, they added. *"The Real Beauty campaign is a game changer for advertising and more should follow in their footsteps,"*[17] said Lianna Brinded, Finance Editor for Business Insider UK.

Some industry observers opined that over the years, Dove's ad campaigns were providing a significant change in redefining advertising standards and the unrealistic ideals for the way women looked. For instance, in its ten years of existence, Dove's Campaign For Real Beauty had changed the perceptions of beauty, won many awards, and pushed sales of Dove products. It had reportedly helped boost Dove sales from US$2.5 billion in the opening year of the campaign (2004) to US$4 billion in 2014.[18] The Dove team was positive that the campaign would continue with its commitment to the idea of making women feel beautiful for years to come. *"Dove is so far ahead of most companies in terms of being in touch with women's actual attitudes, emotions, and frustrations with the beauty industry in general. Companies have to be—and are starting to become—more savvy about understanding the people they're trying to sell to. But women support companies that go above and beyond the commercial motivations and try to make an effort to understand how they think and feel. There's a lesson there that other companies would be well-served in paying close attention to,"*[19] pointed out marketing expert Marti Barletta.

EXHIBIT 11.1   Video Statistics of Dove Sketches Real Beauty Campaign

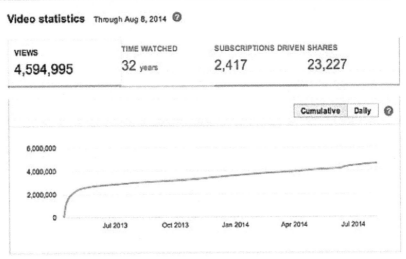

Source: http://blogsession.co.uk/2014/08/dove-real-beauty-sketches/

EXHIBIT 11.2   Real Beauty Sketches

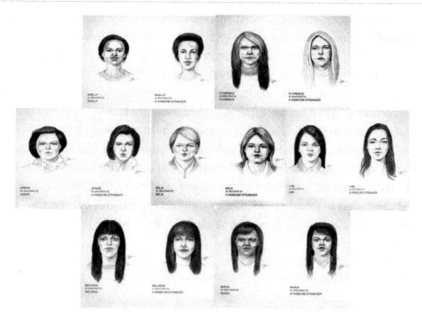

Source: www.dove.com

EXHIBIT 11.3   Share Statistics of 'Real Beauty Sketches' campaign

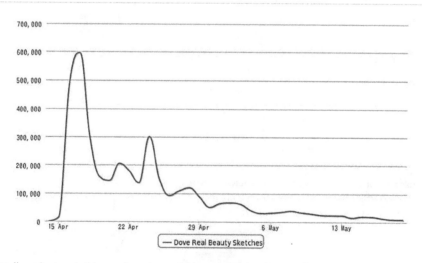

Source: http://www.businessinsider.com/how-doves-real-beauty-sketches-became-the-most-viral-ad-video-of-all-time-2013-5?IR=T

EXHIBIT 11.4   RBS – Participants and Impressions

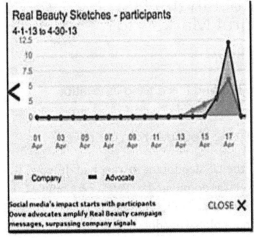
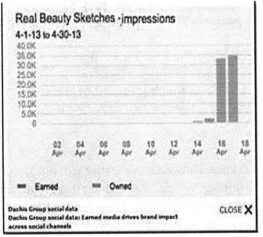

Source: www.asia.mslgroup.com

END NOTES

1   Samantha Murphy Kelly, "Viral Dove Campaign Becomes Most Watched Ad Ever," http://mashable.com, May 20, 2013.

2   Eric Spitznagel, "How Those Dove 'Real Beauty Sketch' Ads Went Viral," www.bloomberg.com, April 26, 2013.

3   "Shamefaced: Reframing the Dove Real Beauty Sketches," www.flowjournal.org, August, 2013.

4   John Noble, "Are Brands a Force for Good?" www.britishbrandsgroup.org.uk, 2004.

5   http://media.wiley.com/product_data/excerpt/14/04708621/0470862114.pdf.

6   www.unilever.com/ourbrands/personalcare/dove.asp.

7   Memac Ogilvy, "Dove Integrated Social Media 2012," www.memacogilvy.com.

8   http://www.dove.com/us/en/stories/about-dove/our-research.html.

9   "Dove "Real Beauty Sketches" Campaign," www.unilever.co.za, June 30, 2013.

10   Jack Neff, "Dove: The Evolution from 'Evolution'," www.adageindia.in, June 11, 2013.

11   Jessica Grose, "The Story Behind Dove's Mega Viral "Real Beauty Sketches" Campaign," www.fastcocreate.com, April 19, 2013.

12   Laura Stampler, "How Dove's 'Real Beauty Sketches' Became The Most Viral Video Ad of All Time," www.businessinsider.com, May 22, 2013.

13   "Dove's Real Beauty Sketch Campaign. An Open Letter by Jill Andrew," www.fatinthecity.com, April 17, 2013.

14   Jazz Bruce, "If you Saw Dove's Latest Ad Campaign, you Need to Read this Response," www.refinery29.com, April 19, 2013.

15   "5 Reasons Why Some Critics are Hating on Dove's Real Beauty Sketches Video," www.adweek.com, April 19, 2013.

16   Will Burns, "Dove, Your 'Sketches' Idea Is More Beautiful than Your Critics Think," www.forbes.com, April 23, 2013.

17   "It's an Ad, but Dove's Real Beauty Campaign is a Game Changer," www.independent.co.uk, April 21, 2013.

18   Kiley Skene, "A PR Case Study: Dove Real Beauty Campaign," www.newsgeneration.com, April 11, 2014.

19   Eric Spitznagel, "How Those Dove 'Real Beauty Sketch' Ads Went Viral," www.bloomberg.com, April 26, 2013.

FOR MEN: Axe Effect in the US: Success Through Viral Marketing?

Aich Vasudha and TR Venkatesh

> "The men's [*grooming*] market is growing and it is driving innovation. It is here to stay without a doubt."[15]
>
> —Will King, Founder, King of Shaves[16]

In 2001, Unilever's (**Annexure 11.1**) position in the US deodorant market had dropped to number six[17] with 5.4% market share. The market was dominated by Procter & Gamble Co. (P&G) and Gillette, which together held 47% of the market. Unilever hoped to break through this domination with the launch of its second largest global deodorant brand AXE.

While there were high end luxury brands (priced around US$50 per can) such as Clinique,[18] Kiehl's[19] and John Allan's[20] catering to men's grooming needs, there were not many meant for the mass market. P&G's Old Spice and Gillette's Right Guard were a few of the popular men's deodorant brands in the market.

> "Young men are spending more time and money on their appearance than ever before, and this trend is expected to increase ... We think the time is right to bring Axe, an incredibly popular franchise in many countries around the world, to North America."[21]
>
> —Alan Jope, COO of Unilever Home and Personal care,
> North America.

AXE male deodorant body spray was launched in the US market in August 2002. The launch signaled the birth of a new male grooming product –body deodorant with odor controlling properties. In 2004, within two years of the launch, AXE became the leading brand in the US$ 1.3 billion US men's deodorant market with 80% market share. Its share in the deodorant market climbed to 13% in 2004. By 2005, AXE was the fastest growing deodorant brand and had achieved sales of over US$ 100 million.

---

15 Antoinette Alexander, "Media, Euro Influence drive growth, helps men's grooming carve solid niche," September 2004, www.findarticles.com
16 Marketer of number two shaving brand in the UK.
17 Behind P&G, Gillette, Colgate Palmolive, Helene Curtis and Carter-Wallace. These companies also experienced a dip of 1.9 to 13% market share in the same period while Unilever experienced a drop of 3.4%.
18 A cologne spray owned by Boots Group PLC, the UK's leading health & beauty retailer.
19 Cologne owned by New York based skin and hair care products marketer, belonged to the L'Oreal Group.
20 A brand owned by a men's club (by the same name) which provided grooming services. There was a whole line of men's grooming products under the brand name in the US.
21 Vavra Bob, "An Axe to Grind", 7 January 2002, Business Source Premier

The success of the brand in the men's grooming market[22] inspired the launch of new brands by P&G and Gillette. P&G launched Red Zone deodorant body spray in 2004. Gillette the other dominant player launched TAG in 2005. Red Zone and TAG brands targeted the same segment which AXE catered to. In 2005, AXE sales experienced a dip and the brand had slipped to number two position behind P&G's Old Spice deodorant. Responding to intensifying competition, Unilever revamped its marketing strategy for AXE.

BACKGROUND

In 2003, the US deodorant market was dominated by four companies each holding market shares in excess of 10%. The market leader was P&G which controlled about a fourth of the market. The market share of the nearest rival Gillette had been declining over the last few years. Colgate Palmolive and Unilever were also significant players with double-digit market shares. The market also saw the growth of new brands floated by leading private super market chains over the last five years, since 1998.

Men's attitude towards grooming in the US seemed to be moving in the same direction as European markets. TV Channels such as MTV and men's magazines were giving out a whole lot of information on male grooming which resulted in increased interest in these products. Men were now more open to buying grooming products and addressing their grooming needs.

LAUNCH OF AXE MALE DEODORANT BODY SPRAY

When it was first launched in France in 1983, AXE was a great success. In the UK, AXE was launched in 1985 and had attained a market share of 17% over the span of seven years. It soon spread to European and Latin American markets where it gained market shares in double digits. In Mexico where it was launched in 1999 the brand captured a market share of 10% with a 120% growth within three years. Unilever had hoped to gain a similar foothold in the US market.

> "Axe does what a standard deodorant does, but its six fragrances don't smell like deodorants ... We have finely tuned our marketing model, have used it in many countries with great success, and have done so in a way that no other brand has been able to duplicate."[23]
>
> —Alan Jope, COO of Unilever Home and Personal Care –North America.

---

22 Included shaving products (aftershave, pre-shave, shaving cream), fragrances, deodorants/antiperspirants, hair care products (for styling, grooming and coloring hair), and skincare products.
23 Vavra Bob, "An Axe to Grind", 7 January 2002, Business Source Premier, www.search.epnet.com

AXE was not merely a deodorant to be sprayed under the arms or cologne to be dabbed behind the ears or at the pulse points. The brand promised extended deodorant benefit of 24 hours odor control. In the US, the pricing matched its positioning strategy, US$4 to US$5 for a four oz spray canister which was higher than that of a deodorant stick priced at US$2.76 and much lower than US$50 for a bottle of cologne.

The AXE launch was supported by an aggressive and unconventional ad campaign. The company also worked with retailers to get across the strong brand message to its consumers. Though the product was initially targeted at 18 to 34 year old men, it was also popular among the 11 to 13 year olds which demonstrated the age compression factor, where 12 year olds wanted to behave like 21 year olds.

Available at food, drug and mass outlets, AXE was packaged in black cans and available in 8 different masculine fragrances: Apollo, Kilo, Orion, Phoenix, Tsunami, Voodoo, Essence and Touch. The company used innovative in-store merchandising and positioned it at visible points next to Automotive and Electronic department displays. The product launch activities, in the US, were handled by New York based Bartle Bogle Hegarty, the ad agency which also handled the AXE brand in the UK.

At the launch stage the brand focused on TV advertising. The main ad pitch was that using AXE made men irresistible to women. The ads were designed to be provocative enough to catch the attention of young men. The first ads released, showed beautiful women ravishing male mannequins sprayed with AXE deodorant. Unilever also gained attention by getting young males sprayed with AXE by skimpily clad women called "AXE Angels" in shopping malls. There were also TV ads which showed women demonstrating the use of the deodorant on mannequins. These spots also served the purpose of educating the viewers on product usage.

Learning quickly that conventional TV advertising was not making a big impact on the young and that 95% of the target group[24] spent at least four hours a day online, the company launched Web based initiatives. The main target group was left to "discover" the brands for themselves and spread the word amongst their peer groups (viral marketing). The company also resorted to banner ads on the web sites of men's magazines such as *Maxim, FHM* and *AtomFilms* (a web host of short films and animations). The banners directed users to the AXE website.

The AXE website, launched in 2002, displayed exclusive commercials, which were considered too racy for television viewers. The website was expected to draw about 100,000 visits in the first month but drew seven times that number of visitors. In four months the site had registered about 1.7 million visits. A third of these visitors were referred to the site by friends.

The AXE launch campaign won the Business 2.0 Sweet Spot Award which recognized most innovative and successful marketing campaigns award given by Monthly magazine in 2003.

---

24 Thomas Mucha, "Spray Here. Get Girl.", www.business2.com/b2/web/articles, June 01, 2003 11

THE AXE HOUSE PARTY: MARCH 2003

AXE hosted an extravagant house party at a mansion outside Miami featuring latest music, TV and lifestyle celebrities. The event, which was handled by GMR Marketing Agency, the largest event marketing firm in the US, was the main attraction in the promotion of the brand. The initial information about the consumer destination event was let out into the market in December 2002 itself.

Unilever targeted millions of students and men in the age group of 11 to 24, who received trial size samples and information about the party. There was a radio campaign and an online push for young men to register at the website and participate in an online video game at the www.axehouseparty.com website (launched in 2003) in order to win invitations to the party.

The website received about 943,000 visits up to March 2003. Flyers advertising the event were posted at strategic locations in night clubs and print ads were run in *Rolling Stone* and *Spin* magazines. 100 of the chosen ones were flown in to attend the party along with young girls who were also invited.

The event enjoyed a 1-hour special TV airing on "The New TNN" channel. Popular TV shows, websites of men's magazines and channels such as The Jimmy Kimmel Show, MTV, VH1, FHMUS.com, Vibe.com covered the event. The event also won two 2004 Gold Reggies[25] in the "New Media Promotion" and "National Consumer Promotion (US\$ 1million- US\$ 5 million budgets)" categories. This resulted in a 22% increase in general brand awareness among 11–24 year old men and 3.0% to 3.7% dollar share increase[26] (within the Antiperspirant /Deodorant category) soon after the promotional period. Unilever capitalized on the popularity of the event by offering free CDs of musicals that were featured at the party along with sale of two cans of the deodorant spray.

SUBSEQUENT MARKETING ACTIVITIES

Unilever kept up the interest and awareness of the brand with continuous action. New fragrance variants were launched and the brand was extended to products such as antiperspirants, shower gels and under-arm-only deodorants.

In 2004, competition intensified when new brands entered the market on the same platform, targeting the young male population. P&G launched Old Spice's Red Zone deodorant body spray (**Annexure 11.2**) in 2004 and Gillette launched TAG (**Annexure 11.3**) in 2005. In February 2005, Unilever launched 'Degree For Men' under the Degree (leading brand in the antiperspirant/ deodorant category) brand with the purpose of further strengthening the brand's position in the deodorant market. The line included Ultra Clear Degree

---

25 Awarded by the Promotion Marketing Association to honor the best promotional programs in the US.
26 Patricia Odell, "The Mating Game", www.promomagazine.com, May 1, 2004

deodorant in stick and gel versions and Ultra Dry Degree antiperspirant[27] in stick, soft solid or aerosol forms.

In 2004, the company distributed an innovative sales kit to 300 Unilever sales people, which won the Promotional Product Association Florida (PPAF)[28] Award in the Consumer Promotion category. Unilever hired a promotional consultant Mike Simms to design the sales kit. The kit comprised of a custom designed skateboard along with a backpack to carry it and other items appealing to 12 to 24 year olds. The back pack also contained product samples, CD-ROM with ready made sales presentations, product images, price lists ... A letter to the sales person from the AXE brand manager was also part of the kit.

Unilever did not neglect the traditional media altogether in its Web focused efforts, but made innovative use of the print media too. AXE deodorant and body spray won a Media Lion at the Cannes Festival in 2005, for the execution of an interactive print ad. The cover girl on a Colombian men's magazine had a removable top which was meant to demonstrate the "AXE Effect." Unilever had also put on display hoardings carrying scenes resulting from the usage of AXE.

In 2005, the company also recruited brand ambassadors from young male students in an unconventional manner by leaving a pair of black thongs in their laundry basket along with a note saying: "Do you have what it takes to be the next AXE ambassador?" The ambassadors were paid by the company to entertain friends and distribute samples of the product.

In 2005, AXE's sales underwent a slight dip and the brand slipped to number two position next to Old Spice. In the summer of 2005, Unilever launched a fragrance variant, AXE Unlimited. The release of Mojo Master, which coincided with the launch of the fragrance variant, attempted to use digital media and enhance its popularity via viral marketing.

The Mojo Master, an online game meant for young men, was available freely at the MojoMastergame.com website. The Mojo Master was a fantasy game where players could use their playboy skills in encounters with "unique" women (one of them was Tiffany Fallon, the 2005 Playboy Playmate of the Year) at various virtual venues located in cities like New York City and Los Angeles. In July, the game was to be upgraded with more venues and more girls and in August the players would be able to test their playboy skills against each other.

The company took the help of Conductor, a Santa Monica based marketing firm that had done the promotion work for Spiderman films, to launch the site. The marketing firm engaged Wild Tangent, the industry leader in online games, to develop this fantasy video game.

> "Mojo Master is a deep, feature-rich, console-quality downloadable
> game that introduces the best crossbreed of two hit genres, simulation

---

27 Priced at for a 2.7 oz soft solid pack 14
28 Founded in 1972 the PPAF is a regional association which strived to achieve highest standards of professionalism and create growth opportunities in the promotional products industry.

and role-playing, all for free. It is the most ambitious development of branded entertainment that any marketer has ever undertaken and we're delighted to finally unleash it for gamers to play."[29]

—Alex St. John, Chief Executive Officer and Founder, WildTangent.

One distinguishing feature of the Mojo Master website was the reality based blog titled "EvanAndGareth.com", which detailed the real life experiences of two young men, Evan and Gareth, through video clips. The clips captured the young men's encounters with women during their trek across the US. Unilever hoped the short video clips would become popular among young men and be emailed around, creating a viral marketing effect. The video clips of Evan and Gareth's campaign could also be viewed on Heavy.com[30] or downloaded from Heavy.com and viewed on a PSP.[31]

THE NEXT MOVE

In the four years since 2000, the men's grooming market had grown at the rate of 285%[32] even outdoing the growth of the women's grooming products segment. There were 194 new products introduced in the men's personal care segment during this period. TAG, the brand launched by Gillette to take on AXE, was also gaining popularity among the teens in 2005. According to industry experts[33] the men's toiletries segment, in the US, was expected to grow from US$ 1.30 billion in 2004 to US$ 1.64 billion in 2008. The age group (15 to 34 years) which contributed to the sales in this segment was also expected to grow roughly at the rate of 4.2% through this time period.

Kevin George, Unilever's Marketing Director for deodorants in the US, envisioned the brand as a cult icon for the younger generation along with the likes of MTV, Nike and iPod.

"Our ambition is to live in the world of brands like [Nike, MTV and Xbox] not in the world of package goods. We want to live in the world of cool brands."[34]

—Carlos Gil, Brand Development Director, AXE

29   Mike Larson & Erin Shiba, "Mojo Master(TM)—The First Virtual Fantasy Game of Seduction Goes Live for Free", www.prnewswire.com, June 20, 2005
30   A Web host of short films and animation which allowed free downloading of its video clips.
31   Sony's Portable Station Player, a handheld game device which could also play music and movies.
32   Theresa Howard, "A nice Smelling Man is Hard to Find", http://www.usatoday.com/money/advertising/adtrack/2005-07-17-axe-track_x.htm
33   Antoinette Alexander, "Media, Euro influence drive growth, help men's grooming carve solid niche", www.findarticles.com, Sept 27, 2004
34   Jack Neff, "Axe board helps find 'whack juice'", *Advertising Age*, search.epnet.com, October 18, 2004 21

Unilever had spent more than US$ 100 million between 2003 and 2005 to market the brand. The company felt that since the target segment was a multimedia user they had to cover a range of media options such as television, Internet and mobile devices.

> "He (*18 to 24 year olds*) is still watching television, but even when he's doing that, he's online or might have his PSP on in front of him. The more pieces you can reach, the better ... If you were to just do television or print, which do play a very important role, you miss the opportunities that other media allow."
>
> —David Rubin, Development Manager, Axe, Unilever.[35]

Marketers were resorting to newly emerging media as effective channels for communication to reach young consumers whose use of traditional media was rapidly decreasing. Podcasting[36] which was virtually ad free in 2005 was one such medium which was gaining popularity among advertisers. Unilever and P&G were both considering sponsored entertainment in this medium as a future option. Unilever had released its first AXE body spray podcast ad in August 2005.

> "As original as the Axe strategy has been, it will be an enormous challenge to keep the campaign fresh. Evan and Gareth's tour ends in August; by that time the two could well be played out. After that, Unilever knows it can't revert to pitching 24-hour underarm protection. Whatever the next stage of the Axe strategy is, look for it on the Internet and on cell phones, not on television."[37]
>
> —Robert Berner, Business Week

In January 2005, P&G acquired Gillette. Though Unilever retained the number one slot globally, the acquisition narrowed the gap between P&G (which was in second place) and Unilever, thus providing P&G with a better bargaining position with retail outlets like Wal-Mart. Unilever executives wondered what more marketing innovations would be needed for AXE.

---

35 "PSP as a new marketing media",marketingangles.blogspot.com, May 3, 2005
36 Method of transferring audio files over the Internet for download to multimedia players.
37 Robert Berner, "How Unilever Scored with Young Guys", *Business Week*, May 23, 2005

ANNEXURE 11.1: UNILEVER GROUP

Unilever, an Anglo-Dutch company, was one of the world's largest sellers of fast moving consumer goods. Unilever had two parent companies, Unilever NV in Rotterdam, Netherlands and Unilever PLC in London, UK.

The genesis of the company could be traced back to the 1890s when William Heskith Lever, founder of Lever Bros., the British soap maker, developed Sunlight soap, a product which popularized cleanliness and hygiene in Victorian England. Although Unilever was not formed until 1930, the companies that joined to create the group were already established before the start of the 20th century. In 1930 the Lever Bros. merged with Margerine Unie, a Dutch margarine producer. Since then the Unilever group had grown with a series of acquisitions and mergers across the world. The company also sold off a number of brands and businesses during this period. In 2005 its portfolio consisted of 400 brands, both global and regional. Unilever had established itself into two global divisions: Foods and Home and personal care.

In 2004, in the Personal care category, Unilever was the leader in the skin cleansing and deodorants markets. It was one of the top three players in daily hair care and mass-market skin care categories. The six global brands: Dove, AXE, Lux, Rexona, Ponds and Sunsilk formed the core of its personal care division.

Unilever in the United States, in 2005, employed more than 15,000 people in 74 offices and had manufacturing sites in 24 states and Puerto Rico, generating approximately $11 billion in sales.

The personal care division in the US comprised of the following main brands:

- Skin care products: Caress, Dove, Lever 2000, Pond's, Suave and Vaseline
- Deodorant and antiperspirant products: AXE and Degree
- Hair care products: Dove, Finesse, Suave and ThermaSilk.

Compiled by case author

ANNEXURE 11.2: PROCTER & GAMBLE'S OLD SPICE

Old Spice was launched in the year 1938, by the Shulton Company, as cologne which was considered a "man's man" product. The brand was acquired by P&G in the year 1990, and since then has grown rapidly. The brand used Sporting events as the main platform for targeting young males.

The Old Spice brand included:

- Old Spice Classic Deodorant launched in 1950 offering round-the-clock protection
- High Endurance Deodorant with a cutting edge formula launched in 1993
- High Endurance Gel Solid Antiperspirant launched in 1998 with a powerful antiperspirant
- Red Zone Antiperspirant launched in 2000 meant for men whose perspiration rate was very high.
- High Endurance Body Spray launched in 2002, providing odor protection for the whole body
- Red Zone body spray launched in 2002. It was available in four scents: Pure Sport, Glacial Falls, Aqua Reef and Metallic Ice.
- Red Zone Invisible Solid and Invisible Stick launched in 2004

Red Zone came with a new Odor Defense System which helped neutralize odor at source and used a Controlled Release Technology that released scent which was longer lasting. The Red Zone deodorant was priced at $4.99 per 4 oz can.

Old Spice as a brand had evolved over the years and in the year 2002 was targeting young males in the age group 12 to 34. In 2002 the brand was revamped with major changes in product packaging and advertisements. The old "whistling sailor" theme which was the main stay of ad campaigns till then was traded in for scantily clad young women who were being whistled at.

In 2002, P&G also introduced the "Cool Contact" marketing campaign when it introduced Cool Contact refreshment towels a new product available in fresh, pure sport and mountain rush scents. The campaign included the "Towel Girls Tour 2002, where three girls dressed in tight fitting sports clothes with the Cool Contact logo on the front were seen at major sporting events nationwide.

In 2004 P&G teamed up with Electronic Arts, where EA used the "Red Zone" theme in its NCAA 2004 football game with the tagline "When performance matters most". The ad campaign launched in 2004 carried the message "Scent is the strongest sense tied to memory" which demonstrated that the scent of Red Zone triggered positive memories in mind of the user's girlfriend making her recall the good times spent together.

Compiled by case author

ANNEXURE 11.3: GILLETTE'S RIGHT GUARD & TAG

Right Guard was the first deodorant brand to be marketed by Gillette in the year 1960 when it was introduced as an aerosol. Over the years, Right Guard had become the umbrella brand for a number of product variants:

- Right Guard Antiperspirant in 1968
- Right Guard roll-on in 1975
- Right Guard pump in 1977
- Right Guard solid Antiperspirant in 1981
- Right Guard clear gel in 1993
- Right Guard Xtreme Sports (specifically meant for active people) in 2000
- Right Guard Cool Spray in 2004

Right Guard Cool Spray was launched in 2004 with an advanced high-performance formula with guaranteed results even under extreme situations. The brand came in a new can with benefits such as a "point-and-shoot" vertical dispenser and easy-to-use, thumb-activated side trigger. The ad appeared exclusively in theatres. It then moved onto cable stations such as MTV, Comedy Central and ESPN's X games coverage.

Gillette launched its new brand of male deodorant, TAG as direct competitor to AXE in March 2005. The ad campaign for the brand with the tag line "Consider yourself warned" included television, print and online advertising. The print ad showed a young man being mauled by a team of women volley ball players. The television ads appeared during popular American shows such as "American Idol", FOX's "24" and "The Simpsons," CBS' "Late Show with David Letterman" and ESPN's "Sportscenter."

The print ads were released in popular men's magazines such as *FHM, Maxim, Rolling Stone, Stuff and Blender.* One execution of a print ad carried a unique takeaways for readers in the form of a pocket card carrying the sentence, "No sir, I did not have foreign relations with your daughter," and its translation in four languages.

The company also made use of Radio advertising and online ads posted on popular Web sites such as Bolt.com, AOL Red, Comedy Central, MTV, Gamespot, Shockwave, and Google. An online game meant for young men was available at the www.consideryourself-warned.com website. In July 2005, sales of TAG had reached US$ 7.4 million and the brand had become the second best selling male deodorant next to AXE.

TAG Body Spray was available in four scents Lucky Day, First Move, Midnight and After Hours. The product was sold at food, drug and mass merchandise stores across the U.S. for a suggested retail price of US$ 4.49 for a 4 oz can.

Compiled by case author

REFERENCES

1. Theresa Howard, "Viral' advertising spreads through marketing plans", USA Today, June 2005
2. Deodorants in the US, Industry Profile, www.datamonitor.com, Feb 2004
3. Global Deodorants, Industry Profile, www.datamonitor.com, Feb 2004
4. "A new Brand World", www.larsbjorge.com, May 2005
5. Baptistemar, "PSP as a new marketing media", themarketingangles.blogspot.com, May 03, 2005
6. Theresa Howard, "Ads take bite out of political sensitivity", www.usatoday.com May 2005
7. Theresa Howard, "Advertisers try new ways to always get their man", www.usatoday.com, June 2005
8. Vavra, Bob, "An Axe to grind", Vol. 81, Issue 10, Database: Business Source Premier, www.search.epnet.com, 7/1/2002
9. Neff, Jack "Axe board helps find 'whack juice", By:, Advertising Age, October 18, 2004, Vol. 75, Issue 42, *Business Source Premier*, www.search.epnet.com
10. Laurel Wentz & Jack Neff, "The Lynx effect may affect U.S.", Advertising Age, July 30, 2001, Vol. 72, Issue 31, *Business Source Premier*, www.search.epnet.com
11. Kristina Dell, "Just for Dudes", www.time.com, Feb. 06, 2005
12. David Kiley, "Mad Ave's Rush to Podcasts", May 25, 2005, www.businessweekasia.com
13. Christine Bittar, "Razor-Sharp Marketing at the New *P&G?*", Brandweek, 10644318, 6/20/2005, Vol. 46, Issue 25, *Business Source Premier*, www.search.epnet.com
14. "The Mating Game", Patricia Odell www.promomagazine.com/campaigns, May 1, 2004
15. Top Ten Deo Brands, Global Report: Personal Care, GCI April 2005, www.search.epnet.com
16. The Smell of Success, By: Lippert, Barbara, Adweek, 01992864, 3/28/2005, Vol. 46, Issue 13, *Business Source Premier*, www.search.epnet.com
17. Jerry Large, "Evil Axe-is: sexy ads, stinky teens", www.seattletimes.com, June 23, 2005
18. Thomas Mucha, "Spray here get girl", www.business2.com, June 01, 2003
19. "Old Spice introduces Red Zone", Press release, www.oldspice.com
20. Don Baker, "Reviving a Classic: Today's Old Spice is just isn't for the old guys," February 21, 2002, Post Cinncinatti, www.oldspice.com
21. Barbie Casasus, "Guys gain a new edge in the dating game with axe deodorant warning: not your grandfather's old stick," www.hispanicprwire.com, August 20, 2002
22. Antoinette Alexander, "Media, Euro influence drive growth, help men's grooming carve solid niche", www.findarticles.com, Sept 27, 2004
23. "Media, Euro influence drive growth, help men's grooming carve solid niche", www.findarticles.com, September 2004
24. The Associated Press, "Gillette's Body Spray a Hit with Teens," www.telegram.com, 7 August 2005
25. Suzanne Wu, "Podcasting for The Man", www.wired.com, August 2005

WEBSITES

1. www.oldspice.com
2. www.gillette.com
3. www.theaxeeffect.com
4. www.mojomaster.com
5. www.unilever.com
6. www.ad-rag.com
7. www.business2.com
8. www.eventmarketermag.com

SECTION III: WRAP UP AND REVIEW

KEY TIPS TO HELP SELECT THE RIGHT SOCIAL MEDIA MARKETING PLATFORM

- What is the ultimate goal behind your viral media marketing campaign? Tightly defining your primary online objective will help you to define exactly what type of approach to use. Is it to raise brand awareness? Drive increased web traffic? Do you see it as a tool that lets you stay in direct communication with your client and user base? For example, as a journalist, will you be creating a hard news site, one for celebrity gossip, a sports report, or a personal opinion blog? Having a well-defined objective is instrumental in crafting the correct social media marketing strategy. It boils down to this, what do you want your followers to know about your brand?

- Determine the scale of resources that you are willing to commit to the marketing effort. How ambitious are your viral media marketing goals? For a small business owner or a sole proprietorship, how much free time will you personally be able to dedicate to social media? It is one thing to build the company website or create its initial Twitter account, but something else entirely to commit to a round-the-clock social media marketing operation. It is important to be realistic about what level of social media sophistication your budget will allow.

- Identify your target demographic. With an online marketing plan and the proper online infrastructure in place, it is now time to identify your brand's true target audience. Remember that the team behind Axe targeted 18–25-year-old males, only to find that their ads were actually appealing to teens as young as 13–14 years of age. So, you will also want to distinguish exactly who your target demographic is, which social media platforms (Facebook, Instagram, etc.) they use, and how much time they tend to spend on their preferred sites. It is also not a bad idea to investigate which social media platforms your main competitors are currently using. What do they know that you do not?

- Consider the importance of selecting your platform's content and design features. What is the best way to catch the attention of your target demographic and maximize audience engagement? Visual appeal is what sells, but what visuals will you feature: solely high resolution, HD video content, or will it also consist of photos, graphics, video links, and PowerPoint presentations (or perhaps even interactive multimedia content and games). Will it feature a breaking news ticker or sports and financial-related updates somewhere on screen? Will you have an e-commerce component of some kind? How easy is your site to navigate? Does your media content playback smoothly on a variety of media platforms ranging from laptops to widescreen TVs, and from smartphones to video game consoles?

- Choose the social media platform(s) that best suit your particular needs. All social media platforms are not created equally, with some sites looking to serve a wide, general audience, while other alternative sites concentrate on providing narrow types of customized information. Some sites are informative in nature, while others aspire to be a destination site; some platforms are for social networking, while others are mainly for business, and some platforms allow advertising, still others forbid it outright. So, before making a commitment, examine the different platforms and who their typical users are. Also check into the quality of the platform's data analytics (how accurate are their measurements of visitors to your site and the frequency of those visits?).

- Pay close attention to your online audience and you will build a lasting connection with your users. One of the great benefits of viral media marketing is that it can provide a fantastic way to provide direct, round-the-clock access to your audience. Showing how responsive your organization is to customer concerns also helps to build brand loyalty and retention. However, to maintain these close ties to your followers, it is important for your social media team to be very responsive in their dealings with the public. Take the time to monitor your various social media platforms on a regular basis. What is being posted? How well is your staff interacting with the general public online? Stay in touch with the virtual side of your business. Make sure proper standards are being enforced.

- Regularly evaluate, analyze, and refine your social media strategy. Company needs or goals can change rapidly, often without any warning. Flexibility becomes key, particularly in an online environment in which breaking news can forever sway the fortunes of individuals or even entire industries in the time it takes to clip on a weblink or forward someone's ill-thought-out tweet. As mentioned above, make sure to review the analytical data associated with social media platforms. How many new visitors are coming to your site? Which links are they using to get there? How long are those visitors staying? If the numbers are not generating the results that you hoped for, look at improving your message by making any adjustments or refinement, as needed.

QUESTIONS

1. How do online and viral marketing campaigns compare in effectiveness to more traditional print or broadcast advertisements? According to the text, what are some of the main principles or arguments in favor of using viral video-style ads? What

are some of online myths most associated with viral videos? Of the two advertising approaches (viral versus traditional), explain which method relies more on a passive audience and which one needs a more participatory audience? Between the two strategies, which seems to generate the most marketing buzz?

2. According to the text, what are the names of some of the top, current social media platforms? What types of unique media content are these particular sites best known for? What is meant by the term dense content and how does it impact audience retention? How can viral video producers and directors start to use new technologies to make their viral content more of an immersive experience for their online users?

3. In what ways has the journalism profession had to adapt because of the emergence of social media networks, citizen journalists, and the instantaneous trends created by viral content? How have these new media platforms changed the economics of delivering the news? Long term, should these adaptions be viewed in a positive or negative light? Please explain the thoughts and reasonings behind your views.

4. Ask students to identify areas of both their public and private lives that are now dependent upon, if not outright dominated by, the presence of the Internet and social media? For example, video stores and record shops are a thing of the past since most media content is now streamed, while many banking transactions no longer even require human interaction, and automobiles have morphed into roving Wi-Fi hotspots with onboard sensors that automatically apply the brakes to avoid a collision. Discuss how the growth of the Internet and social media have changed your own consumer purchasing and consumption habits. Also discuss whether or not we all should be more concerned about the growing lack of privacy, as our personal lives are live steamed to the world, and our movements constantly tracked by GPS devices and the increasing number of public surveillance cameras? Is social media potentially more of a threat to us as a society, than it is a remedy to our ills?

RELATED PROJECTS AND EXERCISES

- Have individual students track their media usage over the course of a single, 24-hour day. Have the students keep a running log of how and when they are exposed to different forms of media, from the moment that they wake up in the morning to the sound of their smart phone's alarm to their last Twitter post before bedtime. Have them track their individual amounts of media consumption, be it listening to music on their commute into school, when they play a quick round of online video games with friends, conduct research on the Internet for a homework assignment, or even when they are simply streaming their favorite TV show or viral video. Have them be as thorough as possible. Have them submit the completed video log along with 700–1,000 words of analysis.

- If you have not already done so, break the students into teams comprised of four to six individuals and then have each team conduct detailed research on a well-known advertising campaign of their choosing. Ideally, the campaign chosen should be one that is, or was, multimedia in nature, stretching across various media platforms (viral marketing, print, broadcasting, online websites, social media, cinema, video gaming, etc.) for a well-known brand. Ask the students to breakdown the marketing campaign based on a number of creative factors, including the ad's visual design and layout, shot and color composition, font size and style, slogan used, etc. Ask students to put into their own words why it is they think that the advertiser made these specific choices. Did the choices that the advertiser made, ultimately prove to be effective? Did brand recognition or sales actually increase as a result of the marketing efforts?

- As an alternate or complementary assignment to the one listed above, ask each of the student groups to create their own multimedia advertising campaign. Suggest that they pick an older, established brand whose image has grown stale and then remake or reimagine that particular brand with a newer, more modern approach that appeals to a typical college-age demographic. Have students explain why they made the choices for the ad campaign that they did. What impression do they hope to leave with the viewer in regard to the featured brand? What do they believe that their ad campaign has done well? What areas, if any, would they liked to have improved on? The goal of this project is to have students focus on basic branding and layout skills. For advanced classes, have each group also create a press release to help promote their new ad campaign.

SECTION IV

Ethical Journalism for the Viral Age

INTRODUCTION

The ethical standards of journalistic behavior that are outlined in Section IV are principles that many of us take for granted. The tendency is to believe that appropriate measures are already in place and that these ethical standards are always being enforced. Truth be told, most news consumers probably never give much thought to the newsroom supervisors, producers, and editors-in-chief who act as gatekeepers of the news. These are the individuals who put in long hours covering breaking news and then have to make the difficult judgment calls as to which stories should or should not make it to print, or on to broadcast. These are the same individuals who will have to take the heat if they make the wrong call and circulate a report that later proves to be false or unsubstantiated.

There are also regulatory organizations like the Federal Communications Commission (FCC) that work to ensure that all federal rules and guidelines are being met. Professional organizations like the Radio TV News Directors Association (RTNDA), the Society for Professional Journalists (SPJ), and the Center for Journalism Ethics (CJE), also take a lead role in promoting ethical codes of conduct for journalists to adhere to. Unfortunately, there is no single, unified set of global ethical standards for journalists, primarily because of the varying cultural norms and levels of press freedom found in countries throughout the world.

KEY TERMS

- the Absolutist Theory of Right and Wrong
- artificial construction
- citizen journalist
- checkbook journalism
- documentary photograph
- ethnographies/ethnographic
- the Golden Rule (the ethics of reciprocity)
- the Greater Good Rule
- juxtaposing clips
- narrativize/narrativizing
- pictorial photograph
- preconceptualized/preconception
- pseudo events
- recontextualizing
- slipping sound
- tableau vivant
- video journalism versus docudramas
- visual trope

Nevertheless, even with regional disparities, journalists on a broad scale agree on the need for stories to be produced in an even-handed and objective manner; one that reflects all of the legitimate parties and perspectives involved on an equal basis.

The problem is that many of the standard ethical protocols related to journalism were first envisioned with large news operations in mind, where there would be ample support staff to help ensure that all of the proper guidelines were followed. However, that traditional news production paradigm has now been altered, due in large part to the influence and 24/7 content demands of social media. Many viral news productions are so small that they have little to no support staff, meaning that there are no editors to check the veracity of sources, no legal team to review possible defamatory material, and no experienced ombudsman or news director to question the appropriateness of the story's final content. The question becomes, for the independent citizen journalists and online bloggers of the world, what ethical code of conduct must they be expected to follow, given that they answer to no one except themselves?

Compounding this dilemma is the fact that this new breed of reporter lacks any formal journalistic training and, therefore, they lack awareness of the profession's ethical standards and expectations. Still, other viral news producers come from activist backgrounds, suggesting that preordained biases or agendas may be present in their reporting. These are all trends that run counter to journalistic ideals, yet, in this type of viral news environment, how can we be sure that the individuals depicted in news reports are being treated with the same level of respect and objectivity that any of us would want to be shown under similar circumstances?

Another concern is that, without the support of a large news organization behind them, how ethics-focused can a small viral news operation afford to be? Will online journalists be able to stand their ground and remain truly independent when reporting on politically charged stories or when issuing controversial editorials if, by doing so, they jeopardize their main revenue source of online income? Does a small news website run the risk of being sued out of existence, a la what happened to Gawker? At some point, does it become easier for an independent viral journalist to set their scruples aside in favor of simply killing a story outright, despite its importance to the public? If your online report leads to physical harm occurring to someone, who takes responsibility to see that the right decision is made beforehand?

Obviously, situations like these illustrate the profound changes occurring within journalism profession right now. They provide a glimpse into the near future, showing how difficult it will be to administer a consistent set of ethical standards in a digital world where content can be manipulated in virtually undetectable ways and then be transmitted instantaneously around the globe via the Internet. As a consequence, Section IV examines how even trying to define the term *ethical journalism* has taken on a new level of complexity in a viral media era distinguished by claims of fake news, alternative facts, hyperpartisan reporting, particularly with the press now labeled as "an enemy of the people."

These developments provide a cautionary tale for viral journalists who have to make spur-of-the-moment decisions about what is proper to upload and stream online and what is not. Do journalists have an inherent responsibility to expose the facts of a case responsibly and in the most unbiased way possible? Do journalists always have a deep-rooted responsibility to fact check any and all information, regardless of the source's credibility? Should social media platforms, bloggers, and citizen journalists all be held to the same ethical standards as established journalistic entities, or have the rules changed so much that they now permit a two-tiered system of ethical behavior?

Section IV challenges you, as an up-and-coming journalist, to raise your own standards to the point that they exemplify the highest principles of ethical journalism. This section of the text will explain the three main philosophical precepts associated with ethical journalism: The Golden Rule, The Greater Good Rule, and the Absolutist Theory of Right-and-Wrong Rule. When can journalists apply these ethical principles to help themselves avoid falling into ethical traps or becoming a party to unintended conflicts of interest? Why is it that these differing philosophical approaches can sometimes be at odds with one another, and how does an inexperienced journalist know when to apply one set of philosophical tenets over the other? Section IV will try to provide the reader with valuable insight into all of these journalistic topics of ethical concern.

CHAPTER 12

Ethics

Donald R. Winslow; ed. Kenneth Kobre

As storytellers in a competitive environment, our goal is always to tell a fair, complete and accurate story. But at the same time, don't we also hope to tell a story in such as way as to snatch and hold viewers' attention? Can those be conflicting goals?

How do you stay within the ethical boundaries of the profession and still produce eye-grabbing video stories?

PHILOSOPHY OF ETHICAL DECISION MAKING

Videojournalists make ethical decisions based on three different principles: **the Golden Rule**, **the Greater Good Rule**, and **the Absolute Right and Wrong Rule**. Sometimes following these principles can lead to the same conclusion; at other times, they point to very different courses of action.

THE GOLDEN RULE

"The Ethics of Reciprocity," of Greek origin, is also known as "the Golden Rule." It says, "Do unto others as you would have them do unto you."

Ethicists have interpreted this rule to mean that we should treat others as we ourselves would like to be treated in the same situation. We must understand the implications and impact that our choices will make on the lives of others. Translated to videojournalism, that rule would state, "Take other peoples' pictures in the same way you would want your picture to be taken." If you were severely injured in a car accident, how would you feel about a videojournalist photographing you bleeding and injured, and then showing the footage on the evening news?

THE GREATER GOOD

The Utilitarian concept of the greater good, which can be traced to the Greek philosopher Epicurus, was popularized by British jurist Jeremy Bentham and English philosopher James Mill in the 1800s. The principle holds that within the potential rules of action, one should act only based on what the outcome will be, and that one's choice should be determined by which outcome will do the greatest good for the greatest number of people.

Journalism generally operates on the Utilitarian principle of making decisions in which the end result does the greatest possible good for the greatest number of people. For instance, you might be photographing a car accident. The very act of shooting pictures of victims might bring temporary emotional harm to the injured, but it might also save hundreds of lives if seeing the final footage serves to make viewers more cautious in the future.

THE ABSOLUTE

The Ten Commandments serve as an example of an absolutist set of rules. For instance, "Thou shall not kill" is a fixed notion, with no leeway whatsoever. Regardless of the benefits to society (the greater good) such as killing during war or in self-defense, all killing is viewed as unjust. From the Absolutist point of view, killing is always forbidden—regardless of any possible benefit to society.

In the videojournalism profession, the National Press Photographers Association (NPPA) provides a code of ethics that might be considered the Ten Commandments of visual journalism. The code's Absolutist principles are listed on NPPA's website.

WHEN PRINCIPLES COLLIDE

You will often hear that "people have a right to their privacy." How does that notion work in conjunction with the idea of journalism serving a greater good? A video clip depicts family members in the throes of horrible grief, reacting to the drowning of a child. Those operating on the idea of a greater good might believe that broadcasting this scene will make people think more carefully about swimming safety and accident prevention; those who adhere to the Absolutist principle of privacy would oppose publishing the picture. The absolutists would argue that regardless of any possible social benefit, the family's right to privacy might now trump the possible social gain. "Privacy" means exactly that—not having one's personal space in any way violated. Privacy is private. The Golden Rule would lead you to ask, "If this were my child who died, would I want a video camera recording my grief and would I want millions of people to see me breaking down?" Obviously, different videojournalists would have different reactions to the Golden Rule in this situation. Ironically, any of the choices might be ethical, depending on who you are and which underlying principles you choose to apply in this each case.

FIGURE 12.1 **Preventing Future Deaths?**
The boy in the body bag had just drowned. This family was grief stricken. Might running the picture in the paper, on TV, or the Internet help prevent future accidents? (Photo by John Harte, Bakersfield, California)

TELEVISION JOURNALISM ETHICS IN THE "GOOD OLD DAYS"

Today's ethical standards of storytelling evolved during a time when television ethics weren't so clear-cut. When Darrell Barton started in television news in 1967 for KAKE, Channel 10 in Wichita, the ethics of doing feature stories were very loose. "You could bring along your own characters," Barton recalls, "to role-play story-lines as needed in order to create or recreate the visuals you needed for storytelling."

Barton knows of a story in which two journalists were doing a piece on a giant slide in Wichita. To make it interesting, they "developed" a storyline about a girl being afraid of the slide and her boyfriend convincing her to go down it. They selected a pretty girl and her boyfriend to act out the roles. Set to triumphant music, she conquered her fears "and they lived happily ever after."

Barton recalls another incident in which two relatives of a photographer were used to impersonate the characters in a state fair feature about a lost boy on the midway and his big sister, who finds him. In both instances, the use of role-playing subjects was condoned because it abided by the ethical standards of the times.

"I won an award with a dance contest feature story where I took the winners to a park and let them dance to a tape," Barton says. He set up the scene and shot the video. "That was the last time I ever did anything like that because it won first place in a Gulf Coast News Photographers competition. Bob Brandon's story on a train derailment explosion won second. I got the award, and Bob spent three weeks in a hospital. I was 'shamed' into honesty," he says.

Though the networks' definition of "staging" was pretty broad, there was a lot of "creativity" being applied until the day CBS News issued a Standards & Practices policy that said no one could stage events—ever—without being fired. And anyone who failed to report another journalist staging could also be fired.

FIGURE 12.2 **The Radio Television Digital News Association (RTDNA).** RTDNA is a professional organization exclusively serving the electronic news profession, and consisting of more than 3,000 news directors, news associates, educators and students.

FIGURE 12.3 **The National Press Photographers Association** is an organization consisting of still photographers, TV photographers, and videojournalists.

FIGURE 12.4 **The Society of Professional Journalists** includes among its members professional writers, producers, photojournalists, videographers, and videojournalists.

FIGURE 12.5 **Demotix: News by You** is a website that allows citizens to put up their images and helps them sell the pictures to news agencies.

"The amazing thing was," Barton recalls, "they meant it. I mean you couldn't even ask someone to wait a moment while you moved ahead of them. Then I found out it was a great way to work. It made you sharp. It made you feel 'clean.' If it happened, you shot it. If you missed it, you missed it. If it didn't happen, it didn't happen."

JOURNALISM CODES FOR STANDARDS AND ETHICS

As a profession, journalism has created and followed its own set of ethical standards. Professional journalism organizations such as the National Press Photographers Association (NPPA), the Society of Professional Journalists (SPJ), and the Radio Television Digital News Association (RTDNA) have over time written and refined codes of ethics that individuals and entire news organizations can elect to embrace. Despite varying slightly from group to group and outlet to outlet, journalism's ethical standards all share some basic principles: truthfulness, accuracy, objectivity, fairness, and accountability (which lately has been called "transparency").

CITIZEN JOURNALISTS

Web bloggers and citizen journalists could follow a similar prescribed code of conduct if they decide to adopt such standards. *Cyberjournalist.net* has developed a code for citizen journalists. The code is a good road map, but the difference between the blogger and the professional working for a salary from an outlet such as a newspaper, broadcast network, or online publication is that the professional has editors and managers to supervise and enforce ethical standards. Freelancers, solo videojournalists, and independent web bloggers are, by definition, "self-regulating."

If you are working for an established journalistic organization, an ethical breach usually results in discipline from your employer. Disciplinary action can range from a relatively minor reprimand to the loss of a job. Regardless of where you work, though, if an ethical breach crosses legal boundaries such as committing a crime; slandering or libeling someone; or infringing someone's copyright, the issue may actually lead to criminal or civil proceedings.

For the sake of journalism's credibility, many traditional editors of established publications believe it's necessary to take extra precautions when publishing the work of "citizen journalists." Editors point out that self-appointed journalists don't have a track record or established trust and credibility. In fact, there are those who go to great lengths to dupe news organizations or foist a hoax. So citizen journalists' work must be held to a tighter standard, if only because a news organization has no leverage over the individual if the reporting turns out to be false.

The Web has its own way of punishing wrongdoers. Although the editor of a traditional publication can't fire a citizen journalist, watch guards on Web certainly can expose doctored stories or pictures. Web mavens have exposed a number of fake pictures and called them out as ethical missteps.

AVOID GIFTS OR BRIBES

When completing a piece on a story about, say, a homeless man in your town, you might be tempted to give an obviously needy person money in exchange for recording some pictures and asking a few questions about his life.

You feel sorry for him. He could use a solid meal and a place to stay. Why not give him a bit of cash?

Don't do it!

The journalism profession has a strict code that prohibits reporters, photojournalists or videographers from paying subjects for interviews, information or access. This code of ethics does not allow giving gifts in exchange for an onor off-camera interview. Journalists simply must refrain from the temptation to hand over money. Some media organizations even prohibit buying a prospective subject a meal.

Why? First, let's call it what it is, or at least what it is seen to be: A bribe.

The reason for the "no bribe" rule is that once journalists pay for information, their relationship with a subject becomes a business proposition. This business arrangement can impact the veracity and accuracy of information conveyed.

The street person, for example, might not tell the whole truth or the "same truth" if he knows his answers are tied to a monetary reward. He might say what he hopes the interviewer wants to hear in hopes of getting a still greater payoff.

Also, a bribe sets a precedent. Subsequent journalists are likely to be asked for more and more money in exchange for an on-camera appearance.

Perhaps most important, the public has less trust in a report that involves exchanging money for an interview.

Bottom line. Avoid "checkbook" journalism by never offering and, if asked, refusing to give cash for contacts.

ETHICAL TRAPS

TO SHOOT OR NOT TO SHOOT?

When an unexpected event unfolds rapidly in front of the camera, photographers must decide whether they should be shooting. Almost always, the answer is "shoot." The rule is to shoot now and decide (discuss and edit) later. The moment can never be recovered if it's lost. Ethical decisions about what to show and how to show it can always be discussed long after the fact. But from the videojournalist's point of view, if the picture or the moment is not captured, it may as well never have happened.

When Darren Durlach, senior multimedia producer for the *Boston Globe* and an Ernie Crisp NPPA Television News Photographer of the Year, arrives on the scene of a story—if there's not something "blowing up or burning" that he has to capture immediately—he first assesses the sounds he's hearing. He wants to determine what sounds are going to be happening only for the next few moments so that he can record them before they go away. He then tries to evaluate what sounds will still be going on in ten minutes or even an hour later.

First things first. After ranking those sounds according to potential longevity, he goes about the task of capturing the audio that is likely to cease soon, followed by the audio that will still be around later. This way, Durlach never panics from realizing, "That sound is gone; I should have captured it first." Also by using this approach, Durlach doesn't place himself in a position of feeling pressed to ask someone to "do it again."

Suppose Durlach misses good video when he is busy shooting his audio? "Those are the breaks," he says.

FIGURE 12.6 **Darren Durlach,** WBBF-TV Baltimore, at the scene of a car accident that killed a 16-year-old pedestrian the previous day. (Photo by Mike Buscher)

JUXTAPOSING CLIPS CAN CHANGE THE MEANING OF THE STORY

There are hundreds of edits in a video even as short as 90 seconds, points out Jorge Sanhueza-Lyon, multimedia producer and photojournalist at the *Austin American-Statesman.* "There are so many ways to juxtapose clips that could make a story seem to go one way or another."

Sanhueza-Lyon, who also teaches at the University of Texas–Austin, tells his upper-level and graduate students about how easy it would be to alter the reality of a story by merely changing the context of video clips during editing. To illustrate his point, he shows the students raw footage from his stories, unedited. Then he shows them the various ways those clips could be assembled to tell entirely different stories by changing the order of their viewing.

For example, Sanhueza-Lyon shows raw video from a fire scene including a series of crowd and reaction shots. At most news scenes, a photographer can find a selection of people reacting differently: grieving bystanders, nonchalant gawkers, or maybe even people who are having a good time and laughing about something unrelated to the fire.

"How you pick which one of those shots to show next, after the fire pictures, gives context to the story," Sanhueza-Lyon says. "You are telling the viewer that the crowd was either just hanging out and 'doing their thing,' or were really angry or hurt or concerned, or were trying to make sense out of what was happening, or alternatively, were reacting inappropriately ... whichever shot you pick to show next can result in a completely different story."

SLOWING DOWN OR SPEEDING UP VIDEO

While editing, says Stan Heist, former videographer for channel WBFF in Baltimore, "changing the speed of video can have a substantial effect on how it is perceived. It can be tempting to slow down or speed up video to fit a specific need or want," he says. For instance, you might not have enough arrest footage in front of the courthouse to cover the voice-over script. Should you stretch out the arrest video, running it slower than normal, to cover the voice-over track?

"Take a video of someone walking and slow it down—oftentimes the viewer's perception of that person will seem ominous, sinister, or somehow guilty. That same scene, sped up, can give the appearance of someone who is harried, foolish, or superhuman. In

FIGURE 12.7   **Stan Heist,** Channel WBFF Baltimore.

this case, the audience may be in on the joke, but are you intimating something about your subject's character by using this effect? Is it a fair effect?

"The question I ask myself centers on intention and how I believe the viewer will view the edit," say Heist. "Am I trying to 'fool' the viewer into believing something is real that isn't, or are they in on it?"

COLOR BALANCE CAN COLOR THE OUTCOME

Heist also notes that adjusting color balance in the camera and in postproduction involves ethical choices. He poses this theoretical question: "What would happen if the videographer made a mistake when setting the white balance in the field. Let's say it was set to a cooler than natural color. Then the footage would have a blue cast. If the shooter warmed up the footage during editing by adding red and yellow filtration to the color balance, is this video-journalist fiddling with the truth? The footage will ultimately be neutrally colored but will it have been artificially manipulated?

Heist believes that correcting a mistake in color balance during editing is acceptable behavior because you're trying to match reality. But he says making a shot in the edit bay "cooler" (more blue) than the original scene to make it appear more "sinister" or "unhealthy" is an example of an ethical mistake. There is a subtle but clear-cut difference between the two. Correcting mistakes is ethical, but giving the footage a sinister look that was not present in the original scene is not.

TURN DOWN DISTRACTING BACKGROUND SOUNDS

Indiana University journalism associate dean James W. Brown shot a video story on a bicycle shop. In his edited piece, there is distracting background sound from a radio. He took his piece to WISH-TV veteran videojournalist Steve Sweitzer for a critique. Sweitzer told Brown that he needed clean audio to go with his video. Due to the radio sounds in the background on his recorded tape, he simply didn't have it. "Do you mean I should have turned the radio down or off?" Brown asked.

"Yes, under certain circumstances," Sweitzer replied. "Ask yourself what the story's about; if the radio's a part of the story, then by all means, leave it in. But if the sounds coming from the radio are just a distraction from your story (the sound drowns out the dialog between the repair-man and the customer, for example), "you might have to exercise some control over the background noise caused by the radio," said Sweitzer.

In other words, turn down the radio.

Sweitzer says that if you did not want to change the radio volume for ethical reasons, then maybe you could use a lavalier microphone rather than the stereo microphone on the camera. Even changing mics doesn't solve all distracting noise problems, Sweitzer says. "Sometimes you have to tell someone to quit talking or shut a window to eliminate lawn mower noise outside."

In the case of the radio blaring in the bicycle shop, the ethical concept of "the greater good" is behind Sweitzer's advice of turning down the sound—most viewers will benefit more from hearing the dialog clearly than from having the music interfere with what is being said.

However, the Absolutist who says "thou shalt not alter anything" might warn the videojournalist not to touch the radio dial. This approach requires finding some other way to shoot in the noisy environment or not shoot there at all.

For the Associated Press, the world's largest news gathering organization, its standard for audio is very clear-cut: "Audio actualities must always tell the truth. We do not alter or manipulate the content of a newsmaker actuality in any way. Voice reports by AP correspondents may only be edited to remove pauses or stumbles."

As for audio editing, "AP does permit the use of the subtle, standard audio processing methods of normalization of levels, general volume adjustments, equalization to make the sound clearer, noise reduction to reduce extraneous sounds such as telephone line noise, and the fading in and out of the start and end of sound bites—all of the above provided the use of these methods does not conceal, obscure, remove or otherwise alter the content or any portion of the content of the audio." For anything other than these adjustments, any AP employee must consult with a supervisor.

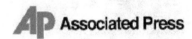

FIGURE 12.8 **The Associated Press** "Standards and Practices" statement lays out clearly the rules of the road for videojournalists working for the world's largest news-gathering agency.

CLEANING UP QUOTES

In audio, you can edit someone's quote for clarity, as is done on NPR and PRI. Yes, you can get fired for editing that same quote in a print article. In written text, however, you can paraphrase or add ellipses to indicate omitted material, neither of which is possible with radio.

Senior photographer and picture editor James Estrin of the *New York Times* says that he and his *Times* colleagues have settled on "not cleaning up audio too much. We tend to like to rely on giving the listener the subject's patterns of speaking, even if that includes a few 'ums' and 'aws' in their delivery."

SLIDING SOUND AROUND

Unlocking the audio and video tracks during editing allows you to slide the sound bite or natural sound under other video shots that were taken at a different moment. The act of moving the sound file around, unhooked from the original video file, is called "slipping sound."

With interview footage, most professionals have no problem with unlocking the sound track from the video track. The audio can be combined with B-roll video that illustrates the thrust of the interview. That technique, as old as theatre newsreels before the dawn of television, is called editing with an A-roll (voice from the interview) and B-roll (supporting film clips). (See Chapter 10, "Shooting a Sequence.")

The ethical dilemma for some journalists arises when the editor combines natural sound recorded at one moment with video recorded at another moment. For example, during

FIGURE 12.9 **Jorge Sanhueza-Lyon,** *Austin American-Statesman*, recording video of a circus in Austin, Texas. (Photo by Donald R. Winslow, *News Photographer Magazine*)

clashes in Israel between the Israeli army and Palestinian youth throwing rocks, the sound of gunfire was going off all the time. When the camera was pointed at the soldiers, the sound of the gunfire was loud, but when the camera was pointed away, toward the protesters, the gunfire sounded muffled. Obviously, the sound of gunfire was constant during the uprising, and the only reason the sound dipped in volume was that the camera and shotgun mic had been turned from the source of the sound. Is it ethical to transfer the sound of the gunfire to accompany all the footage of the clashes, whether the video showed the soldiers or the youth? If you were present during the conflict, you would have heard a steady rata-ta-tat beat of shots being fired regardless of the direction in which you were looking. Continuing the audio sound track with all video footage of the conflict was nearer to reality than having the sounds of gunfire fade in and fade out as they were actually recorded.

Some visual journalists see no problem with the practice of "sliding sound." Multimedia producer Sanhueza-Lyon in Texas says sliding sound from one image to another is a necessary technique: "Viewers have been programmed or educated to understand that in anything and everything they see, hear, read or view, some editing and some efforts at presentation have—at some level—taken place. It's *all* a construction of some kind or another".

The multimedia piece consisting of still images with narrative sound, for example, is by definition an artificial construction. Unless the photographer is capturing natural sound while shooting still images and is using the image time code and the audio time code to match them perfectly in presentation, it is an artificial combination of elements. The capturing of perfectly synchronized still images and separately recorded audio is highly unlikely. If it were to occur at all, it would merely be a happy accident.

NPPA's ethics chair, John Long, however, is very clear-cut in his opposition to sliding sound, whether in video or multimedia. He says there's no place for it in journalism. "Whether it's moving the sound of thunder closer to the image of a lightning bolt, or adding siren noise from another source, or rerecording audio after a still camera has stopped its annoying habit of making motor drive noise ... this is lying," he says. "If the initial audio fails, find another way (such as using a voice-over), but be careful not to create the impression with the viewer that the audio and visuals are from the same moments."

In the emerging field of videojournalism, handling audio raises questions that have different answers at different organizations. Some editors have no problem with sliding sound if it doesn't change the story, create a different reality, or deceive viewers. For some news organizations, sliding sound is an "editing" decision and not an "ethical" choice. Other journalists put their foot down on allowing this procedure at all.

If you're not working for an established organization and you're a solo videojournalist, you're going to have to decide on your own where to pitch your ethical tent because the industry has believers in both camps. If you feel you're deceiving your viewers, or if you would be uncomfortable with them knowing the methods you've used to create the combination of pictures and sound, don't make the dubious edit. Find another way around the problem.

MUSIC—PRESENT OR ADDED DURING EDITING?

Some video producers add music to the story after it has been shot to heighten the mood of a piece. Adding additional music that was not captured during the original shoot is controversial. Many documentaries use music added after the fact. *This American Life,* on PRI, often adds music to further the effect of the reporting. Of course you wouldn't want to add "Light My Fire" by the Doors to a story about a two-alarm blaze that occurred last night. Discretion and good taste must prevail.

KUSA-TV Denver veteran solo videojournalist Dave Delozier says that although music doesn't always exist in the field, he thinks viewers are smart enough to understand when music has been added to work with the feeling of the story.

FIGURE 12.10　**Dave Delozier** KUSA-TV's videojournalist. (Photo by Matt McClain)

"Does it work with the story or does it interfere with the story? If it works with the true feeling of the story and doesn't get in the way, I have no problem with the use of music in a feature story," Delozier says.

STAGING STILL GOES ON TODAY

First Lady Michelle Obama came to Camden Yards (a Baltimore baseball stadium) to encourage obese children to become more active. It was a highly organized public relations event,

FIGURE 12.11 Staging the Moment When First Lady Michelle Obama came to Baltimore, one of the network photographers yelled out during the event, "Can you make her play with the kids!" Was that okay?

and she was supposed to play with the kids. Instead of playing, she just stood with them and talked. But one of the network photographers yelled out during the event, 'Can you make her play with the kids!' "Aside from being very rude, it was completely unethical," says Darren Durlach, who worked for WBFF-TV in Baltimore.

Durlach points out that sometimes on shoots that involve an interview, a reporter or producer may ask the subject to do something like walk down a hall or to take a book down from a bookshelf. "I haven't gotten a shot like that in five years, and when I get back to the edit bay I've never said to myself, 'I wish I had a goofy shot of them walking down a hallway, it would really make this story.' I think shots like that make a story reek of fakeness."

So instead of asking the subject walk down the hallway, Durlach asks, "What would you be doing if we weren't here right now?" The takeaway for videojournalists: let the subject go back to his or her normal routine. Begin photographing once "normal" is back under way.

Still, the subject is doing something for the camera. Even if what he's doing is what he'd be doing normally, just being there shooting makes the situation contrived. The difference is subtle and may split hairs, but capturing images of someone doing what they'd normally be doing still is more honest and more accurate than fabricating a situation like walking down the hall for extra visuals that may be useful during the editing process.

Just sitting at a desk, "sitting there," as Durlach says, may not be visual fireworks, but it's more truthful than the total fabrication of asking someone to walk a particular way down a hallway.

"For me," says Durlach, "it comes down to doing my best to blend in and avoiding manipulation and influence over the scene. I find that the best approach is to try to stay out of the way and avoid giving direction even if the subject asks for some. Instead, I do my best to anticipate action and be prepared to shoot the breaking moment before the action happens. The moments I capture are much more genuine and natural than if I had created them.

"For instance, ask someone to pick up a phone so you can shoot them doing it and they'll do it in a way that will be trying to please you—which usually looks fairly awkward and unnatural. However, if you wait for the phone to ring and catch it on video as it happens, it will be natural. Sometimes keeping this mindset of limiting shooting to real moments makes for a slower shoot, but that's okay with me."

Former TV professional Heist, now a professor at the University of Maryland, says, "Knowing what to expect in any given situation will help you anticipate and be prepared for the action. Before shooting, I like to ask my subjects what I may expect to see while I am with them. It helps me anticipate what will happen so I don't miss the natural moments or become tempted to ask the subjects to do something for me."

TEST FOR ETHICS

Here are a couple of quick self-tests for trying to solve an ethical dilemma:

Test 1: "Am I comfortable with the viewer knowing how my images and audio were made?" If you, the videojournalist, can honestly answer that question with a frank "yes," then what you've done is probably okay.

Test 2: Test your decision by asking yourself, "Who benefits?" Often the manipulation you plan on making does not benefit the viewer but rather satisfies your own esthetic sensibility. "Does asking someone to walk down the hall a second time so you can shoot video you missed the first time really benefit the viewer?" Be careful that the decisions you make are made in order to improve viewers' ability to understand a story and not to impress your boss or win a prize.

CASE STUDIES

Here are two case studies to test your understanding of journalism ethics. After reading the facts of each case, ask yourself what you would have done in a similar situation before knowing the outcome of the case.

FAKE DOGFIGHT, REAL RAMIFICATIONS

Emmy Award-winning KCNC-TV reporter Windy Bergen and videographers Jim Stair and Scott Wright produced a four-part series on dog fighting called "Blood Sport." The series was to run on the NBC affiliate during "sweeps week," one of the three periods of time each year when viewership is measured to determine a station's annual ratings. Competition during sweeps can be fierce, because market ranking can determine advertising rates.

When authorities discovered that the trio had used footage of staged dogfights and dog training scenes for their series, not only did the reporter and videographers lose their jobs, but a grand jury probe also led to Bergen being charged with multiple counts of perjury. Because they attended the staged dogfights in order to film them, Stair and Wright also faced additional charges of dog fighting and conspiracy.

Wright and Stair both pled guilty to being an accessory to dog fighting and got probation. KCNC news director Marv Rockford was reprimanded for not adequately supervising his staff. Bergen was convicted of staging a dogfight, being an accessory to a dogfight, and conspiring to commit dog fighting. She was fined $20,000 from a maximum sentence of 10 years in prison and $300,000 in fines.

Bergen's ethical decision-making process was corrupted by the competition and pressure of sweeps week and by the pressure to maintain her award-winning reputation in a highly competitive TV market like Denver. "It was just one small, bad decision after another," Bergen told the *American Journalism Review*. "I knew it was wrong, but no one ever believed it would escalate to this level."

In hindsight, which is always 20/20, many ethical minefields can be seen clearly, but only after great damage has been done to journalism's reputation and careers ruined. Because of the "star" system embraced by many television network news operations, and this particular reporter's award-winning track record, at first her dog fighting stories, footage, and sources went largely unchallenged.

Also, had videojournalists researched their own legal standing, they would have learned that merely attending a dogfight was illegal and was not an activity protected by any First Amendment exemption. And the pressure-packed work environment of television news, which Bergen later characterized as a "two-minute review" of news stories by a line producer just before they air, certainly contributed to the ease of getting the fabricated package into the station's story lineup.

THE BRIEFCASE HAND-OFF

A famous example of an attempt at using a reenactment that turned out badly occurred in 1989 when ABC News on the *World News Tonight* broadcast featured ABC employees acting out a scene that depicted suspected spy and State Department employee Felix S. Bloch exchanging a briefcase with a Soviet diplomat. The constructed scene was based on words from an FBI document that said Bloch had been seen passing luggage to a known Soviet agent. In editing, the ABC film was treated to look like an FBI undercover tape, the original color video was turned into black-and-white footage, and the quality was decreased to make it look more grainy. Crosshairs were superimposed on the screen to make it look like surveillance film. During the East Coast broadcast at 6:30 p.m., the label "SIMULATION" was inadvertently dropped. "SIMULATION" was added to the 7:00 p.m. feed, but most of the country saw the first telecast, not the second.

Bloch was never charged with any crime. There was no trial, but he lost his government job. Although ABC News executives were split over whether they'd ever use the technique again, ABC News correspondent Sam Donaldson had no question in his mind that the technique was wrong and unethical.

"It's important not to mix straight reporting with things that are not factual," Donaldson told the *New York Times*. "People who saw that story are liable to say: 'I know Bloch's guilty. I saw him pass the briefcase.' Of course, they didn't see that at all."

FIGURE 12.12 **Too Big to Fail.** This docudrama was based on real events. Don't confuse docudramas that use actors with videojournalism, which records and presents the "real thing." (Directed and Produced by Curtis Hanson, HBO)

Most journalists now consider "simulations," even those labeled as "simulation" or "reenactment," to be unethical because any simulation—labeled or not—can mislead viewers. The danger, of course, in acting out a story is that doing so can lead viewers to conclude that something probably happened, and happened the way it was portrayed because, after all, "seeing is believing."

VIDEOJOURNALISM VERSUS DOCUDRAMAS

Many producers select reenactments of an historical event as the method of choice. Actors dress up, for instance, as 19th-century historic figures like Abraham Lincoln or Ulysses S. Grant and play parts and speak lines that the author thinks might have taken place 150 years ago. With actors in wigs and costumes, viewers will not mistake the scenes as the real thing. The result, a **docudrama**, is an amalgam of a documentary based on facts and a drama that adds fictional elements.

Movies, of course, often show reenactments of historical events—even some very recent news events. HBO, for instance, created a docudrama of the monetary crisis that almost brought a second Great Depression to the United States. The producers used famous actors playing living personalities. Based on the book by Andrew Ross Sorkin titled *Too Big to Fail,* the movie purported to show what happened in a series of closed meetings that took place in New York and Washington when the future of the U.S. economy was on the line. The movie

FIGURE 12.13 **Covering the Police in Action.** Police use pepper spray to keep protesters from crossing a line at California State University, Northridge, during a demonstration against the appearance of former Ku Klux Klan Grand Wizard David Duke. In the United States you can legally film the police or anyone else, even when they are making an arrest, as long as you are in a public place such as sidewalk, street, or park. (Pete Erickson, *Golden Gater*, San Francisco State University)

made clear that although it was based on fact, the docudrama was fiction played by actors including Paul Giamatti, William Hurt, Ed Asner, and others.

There is a vast difference between videojournalism (which records reality) and other forms of entertainment such as docudramas and "Hollywood" movies. The bottom line is that videojournalism rests on the ethical foundation that viewers can have absolute confidence that what they are watching took place. The videojournalist was there, on the scene, to record the moment as it is presented to the audience. Videojournalists don't invent anything. Viewers hear the actual voices of real characters. The people they are seeing are not scripted actors.

A videojournalism story is not a docudrama.

Journalism, photojournalism, and videojournalism get their power from showing the unmanipulated, raw, candid truth. If videojournalists cross the ethical line, viewers will question whether what they are seeing really happened—and may one day turn away from the medium altogether.

CHAPTER 13

You Really, Truly, Have to "Be There"

Video Journalism as a Social and Material Construction

Mary Angela Bock

News organizations are turning increasingly to video journalism as survival strategy in the era of convergence. Video journalism, the process by which one person shoots, writes, and edits video stories, represents both a socially and materially constructed form of news and adds a new dimension to daily work practices. This qualitative project examines the daily work practices of video journalists in a variety of organizational settings, including newspapers and television stations. This project found that the material requirements of video journalism have the potential to shift control of some aspects of news narrative away from journalists and toward their sources.

Video journalism is in many ways the human representation of convergent media. Although at one time there existed a division of labor within and among newsrooms, with some journalists specializing in the gathering of facts, others in the gathering of audio, and still others in the gathering of video or still images, the current environment demands that journalists do all of these things, often alone. Once limited to deployment in very small television markets and scorned as "one-man bands," video journalists now work in the largest metropolitan areas for television stations, radio networks, newspapers, and citizen activist groups.[1] What happens when one person shoots, writes, narrates, edits, and, in some cases, posts those stories to the web alone? Are the adjustments limited to practice or does the product change as well?

VIDEO JOURNALISM ORIGINS

The trade press for photojournalism has covered the spread of video journalism extensively, but the topic has received less attention in the academic literature. Nevertheless, many sociological and cultural studies of journalistic practice can help contextualize this study.

"One-man bands," as they've sometimes been derisively named, have long existed in the world of local television news. Generally, singleperson newsgathering was the norm in smaller markets: journalists would shoot, write, and edit alone with the goal of eventually working their way into larger markets to work as part of a team with a video photographer and (much longer ago) sound technicians.[2] Conventional television newsgathering in the United States commonly uses heavier cameras than those used by those who call themselves "MMJs" (multimedia journalists), "BPJs" (backpack journalists), "Solojos" (solo journalists), "Mojos" (mobile journalists), or, most simply and with the phrase that will be used here, "video journalists" or "VJs."[3]

The term *video journalism* can be traced to a former network television producer, Michael Rosenblum, who used it to title an adjunct course he taught at Columbia University in the late 1980s.[4] Rosenblum also established a short-lived international news network using only VJs, called Video News International.[5] *News Photographer,* the professional trade magazine for the National Press Photographers Association, started using the phrase regularly in 2005,[6] and in 2006, the organization announced a new category for (solo) video journalists in its annual *Best of Photojournalism* contest.[7]

Today it is hard to find a media organization or market that is not adopting some form of video journalism. Two features distinguish its practice from other forms of news production. First, it is a *singular practice,* in that one person shoots, writes, and edits the entire piece. Secondly, it combines intangible, discursive practices, such as writing or interviewing, with *material* practices involving the body in interaction with the realtime environment.

NEWS PRACTICE AND NARRATIVES

The proposition that journalism is a social construction defined by human practice, hardly new, remains useful for scholarly inquiry. One approach has concentrated on the sociology of the professions and the degree to which journalists conform to group norms and ethical ideals.[8] Other scholars use a critical or cultural lens, noting the ways journalists shape their practices to maintain an "interpretive community" whose work, in the words of Riegert and Olson, serves to "reinforce the legitimacy of journalists as central actors in the mediation of truth."[9] Conceptualizing news as a construction has led to rich ethnographies that explain how the day-to-day nature of news work shapes its product.[10]

Gatekeeping theory has also been especially helpful for investigating the way happenings and events are sorted through, categorized, and chosen for presentation.[11] Sigal found that gatekeeping routines caused about half of the stories for national newspapers to originate from "routine" channels, such as news releases or wire services.[12] Television research has also shown that the need for visuals constitutes a critical "gate," leading to a preference for easily found and shot events, such as fires and car accidents.[13]

The impact of new technologies on news practice has inspired its own strand of scholarship.[14] Studies of convergent newsrooms have not only examined the way general work routines have adjusted in the wake of Internet technology, but the ways various journalistic subcultures, i.e., print and television, are contending with one another. For example, Deuze and Singer focused on the dynamics of the newsroom in light of role convergence, new pressure, and the clash of organizational cultures that occurs when lifelong print journalists suddenly work side-by-side with their former competitors from television.[15]

Few scholarly works focus on photojournalists and the related, oft-neglected tension between word-based practices, such as writing and fact-checking, and material practices, such as attending meetings or photographing events.[16] Gatekeeping studies tend to focus on the intangible choices made regarding story topics, facts, or photo-publication.[17] Accounts of decisions in the field by individual photojournalists are usually confined to biographies or discussions of photo ethics.[18] Constructivist accounts of journalism tend to focus on the flexibility of language in its presentation of discourse, without adequate attention to the role of the "body" in news work. This is problematic, since journalists often use "witnessing" as a source of their authority even though writing a story does not necessarily require bodily presence.[19] Zelizer found that claims of journalistic witnessing were often not tied to actual physical witnessing at all.[20] Indeed, reporters often use the phone to collect information and, in some cases, use video monitors to cover legislatures or major speeches remotely.[21] Some scholars are concerned that the contemporary media environment is diminishing the gatekeeping role of journalists as the relationship between the audience and news organizations becomes increasingly porous.[22]

Even in the tumultuous context of twenty-first century journalism, however, individual journalists continue to make choices regarding words, phrases, shots, and angles—choices that limit options further down the gatekeeping chain—and these choices are significant to the overall product.[23] For journalists who work with images, these choices are in the *material*, physical realm as often as they are the intangible. The ontology of a photographic image is rooted, in part, in this material nature, which *can be best thought of as that moment in which a human body, using technology, interacts with the physical environment in a specific moment of time.* Such moments are ephemeral. Cartier-Bresson imbued such "decisive moments" with mythic qualities.[24] This study attempts to ignore the romance, and focuses instead on the intersection of body-camera-time-place, the role it plays in photographic meaning, and its implications for the practice of video journalism. More specifically, this study focuses on the following research questions:

RQ1: How does the process of video journalism compare with other forms of news work?

RQ1a: How does the material nature of photographic work affect the process?

RQ1b: How does the singular nature of the work, that is, the way one person shoots, writes, and edits the story, affect the process?

RQ2: How might the process of video journalism affect its product?

As Zelizer has pointed out, the newsroom study has become, in many ways, an "overused frame."[25] Especially for the study of video journalists, it seems essential for attention to be shifted to their individual, daily, and material routines in the field as well.

METHOD

This study endeavors to provide a rich understanding of video journalism and its routines. It combines ethnographic methods, such as participant observation and long-form interviews, with qualitative analysis of the stories produced by the VJs under observation.

Data were collected over the course of two years using a strategic sample designed to allow for comparison of organizations and institutions. The corpus includes ninety-three extended interviews with VJs, would-be VJs, photojoumalists, newsroom managers, trainers, reporters, and public relations representatives who coordinated with VJs. The loosely structured interviews included questions about the subjects' background, how they came to be video journalists, their daily routines, and the equipment they use. The sample represented men and women, large markets and small, with career experience ranging from beginner to near retirement. In nearly all cases, VJs were questioned about their specific decision-making process for a particular story, while viewing stories together in person or online.

The BBC's news training center was among the observational sites, as the publicly funded institution was one of the first in the world to experiment with video journalism in its local newsrooms. Data were collected at the BBC's training facility in Newcastle upon Tyne, its local news operation in Oxford (staffed by VJs), and its local news operation in Bristol (partly staffed with VJs). Other observational sites included a week-long field visit to a training session sponsored by an ownership group for its newspaper staff to learn about video, the video unit at the *New York Times,* a large-market all-VJ cable news operation, and a local television station which hires VJs and traditional photographers. VJs were observed in the field covering such events as a community news conference, a political rally, an urban shooting and a teenager's funeral.

FINDINGS AND DISCUSSION

No matter where they worked, no matter whether they came from a print or broadcast background, VJs were found to follow a similar cyclical process. Data from the interviews and observations were instrumental in answering the first set of research questions, that is, how video journalism compares with other forms of newsgathering and how its materiality and singularity affect its practice. Their stories served to inform the second research question, regarding how the process affects the product.

First, to answer the first research question, *"How does the process of video journalism compare with other forms of newswork?"* and its sub-questions regarding the impact of materiality and singularity on the process, it is helpful to briefly describe the routine for a typical VJ.

One VJ's Day. [NC] works for a middle-market commercial broadcast television station in the northeastern United States. During the newsroom's editorial morning meeting, [NC] was assigned to produce a story about a local school building that had been declared an historic site. This information was in a newspaper story that the assignment editor clipped for consideration during the station's morning planning session. (Assignment editors are the logistical managers of coverage for television newsrooms.) Both [NC] and her managers *pre-conceptualized the story.*[26] In this case, the situation is pre-conceptualized as a story about the way buildings are designated as historic. Since she knew of at least one other architecturally unique and old school building in the city, [NC] decided to add a bit more to what would otherwise be a simple feature story, by contrasting the school that was designated as historic (which is in a wealthy, privileged district) with one from a less privileged urban center *not* on the historic registry.

During this time at her desk, [NC] made the phone calls necessary to arrange for interviews and access to the building—to *locate and access the elements* needed to construct the story as it was pre-conceptualized. Soon [NC] was packing her photographic equipment, a tote with hair care and cosmetic items, and a portable GPS unit (paid for out of her own pocket, something she considers a good investment for the time and trouble it saves her each day). [NC] explained that since she's solo, her schedule is tight: "Everybody's day revolves around time. Mine does even more so ... My goal every single day is to be back in the station by 3 o'clock ... If I'm not out the door by noon I get nervous."

On this day, the pressure was manageable: the school granted her access early, and she was there by 11 a.m. She immediately assessed the scene, unloaded her camera, and set up her tripod on the lawn to begin *shooting* some exterior shots of the school. Minutes later when the representative came out to greet her, [NC] collected her equipment to go inside for more B-ROLL (illustrative video) and interviews with school representatives. The school's communication officer did not know very much about the historic designation process, something a bit disappointing to [NC]. She was still working with the pre-conceptualization of a story that highlighted the conflict between rich and poor, while the communications officer seemed more interested in highlighting the bell tower's architectural features.

By 12:45, [NC] was on her way back to the station to *narrativize* her elements, re-contextualizing them into a linear story structure that combined her voice, clips from the interviews she collected, and illustrative images of the school buildings. She edited on a computer system in a small windowless room (to better view computer screens) and spent about an hour crafting a story that was not much more than a minute long.

At 5 p.m., she *presented* her story during the newscast, another form of re-contextualization. [NC] stood in the studio, where she was introduced by a studio anchor, and presented her own live introduction. After her brief time in the studio, she returned to her desk to create a web version of her story. When she finished around 6 p.m., she had worked straight through without a lunch break. Nevertheless, she considered this to have been "a nice, neat day."

Unpacking the Process. The steps that [NC] and other informants followed in their daily routines can be described as follows:

1. Pre-conceptualizing a story based on preliminary information and news norms
2. Locating and gaining access to interviews, happenings, or scenes
3. Recording those interviews, happenings, and scenes
4. Arranging those elements into narrative form
5. Re-contextualizing the story into a presentation for an audience[27]

This process is not unlike the one identified by Bantz, McCorkle, and Baade in their description of TV news production for an organization.[28] The steps described here, however, pertain to the *individual* work of a video journalist. The data reveal some crucial differences for a solo video journalist compared with other news workers, particularly in light of the material and singular nature of their routines.

(1) Pre-Conceptualizing the Story. As many newsroom scholars have observed, the demands of a medium's form (Altheide calls it "media logic") determine how journalists decide what stories to tell and how to narrativize a particular set of circumstances.[29] Thus, highly visual fires or automobile crashes are considered "news" for local television, while stories involving abstract economic concepts are traditionally considered better for print. For video journalists, this factor goes beyond merely *part* of the definition to being *central* to the definition of news. Their entire day's work product is built around images that they collect.

Having a narrative pre-conceptualization also favors events that can be presented as unusual or as conflicts, with interesting characters and action. Another VJ, [NQ] made the choice of taking an hour-long round trip for an interview that would add an opposing view to his story about the Love Canal anniversary, and as seen above, [NC] built her narrative around a conflict between rich and poor school districts.

The data indicate that working alone and the physical demands of their work cause pre-conceptualizations for video journalists to be rather rigid. At [NBHD CABLE], [ES] was assigned to cover the funeral of a shooting that killed a promising high school athlete, a type of story that is sadly common in urban areas. He wrote his entire script before leaving his newsroom to shoot a frame. He joked that it's "cheating," but it is common practice for certain types of stories, and it can be done because of the way stories are so tightly pre-conceptualized according to a formula. [HT], who works for a television station and must construct a story every day (three versions of it, in fact) also plans out his stories in detail before leaving the station: "You need to know how you're going to approach it and do it, partly because as a VJ you have so little time to do everything yourself, you have to pre-decide how you're going to do it before you can leave the building or the meeting, or you won't make your deadline. It's not like the old days when you'd go out and see what was actually happening and then decide how to cover it."

(2) Locating & Gaining Access to Elements. Once the narrative is preconceptualized, its elements must be identified and located. Such elements include the audio and video

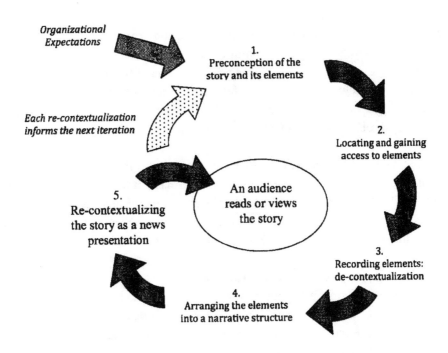

FIGURE 13.1   The Video Journalism Process

Note that the process is self-renewing in that the presentational recontextualization informs the pre-conception phase.

recordings of tangible objects: the setting(s), happenings, or relevant action; the objects or examples acted upon, and the human "characters" whose actions and/or interviews help constitute the story. Note the way these tangible elements line up with the very basic components of narrative.[30] The added burden for a video journalist is that these components *must somehow be represented visually.* The components must somehow be recorded in order to be rearranged. With the exception of typed title graphics (and the use of file tape), each element must be recorded with the camera, which, of course, requires the VJ to be able to be materially present.

Several instances noted during observational visits indicate that while a story's pre-conception drives the overall process, it is malleable and might be re-considered in the face of material considerations. For instance, when [LT] was assigned to cover the presidential primary as experienced by people in the Bronx, she first tried to reach Democratic Party leaders in the area. They would not, and could not, be interviewed. [LT] still had an assignment. So, after consulting with her managers, she decided to base her story on the way local high school (nonvoting age) students were learning about the primary because she was able easily to gain access to a private school.

For many print reporters, "access" is largely a metaphor for being able to reach and talk to the right sources. For video journalists, however, access is both a matter of physical loco-motion and social interaction. Traveling to and getting close enough to elements in order to photograph them often takes more time than the shooting process itself. Most informants drove some sort of news car and printed out directions from an Internet mapping site as part of their routine. [NQ] spent more time driving to one of his interviews than actually conducting the interview, cutting his time for writing and editing the story very close to deadline. Traveling from location to location efficiently and on time was not only a source of stress for the VJs observed, but a factor that influenced their choices of where to go and whom to interview.

(3) *Shooting.* Once a VJ has access to shoot the elements required for a narrative, a series of technical, mechanical, and aesthetic choices must be made in what is essentially a process of de-contextualization. A VJ pulls pieces from the environment he hears and sees in order to construct a filmic story; he is the human bridge between scene and viewer. This step has considerable impact on the overall gatekeeping process of story construction, and requires both discursive and material decisions. As Shoemaker and Vos note, "... perhaps the most important aspect of gate-keeping is that issues and events that are not covered are absent from the worldviews of most audience members."[31] What was chosen depended on story pre-conceptions, of course, but it was also guided by aesthetic and informational criteria. Certain portions of the scene might be relevant to the story at hand, for example, [NCJ]'s historic school building. She chose to shoot her wide shots of the building from the school's lawn and not across the street in order to reveal only the building and not the parked cars in front of it. Other choices may be based on symbolic understandings. A VJ might choose to replicate a culturally relevant visual trope, such as a soldier cradling a child in the manner of the Pietà, or firefighters at the World Trade Center site hoisting a flag at ground zero in the same manner as the soldiers portrayed by Joe Rosenthal at Iwo Jima,[32]

The essential difference between a literary narrative and a VJ narrative is a matter of *materiality:* objects, actions, and happenings in a filmic narrative must somehow be illustrated or described audibly using artifacts constructed by a human operating in concert with a camera. If the story is a profile of a local barista, at some point the VJ must shoot video of *a* cup of coffee being made; if the story is about an abstract concept such as "unemployment," the VJ must find a way to illustrate the abstraction, usually by recording video of people in line at an unemployment office, or filling out applications at a job fair. VJs cannot do any of this remotely; they must physically interact with the environment. One veteran VJ-turned-manager [NJ] goes so far as to call a VJ's body part of the gear pack.

Some of the skills that further differentiate VJs from other news workers are somewhat unusual: opening doors while holding a tripod, steadying a camera when the tripod isn't available, or knowing how to shoot one's own standup (a presentation in the story where the reporter appears). Finally, the demands of working alone constituted a source of stress. Every VJ who participated in this study reported the work to be physically taxing. [CH] and [KB], who have decades-long careers in solo-filmmaking, acknowledge that they have had to stay in shape. [KB] and his staff do calisthenics as part of their work routine. [CH]: "It's really physical ... This is a craft that demands not only intellectual capacity but real physical stamina and a lot of people are not going to be able to do this simply because they haven't got the stamina."

The chief complaint seemed not to be the equipment itself, but of *manipulating* that equipment on site and contending with transportation issues.

(4) Narrativizing. Once a VJ has recorded the necessary elements to compose a narrative that can be understood by others, the physical work of narrativizing can begin. The word *narrativize* distinguishes this process from vocally narrating a story, which might or might not be part of a particular VJ's process. All VJs, however, must narrativize, or create a linear sequence of sound and images that is understood as a news story. There are two dimensions to the work of editing a video narrative: the physical and mechanical work that employs digital software, and the textual work of composing a narrative. Narrativizing a video story may or may not require VJs to actually type up a script or plan, but they must have a mental plan (rooted, of course, in their original pre-conception) of a narrative as they start reviewing their tape and downloading it into their edit system.

VJs observed while in training often reported this to be one of the most challenging aspects of the process. Shooting video is hardly special anymore now that the smallest pocket cameras and even cell phones can record clips, but video editing on a computer requires a more extensive skill set. When [DT] started, he'd spend hours in the editing room until he learned how to better manage his time: "... when I first started doing them I was, you know, trying to be Martin Scorsese on every one of these things—and I realized, first of all, that's not what's required, second of all, I can't do that."

The training session for newspaper journalists devoted far more time to digital editing than to camera technique, and more than one informant expressed frustration with the system. Once conquered, however, informants also reported a level of pleasure in creating multilayered stories.

(5) Re-contextualizing. Video stories are re-contextualized anew when they are put into a presentation by an exhibiting organization. Turow identified exhibition as one of the primary activities of media organizations, which have historically been divided according to their presentational form: newspapers delivered news printed on paper, and television news was presented as a scheduled program?[33] This is changing in the twenty-first century as all media converge to the web production, but old divisions remain. Procedural and intra-cultural differences rooted in historic divisions were observed in the various organizations employing VJs. Newspaper VJs send their work to a website, but in concert with the printed form of the newspaper. VJs at [MID-TV] post their stories to the web *after* those stories are broadcast within a news program. The timing for posting or broadcasting stories ranges from a system without hard deadlines, granting the VJ freedom to decide when a story is ready for view, to very stringent and demanding daily deadlines, which force a VJ to adjust work practices to fit those demands. The amount of time a story can run also varied, with newspaper VJs having the greatest freedom to give their stories some longer creative elements.

SUMMARY

The process of video journalism differs from other forms of news work because of its singular and material characteristics. VJs working alone created production plans before starting their work. The material and singular demands of die work made it physically taxing, occasionally stressful. More important, perhaps, materiality and singularity affected the way VJs planned and executed their stories.

The Product. So far, this discussion has focused on the first research question, regarding process. The second question (How might the process of video journalism affect its product?) remains. From the perspective of the viewing audience, this may be the question that matters most, and the data point to three story trends.

Tighter Pre-conception. For VJs who are expected to produce a story a day (or more), the first step of "pre-conception" was intensified. Generally speaking, *the more constraining the demands of the final presentation, the more intensely a VJ will work within the mental framework of a pre-conceptualization.* Because they work alone, VJs report they are more likely to look for quick and easy access to story elements and less likely to stray from their pre-conceptualization. Rather than being empowered to take chances with smaller cameras and simpler software, television VJs contend they have *less freedom* to take chances with their stories. That's not to say that video journalism does not open possibilities for new sorts of narratives; newspaper VJs are trying to break new ground. VJs who do not produce a story a day can be flexible, but organizations that demand daily filings seem less likely to foster innovation.

Greater Dependence on Sources. Because video journalism requires material access to locations and events, those who hold power to open the literal gates have considerable influence on whether a story idea lives or dies. Without access to an amusement park, [UI] would not have been able to produce his feature story (though a print reporter could simply write for pages). VJs were observed spending considerable time negotiating and arranging for access to locations, and they changed topics when denied that access. This serves to shift more power into the hands of sources who control locations, thereby generating an even greater reliance on what Boorstin called "pseudo" events.[34] True, for some VJs a smaller camera was helpful in getting past authorities in countries with less press freedom, but for day-to-day newsgathering, controlling space was tantamount to controlling the narrative.

Narrative Freedom. The video journalists who reported the greatest satisfaction with their jobs were those without daily deadlines. Those who worked for newspapers, while frustrated in some ways by technical difficulties, found it liberating to be able to add a visual or aural dimension to their stories. Without a daily deadline, they were able to create the type of stories that video journalism's proponents advocate: intimate, slower-moving narratives that "breathe." Their stories could be longer than those on television, could be posted to the web only when the subject matter compelled multi-media treatment, and could use a variety of narrative techniques. While giving a detailed presentation on how to use a video camera, tripod, and microphone cables, one veteran newspaper VJ proclaimed, without irony, "This is not TV," and, indeed, the stories newspaper VJs produce for the web often have a very different look and feel from the typical TV newscast.

CONCLUSION

The news industry's current financial downturn is likely to continue to foster a reliance on video journalists who can multitask. As video journalism's proponents have noted, there are creative advantages to having one person shoot, write, and edit stories for the web that go beyond economics. Having the skill to marry video, sound, text, or graphics according to the demands of a story can enhance the journalistic product, and some informants report enjoying more narrative freedom.

This study also presents a cautionary tale in that it locates trends that run counter to journalistic ideals. The singular and material nature of video journalism can intensify the need to rely on formula and craft simple stories with easy access to visuals (what's known in newsroom lingo as "one-stop shopping"). It also shifts more power over a story's construction to image handlers. As video journalism continues to grow as a profession, it is essential for journalistic institutions to prevent what might be a cheaper way to produce news into cheapening the product.

NOTES

1. Paul J. Gough, "ABC News Opening One-Man Foreign Bureaus," *Yahoo News/Reuters*, October 3, 2007; Brian Stelter and Bill Carter, "ABC News to Cut Hundreds of Staff," *New York Times*, February 23, 2010, sec. B, p. 5.
2. Throughout this paper, the word "photographer" is used to describe the work of still and video photographers. When a distinction is necessary the preface still- or video- is added.
3. Peter H. Martyn, "The Mojo in the Third Millenium," *Journalism Practice* 3 (2, 2009): 196–215.
4. Michael Rosenblum, personal communication, June 23, 2008.
5. Rosenblum, personal communication, 2008.
6. As determined by a text search using the terms "video journalist," "video journalism," "mobile journalist/ism" and "backpack journalist/ism."
7. Merry Murray, "Best of Photojournalism 2007 TV Contest Rule Changes and Additions," National Press Photographers Association, http://www.nppa.org/news_and_events/news/2006/11/2007_tv_bop_rules.html (accessed January 12, 2011).
8. Mark Deuze, "What Is Journalism?" *Journalism* 6 (4, 2005): 442–64; Mark Deuze, "What Is Multimedia Journalism?" *Journalism Studies* 5 (2, 2004): 139–52; Michael Schudson, *Discovering the News: A Social History of American Newspapers* (NY: Basic Books, 1978); Michael Schudson, "The Objectivity Norm in American Journalism," *Journalism* 2 (2, 2001): 149–70; Michael Schudson, *The Sociology of News* (NY: Norton, 2003); Jane B. Singer, "The Political J-Blogger: 'Normalizing' a New Media Form to Fit Old Norms and Practices," *Journalism* 6 (2, 2005): 173–98; Jane B. Singer, "Who Are These Guys? The Online Challenge to the Notion of Journalistic Professionalism," *Journalism* 4 (2, 2003): 139–63.
9. Kristina Riegert and Eva-Karin Olsson, "The Importance of Ritual in Crisis Journalism," in *Cultural Meanings of News: A Text-Reader*, ed. Daniel A. Berkowitz (Thousand Oaks, CA: Sage 2009), 137–50, 140; Stuart Allan, "News from Now Here: Televisual News and the Construction of Hegemony," in *Approaches to Media Discourse*, ed. Allan Bell and Peter Garrett (Oxford, UK: Blackwell, 1998); Todd Gitlin, *The Whole World Is Watching: Mass Media in the Making and Unmaking of the New Left* (Berkeley: University of California Press, 1980); Singer, "The Political J-Blogger"; Barbie Zelizer, "Journalists as Interpretive Communities," *Critical Studies in Mass Communication* 10

(3,1993): 219–37; Barbie Zelizer, *Taking Journalism Seriously: News and the Academy* (Thousand Oaks, CA: Sage, 2004).

10 Charles R. Bantz, Suzanne McCorkle, and Roberta Baade, "The News Factory," *Communication Research* 7 (1, 1980): 45–68; Herbert Gans, *Deciding What's News: A Study of CBS Evening News, NBC Nightly News, Newsweek and Time, 25th Anniversary Edition* (NY: Random House, 2004); Gaye Tuchman, *Making News: A Study in the Construction of Reality* (London: Macmillan, 1978).

11 Pamela J. Shoemaker, *Gatekeeping* (Thousand Oaks, CA: Sage, 1991); Pamela J. Shoemaker and Tim P. Vos, *Gatekeeping Theory* (NY: Routledge, 2009).

12 Leon Sigal, *Reporters and Officials: The Organization and Politics of Newsmaking* (Lexington, MA: DC Heath, 1973).

13 Phyllis Kaniss, *Making Local News* (Chicago: University of Chicago Press, 1991); Steven Livingston and Lance W. Bennett, "Gatekeeping, Indexing and Live-Event News: Is Technology Altering the Construction of News?" *Political Communication* 20 (4, 2007): 363–80.

14 Pablo Boczkowski, *Digitizing the News: Innovation in Online Newspapers* (Cambridge, MA: The MIT Press, 2004); Deuze, "What Is Multimedia Journalism?"; Deuze, "What Is Journalism?"; Edgar Huang, Karen Davison, Stephanie Shreve, Twila Davis, Elizabeth Bettendorf, and Anita Nair, "Bridging Newsrooms and Classrooms: Preparing the Next Generation of Journalists for Converged Media," *Journalism Communication Monographs* 8 (3,2006): 221–62; Martyn, "The Mojo in the Third Millenium"; Sara Platon and Mark Deuze, "Indymedia Journalism," *Journalism* 4 (3, 2003): 336–55; Stephen Quinn, *Convergent Journalism* (NY: Peter Lang, 2005); Singer, "The Political J-Blogger"; Singer, "Who Are These Guys?"; Blu Tirohl, "The Photo-Journalist and the Changing News Image," *New Media and Society* 2 (3, 2000): 335–52.

15 Platon and Deuze, "Indymedia Journalism"; Deuze, "What Is Multimedia Journalism?"; Deuze, "What Is Journalism?"; Singer, "The Political J-Blogger"; Singer, "Who Are These Guys?"

16 Karin Becker-Ohm, "How Photographs Become News: Photo-journalists at Work" (paper presented at the annual meeting of AEJMC, Corvallis, OR, 1983); D. M. Lindekugel, *Shooters: TV News Photographers and Their Work* (Westport, CT: Praeger, 1994); Barbara Rosenblum, *Photographers and Their Photographs: An Empirical Study in the Sociology of Aesthetics* (Thesis, Northwestern University, 1973); Dona Schwartz, "To Tell the Truth: Codes of Objectivity in Journalism," *Communication* (2, 1992): 95–109; Dona Schwartz, "Objective Representation: Photographs as Facts," in *Picturing the Past*, ed. Bonnie Brennen and Hanno Hardt (Urbana: University of Illinois Press, 1999), 158–81.

17 Kimberly L. Bissell, "A Return to 'Mr. Gates': Photography and Objectivity," *Newspaper Research Journal* 21 (3, 2000): 81–93; William P. Cassidy, "Gatekeeping Similar for Online, Print Journalists," *Newspaper Research Journal* 27 (spring 2006): 6–23.

18 Pierre Assouline, *Henri Cartier-Bresson: A Biography* (NY: Thames and Hudson, 2005); John G. Morris, *Get the Picture* (Chicago: University of Chicago Press, 2002); Julianne H. Newton, *The Burden of Visual Truth: The Role of Photojournalism in Mediating Reality* (Mahwah, NJ: Erlbaum, 2001).

19 John Durham Peters, "Witnessing," *Media, Culture and Society* 23 (6, 2001): 707–23; Barbie Zelizer, "On 'Having Been There': Eyewitnessing as a Journalistic Key Word," *Critical Studies in Media Communication* 24 (5, 2007): 408–28.

20 Zelizer, "On 'Having Been There.'"

21 Mary Angela Bock, "Who's Minding the Gate? Pool Feeds, Video Subsidies and Political Images," *International Journal of Press and Politics* (2, 2009): 257–78.

22 Eran N. Ben-Porath, "Internal Fragmentation of the News," *Journalism Studies* 8 (3, 2007): 414–31; Bruce Williams and Michael X. Delli Carpini, "Unchained Reaction: The Collapse of Media Gatekeeping and the Clinton-Lewinsky Scandal," *Journalism* 1 (1, 2000): 61–85.

23 Shoemaker and Vos, *Gatekeeping Theory*.

24 Henri Cartier-Bresson, *The Decisive Moment* (NY: Simon and Schuster, 1952).

25 Zelizer, *Taking Journalism Seriously*; Zelizer, "On 'Having Been There.'"

26 Identified as "story ideation" by Bantz, McCorkle, and Baade, "The News Factory."

27 To which, of course, the audience brings its own pre-conceptions for decoding the story.

28 Bantz, McCorkle, and Baade, "The News Factory."

29 David L. Altheide, "The Format of TV Network News," in *The Focused Screen,* ed. Jose Vidal-Beneyto and Peter Dahlgren (Strasbourg, France: AMELA/Council of Europe, 1987); David L. Altheide and Robert P. Snow, *Media Logic* (Thousand Oaks, CA: Sage, 1979); Kevin G. Bamhurst and John Nerone, *The Form of News* (NY: The Guilford Press, 2001); Dan Berkowitz, "Refining the Gatekeeping Metaphor for Local Television News," *Journal of Broadcasting and Electronic Media* 34 (1,1990): 55–68; Kaniss, *Making Local News.*

30 Seymour Chatman, *Story and Discourse: Narrative Structure in Fiction and Film* (Ithaca, NY: Cornell University Press, 1978); Seymour Chatman, *Coming to Terms: The Rhetoric of Narrative in Fiction and Film* (Ithaca: Cornell University Press 1990); Luc Herman and Bart Vervaeck, *Handbook of Narrative Analysis* (Lincoln: University of Nebraska Press, 2005).

31 Shoemaker and Vos, *Gatekeeping Theory,* 4.

32 Charles A. Hill and Marguerite H. Helmers, *Defining Visual Rhetorics* (Mahwah, NJ: Erlbaum, 2004); John Huxford, "Beyond the Referential: Uses of Visual Symbolism in the Press," *Journalism* 2 (1, 2001): 45–71.

33 Joseph Turow, *Media Today,* 2d ed. (Boston: Houghton Mifflin, 2003).

34 Daniel Boorstin, *The Image: A Guide to Pseudo Events in America* (NY: Harper and Row, 1961).

CHAPTER 14

Ethical Photojournalism in the Age of the Electronic Darkroom

Nigel Warburton

In the sceptical phase of his *Meditations,* René Descartes entertains the possibility that all his experiences might have been caused by the artifice of an evil demon: 'I will suppose that the heavens, the air, the earth, colours, shapes, sounds and all external things that we see are only illusions and deceptions which he uses to take me in.'[1] This evil demon manipulates Descartes's sensory inputs to give a convincing illusion of direct engagement with reality. Descartes gets the same sort of experiences he would have had had they been caused by engagement with reality; but it is all the work of the demon.

The evil demon finds its modern equivalent in the cynical photojournalist or picture editor who uses new electronic technology to manipulate what the viewer of a news photograph sees. Sophisticated computer technology which converts an image to pixels, each of which can be electronically controlled, allows almost anyone to manipulate photographs convincingly.[2] In a matter of minutes two photographs can be combined seamlessly to give the illusion that, for instance, John Major was rubbing shoulders with Tony Blair, when in fact they were standing on opposite sides of the room. Or, as actually occurred, two pyramids can be shunted electronically closer together in order to fit the portrait cover format of *National Geographic*[3]. Inconvenient details can be extracted without leaving any indication that they were ever there, and new details can be added from other photographs. In fashion photography it is now common practice for the photographs of models to be electronically altered: the pupils of their eyes are often enlarged, or their legs lengthened. We can't trust what we see in photographs any more.

Perhaps the only rational strategy in such circumstances is the Cartesian one of treating as false any belief acquired from looking at photographs, unless we can be absolutely certain that it is true. We have plenty of evidence that the demon-like picture editor is likely, on occasion, to deceive us. This casts doubt on the whole assumption of veracity which has traditionally been the starting-point of reputable photojournalism.

In newspaper and magazine journalism photography has traditionally played a major role, providing visual and memorable evidence for what the accompanying text described. War photography, for instance, illustrated more immediately than print ever could commonplace horrors and individual suffering. The Vietnam War lingers in many of our memories as a series of still photographs which provided evidence of particular events, but at the same time symbolised needless loss of life and cruelty. Malcolm Brown's image of a Buddhist monk's protest self-immolation, Eddie Adams's still of a police chief in Saigon executing a Vietcong officer with his pistol, and, of course, Huyn Cong Ut's unforgettable photograph of a naked girl, burnt by napalm, running towards the camera: these and other images had a profound effect on how that war was understood. But their effect depended upon their being reliable as documentary evidence for what they appeared to depict. Without the causal link back to a real event, these images would have been simply manufactured propaganda and would not have had the eyewitness status that they in fact did have. Readers of the magazines and newspapers in which they appeared quite reasonably took these to be photographs of real events, presenting in a legible way images of what actually happened. The convention of interpreting news photographs was based on trust: trust that the photographer wasn't duping picture editors about what his or her photographs really showed.

Now, in the age of the electronic darkroom, the informed viewer of a photograph should be sceptical about its origins, or perhaps even acknowledge that the old conventions of photography were based on an outdated cliché which we can no longer accept, that the camera never lies. In other words, from today photojournalism is dead. Theorists such as William J. Mitchell suggest that we have already moved into a post-photographic era.[4] It's just a matter of time before the newspaper-reading public catches on. Or so the story goes.

But this pessimistic view is mistaken. It is based on myths about the nature of photojournalism and the kinds of evidence it can provide, and about the kinds of evidence it has traditionally provided. The more optimistic line I want to take is that new technology should force photographers and picture editors to be far more aware of the moral implications of their practices.[5] Far from signalling the death of photojournalism, and particularly of ethical photojournalism, the electronic revolution could be the catalyst for its rejuvenation.

IS NEW PHOTOGRAPHY DIFFERENT FROM OLD?

The claim that we are moving into a post-photographic era is based on the belief that electronic photography is fundamentally different from its opticochemical forebears. With the new technology, so the argument goes, a new relationship between object, image and viewer is set up, and so the conventions surrounding photographic image production and reception must be transformed accordingly. The relevant features of new photography that distinguish it from old photography are:

(1) *Ease of manipulation*: Whilst the manipulation of photographs by means of cropping, dodging, burning in, composite printing and a whole range of darkroom procedures, has been possible for most of photography's history, the electronic darkroom facilitates such manipulation to an unprecedented degree. For instance, in order to produce a plausible photographic image of a footballer committing a handball offence in the penalty area, using as raw material a photograph of the same footballer with the ball at his feet, you would, if you used traditional opticochemical methods, have to be a skilled photographic technician.

Another way of producing a similar effect would be to use an airbrush; but, again, you would have to have quite a high level of skill to do this in a way that would be convincing. With computer-assisted manipulation of images, this sort of transformation of a photograph is relatively straightforward even for a novice. It could probably be done in a few minutes. One consequence of this is that virtually anyone with access to the appropriate machines can perform this sort of transformation.

(2) *Undetectability*: This has two aspects. First, the ways in which an image has been manipulated electronically can be undetectable. Seamless collage is a genuine possibility with the new media, whereas it was something less frequently achieved with the old. In the above example, no evidence of the original position of the ball would remain. Second, the electronic dark-room need not leave anything that you can go back to to check the accuracy of the print. Unlike the traditional forms of photography which, Polaroids and slides apart, left a negative as a touchstone against which subsequent manipulations of an image could be measured, video stills cameras need not leave any such objects. An edited picture file need not reveal that it has been edited, and the original can simply be deleted. Thus anyone attempting to demonstrate how an electronically produced photographic image has been manipulated has a difficult task.

(3) *Change from analogue to digital*: Traditional photographs are analogues of what they represent: every variation on the negative can in principle have a representational function. New photographs are digital, which means that they are genuinely reproducible, since the state of every pixel can be encoded. Perfect reproducibility is a new phenomenon for photography (even though at its inception old photography was hailed as intrinsically reproducible); however, it is not a relevant feature of photography for the present discussion.

(4) *Transmissibility*: New technology allows digitally produced images to be transmitted electronically without loss of quality. This has important implications for how photojournalists work, but is not relevant to the present discussion.

Of the four features of new photography outlined above, only the first and second, the ease and the undetectability of manipulation, are directly relevant to the issue of photographic truth. It should be noted that neither of these constitutes a difference in kind from traditional photography, only of degree. Everything that the new technology does in terms of manipulation has had its equivalent in pre-electronic photography. Skilful technicians have managed to produce equally undetectable images using traditional techniques. Besides which, most of the most successful deceptions using photography have been carried out outside the darkroom. Think of the case of the Cottingley Fairies which duped 'experts' for almost half a century,[6] or of Capa's 'Republican soldier at the very instant of his death', the authenticity of which has frequently been questioned, but never on the grounds of illicit photographic manipulation.[7] The new technology only speeds up what photojournalists could always do anyway: there is no relevant qualitative difference from this point of view between what the new electronic technologies can offer and what the opticochemical ones always provided.

THE ETHICS OF NEWS PHOTOGRAPHY

So, the ethics of photojournalism in general is the real issue, not just of electronically based photojournalism. In order to address the central questions about the ethics of photojournalism, it is necessary to say something about photojournalistic conventions. Photography is clearly used in a wide variety of ways. Here I concentrate on news photography, and in particular on the use of photographs as evidence that an event took place. My concern is not with issues about the subject-matter of photographs, whether news photographers are insensitive, intrusive, irresponsible in their invasion of the private lives of public figures and so on. Rather I want to concentrate on the ethical questions about how they produce the images that they do, and whether or not they dupe viewers of those images about how they have been produced.

Imagine the following scenario. You pick up your morning tabloid on the way to work. On the front page is a photograph of a member of the royal family, a married princess no less, topless and in a compromising position with her bodyguard on a public beach. The picture is not in any way ambiguous. You can see who is involved and precisely what they are doing: no innocent explanation would be in the least bit plausible. The photograph is proof of what they did.

The photograph provides us with proof, or at least that is what we take for granted, because we have, consciously or unconsciously, acknowledged the conventions about how photographs are used accompanying news stories. We assume that the photograph really is a photograph of whoever the caption claims it is; we assume that what looks to be happening really was happening; we assume that the image before us is a photograph and not a skilfully executed painting, and so on. We might exercise a little healthy scepticism about how representative the depicted scene was of what was actually going on on the beach, but, as newspaper readers who have grown up with the conventions of photojournalism, we do not expect anything but a documentary photograph to accompany a news story. The photograph gives us convincing evidence of a special kind about what happened.

Now, consider how the image was made. The photographer climbed a tree with his camera and hung around for several hours until the couple emerged. He could scarcely believe what he was seeing through his telephoto lens. He shot a roll of film, then sneaked off to have it developed, confident that he'd just made a year's salary in a few hours. To his dismay, a fault in the film meant that only half of the shots had come out; none of the more compromising ones were printable. But all was not lost; he scanned the photographs that had come out into his computer and within half an hour he had produced a composite picture showing more or less what he had seen through the telephoto lens. He felt justified in what he had done because he knew that the photograph was not misleading in any important way. He was committed to revealing the truth, and what better way to reveal the truth than with this striking image.

He sent the image electronically to the picture editor of his newspaper, who decided to make it the lead story. However, just to cover himself, the picture editor telephoned back to check that the photograph wasn't misleading. He asked the photographer whether it showed what really happened; the photographer answered, honestly, that it did. So the photograph appeared on the front page of the newspaper the next day. None of the newspaper readers were aware of precisely how the photograph had been made, nor was the picture editor. They assumed that it was a straightforward documentary photograph. Consequently they took it as incontrovertible photographic evidence of the princess's misdemeanours.

Setting aside any issues of invasion of privacy, is there anything wrong with what the photographer did? The answer is surely yes. There are at least three reasons for this:

1.   The image he sent down the wire to the newspaper wasn't *photographic evidence* for the action it seemed to show.
2.   What the photographer did involved *deception* about how the image was made.
3.   His deception took a step down a very *slippery slope* that could lead to the demise of news photography altogether.

We'll consider each of these reasons in turn.

PHOTOGRAPHIC EVIDENCE

Still photographs, because of reasonably direct and traceable causal links, can be good evidence for what they are indexically of (i.e. whatever was in front of the lens and left its trace on the light-sensitive film). Moving images tend to carry much more, and more accessible, information than still photographs; some aspects of most still photographs are ambiguous or indeterminate. But provided that you have external evidence about the conditions under which the photograph was taken, you may well be able to read off all kinds of information.

For instance, think of a photofinish in an Olympic 100 metres final; we can tell who crossed the line first, but only if we are confident that the camera angle is not misleading. We also have to know who was in which lane.[8] Aerial photographs can help us to construct maps if we know the height from which they were taken and possible distortions arising from weather conditions or other factors. X-rays and ultrasound images can give us a great deal of reliable information about the condition of bones, foetuses and internal organs, but they require specialist interpretation and are only usually produced in highly controlled conditions. And so on. The information in each case is there in virtue of such photographs being direct traces of their causes. We read information from these traces almost as if we were looking at the real things. Photographs picture their causes as well as being traces of them. But in some of the above cases appearances alone can be misleading, so we rely on other factual evidence from which we hypothesise the probable causes of the photographs' appearance.

However, most photojournalistic uses of photography differ significantly from the informational ones mentioned above. Typically the viewer does not have detailed information about the conditions under which photojournalistic images were taken. Minimal information is usually carried in captions, accompanying text, or else is implied by the context of presentation. This point is well illustrated by a famous case in France. Robert Doisneau photographed a young woman in a café on the Rue de Seine drinking a glass of wine and sitting next to an older man. The photograph was used to illustrate the dangers of alcohol in a leaflet issued by the temperance league; it was then used to illustrate a story in the magazine *Le Point,* where it appeared with the caption 'Prostitution on the Champs-Elysées'.[9] In both uses, the photograph looked right: there were no incongruous details which undermined the interpretation suggested by the caption. However, in both cases the captions misled: neither of the people photographed was an alcoholic, and neither of them a prostitute. However, viewers of the photograph in these contexts would not have been able to read off these facts from the image itself.

Photojournalistic images have meaning in virtue of three interrelated aspects:

1. what they are of, in the sense of what caused them;
2. what they look to be of;
3. how they are used in a particular context.

The legibility of documentary photography depends on a relation of trust with the photographer or picture editor; in the case of news photography the viewer trusts that he or she is not being misled about the way the image was produced and what it appears to depict. The context of presentation communicates directly (through captions, accompanying stories, etc.) and indirectly (through implicit conventions) a way of interpreting the image. In most cases there is nothing within the photograph which will inform the viewer whether or not the photograph is of what the context of presentation suggests that it is. For example, as I suggested in relation to the Capa photograph of a Republican soldier, external evidence is needed to confirm our interpretation of it as of a Republican soldier at the very instant of his death and not, as has been claimed, of a Republican soldier stumbling in training. So we rely on the sincerity of the presenter and on any external evidence we might happen to have.

In the imaginary case of the photographs of the princess, the image that the photographer used wasn't direct evidence of the event. His wasn't an informational photograph about the event depicted (though if you knew enough about how he actually made the photograph you would no doubt be able to read off many factual details from the direct evidence which the image carries). Nor, however, was it a documentary photograph of the event, since the event did not play the appropriate and implied causal role in the image's construction. Its value as evidence for that event was on a par with an artist's sketch made partly from memory. It was a *pictorial* photograph of that event masquerading as a documentary one:[10] in fact it was a deliberately deceptive quasi-documentary photograph.

DECEPTION

What is most disturbing in such cases is that the viewer is deceived –not deceived about what went on between the princess and the bodyguard, but deceived about how the photograph was made, and so about the kind of evidence being presented. The context of presentation on the news pages of a newspaper implicitly communicates to the viewer that the conventions of documentary news photography have been adhered to. But in fact they haven't. A set of conventions has grown up about photographic communication of news. Roughly, readers of daily newspapers expect that the photographs used alongside news stories are not just photographic illustrations, not simply pictorial interpretations of events, but are reasonably direct traces of what they depict. In other words, if a photograph of a princess and her bodyguard is presented as part of a news story, then the readers will quite naturally assume that they are being presented with a documentary photograph, one which was produced by taking a photograph of the couple in question while they were doing what they appear to be doing in the photograph. Clearly many photographs have the potential to be misleading about what was going on, so it is part of the picture editor's job to select images which are as unambiguous as possible, and at least not misleading on substantial issues. If you present a documentary photograph of a particular princess performing a particular act, then her performing that act must have played a direct causal role in the production of the photograph; if you got a look-alike to enact what had happened and photographed that, it could only serve as a photographic illustration of what happened.

Presenting photographic illustrations is acceptable, provided that you make clear from the context, or explicit in the caption that that is what you are doing. The effect of seeing a photograph apparently of a Second World War bomber crash-landed on the moon is, for most people, disbelief. The front page headline for the *Sunday Sport* on 24 April 1988 was 'World War 2 Bomber Found on Moon', but the headline was no more credible than the photograph accompanying it. This would have been so even if the photograph hadn't appeared on the front page of the *Sunday Sport,* but on the front page of, say, *The Independent.* The photograph reveals itself as pictorial because of the nature of the event it depicts as having actually occurred. It is largely irrelevant as to how the image was produced, whether by composite printing using conventional optico-chemical methods, or by electronic, digitally-based procedures. However, a front page photograph of the princess and the bodyguard would carry different expectations wherever it was published: the photograph depicts an event which could plausibly have taken place. This is the kind of news story deception that we should be concerned about: a form of lying by implication about the kind of visual evidence being presented.

The photojournalist in my example deliberately deceived the picture editor and thus the public about the nature of the photograph. What seems to be documentary evidence, is really just an illustration of the event it purports to reveal. It is a quasi-documentary photocollage. 'So what?', the photojournalist might say, 'I've laid bare a more important truth. What I've done is the equivalent to a white lie. A small lie to communicate a more important truth.'

His point is that the photograph may not be in a direct opticochemical causal link back to the situation it depicts. Nevertheless it does actually convey what did in fact happen. The precise details of posture and nuance may be missing; but they would equally be missing from an eyewitness's testimony of the event, since the photographer did everything in his power to recreate the frame that he had expected to find on his reel of film when it was developed. The photograph communicated the important truth about the events, and that, surely, is what really matters in such cases.

Furthermore, parts of the photograph do have direct causal links to the situation depicted; no actors were involved, for instance, so there is fairly direct evidence about what the two were wearing, their hairstyles, and so on. In other words, parts of the photograph do carry the traditional sorts of photographic evidence. So there are some direct and some indirect causal links back to the depicted people and events, and the truth of what did happen is conveyed in a manner which remains, in all but minor incidental details, true to what took place.

Besides, it seems unreasonable to demand more than this, since in print journalism a certain amount of tidying up of quoted speech is tolerated and even encouraged. For instance, if a hesitant speaker included many 'ums' and 'ers' in his press briefing, no one would be likely to challenge a printed quotation that omitted these. What is important in print journalism is that the content of what was said is not distorted by the process of tidying it up. Newspaper readers don't usually want to read verbatim transcripts of speeches, but rather edited versions of them. Why then worry about whether a photograph presents direct evidence of what it depicts just so long as what it depicts did actually occur?

This sort of response rests on a misunderstanding of the conventions surrounding the use of news photographs and of the consequences of changing those conventions. These conventions include the toleration of minor deceptions in order to produce a legible image; it is usually acceptable to adjust contrasts, to 'burn in' important details and to crop out extraneous details. However, these conventions do not tolerate any manoeuvre which distorts the viewer's appreciation of the relationship between the photograph and its main subject. It is a matter of professional integrity for photojournalists to abide by these conventions. The role responsibilities of the photojournalist must surely include not deceiving the public about how your images were made. In my imaginary case of the princess, the bodyguard and the news photographer, it is not the fact that the photographer used electronic wizardry to produce the effect that makes it unacceptable; it is the fact that the photographer disguised the nature of the causal relationship between what happened and the photograph.

Quite apart from issues of personal and professional integrity, every case in which a deception like this is allowed into print (and subsequently exposed for what it is) serves to undermine the public's trust that the implicit conventions of photojournalism are generally being adhered to. This sort of point has frequently been made about lying in general. For example, it is the line taken by the philosopher G. J. Warnock:

It is, one might say, not the implanting of false beliefs that is damaging, but rather the generation of the suspicion that they may be being implanted. For this undermines trust; and to the extent that trust is undermined, all co-operative undertakings in which what one person can do or has reason to do is dependent on what others have done, are doing, or are going to do, must tend to break down.[11]

In other words, what is wrong with lying is not that it tends to result in people acquiring false beliefs, but that it destroys the trust that is necessary for most cooperation and communication. Applying this sort of point to news photography we get the conclusion that what is wrong with what the photographer did in my example is that he contributed to the undermining of trust and thus of the possibility of photographic communication. If trust were substantially undermined in this area, there would no longer be any point in sending photographers out to take news photographs. Provide them instead with access to a picture library and a computer and they will be able to come up with plausible-looking illustrations of whatever story print journalists care to write up.

SLIPPERY SLOPE?

Toleration of minor deceptions for the sake of truth is the first step down a slippery slope towards general deception with total disregard for the truth. If you allow people to manipulate photographs without informing their viewers, then you will soon find yourself allowing photographers to invent reality. The force of this, like most slippery slope arguments, depends on whether or not you believe it is possible to arrest the descent and say 'Here and no further'. However, in most situations in which slippery slope arguments are used it is relatively easy to say how far down the slope we have already travelled. In the case of photographic deceptions, however, because they can be so difficult to detect, it is not easy to say on what kind of scale and to what degree such deceptions are currently being perpetrated. This in itself provides a reason for discouraging even minor sorties on to the slope.

WHY HAVE THE CONVENTIONS AT ALL?

But why do we have a convention of presenting photographs which picture their causes in a legible way? Why not simply choose the best illustrations for news stories. In other words, what, if anything, is wrong with setting up a plausible tableau vivant and photographing it? What, if anything, is wrong with producing a composite picture by electronic means and publishing it on the front page of a newspaper? Both methods would serve to communicate a fact visually.

There are two principal reasons for preferring documentary photographs to pictorial ones in the context of news reporting. One is related to their status as evidence; the other to the psychology of looking at photographs.

DOCUMENTARY PHOTOGRAPHS AS EVIDENCE

Documentary photographs are themselves evidence, whereas pictorial ones are not themselves evidence; they are like implanted 'memories' which, even if their content happens to be true, are not genuine memories, no matter how realistic they seem to us. News photographs contain all sorts of information which wasn't consciously chosen by the photographer. However, one possible response to this point is that most of this information is inaccessible to the average viewer, requiring as it does a great deal of background information to interpret it. This suggests that there is more to documentary news photography than evidence alone. One additional aspect of news photography is the way that particular depicted events can take on a universal meaning, or at least the part can imply the whole in a kind of visual synecdoche. But this would still be possible if news photography were entirely pictorial. The further aspect of news photography that I believe is essential to understanding the impact of a documentary as opposed to a pictorial image is a feature of the psychology of looking at pictures that we know to be traces of what they depict.

THE PSYCHOLOGY OF LOOKING AT RELICS

Because documentary photographs are traces as well as depictions, they have a reasonably direct causal contact with what they are of and this gives them the status of relics. This is equivalent to the effect of seeing the very shirt that Nelson wore at the battle of Trafalgar rather than a visually indistinguishable one. News photographs are relics of what has happened: events have left their trace on the world, albeit under the direction of a photojournalist. It is just a fact about human psychology that knowledge of such a direct link to events can have a profound effect on the viewer of news photographs. It's not just that the photographs seem to be declaring 'this happened', but rather that they give us the sense of being there when it did happen, and this not simply because of accuracy of detail.

Given the choice, most of us would prefer to have contact with the real world rather than a perceptually indistinguishable one produced by some evil scientist with a virtual reality machine. As Robert Nozick has put it:

> plugging into an experience machine limits us to a manmade reality, to a world no deeper or more important than that which people can construct. There is no *actual* contact with any deeper reality, though the experience of it can be simulated. Many persons desire to leave themselves open to such contact and to a plumbing of deeper significance.[12]

A benefit of contact with reality and not an imaginary version of what someone else takes reality to be is suggested by Harold Evans's remarks made in the context of discussing photographs after Auschwitz had been liberated:

> It is one of the central contributions of photojournalism that it goes beyond the limits of imagination. It makes the unbelievable believable.[13]

In exceptional cases news photography can make us realise the limits of our imagination. Some events are simply beyond our conception until we have seen photographs of them. This is not, of course, to say that the relation between a photograph and what it shows us is an unproblematic one: photographs aren't simply windows on to the past.[14] But they can carry a distinctive kind of evidence, and they can put us into a closer relationship with their subject-matter than any other kind of still picture; and this is why the conventions of documentary news photography are worth preserving even in the age of the electronic darkroom.[15]

NOTES

1 René Descartes, *Discourse on Method and the Meditations,* trans. F. E. Sutcliffe (Harmondsworth: Penguin Books, 1968), p. 100.

2 For a useful bibliography on the subject of digital photography, see *History of Photography* 20 (1996), pp. 336–8.

3 For details of this case and others like it, see Fred Ritchin, *In Our Own Image* (New York: Aperture, 1990).

4 See, for instance, the subtitle of his book *The Reconfigured Eye* (Cambridge, MA: MIT Press, 1992): *Visual Truth in the Post-photographic Era.*

5 For a discussion of Susan Sontag's claim that photographs can't communicate moral knowledge, see Nigel Warburton, 'Photographic communication', *British Journal of Aesthetics* 28 (1988), pp. 173–81.

6 For a detailed and completely convincing account of how these photographs were produced and how so many people were taken in by them, see the series of articles by Geoffrey Crawley in the *British Journal of Photography,* from 24 December 1982 to 8 April 1983.

7 For a discussion of the philosophical implications of this photograph see Nigel Warburton, 'Varieties of photographic representation', *History of Photography* 15 (1991), pp. 203–10.

8 Joel Snyder and Neil Walsh Allen discuss the sort of evidence provided by the photofinish in their important article 'Photography, vision and representation', *Critical Inquiry* 2 (1975), pp. 143–69.

9 This case is described in Gisèle Freund, *Photography and Society* (London: Gordon Fraser, 1980), pp. 178–9.

10 For a discussion of the distinction between documentary and pictorial uses of photography see Warburton, 'Varieties of photographic representation'.

11 G. J. Warnock, quoted in Sissela Bok, *Lying: Moral Choice in Public and Private Life* (Brighton: Harvester, 1978), p. 287.

12 Robert Nozick, *Anarchy, State and Utopia* (Oxford: Blackwell Publishers, 1974), p. 43.

13 Harold Evans, *Eyewitness: 25 Years Through World Press Photos* (London: Quiller Press, 1981), p. 8.

14 For an attempt to show that we can quite literally see through photographs to what they are of, see Kendall Walton, 'Transparent pictures: on the nature of photographic realism', *Critical Inquiry* 11 (1984), pp. 246–77. For a critique of this view, see Nigel Warburton, 'Seeing through "Seeing through" photographs', *Ratio* NS 1/1 (1988), pp. 64–74.

15 I am very grateful for Matthew Kieran's comments on an earlier version of this essay.

KEY TIPS FOR APPROACHING YOUR JOURNALISTIC DUTIES IN AN ETHICAL MANNER

Begin by visiting these websites to review contemporary standards of journalistic ethics:

- The Society of Professional Journalists (SPJ): https://www.spj.org/ethicscode.asp
- The Center for Journalism Ethics (read Stephen Ward's post on *Digital Media Ethics*): https://ethics.journalism.wisc.edu/resources/digital-media-ethics/
- National Press Photographers Association (NPPA): https://nppa.org/code-ethics
- Radio Television Digital News Association (RTDNA): https://www.rtdna.org/content/rtdna_code_of_ethics

Then take the following steps when assembling your story:

- Leave adequate time to review procedures and ensure that the production has not violated any journalistic ethical codes, legalities, or unnecessary moral boundaries.
- Avoid any conflicts of interest; disclose any monetary ties between your story, its subject, and your station or station personnel, and always refuse any offers of gifts or bribes. Remember too, that any promotional courtesies provided to your staff as part of a story, such as travel or overnight accommodations, must be disclosed.
- Avoid the perils of checkbook journalism. Remember that in many instances obtaining proprietary information from sources for monetary gain is prohibited.
- When shooting on location, consider some of ethical demands that come into play while traveling. Journalists can come under increased influence or pressure from local parties when trying to write their narratives or edit an objective news segment, especially if it is an exposé of some kind. Is the safety of your journalists secure and free from undue influence?
- Have you double checked your sources and verified the information that they have provided to you? Are you sure that the source is not purposely feeding you misinformation to discredit some other party? Would reporting such a falsehood make your news organization liable for possible defamation? Have you taken precautions to insulate your staff from these risks?
- Once production does commence, make it a practice to always try to keep your camera or audio recorder rolling whenever possible. Your goal is to document everything that is taking place for accuracy's sake. While in the field, shoot all that you can, then, in postproduction, decide what footage is most appropriate.
- Avoid manipulating any of your video content, except basic adjustments done to improve picture quality. Never digitally alter images by adding or removing content of any kind, merely for dramatic purposes.

- Avoid manipulating audio or a person's soundbite, except basic adjustments done to improve quality, even if that means leaving in some unwanted "ums" and "ahs."
- Along those same lines, always show discretion when adding music into a news story. Music adds an emotional element to the story that would otherwise not be present. So, while it heightens drama, it is also a form of manipulation that could alter the underlying tone or context of the material being presented. Unless the music was recorded at the event that you re reporting on, or is related to a profile of an artist, this is a practice that should be avoided.

QUESTIONS

1. Research some recent examples in which the news media has been accused of altering either audio or visual content in such a way that it was considered deceptive. Detail the specific circumstances of the case and what kind of alteration or editing took place. Discuss when, or if, it is acceptable for a photojournalist to digitally edit a photograph submitted for news publication.

2. Explain what is meant by the term *juxtaposing clips*. How can the use of juxtaposed clips completely change the context of a story? According to the ethics code of most professional journalistic organizations, is juxtaposing clips considered to be an ethical or unethical practice.

3. How does the "one-man band" video journalist affect the final product? What pressures does it put on a journalist when they have to simultaneously act as reporter, camera operator, and sound technician? Does it encourage a journalist to take shortcuts when putting a story together for final consumption? Is there more danger of false or misleading content getting out when there are no production personnel working as gatekeepers of the content's veracity?

4. "Pseudo-events" are the brainchild of public relation firms. Their purpose is to attract media attention for a client's brand or organization without having to pay the formal costs of an advertising or marketing campaign. An example of one type of pseudo-event would be a news station covering the red-carpet premiere of a film that was produced by the same large media company that owns the news station itself. Considering that these events are mostly promotional in nature, and often lack any true news value, how justifiable is it for journalists to cover these events in the first place? How does having to cover these mandated events affect a video journalist's independence and narrative freedom?

5. Why are the context and sanctity of an image so important to photo and video journalists the world over? Why do all the major journalistic codes of ethics take pains to make clear that news photos should never be altered to "mislead viewers or

misrepresent (its) subjects." What are some of the ways in which photographs can be edited to distort or recontextualize the visual evidence that they allege to present?

RELATED PROJECTS AND EXERCISES

- Photographs and context. To gain a better understanding of how editing and photo manipulation can change the intended meaning or context of the image, use an existing photo or an original image taken for this exercise. The photo should be as ambiguous as possible, in terms of representing any overt political or cultural subtext. Then, using digital photo-editing software, give the image a makeover by manipulating any number of aesthetic features, including lighting, color, size, adding effects, cropping and blending, and any additional editing necessary to support the caption. Create at least two to four variations of the same image and supple each image with different caption. Upon completion, supply a copy of both the original "raw" photo and each of the variants that you created. Explain what photographic tricks were used to make the alterations and how those alterations impact the context of the overall story.

- Have your class teams choose a recent news story that they believe is an example of fake news. Have each team prepare a multimedia presentation examining all aspects of the story in question. Where and when did the story first appear? What form did it take (print, video, online blog, broadcast news, etc.)? How much coverage did the story receive when it was first published? Does the story contain eyewitness accounts or include verifiable, named sources to lend credence to its allegations? What other data, if any, is cited to help support the veracity of the story? Have any of the facts contained in the original story now been proven to be false; if so, did the originating news source or any of the other outlets that also posted the story, issue a correction or retraction? As a consumer of news, what are some practical steps that can be taken to verify the accuracy of a news report?

- The Internet and the rise of viral media have had a tremendous impact on long-established journalism practices and standards. One of the most striking changes has been that newsrooms must now rely more on the general public and on self-styled *citizen journalists* to provide the content featured on the nightly news. Unlike in the past when a local TV stations would send their own news team out to get a story firsthand in order to verify its accuracy, now, with social media, news stations depend on user-generated content (footage shot by individuals on their personal cameras or cell phones, closed-circuit security camera footage, etc.) to fill out their programming. Unfortunately, this growing dependence on user-generated footage raises a number of troubling ethical questions. To highlight these ethical concerns, have each of your student teams discuss the viral media production dilemma highlighted below. Have the group pay extra attention to issues such as verification of online sources, the reliability of third-party footage, and proper attribution for use, along with any transparency concerns that a news station might need to address when using such footage. Have the teams further evaluate this scenario by analyzing how the differing ethical principles, including the Golden Rule, the Greater Good Rule and the Absolutist Theory of Right and Wrong may apply:

You are a news editor at a 24-hour cable or online news station when your police scanner picks up a series of emergency calls about a possible hostage situation involving a gunman at a large downtown theater. At about the same time, images and videostreams from both inside and outside of the theater begin to appear on a few social media sites. Until you can dispatch your own news crew to the theater, this online content is the only source of footage that is available to show to viewers. As a journalist, is it ethically permissible to air this online footage or to post it to your own online site? How important is it to include attribution regarding the source of the footage?

Just as you have come to a decision about whether or not to use that online footage, a station intern comes running up to tell you that a woman named "Janet" is on the phone who claims to be inside the theater at this very moment. She will send you a live stream of the ongoing events from inside, but only if you agree to pay her $5,000.00 for the footage.

What should you do next? Posting footage like this, from inside the theater, would be a journalistic coup and help to draw a massive audience to your newscast. Is it ethical to pay Janet the money given the risk that she is taking? If you do pay for the footage, does this constitute an example of checkbook journalism? Furthermore, if you do elect to air the content, and someone is harmed live and on camera, how will you respond? What if Janet is harmed while covering this story for you? What are your legal, ethical, and financial obligations to her, if any harm should befall Janet because of her coverage?

SECTION V

Social Media Advertising— Advanced Case Studies

INTRODUCTION

Section V will revisit some of the social media marketing concepts first introduced in Section III. The difference will be that while Section III focused mostly on consumer-initiated viral marketing strategies, Section V will explore examples of business-initiated viral marketing campaigns. These upcoming chapters will provide an opportunity for students to see just how well commercial entities have fared in crafting transmedia narratives in their initial forays into viral media marketing. This portion of the text will also use real-world case studies as a way of illustrating how the concept of *brand storytelling* has influenced viral media campaigns, on both a national and global basis, with companies ranging from McDonald's and Coca-Cola, to Air France and Capital One.

KEY TERMS

- brand storytelling
- content aggregator websites
- customer acquisition and retention
- #MeetTheFarmers/#McDStories
- online social networking groups
- search engine marketing
- search engine optimization
- transmedia storytelling
- Twitter hashtags
- user-generated content

Case studies are detailed narratives that contain examples of complex, real-world scenarios, including dilemmas that are to be analyzed, explained, and, in some circumstances, satisfactorily resolved. Case studies are a practical way to exemplify an abstract or intricate theoretical principle in the form of an easy-to-grasp, true-to-life situation. Like all good stories, case studies should be centered on a conflict, which is essential for creating dramatic tension and engagement. In a case study, narratives should address some type of timely or insightful content and feature an empathetic protagonist who is tasked with needing to achieve a well-defined goal or to overcome a daunting obstacle.

A quality case study can be based on a single, fact-based event or it be created out of an assemblage of components, including anecdotal references, newspaper headlines, and/or personal experiences—anything that helps to maximize the complexity of the narrative.

The benefit to case studies is that they are very flexible in nature and serve as a marvelous teaching aid that helps to expose students to the realities of the workplace, while staying true to principles of academic theory and discourse. Case studies can be designed in a number of ways, they can provide clues that lead towards a directed result with a preordained outcome that needs to be deduced, or they can be more speculative in configuration, with the featured scenario lacking a clear-cut solution, therefore requiring a more open-ended and abstract response.

Case study analysis encourages students to attack problems in unique and innovative ways; they also provide students with the experience necessary to identifying complex issues, reducing those issues down into more manageable elements and then devising appropriate courses of action to deal with any lingering difficulties. Perhaps professor Paul Lawrence put it best when he described case studies as *"the vehicle by which a chunk of reality is brought into the classroom to be worked over by the class and the instructor. A good case keeps the class discussion grounded upon some of the stubborn facts that must be faced in real life situations."* *Teaching and the Case Method*, 3rd ed., vols. 1 and 2, by Louis Barnes, C. Roland (Chris) Christensen, and Abby Hansen. Harvard Business School Press, Cambridge, Massachusetts, 1994. 333 pp. (vol 1), 412 pp. (vol 2)

Section V will provide you with outstanding case study examples of some recent, high-profile, business-initiated viral marketing campaigns; some that met with notable success and others that suffered from glaring marketing miscalculations. Let's get started.

CHAPTER 15

McDonald's Twitter Campaign
Hype Versus Reality

Jana Seijts and Paul Bigus

On Tuesday, January 24, 2012, at the corporate head office in Oak Brook, Illinois just outside of Chicago, Rick Wion, director of social media for the McDonald's Corporation (McDonald's) was challenged with a tall order. Earlier that month, McDonald's had launched a campaign aimed at better informing the public where its food came from, with a series of videos on TV and in social media showcasing some of the farmers and ranchers that grow food for the company. As part of that promotions effort, the Twitter hashtag "#MeetThe-Farmers" was used to promote connections with family farms and local suppliers. In order to maximize the Twitter Promoted Trends expenditure (a service Twitter offered to display trending hashtags on its homepage), Wion switched the hashtag from "#MeetTheFarmers" to "#McDStories" with the tweeted message, "When u make something w/pride people can taste it."[1] By doing this, he hoped to capitalize the campaign on the Twittersphere. Yet within the first hour of launching the new hashtag, he and his team quickly realized that numerous

---

1   Gus Lubin, "McDonald's Twitter Campaign Goes Horribly Wrong #McDStories," <u>Business Insider</u>, January 24, 2012, www.businessinsider.com/mcdonalds-twitter-campaign-goes-horribly-wrong-mcdstories-2012-1, accessed September 21, 2013.

detractors were using it to express negative comments towards McDonald's. In an attempt to change the course of the campaign, the hashtag was changed back to "#MeetTheFarmers," thereby successfully reducing the number of negative comments and discussions.

However, a few days later, the media started to run negative coverage of the "#McDStories" hashtag using a very formulaic approach. Headlines reading, "#McFail! McDonalds' Twitter promotion backfires as users hijack #McDstories hashtag to share fast food horror stories" were followed by articles providing various screenshots of the negative tweets.[2] Very few of the media articles contained any statistics to demonstrate how many negative versus positives tweets were shared or that explained or put proper context behind the situation.

Moving forward, Wion needed to devise a better social media strategy for McDonald's social media campaigns.

MCDONALD'S HISTORY[3]

The world's most famous fast food restaurant was founded in 1940 when brothers Dick and Mac Donald opened McDonald's Bar-B-Q restaurant in San Bernardino, California. Typical of the time period, the restaurant offered carhop service and featured a large menu. In 1948, the brothers shut down the location for renovations, reopening as a self-service, drive-in restaurant, with a reduced menu featuring just nine items, centred around a 15 cent hamburger.[4] The effectiveness of their operations did not go unnoticed, catching the eye of Ray Kroc, a 52-year-old multi-mixer salesman, during a sales visit in 1954. Kroc discovered that by producing a limited menu, the restaurant was able to focus on quality at every step. He recognized an opportunity and successfully pitched to the two brothers his vision of creating McDonald's restaurants all over the United States, officially founding the McDonald's Corporation in 1955. The first McDonald's location in Des Plains, Illinois featured the eye-catching golden arches along with a red and white tile design. Kroc had a unique philosophy: he desired to build a restaurant system on consistency, high quality and uniform methods of preparation, essentially offering customers food that would taste the same regardless of the location. To help achieve his vision, he promoted the slogan "In business for yourself, but not by yourself" to both franchisees and suppliers, using the analogy of a three-legged stool, with one leg representing McDonald's, the second

---

2   Hannah Roberts, "#McFail! McDonalds' Twitter promotion backfires as users hijack #McDstories hashtag to share fast food horror stories," Daily Mail, January 24, 2012, www.dailymail.co.uk/news/article-2090862/McDstories-McDonalds-Twitter-promotion-backfires-users-share-fast-food-horror-stories.html, accessed September 21, 2013.

3   McDonald's, "McDonald's History," 2013, www.aboutmcdonalds.com/mcd/our_company/mcdonalds_history_timeline.html, accessed September 21, 2013.

4   All amounts represented in U.S. currency unless otherwise stated.

franchisees, and the third suppliers, conveying the point that the stool was only as strong as its three legs.[5]

By 1959, the corporation had experienced rapid success, and McDonald's opened its one-hundredth restaurant. As the restaurant chain continued to expand, it recognized how to better serve its customers, in 1962 offering indoor restaurant seating for the first time. With McDonald's tenth anniversary in 1965, the corporation went public with its first stock offering at a cost of $22.50 per share. Efforts to strengthen the McDonald's brand were made in 1966 with the first appearance of the iconic clown character Ronald McDonald in a national television commercial. In 1967, having achieved significant growth with more than 500 locations across the United States, McDonald's expanded internationally for the first time, opening restaurants in Canada and Puerto Rico. Kroc believed in the entrepreneurial spirit and encouraged his franchisees to communicate their ideas and individual creativity.[6] As a result, in 1968, McDonald's introduced to its national menu the Big Mac, which had been developed by a franchise owner/operator. Under Kroc's vision and leadership as both the company founder and chairman of the board, McDonald's had grown to become the world's largest fast food restaurant chain with more than 7,778 restaurants in 32 countries before he passed away in 1984.

To better appeal to consumer tastes, McDonald's constantly experimented with new food items, introducing fresh salads to its national menu in 1987. The expansion to new locations continued in 1990, with the first McDonald's opening in Moscow and serving more than 30,000 customers on its first day. McDonald's entered the online environment in 1996, launching the website McDonalds.com. Seeking greater customization of menu items and increased kitchen flexibility, the "Made For You" kitchen operating platform was initiated in 1998 and became the standard operating platform for McDonald's kitchens globally. Dedicated to giving back to the communities in which it operated, in 2002 McDonald's started McHappy Day, an annual event that raised proceeds for the Ronald McDonald House Charities and other local children's charities. Throughout its long history, McDonald's utilized a number of popular slogans, with the most recent "im lovin' it" campaign first introduced in Germany in 2003. Further diversifying its beverage line, McDonalds added the McCafe coffees in 2009 and real fruit smoothies and frappes in 2010.

In 2011, after 56 years of successful operations, McDonald's had expanded to employ over 1.7 million employees in more than 33,000 restaurants located in 119 countries worldwide, resulting in an annual operating income of $8.5 billion (see Exhibit 15.1). On average, McDonald's restaurants served nearly 68 million people globally each day.[7] Although many restaurant menu items were uniform, McDonald's also catered to local tastes. Customers

5 McDonald's, "The Ray Kroc Story," 2013, www.mcdonalds.com/us/en/our_story/our_history/the_ray_kroc_story.html, accessed September 21, 2013.

6 Ibid.

7 McDonald's Corporation, "2011 Annual Report," www.aboutmcdonalds.com/content/dam/AboutMcDonalds/Investors /Investors%202012/2011%20Annual%20Report%20Final.pdf, accessed September 21, 2013.

could order a Quiche de Queijo (cheese quiche) in Brazil, Red Bean Pie in Hong Kong and potato-patty McAloo Tikki burger in India.[8] Regardless of the location, McDonald's brand mission was to be its customers' favourite place and way to eat and drink.[9]

RICK WION[10]

Growing up in the Chicago area, Wion attended the University of Illinois where he successfully graduated with a Bachelor of Science in Journalism. He first worked as a journalist for several years with publications including the *Daily Herald* and *Chicago Tribune*. Eventually, he left the journalism industry, taking a position with the association management company SmithBucklin, advancing to the position of director of technology services. In 2006, Wion joined the communications firm GolinHarris as the vice-president of interactive media; that firm's large client list included corporations such as McDonald's. It was then that Wion first started working with McDonald's on different projects and programs. After having spent many years becoming familiar with McDonald's business operations, in 2010, Wion joined the corporation as director of social media.

MCDONALD'S CRITICS

Throughout the duration of McDonald's 56-year history and as it became the world's largest fast food restaurant chain, the corporation had naturally attracted the focus of numerous critics. The animal rights organization, People for the Ethical Treatment of Animals (PETA), had for many years engaged in various campaigns that claimed McDonald's chicken suppliers used outdated and cruel slaughter methods, with the most recent "McCruelty" campaign continuing in 2012.[11] Despite efforts to add grilled chicken wraps, yogurt parfaits, an assortment of salads and a variety of other menu items with more fruits and vegetables to keep up with changing tastes as people increasingly opted for foods they felt were fresh or healthy, McDonald's still faced criticism that it was a purveyor of junk food.[12] In 2004, McDonald's became subject to immense public scrutiny following the release of Morgan Spurlock's movie "Super Size Me," which documented an investigation into the increased spread of obesity throughout U.S. society, with the filmmaker himself monitoring his own health after

---

8 McDonald's, "Catering to Local Tastes," 2013, www.aboutmcdonalds.com/mcd/our_company/amazing_stories/food/catering_to_local_tastes.html, accessed September 21, 2013.
9 McDonald's, "Mission & Values," 2013, www.aboutmcdonalds.com/mcd/our_company/mission_and_values.html, accessed September 21, 2013.
10 All personal information and quotes from Rick Wion were obtained during an interview on July 9, 2013.
11 McCruelty, "MCCRUELTY: IM HATIN' IT," 2013, www.mccruelty.com/default.aspx, accessed September 21, 2013.
12 Maclean's, "As McDonald's tries to evolve its image, criticism over nutrition persists at annual meeting," May 23, 2013, www2.macleans.ca/2013/05/23/as-mcdonalds-tries-to-evolve-its-image-criticism-over-nutrition-persists-at-annual-meeting/, accessed September 21, 2013.

eating all of his meals at McDonald's for 30 days straight.[13] A barrage of speculation also surrounded the types of ingredients and additives contained in McDonald's food items, despite assurances from the company that the freshest ingredients were used, with its menu based on staple foods such as meat, fish, potatoes, eggs, milk and grain.[14]

MCDONALD'S "MEET THE FARMERS" TWITTER CAMPAIGN

As part of their overall communication strategy, McDonald's consistently communicated its food quality to the public, let people know who the corporation was and what it stood for and outlined what ingredients were in its food. The main driver of the most recent campaign was a series of television commercials that showed and featured farmers who were directly associated with McDonald's. In creating the campaign, McDonald's conducted interviews in a documentary format with a potato grower in Idaho, a lettuce grower in California and a cattle rancher in Illinois. The interviews were produced into a series of television commercials and video vignettes to upload onto the Internet, with each farmer telling a personal story about McDonald's food and where it came from. While it was a fairly traditional driven campaign, McDonald's looked to social media to help spread awareness of it and to keep it going. As Wion commented:

> One of the tactics in the campaign was figuring out how we could use Twitter to get more people to watch the videos and generate conversation, and so "#MeetTheFarmers" was the first hashtag that we used. The thought process behind it was that if we used the hashtag "#MeetTheFarmers," people would be curious and say, "Oh, who are these farmers? I want to find out what this is all about," because a lot of Twitter is built on discovery. And so when you would click on the hashtag, you would see some of our tweets and links to some of the videos to watch.

As part of the campaign, McDonald's planned to take advantage of Twitter Promoted Trends, which for a fee allowed organizations to place their hashtag message at the top of Twitter's trends list, which appeared on the main screen of the social media site on both desktop and mobile devices. Providing maximum exposure, the Twitter Promoted Trends feature was often used by various organizations to kick off an event, a major announcement or even a product launch, giving Twitter users something new and exciting to discover, participate in and share.[15]

13   John Stossel, "'Super Size Me' Carries Weight With Critics," ABC News, June 18, 2004, abcnews. go.com/2020/Oscars2005/story?id=124265&page=1, accessed September 21, 2013.
14   Martin Hickman, "On the menu at McDonald's: 78 additives (some may be harmful)," The Independent, January 1, 2008, www.independent.co.uk/life-style/food-and-drink/news/on-the-menu-at-mcdonalds-78-additives-some-may-be-harmful-767533.html, accessed September 21, 2013.
15   Twitter, "Promoted Trends," 2013, business.twitter.com/products/promoted-trends, accessed September 21, 2013.

McDonald's had utilized Twitter Promoted Trends in several previous campaigns, and Wion and his team had realized that if they changed the promoted key words at some point during the day, they could get a little bit more "bang for their buck." As Wion explained, "We would literally get more engagement from two different words versus one word throughout the day. This actually goes back to the curiosity factor on Twitter. Once you see something on a trend list and click on it, you know what it is and you probably aren't going to go back there again."

On Wednesday, January 18, 2012, at 12:00 a.m., Central Standard Time (CST), McDonald's officially launched the "#MeetTheFarmers" hashtag using Twitter Promoted Trends along with the tweeted message "Meet some of the hard-working people dedicated to providing McDs with quality food every day #McDStories http://mcd.to/ylOG3a."[16] When describing the hashtag strategy, Wion stated, "The thought process was we start with #MeetTheFarmers" to introduce these people, the farmers who are telling their stories about McDonald's, and then switch to #McDStories" at about midpoint during the day." When using Twitter Promoted Trends, a hashtag could only be changed at the top of each hour. Thus, at 1 p.m., CST, the McDonald's Twitter Promoted Trends hashtag was changed to "#McDStories" along with the tweeted message, "When u make something w/pride people can taste it," creating an opportunity for the public to share their own McDonald's stories online.

After successfully changing the hashtag, Wion and his team monitored the ensuing online Twitter activity closely. They quickly discovered over the duration of the next hour that the tweets appearing under the "#McDStories" hashtag were not the kind that they desired, as detractors had in fact hijacked the hashtag by posting negative messages, such as the following:

> @jfsmith23 wrote: "Watching a classmate projectile vomit his food all over the restaurant during a 6th grade trip. #McDStories."[17]

> @MuzzaFuzza wrote: "I haven't been to McDonalds in years, because I'd rather eat my own diarrhea."[18]

> @nelo_taylor wrote: "These #McDStories never get old, kinda like a box of McDonald's 10 piece."[19]

> @peta wrote: "#McDStories: Liquid chicken nuggets http://t.co/S6YB4Lun Who's hungry for @McDonalds?"[20]

16   Brad Friedman, "McDonald's Promoted Twitter Campaign #McFailed," Social Media Today, January 30, 2012, socialmediatoday.com/bradfriedman/436608/mcdonald-s-promoted-twitter-campaign-mcfailed, accessed September 21, 2013.

17   TNT Magazine, "McDonalds Twitter fail as #McDstories spawns backlash," January 24, 2012, www.tntmagazine.com/news/world/mcdonalds-twitter-fail-as, accessed September 21, 2013.

18   Ibid.

19   Ibid.

20   Sara C Nelson, "McDonald's #McDStories Twitter Campaign Fails," The Huffington Post, January 24, 2012, www.huffingtonpost.co.uk/2012/01/24/mcdonalds-mcdstories-twitter-campaign-fails-_n_1226811.html, accessed September 21, 2013.

@Siriusjay wrote: "My wife can always tell when I've been to McDonalds by the smell of the farts #McDstories."[21]

@mmemordant wrote: "Eating a Quarter Pounder value meal makes me feel the exact same as an hour of violent weeping. McDStories."[22]

@natebramble wrote: "My father used to bring us to McDonald's as a reward when we were kids. Now he's horribly obese and has diabetes. Lesson learned #McDStories."[23]

@healthy_food wrote: "I ate a @McDonalds cheeseburger a few years ago and got food poisoning so bad that I had to get hospitalized. That is my #mdstories.[24]

@michellevegan wrote: "#McDStories @McDonalds scalds baby chicks alive for nuggets #MeetTheReality here & take action: McCruelty.com #UnhappyMeal"[25]

@bernvendlinski wrote: "Which has more chemicals: Marlboro cigarette or egg mcmuffin? Flip a coin. #mcdstories."[26]

@winsoar wrote: "I once worked at McDonalds. I have never eaten there since. #McDStories."[27]

With each Twitter campaign, Wion and his team were well aware that taking the McDonald's brand into an online environment meant dealing with a mix of both positive and negative comments. However, when describing the influx of negative tweets under the "#McDStories" hashtag, Wion stated, "Over the next half hour or so, we saw some people start to take the hashtag in a different direction, by cracking jokes, making funny stories and just trying to bash us." He added, "It got to a point where I was like, you know what, we know we are going to deal with negatives, but this just seems to have more potential to be more negative than we would like it to be, so let's change it back." In keeping with all McDonald's social media campaigns, a contingency plan existed should the conversation not go as planned; therefore, the ability to change midstream helped the small blip of negative comments from becoming something larger. At 3:00 p.m., CST, Wion and his team officially switched the "#McDStories" hashtag back to "#MeetTheFarmers." Within an hour, the number of mentions about the "#McDStories" hashtag on Twitter decreased from a peak of 1,600 to just a few dozen.[28]

21 HyperVocal, "10 Funniest Tweets From the #McDStories Disaster," January 25, 2013, hypervocal.com/news/2012/mcdonalds-tweets-twitter-mcdstories-fail/, accessed September 21, 2013.
22 Ibid.
23 Ibid.
24 Ibid.
25 Kelly Ferrier, "When warm & fuzzy goes dark & ugly, a #bashtag is born," communicatto, January 26, 2012, www.communicatto.com/2012/01/26/when-warm-fuzzy-goes-dark-ugly-a-bashtag-is-born/, accessed September 21, 2013.
26 Sydney Morning Herald, "I'm Not Lovin' It: McDonald's Twitter campaign backfires," January 25, 2013, www.smh.com.au/technology/technology-news/im-not-lovin-it-mcdonalds-twitter-campaign-backfires-20120125-1qgj2.html, accessed September 21, 2013.
27 Ibid.
28 Lubin, "McDonald's Twitter Campaign Goes Horribly Wrong #McDStories."

Overall, it was important to keep the numbers in perspective. The online activity surrounding the two hashtag names resulted in a total of 72,788 mentions of McDonald's that day, only 2,000 of which mentioned #McDStories.[29] On a typical day, McDonald's averaged 25,000 to 30,000 mentions on Twitter. While the "#McDStories" hashtag did not go as planned, the "#MeetTheFarmers" hashtag used for the majority of the day was quite successful in raising awareness of McDonald's supplier stories campaign.

THE MEDIA

As the "#McDStories" trend decreased, Wion and his team believed that the Twitter hashtag issue had been successfully resolved. Then, several days later, on Tuesday, January 24, 2012, some negative media coverage surrounding the matter started to appear. Headlines included: "McDonald's Twitter Campaign Goes Horribly Wrong #McDStories"[30] and "McDialysis? I'm Loving it!': McDonald's Twitter Promo Fail"[31]

On top of the negative headlines and various screenshots of detracting tweets, many of the articles used a very formulaic approach. In fact, very few of the media articles contained any statistics that explained or put any proper context behind the recent McDonald's hashtag situation. As a former journalist, Wion became frustrated when the media picked up a story without getting accurate and important details. He personally contacted the reporter of one of the first high-profile articles that appeared in the media, providing the key trending statistics and information surrounding the "#McDStories" hashtag, but the reporter refused to make a correction to the initial article. As Wion said, "The reporter was just interested on capitalizing on the out of context information that would make headlines." He bemoaned the fact that "We're in a situation where certain publications would rather pick and choose what stats they want to put into a story, so that it can get traffic over telling a full big story." As the media attention surrounding the "#McDStories" hashtag increased, Wion was contacted for comment by various publications around the globe.

DECISION

Reflecting back on McDonald's social media campaign, Wion acknowledged that not everything had gone according to plan, stating, "As Twitter continues to evolve its platform and engagement opportunities, we're learning from our experiences."[32] The campaign had

29 Ibid.
30 Ibid.
31 Colleen Curry, "'McDialysis? I'm Loving it!': McDonald's Twitter Promo Fail," ABC News, January 24, 2012, abcnews.go.com/blogs/headlines/2012/01/mcdialysis-im-loving-it-mcdonalds-twitter-promo-fail/, accessed September 21, 2013.
32 Kashmir Hill, "#McDStories: When a Hashtag Becomes a Bashtag," Forbes, January 24, 2012, www.forbes.com/sites/kashmirhill/2012/01/24/mcdstories-when-a-hashtag-becomes-a-bashtag/, accessed September 21, 2013.

started with a simple goal, to tell people where McDonald's food came from. Wion knew there were certain detractors out there, people who didn't like McDonald's for whatever reason, people who were going to try and make McDonald's look bad or have fun at the corporation's expense. However, there were also a lot of fans and dedicated customers out there as well. People each week tweeted, "Hey McDonald's I love you!" Wion commented, "We don't want to be focused so much on the detractors that we lose sight of customers." As the director of social media, Wion needed to devise a better social media strategy for McDonald's social media campaigns while also preventing potential media fallouts by facilitating better media relations, thus encouraging more accurate reporting. Action was needed, as one thing was clear when designing a social media campaign—there was never a guarantee that everyone would be "lovin' it."

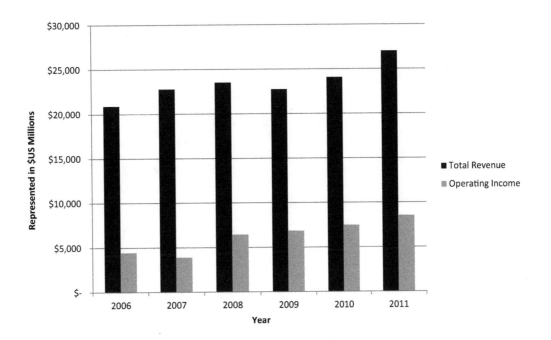

EXHIBIT 15.1   McDonald's corporation annual revenue and operating income.

Source: McDonald's Corporation, 2011 Annual Report, www.aboutmcdonalds.com/content/dam/AboutMcDonalds/Investors/Investors%202012/2011%20Annual%20Report%20Final.pdf, accessed September 17, 2013.

CHAPTER 16

Capital One

Launching a Mass Media Campaign

Robert J. Fisher and Ken Mark

Ken Mark prepared this case under the supervision of Professor Robert Fisher solely to provide material for class discussion. The authors do not intend to illustrate either effective or ineffective handling of a managerial situation. The authors may have disguised certain names and other identifying information to protect confidentiality.

Ivey Management Services prohibits any form of reproduction, storage or transmittal without its written permission. Reproduction of this material is not covered under authorization by any reproduction rights organization. To order copies or request permission to reproduce materials, contact Ivey Publishing, Ivey Management Services, c/o Richard Ivey School of Business, The University of Western Ontario, London, Ontario, Canada, N6A 3K7; phone (519) 661-3208; fax (519) 661-3882; e-mail cases@ivey. uwo.ca.

INTRODUCTION

At the end of March 2005, Clinton Braganza, senior brand manager, was preparing to present his recommendations to his Canadian senior management team at Capital One's Toronto office. Braganza had been tasked with determining Capital One's strategy for its first mass media advertising campaign in Canada. He had spent the last few months conducting and analysing consumer research, and had started to adapt several U.S. and U.K. television ads for use in Canada.

Capital One's intent was to maintain its competition with Canadian banks, which defined the objective of this mass media advertising campaign: *To raise Capital One's awareness and communicate a position in the marketplace in order to achieve growth and change the market's perception of its financial products.*

Robert J. Fisher and Ken Mark, "Capital One: Launching a Mass Media Campaign," pp. 1-18. Copyright © 2006 by Ivey Publishing - Richard Ivey School of Business. Reprinted with permission.

With a limited budget, Braganza knew he couldn't invest in all the options in front of him. To design his strategy, Braganza revisited the consumer research findings he had compiled. Braganza faced three major challenges:

1. Choosing the appropriate target segments;
2. Selecting different advertisements for a nationwide launch;
3. Drafting an advertising plan that best delivered the message to Capital One's target audience groups.

THE CANADIAN BANKING INDUSTRY

In 2005, the Canadian banking industry was made up of 13 domestic banks, 34 foreign bank subsidiaries and 11 foreign bank branches. The six major domestic banks—Royal Bank, Bank of Montreal, TD Canada Trust, Canadian Imperial Bank of Commerce, Scotiabank and National Bank—accounted for more than 90 per cent of the assets held by the banking industry. In Canada, these six banks operated a total of 8,000 branches and nearly 17,000 automated banking machines. The other seven domestic banks were significantly smaller and, as a group, accounted for less than two per cent of the total assets held by the Canadian banking industry. With a combined seven per cent share, foreign banks that operated in Canada accounted for the remaining assets of the Canadian banking industry.

Ninety-three per cent of Canadians had banking relationships, and it was common for customers to consolidate their mortgage, car loan, personal loan, line of credit, investments and credit card at the same retail bank.

In contrast, the U.S. retail banking industry was less consolidated, owing to the legacy of interstate banking regulations and the preference of U.S. consumers to use different financial institutions for their various financial needs.

CREDIT CARDS

Credit cards provided consumers a means of payment, a source of consumer loans and were used as marketing tools by companies. By 2005, credit cards were accepted at more than 1.1 million merchant outlets in Canada. Issued through banks and financial services firms, credit cards belonged to one of the following payment solution organizations: Visa, Master-Card (the two most dominant players), American Express or Diners Club. Merchants remit between one and two per cent of the total transaction charged to Visa or MasterCard. The exact fee charged varies depending on the size of the merchant, with larger firms paying close to one per cent and smaller firms paying close to two per cent. In Canada, the 23 principal issuers of Visa or MasterCard branded credit cards were banks, credit unions, caisses populaires and retailers. For an overview of Visa and MasterCard statistics, see Exhibit 16.1. For the market shares of Visa and MasterCard, see Exhibit 16.2.

The Canadian credit card industry had been traditionally controlled by the six major banks, but, in recent years, had experienced higher levels of competition because of several

U.S.-based players, such as Capital One and MBNA, who had entered the market. From 1996 to 2004, as the number of Visa and MasterCard issuers grew from 15 to 23, the circulation of cards in Canada grew from 30.2 million to 53.4 million. In 2004, about 23.2 million of these credit card accounts were considered "active," which meant they held balances, including those that were paid off every month.

A common trait shared by U.S. and Canadian retail banks was their tendency to run their credit card business as part of an integrated operation. Managers at North American retail banks relied on a combination of these four objectives to run their line of business and optimize profits:

1. Improving marketing to new accounts
2. Retaining existing accounts
3. Minimizing credit losses
4. Minimizing costs

Retail banks in both countries primarily tended to market their credit cards to their own customers through their extensive branch networks. In addition to their trusted brand names, retail banks had lower costs of capital—up to 75 basis points lower—than the U.S. issuers, such as Capital One and MBNA. It was not surprising to see that retail banks garnered the greatest share of new acquisitions in 2004. More than half of the 2004 card applications were received through store and bank branch channels (see Exhibit 16.3).

CREDIT CARD CUSTOMERS

Customers were typically divided into three categories depending on their default risk:

- Super prime
- Prime
- Sub prime

At one extreme, super prime customers were considered a low risk for default; at the other end, sub prime customers were considered a high risk for default. As a result, Canadian retail banks typically offered credit cards only to prime or super prime customers. For a look at selected statistics available on the three segments, see Table 16.1.

TABLE 16.1

RISK SEGMENT	RISK SCORE	% OF CDN ADULTS	AVERAGE CREDIT CARD DEBT	AVERAGE CREDIT AVAILABLE ON CREDIT CARDS	AVERAGE NUMBER OF CREDIT CARDS
Sub prime	<660	17%	$4,500	$6,600	1.8
Prime	660–719	17%	$5,300	$12,500	2.2
Super prime	>720	66%	$2,000	$13,700	1.8

Source: Equifax eIB Tool, June 2005.

Within each segment, customers could be further divided into "transactors" and "revolvers." *Transactors* typically paid off their entire credit balance every month and tended to avoid interest charges. *Revolvers* generally carried a balance from month to month and would pay their minimum monthly payments (which was two or three per cent of the total amount owed) but not their full amount. Because customers paid interest on the balances they carried forward, as a group, *revolvers* were a significant source of revenue for credit companies. An Ipsos Reid survey estimated the average customer carried a balance between $2,400 and $2,900 (see Exhibit 16.4).

Customers who had more credit cards were likely to have higher monthly spends (see Exhibit 16.5). Regardless of how many credit cards customers possessed, however, they typically relied on one primary card. While customers had key reasons for using their primary cards, some were willing to replace their primary card with another if they were offered the right value proposition. (see Exhibit 16.6).

CAPITAL ONE

In 2005, Capital One had a global customer base of 49 million and managed loans of $105 billion. In addition to issuing credit cards, Capital One offered other financial products and services, such as auto loans, home equity loans, small business loans, installment loans, consumer financing for elective medical and dental procedures and savings products.

Established in 1995, Capital One had developed into a global diversified financial services provider with operations in the United States, Canada and the United Kingdom. The firm was founded by Richard Fairbank on his belief that the power of information, technology, testing and great people could be combined to deliver highly customized financial products directly to customers. Capital One was known for its proprietary Information-Based Strategy (IBS), which referred to its practice of relying heavily on data to make management decisions. Using scientific testing on a large scale, Capital One gathered huge amounts of information to help tailor products and services to the individual consumer, rather than simply offering one product to broad socio-economic groups. Capital One attributed its financial services success to its focus on information technology, customer acquisition and customer retention. Less than one decade after it had been established, Capital One joined the Fortune 500.

In 1996, Capital One entered Canada but, unlike its U.S. parent, the focus was issuing credit cards. With a foothold in Canada, Capital One leveraged its IBS to take advantage of the opportunity to offer all Canadians—in all risk segments—low-interest rates and access to credit. Capital One's initial strategy was to present a unique credit card offer to Canadians. When it began operations, Capital One relied on an initial 9.9 per cent introductory offer to rapidly gain market share. As a comparison, its competitors were offering fixed-rate credit cards with interest rates of 16 per cent and higher. In subsequent years, Capital One's low-price offerings became attractive to prime customers who "revolved." For the sub prime segment—a segment the major banks tended to ignore—Capital One offered products not previously available, giving sub prime customers an opportunity to build their credit history.

Canadians responded to Capital One's unique products and, by 2004, they had US$2.4 billion in outstanding balances. To manage its growth, Capital One increased its staff to 100 employees in its Toronto office. Capital One's main focus in 2005 was to establish a clear positioning in the marketplace and to expand its credit card product offerings and channels to acquire new customers.

THE CAPITAL ONE CUSTOMER

Capital One customers used credit cards for several reasons:

- For convenience
- To avoid carrying cash
- To keep track of expenses
- For collecting loyalty reward points

If customers chose not to use credit cards, they either wanted to avoid interest and debt, or had a preference for cash or debit payment methods. Of note, Capital One customers were as equally likely to use credit cards for special occasion purchases as they were for business-related purchases; whereas, the general populace was more likely to use credit cards for the latter purpose.[1] For a list of Capital One credit cards available to Canadian consumers, see Exhibit 16.7.

CUSTOMER ACQUISITION AND RETENTION USING IBS

Capital One relied heavily on its IBS for growth. An entrepreneurial structure supported the culture of testing and learning, which was at the heart of the IBS. The responsibilities for the two core activities of customer acquisition and retention resided with the Acquisitions division and the Account Management division, respectively. Capital One built consumer tests, analysed and applied results from large quantities of data to reduce credit risk, provided customized products for consumers and improved operational efficiency.

In the United States, Capital One combined public bureau data with its private data. In contrast, the Canadian branch only had access to bureau data in Canada after a consumer had completed an application for a credit card. Thus, from a consumer targeting perspective, Capital One felt the management of direct mail was its largest tactical challenge across all segments. As a result, to better target consumers with appropriate direct mail, Capital One had to rely on other means to segment consumers. By actively testing a wide variety of products and service features, marketing channels (in Canada, Capital One utilized both direct mail and

---

1   G. Bhalla & Associates, <u>Canadian Consumer Survey</u>, commissioned by Capital One, January 22, 2001.

the Internet to solicit applications) and other aspects of offerings, Capital One enhanced the response levels and maximized returns on investment within its underwriting parameters.

Credit evaluation began during the application process. Generally credit card issuers used a combination of credit bureau information, statistical models and decision rules to approve or decline applicants. These procedures were constantly changing in response to dynamic market conditions and new insights.

Driving innovation was always a key concern at Capital One, because it was the foundation of the company's success. Communicating Capital One's innovation was equally important, as Sartaj Alag, president of the Canadian branch of Capital One, pointed out:

> How do we come up with an advertising strategy that 1) speaks directly to our target segment, 2) is distinctive from our competitors and 3) is a position we can immediately deliver on?

Youssef Lahrech, Capital One's head of Marketing and Analysis in Canada added:

> How can Capital One change Canadian consumers' negative attitude towards credit cards through our advertising campaign? Can Capital One build one campaign for all consumer segments or do we need to differentiate our ads?

To determine whether their programs were on the right track, Capital One relied on quantitative measures, such as net present value per marketing dollar. After a customer was acquired, the Account Management Division ran tests to determine which marketing programs would either increase revenues or decrease default. Some of these programs included building balances, credit line increases and cross-selling products.

DAY-TO-DAY CHALLENGES
COMPETITIVE RESPONSES BY RETAIL BANKS

In 2004, major banks continued to issue the majority of new credit cards. With their infrastructure of branches and relationships with banking customers, acquisition costs for banks were lower than similar costs for U.S. credit card issuers. To respond to products offered by U.S. issuers, retail banks didn't need to innovate, advocate or educate. All they had to do was watch and follow. For example, while balance transfers had been a market niche for Capital One, retail banks had since entered the market.

Although Capital One was constantly inventing new products to keep ahead of its competitors, one advantage it maintained over retail banks was its ability to target offers to select consumers. A second advantage that favored Capital One was its expertise in credit cards, among other financial services offered. Because retail banks ran their credit card operations as part of a diversified portfolio of products, they seemed disinclined to grow their credit card operations if it meant cannibalizing other products in their portfolio.

A FOCUSED OPERATION THAT HAD NOT PARTNERED
WITH A REWARDS PROGRAM

For other card issuers, a strong rewards program, such as Air Canada's Aeroplan (to which 21 per cent of all Canadian card holders belonged in 2004, up from 12 per cent in 2002), provided quantifiable incentives to customers to increase their spending in the hunt for reward miles. Such programs also allowed partners to exchange mailing lists. There were several rewards programs in Canada other than Aeroplan, including Air Miles (by Loyalty Management Group), Hudson's Bay Company's HBC Rewards and Club Z program, Shoppers Drug Mart's Optimum program and Canadian Tire money. Twenty-three per cent of respondents cited the availability of a rewards program as a reason for using their primary credit card. By 2005, Capital One had built a strong business without having to rely on a rewards program or partner in Canada.

WORKING WITHOUT PHYSICAL BRANCHES

Capital One's lack of physical branches in Canada posed a unique challenge. Without face-to-face contact, several Capital One associates reasoned, it could be difficult to build a relationship with customers that appreciated and fulfilled their needs.

SUBSTITUTES FOR CREDIT CARDS

For customers who used credit cards purely as transaction vehicles, cash, cheques, debit cards and direct deposits were used as substitutes. Although they didn't demonstrate a cardholder's creditworthiness, debit cards allowed consumers to withdraw cash from the point of sale, giving them "cash back," while making purchases. For customers who carried balances on their credit cards, product substitutes included bank lines of credit, bank installment loans, home equity loans (with lower interest rates), retail layaway plans, retail store credit (such as Leon's and The Brick), cash advances against pay cheques from companies such as Money Mart, and vehicle loans from automobile manufacturers or leasing organizations, such as GE Capital.

THE MARKETING AND PROMOTIONS CHOICES

Capital One's global value proposition had been centered on the tagline "What's in Your Wallet?" positioning Capital One as offering "great value without the hassle." This proposition had been conveyed to customers through a series of long-running television ads in the United States and, more recently, in the United Kingdom. In both the United States and the United Kingdom, Capital One's locally made advertisements had proven extremely successful, with awareness levels of 98 per cent in the United States and 95 per cent in the United Kingdom. Up until now, Canadians primarily knew Capital One as a price player, with some Canadians aware of "great value without the hassle" because of U.S. advertising spillover.

Braganza wondered about the implications of using the U.S. positioning in Canada, and asked himself several questions:

- Could "great value" refer to price or should it refer to rewards?
- How important were rewards to Canadians and what were the implications for Capital One?
- What were the "hassles" that Canadian consumers wanted to avoid and how could Capital One show that it was providing "great value without the hassle" to Canadians?

To sum it up, was "great value" the right positioning for Capital One in Canada?

Aside from determining the right positioning, Braganza also had to decide if he would adapt U.S. and or U.K. advertisements, or develop advertisements unique to Canada. He recalled that consumer packaged goods companies (Procter & Gamble, for example) developed a significant portion of their advertising in the United States, and then adapted the same advertisement for various countries. In contrast, MasterCard's "priceless" campaign, gave flexibility to individual countries' organizations to develop their own unique advertisements based on a common global theme (tagline: "There are some things money can't buy; for everything else, there's MasterCard").

Braganza projected a minimum of four months to develop new advertising. He would need to find and hire an advertising agency, organize consumer research and obtain internal approvals at various stages. These tasks would require Capital One to shift precious marketing management resources from other programs designed to enhance customer acquisition and retention. And, according to Millward Brown's research, there was a greater than 50 per cent probability that a new advertisement in the financial services industry would score below the Canadian average. But the opportunity to develop an advertisement that truly "cut through the clutter" of average advertising had a strong appeal. Adapting a U.S. or U.K. advertisement would include paying licensing fees and could be accomplished in four weeks or less. However, it wasn't clear that the portfolio of available advertisements would enable Capital One to meet its objectives in the Canadian market.

But which segment should Capital One focus on? According to the Canadian test results, the various executions appealed to different target segments. Although competitors had largely ignored the sub prime customer (who seemed more responsive to offers), Capital One could also target prime and super prime customers (who were less responsive to offers, and were targeted by retail banks). Also should Capital One aim to book additional accounts or target existing customers? Put another way, should the television advertisements boost Capital One's direct mail response rate, or should they encourage current customers to use their cards more often?

Generally, different advertisement executions were needed to achieve either target. For example, focusing on an introductory interest rate could be enticing to new customers but not to existing ones. However, there were some advertisements—such as those focusing on fraud protection—that could be used for either segment. But would focusing on fraud protection be too general? Also, could any of the U.K and U.S. advertisements be relevant to a Canadian audience? Capital One was a relatively small player in Canada, as could be seen by Canada's contribution to the firm's overall loan portfolio (see Exhibit 16.8).

With regard to executing the strategy, John McNain, head of Brand and New Ventures at Capital One, wondered:

> How do we build a sustainable brand in Canada yet recognize our current limitations such as resources, infrastructure and product offerings? Also, how do we balance the growth of general awareness versus quickly demonstrating the returns from a more direct advertising campaign? We have to consider three dimensions. First, geography: Should we target just Toronto or the entire country? Second, how do we target our customer segments—Do we offer something general or consider a rewards or price play? Third, to what extent should our advertisements target new accounts or existing customers?

CONCLUSION

Braganza knew that a presentation to Capital One's senior management team would be more convincing if he could back up his recommendations with numbers and logic. While other firms could choose to invest in brand development over a longer time frame, Capital One's senior management team would want to see how the company's investment would pay out in the short to medium term. Braganza knew that advertising in the United States and United Kingdom would continue—clear evidence that their campaigns were paying out. But Braganza didn't want to focus solely on payout because it could compromise Capital One's brand-building efforts. His challenge was to balance the needs of driving new customer signups with the longer term goals of influencing customer behavior, increasing satisfaction rates and reducing attrition.

Braganza outlined the decisions he faced:

- On which customer segments should Capital One focus?
- What value proposition should Capital One be signaling to these segments?
- What advertisements should be used to deliver these messages, and what customization efforts were needed?

Braganza took a look at the competitive media spend for Canadian credit cards, as compiled by Neilsen, a media research firm (see Exhibit 16.9). Next, he looked at a list of competitive cards and their features, as can be seen in Exhibit 16.10. He also reviewed results from Capital One's U.K. and U.S. advertising copy tests in Canada for both the prime and sub prime segments (see Exhibit 16.11).

This was the first time that Capital One would be investing in mass media advertising. Braganza wanted to recommend the best set of options to his senior management team.

EXHIBIT 16.1 Credit card statistics

CANADIAN BANKERS ASSOCIATION
Credit Card Statistics—VISA and MasterCard

DB 38—PUBLIC

FISCAL YEAR ENDED OCT. 31	NUMBER OF CARDS IN CIRCULATION (1A) (MILLIONS)	*NO. OF ACCTS WITH BALANCES (MILLIONS), INCLUDING THOSE THAT ARE PAID OFF EVERY MONTH (1B)	NET RETAIL VOLUME (2) (BILLIONS)	AVERAGE SALE	% DELINQUENCY 90 DAYS & OVER (3)(7)	NUMBER OF CARDS FRAUDULENTLY USED (2)	$ AMOUNT OF FRAUDULENT ACCOUNTS WRITTEN OFF (6) (MILLIONS)	MERCHANT OUTLETS (5)	VISA/MCI PRINCIPAL ISSUERS
1977	8.2		$3.61	$30.46	1.3%	-	-	271,150	-
1978	9.0		$4.90	$32.50	1.3%	-	-	290,692	-
1979	9.9		$6.64	$35.72	1.2%	-	-	322,115	-
1980	10.8		$8.82	$39.47	1.3%	-	-	347,845	-
1981	12.0		$10.59	$42.43	1.0%	-	-	371,831	-
1982	11.6		$13.83	$50.30	1.7%	-	$15.88	382,206	-
1983	12.1		$14.84	$49.88	0.9%	19,200	$17.39	419,610	10
1984	13.1		$16.92	$52.05	0.7%	21,332	$16.79	442,928	10
1985	14.0	7.3	$19.35	$51.90	0.7%	21,026	$17.54	527,042	10
1986	15.5	7.9	$23.01	$55.15	0.8%	22,326	$18.61	571,771	10
1987	17.6	8.8	$26.37	$58.52	0.7%	23,913	$15.78	642,429	12
1988	19.4	9.5	$30.33	$61.90	0.7%	25,773	$15.63	646,844	13
1989	20.4	10.3	$36.10	$66.00	0.9%	30,919	$19.20	709,674	14
1990	23.2	11.1	$38.60	$67.22	1.8%	32,851	$28.90	786,288	14
1991	24.3	11.8	$40.45	$67.40	1.3%	53,968	$44.60	857,159	14
1992	24.4	12.2	$43.10	$69.30	1.0%	61,234	$63.50	896,365	14
1993	25.0	12.4	$47.90	$70.50	0.7%	63,442	$75.20	904,689	13
1994	27.5	13.2	$55.10	$72.40	0.9%	63,635	$70.60	955,993	13
1995	28.8	13.6	$61.26	$74.51	0.9%	66,109	$72.64	981,851	13

EXHIBIT 16.1 Credit card statistics (continued)

FISCAL YEAR ENDED OCT. 31	NUMBER OF CARDS IN CIRCULATION (1A) (MILLIONS)	*NO. OF ACCTS WITH BALANCES (MILLIONS), INCLUDING THOSE THAT ARE PAID OFF EVERY MONTH (1B)	NET RETAIL VOLUME (2) (BILLIONS)	AVERAGE SALE	% DELINQUENCY 90 DAYS & OVER (3)(7)	NUMBER OF CARDS FRAUDULENTLY USED (2)	$ AMOUNT OF FRAUDULENT ACCOUNTS WRITTEN OFF (6) (MILLIONS)	MERCHANT OUTLETS (5)	VISA/MCI PRINCIPAL ISSUERS
1996	30.2	14.1	$67.70	$77.80	1.0%	77,740	$83.60	1,076,694	15
1997	31.9	15.0	$76.00	$82.50	0.9%	89,982	$88.08	1,106,141	17
1998	35.3	16.0	$84.10	$89.96	0.9%	126,384	$104.80	1,143,110	19
1999	37.7	17.3	$94.30	$90.35	0.9%	132,836	$134.10	1,139,228	18
2000	40.1	18.5	$109.87	$95.57	0.7%	112,070	$156.38	1,187,745	19
2001	44.1	19.6	$121.82	$99.16	0.8%	116,139	$142.27	1,206,779	19
2002	49.4	20.8	$135.69	$100.51	0.7%	136,598	$128.42	1,265,157	23
2003	50.4	22.2	$150.49	$102.00	0.8%	146,310	$138.60	1,187,384	23
2004	53.4	23.2	$168.78	$104.00	0.8%	177,081	$163.18	1,128,410	23

(1a) As at last day of the fiscal year-end
(1b) As at last day of the fiscal year-end, including accounts with balances paid off every month.
(2) Reported total for the fiscal year.
(3) Percentage of outstandings as at fiscal year-end.
(4) Total of Net Retail Volume ($ sales) and cash advance volume ($).
(5) Merchants accepting VISA and/or MASTERCARD. Note that merchants accepting both cards have been reported by each plan. To estimate # of merchant outlets accepting VISA or MASTERCARD, divide Merchants Outlets by 2 and multiply by 1.1.
(6) Includes total cardholder and merchant fraud for the fiscal year.
(7) Effective October 31, 1991, a new interpretation of "90 days & over" was adopted. This resulted in a one-time reduction in the delinquency ratio of approx. 0.2%.

PRINCIPAL VISA AND MASTERCARD ISSUERS:

VISA Bank of America, Bank of Nova Scotia, Caisses Populaires Desjardins, CIBC, Citizens Bank of Canada, Home Trust, Laurentian Bank, Royal Bank, TD Bank, US Bank, Vancouver City Savings Credit Union.

MCI Alberta Treasury Branches, Bank of Montreal, Canadian Tire Acceptance Ltd, Capital One, Citibank Canada, Credit Union Electronic Transaction Services Inc., G.E. Capital Corp., MBNA Canada., National Bank of Canada, President's Choice Financial, Wells Fargo/Trans Canada, Sears Canada

   (Data from Affiliated Issuers reported through Principal Issuers)

Source: Canadian Bankers Association, Table includes data from all VISA & MASTERCARD issuers.

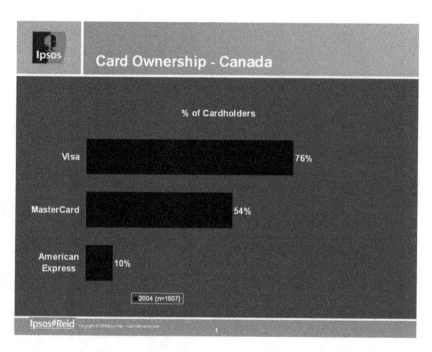

EXHIBIT 16.2 Card ownership—Canada

Source: Ipsos-Reid

Channel used:	2002 (n=289) %	2003 (n=256) %	2004 (n=322) %
In store	26	26	32
At bank branch	20	17	26
Kiosk/shopping centre	-	-	3
Through the mail	33	26	18
Inbound telephone	9	6	10
Outbound telephone	4	7	4
Over the Internet	3	6	7

EXHIBIT 16.3 Distribution channel for card applications

Source: Ipsos-Reid

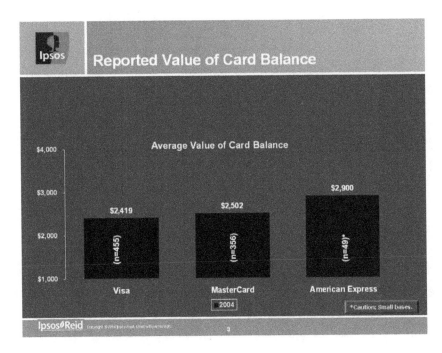

EXHIBIT 16.4   Reported value of card balance

Source: Ipsos-Reid

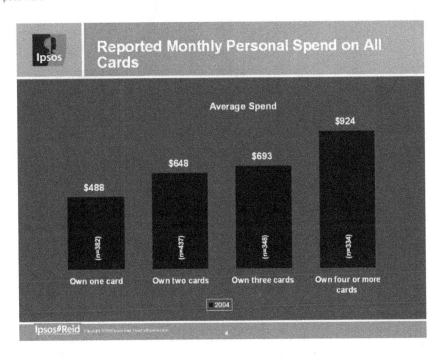

Exhibit 16.5   Reported monthly personal spend on all cards

Source: Ipsos-Reid

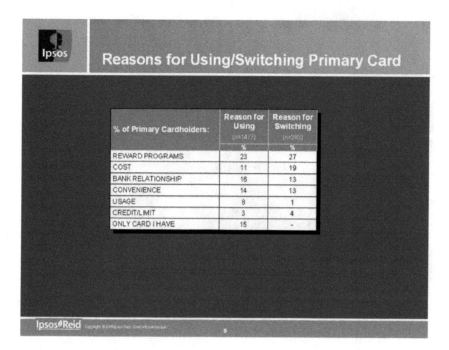

Exhibit 16.6   Reasons for using/switching primary card

Source: Ipsos-Reid

Exhibit 16.7   capital one's credit cards available to canadians

CREDIT CARD	CAPITAL ONE® LOW-RATE PLATINUM MASTERCARD®	CAPITAL ONE 1% CASH REBATE PLATINUM MASTERCARD	CAPITAL ONE GOLD MASTERCARD	CAPITAL ONE SECURED MASTERCARD
This card is right for you if	You have excellent credit and have had Canadian cards for at least 3 years	You have excellent credit and have had Canadian cards for at least 3 years	You would like to strengthen your credit and have had Canadian cards for at least 3 years	You want to establish credit
Annual Purchase Rate	6.99%	17.90%	9.9% until May 2006; 19.8% variable thereafter (a variable annual interest rate of Canadian Prime plus 15.55%, currently equal to 19.8% as of July 2005)	19.8% variable (a variable annual interest rate of Canadian Prime plus 15.55%, currently equal to 19.8% as of July 2005)
Annual Fee	None	None	$59	$59
Security Funds Required	None	None	None	Either $75 or $200

Source: www.capitalone.ca, accessed January 27, 2006.

EXHIBIT 16.8 Capital one financial corporation: contribution by geographic region (US$)

| | DECEMBER 31 | | | | |
| | 2004 | | | 2003 | |
	LOANS	PERCENTAGE OF TOTAL		LOANS	PERCENTAGE OF TOTAL
Geographic Region:					
Domestic					
South	$ 25,034,582	31.34%		$ 23,262,643	32.65%
West	15,873,159	19.88		14,662,193	20.58
Midwest	15,220,162	19.06		13,643,202	19.15
Northeast	13,198,619	16.53		12,029,894	16.89
Total Domestic	69,326,522	86.81%		63,597,932	89.27%
International					
U.K.	8,163,109	10.22%		5,546,644	7.78%
Canada	2,360,297	2.96		1,935,396	2.72
Other	11,371	.01		164,824	0.23
Total International	10,534,777	13.19%		7,646,864	10.73%
	79,861,299	100.00%		71,244,796	100.00%
Less securitization adjustments	(41,645,708)			(38,394,527)	
Total	$ 38,215,591			$ 32,850,269	

Source: Capital One Annual Report.

EXHIBIT 16.9 2004 Competitive media spend (NIELSEN)

CLASS	COMPANY	TOTAL MEDIA ($)	MT SHR%	DAILY PAPER ($)	MAGAZINE ($)	OUT OF HOME ($)	RADIO ($)	TOTAL TV ($)	NETWORK TV ($)	SELECTIVE TV ($)
Cards: Credit; Debit;	(Jetsgo Corporation)	25,000	0.0	0	0	25,000	0	0	0	0
Cards: Credit; Debit;	Alaska Air Group, Inc	592,699	0.8	222,202	0	0	10,650	359,847	0	359,847
Cards: Credit; Debit;	American Express Company	13,477,478	17.2	4,433,944	2,049,491	519,502	215,011	6,259,530	5,373,450	886,080
Cards: Credit; Debit;	Bank Of America	56,792	0.1	0	0	0	56,792	0	0	0
Cards: Credit; Debit;	Bank Of Nova Scotia	330,160	0.4	29,524	15,316	0	0	285,320	193,616	91,704
Cards: Credit; Debit;	Bayview Credit Union	3,303	0.0	3,303	0	0	0	0	0	0
Cards: Credit; Debit;	Benq America Corp	4,757	0.0	0	4,757	0	0	0	0	0
Cards: Credit; Debit;	Bmo Financial Group	3,221,715	4.1	2,355,300	191,540	0	372,866	302,009	294,529	7,480
Cards: Credit; Debit;	Canadian Automobile Association	43,069	0.1	0	26,673	0	0	16,396	0	16,396
Cards: Credit; Debit;	Canadian Cooperative Agricultural Finan	30,179	0.0	0	0	30,179	0	0	0	0
Cards: Credit; Debit;	Canadian Imperial Bank Of Commerce	7,068,982	9.0	2,122,847	1,910,396	293,255	758,920	1,983,564	1,349,306	634,258
Cards: Credit; Debit;	Canadian Tire Corporation Limited	41,304	0.1	41,304	0	0	0	0	0	0
Cards: Credit; Debit;	Choice Rewards	42,783	0.1	39,079	3,704	0	0	0	0	0
Cards: Credit; Debit;	Citigroup Inc	373,472	0.5	56,234	11,520	305,718	0	0	0	0
Cards: Credit; Debit;	Corp-Rate	2,998	0.0	0	2,998	0	0	0	0	0
Cards: Credit; Debit;	Credit Union Electronic Transaction Serv	14,578	0.0	14,578	0	0	0	0	0	0
Cards: Credit; Debit;	Dexit Inc	563,220	0.7	0	0	357,452	205,768	0	0	0
Cards: Credit; Debit;	Gm Corp	1,945,383	2.5	873,921	1,043,734	23,960	3,768	0	0	0

EXHIBIT 16.9 2004 Competitive media spend (NIELSEN) (continued)

CLASS	COMPANY	TOTAL MEDIA ($)	MT SHR%	DAILY PAPER ($)	MAGAZINE ($)	OUT OF HOME ($)	RADIO ($)	TOTAL TV ($)	NETWORK TV ($)	SELECTIVE TV ($)
Cards: Credit; Debit;	Groupe Marie Claire, Le	20,552	0.0	0	20,552	0	0	0	0	0
Cards: Credit; Debit;	Island Savings Credit Union	7,834	0.0	7,834	0	0	0	0	0	0
Cards: Credit; Debit;	Kootenay Savings Credit Union	3,055	0.0	3,055	0	0	0	0	0	0
Cards: Credit; Debit;	Mastercard International Inc	10,717,720	13.7	787,066	111,522	127,325	187,701	9,504,106	5,692,158	3,811,948
Cards: Credit; Debit;	Mbna Canada Bank	576,959	0.7	246,342	0	0	0	330,617	68,981	261,636
Cards: Credit; Debit;	Morgan Stanley & Co Ltd	116	0.0	0	0	0	0	116	0	116
Cards: Credit; Debit;	Mouvement Des Caisses Desjardins	534,326	0.7	249,425	17,264	267,637	0	0	0	0
Cards: Credit; Debit;	National Bank Of Canada	284,991	0.4	138,877	146,114	0	0	0	0	0
Cards: Credit; Debit;	Pattison Group, Jim	40,223	0.1	40,223	0	0	0	0	0	0
Cards: Credit; Debit;	Petro Canada Ltd	4,065,060	5.2	1,642,395	0	0	695,976	1,726,689	667,088	1,059,601
Cards: Credit; Debit;	Rbc Financial Group	9,670,473	12.3	3,920,508	1,017,955	296,857	540,463	3,894,690	2,904,384	990,306
Cards: Credit; Debit;	Rona Inc	4,037	0.0	4,037	0	0	0	0	0	0
Cards: Credit; Debit;	Sears Canada Inc	77,305	0.1	77,305	0	0	0	0	0	0
Cards: Credit; Debit;	Solstice Publishing Inc	4,320	0.0	0	4,320	0	0	0	0	0
Cards: Credit; Debit;	Td Bank Financial Group	4,020,993	5.1	1,988,483	1,018,804	287,718	276,230	449,758	449,758	0
Cards: Credit; Debit;	Valero Energy Corporation	33,396	0.0	0	0	0	33,396	0	0	0
Cards: Credit; Debit;	Visa International	20,448,857	26.1	1,461,989	1,286,796	135,213	354,561	17,210,298	12,548,090	4,662,208
Cards: Credit; Debit;	Weston Limited, George	3,334	0.0	3,334	0	0	0	0	0	0
TOTAL	*TOTAL*	78,351,423	100.0	20,763,109	8,883,456	2,669,816	3,712,102	42,322,940	29,541,360	12,781,580

Source: Nielsen Media Research Canada

EXHIBIT 16.10   Competitive credit cards—five major banks

CREDIT CARDS*	INTEREST RATE	ANNUAL FEE	INSURANCE PROGRAMS	REWARD PROGRAMS	GUARANTEED HOTEL RESERVATIONS	EMERGENCY CARD REPLACEMENT	DISCOUNTS
BMO Bank of Montreal							
Mosaik MasterCard (customizable)							
12 different combinations possible	Variable	Yes	√	√			
CIBC							
Visa Cards							
Aventura Gold	19.5%	120	√	√	√	√	
Aerogold	19.5%	120	√	√	√	√	√
Aero Classic	19.5%	29	√	√	√	√	√
Classic	18.5%	Free	√		√	√	√
Select	10.5%	29	√		√	√	√
Dividend	19.5%	Free	√		√	√	√
Dividend Platinum	19.5%	79	√		√	√	√
Gold	18.5%	99	√	√		√	√
Shoppers Optimum	19.5%	Free	√	√		√	√
Classic for Students	18.5%	Free	√			√	√
US Dollar	18.5%	35	√			√	√
Royal Bank							
RBC Rewards Cards							
Visa Platinum Avion	19.5%	120	√	√	√	√	√
Visa Platinum Preferred	18.5%	110	√	√	√	√	√

EXHIBIT 16.10 Competitive credit cards—five major banks (continued)

CREDIT CARDS*	INTEREST RATE	ANNUAL FEE	INSURANCE PROGRAMS	REWARD PROGRAMS	GUARANTEED HOTEL RESERVATIONS	EMERGENCY CARD REPLACEMENT	DISCOUNTS
Visa Gold Preferred	18.5%	110	√	√	√	√	√
Visa Classic II	18.5%	35	√	√	√	√	√
Visa Classic II Student	18.5%	35	√	√	√	√	√
RBC Rewards Visa Classic	18.5%	Free	√	√	√	√	√
US Dollar Visa Gold (US$)	18.5%	65	√	√	√	√	√
RBC Mike Weir Visa Card	19.5%	35	√	√	√	√	√
Partner Rewards Cards							
Advantage Visa Gold	20.5%	70	√	√	√	√	√
British Airways Visa Platinum	20.5%	75	√	√	√	√	√
Cathay Pacific Visa Platinum	20.5%	75	√	√	√	√	√
Esso Visa	18.5%	Free	√	√	√	√	√
Starbucks Duetto Visa Card	19.5%	Free	√	√	√	√	√
Everyday Convenience Cards							
Visa Platinum	18.5%	Free	√		√	√	√
Visa Gold	18.5%	Free	√		√	√	√
Visa Classic Low Rate	11.5%	20	√		√	√	√
Visa Classic	18.5%	Free	√		√	√	√
Visa Classic Student	18.5%	Free	√		√	√	√
Scotiabank							
Visa Cards							
ScotiaGold Preferred Visa	17.9%	95	√	√	√	√	√

(continued)

EXHIBIT 16.10 Competitive credit cards—five major banks *(continued)*

CREDIT CARDS*	INTEREST RATE	ANNUAL FEE	INSURANCE PROGRAMS	REWARD PROGRAMS	GUARANTEED HOTEL RESERVATIONS	EMERGENCY CARD REPLACEMENT	DISCOUNTS
No-Fee ScotiaGold Visa	18.5%	Free	√		√	√	√
Scotia Moneyback Visa	17.9%	8 or Free		√	√	√	√
ScotiaLine Visa	Variable	Free	√		√	√	√
Scotia Value Visa	10.4%–12.9%	29			√	√	√
TD Canada Trust							
Reward Cards							
TD Gold Travel Visa	19.5%	120	√	√	√	√	√
TD Gold Elite Visa	19.5%	99	√	√	√	√	√
The GM Card	19.5%	Free	√	√	√	√	√
Low Rate Cards	√	√	√				
TD Emerald Visa**	7.15%–12.15%	25	√		√	√	√
Other Cards							
TD Green Visa Card	19.8%	Free	√		√	√	√
TD Gold Select Visa	19.8%	Free	√		√	√	√
TD U.S Dollar Advantage Visa (US$)	18.5%	25	√		√	√	√
Small Business Credit Cards							
TD Business Visa Card	19.8%	50	√		√	√	√
TD Venture Line of Credit Visa	9.3%	Free			√	√	√

**Based on TD Prime of 5.25%*

Source: This list was created from information gathered from the various bank websites on 20th Feb 2006. Some features may differ from card to card, and between banks. In addition, more features may be available than are depicted in this list.

EXHIBIT 16.11 Canadian test scores for capital one ads

The Link™ Copy Test was designed to provide a complete understanding of how an ad is likely to perform in-market. It provides both evaluative and diagnostic measures and uses a standard questionnaire targeted at a custom sample. Respondents are screened against appropriate criteria; exposed to a reel of four ads with the Test Ad in the second position; re-exposed to the first ad and asked warm-up questions; re-exposed to the Test Ad and asked a full set of questions; and then re-exposed to the Test Ad again for Interest Trace. Link quantifies branded impact through the Awareness Index (AI). AI is the awareness generated per 100 GRPs (gross rating points). The AI indicates how efficient the ad is at generating awareness. The components of the AI are as follows:

- Branding: Is the brand integral to the storyline? Does the brand play the 'hero'? Is the brand character a fit with the brand? Are there brand cues such as colors, icons, mnemonics, music/jingles, slogans, executional branding (e.g. Gap), package shots?
- Enjoyment: Do the aspects of the creative lead to the ad's enjoyment? Some include: music, talent, animals, kids, scenery/visuals, storyline, humor, surprise
- Active Involvement: Determine the ad's ability to engage the viewer; its 'stopping power'; its style or message of ad; the level of emotional involvement. The ad can also be negatively involving. For many brands, this is likely not desirable.

Millward Brown relied on its large database of ads tested: 11,000 tests had been conducted worldwide and, of those, over 600 tests had been in Canada, with two-thirds being English ads.

Source: Millward Brown.

Below are the Canadian test scores for Capital One's U.S. and U.K. commercials.

Prime + Super Prime Segments (Percent Of Respondents Agreeing)		Bee	Catapult	Cinderella	Crab	Envelope	Poppers	Troll	Visigoths	Canada* Ever Aired Norms
Branded Impact	Branding (Most important)	44	42	38	40	37	30	45	42	**38**
	Enjoyment (2ndary Importance)	42	45	50	44	35	30	45	37	**39**
	Involving/Unique/Interesting	56	56	58	55	50	38	55	60	**55**
	Irritating/Unpleasant/Disturbing	2	10	12	2	5	2	25	13	**7**
Communication	Unaided recall	36	38	45	35	35	30	50	40	**37**
	Aided recall	57	44	65	68	49	35	70	55	**49**

*Average for all industry ads tested by Millward Brown

Underserved Segment (Percent of respondents agreeing)		Bee	Catapult	Cinderella	Crab	Envelope	Poppers	Troll	Visigoths	Canada* Ever Aired Norms
Branded Impact	Branding (Most important)	45	42	38	40	37	30	43	38	**38**
	Enjoyment (2ndary Importance)	45	50	50	55	39	30	55	45	**39**
	Involving/Unique/Interesting	57	56	58	55	57	35	55	60	**55**
	Irritating/Unpleasant/Disturbing	2	10	15	2	5	2	20	13	**7**
Communication	Unaided recall	34	34	40	32	37	25	55	50	**37**
	Aided recall	55	47	70	48	49	32	75	69	**49**

Source: Casewriter
Note: Results have been disguised, including Canada Ever Aired Norms.

CHAPTER 17

The Hunger Games: Catching Fire
Using Digital and Social Media for Brand Storytelling

Mohanbir Sawhney and Pallavi Goodman

The Hunger Games film series began in 2012 with the launch of the first movie in the franchise.[1] In 2013 the second film, called *The Hunger Games: Catching Fire*, was released and set the record for the biggest opening weekend for any movie ever released in November.[2] The marketing campaign for the film was launched well in advance of its opening and employed a promotional campaign that leveraged digital and social media in a coordinated and holistic way to tell a brand story and to engage existing fans of the first movie. Lionsgate Entertainment and Ignition Creative collaborated to create a new type of marketing campaign that relied on storytelling in a digital world and blurred the lines between reality and fiction. This novel marketing strategy, called brand storytelling, consisted of a mix of social media campaigns undertaken across a variety of platforms such as YouTube, Tumblr, Facebook, Twitter, and Instagram, while bringing into sharper focus brand and designer partnerships in the film, and attracting enthusiastic fan participation.

While many aspects of the campaign marked new ground for a film promotion, it raised some unanswered questions. What did the campaign do well, and what could have been done better? Did the campaign really enhance the Hunger Games brand and audience participation? Was brand storytelling the future of film promotion, or was it a one-off concept that lent itself well to this particular film?

THE HUNGER GAMES

The Hunger Games got its start in the form of three novels written by American author and screenwriter Suzanne Collins. First in the trilogy was *The Hunger Games*, published in 2008. Next came *Catching Fire*, in 2009, followed by *Mockingjay*, in 2010. The novels were set in the imaginary, post-apocalyptic nation of Panem, which consisted of a wealthy Capitol and twelve districts, in varying states of poverty and starvation, which were ruled by the Capitol.

---

1   The trailer for the first Hunger Games film can be viewed at https://www.youtube.com/watch?v=4S9a5V9ODuY.
2   The trailer for *The Hunger Games: Catching Fire* can be viewed at https://www.youtube.com/watch?v=EAzGXqJSDJ8.

The citizens of the districts were forced to participate in an annual televised competition called the Hunger Games.

The novels combined the genres of science fiction, adventure, drama, and action. The series quickly captured readers' imagination, especially that of young adults, becoming a top seller on Amazon.com and besting the Harry Potter book series.[3] By 2014, the novels had sold more than 65 million copies in the United States.

BRAND STORYTELLING

Brand storytelling uses new distribution platforms to create personal and unique consumer experiences. Although the branded content is created independent of the audience's needs, the storytelling used to deliver that content connects with the audience's imagination and evokes powerful emotions that linger in their minds. Brand storytelling uses characters and injects personality, humor, and emotion to keep audiences engaged and entertained. It appeals to the audience to imbue a story—and by extension, a brand—with meaning. In a hyperconnected and social world where consumers can find out everything there is to know about a brand or product, evoking emotions about a brand's value can be a powerful way to connect with the audience.

Transmedia storytelling is a technique that allows a story to unfold across multiple media platforms and that solicits the active participation of fans and end users in the story's expansion across these media.[4] In transmedia storytelling, the "spreadability" of the narrative is an important consideration and is accomplished through "viral marketing" practices in social media channels. In transmedia storytelling, finding the core fan base that will share and disseminate the narrative is a crucial element of the campaign. Transmedia storytelling strives for continuity of the narrative as the story expands across multiple channels, thus giving fans an immersive experience in the story. Transmedia storytelling as we know it today emerged in the entertainment industry with films such as *The Blair Witch Project* (1999), whose promotional campaign incorporated televised "documentaries" on the history of the (fictional) Blair Witch and on-the-street personnel who distributed missing-person flyers for the characters who disappear in the film. The technique was rapidly adopted by brand marketers across a wide range of industries. The rise of transmedia brand storytelling was fueled by the ability of digital and social media channels to connect with diverse audiences across the world. *The Lizzie Bennet Diaries*, for example, used a combination of vlogs, Twitter, Facebook, Instagram, and Tumblr to retell the story of Jane Austen's *Pride and Prejudice* in the twenty-first century, which created innovative opportunities for fans to interact with the story.

---

3 Julie Bosman, "Amazon Crowns 'Hunger Games' as Its Top Seller, Surpassing Harry Potter Series," *New York Times*, August 17, 2012.

4 For an overview of transmedia storytelling, see Henry Jenkins, "Transmedia Storytelling 101," *Confessions of an Aca-Fan* (blog), March 22, 2007, http://henryjenkins.org/2007/03/transmedia_storytelling_101.html.

An early example of transmedia brand storytelling was the Audi A3 "Art of the Heist" campaign (see **Exhibit 17.1**). This campaign, designed and executed by marketing agency Campfire in 2005, featured an interactive story about a stolen Audi A3. The campaign involved the audience by making them part of the investigation to find the vehicle. It was like a spy movie, except that this drama moved back and forth between the virtual world and the real world, with the audience as active participants in the story. It began with live footage of a car theft in progress at an Audi dealership on Park Avenue. The thieves made off with a brand-new Audi with the police in hot pursuit. The chase was unsuccessful and flyers were later handed out describing the stolen vehicle. The next day, Audi posted signs at the New York International Auto Show asking for information on the vehicle.

Bloggers around the world posted stories about the stolen vehicle and billboard and messages appeared asking for the public's help in finding the vehicle. A TV commercial was even created about the car's disappearance that described some of its features: "open sky system," "dual clutch DSG," "Audi Nav Plus," and "two SD card slots." Finally, the A3's website revealed that the company had hired a firm specializing in the recovery of high-end art items, Last Resort Retrieval, to find the missing car. Last Resort had advertised its services in several high-end magazines to strengthen the illusion of its authenticity. Audi even enlisted the help of a videogame designer to design a game/app that would help to find the missing car. An influential blogger had also compiled details of the case and a curious visitor to the site would have found videos and clips about the theft and details about the public's participation in the recovery of the car. Anyone following the story could watch events unfold as in a movie. A visit to Audi's site would have revealed that the "stolen" car had been recovered and why it had been stolen in the first place. The audience had participated in the largest and most experiential "reality blurring" campaign ever executed. The campaign resulted in 45 million PR impressions, 500,000 story participants, over 10,000 leads to dealers, and over 2 million unique visitors to AudiUSA.com.

Other transmedia brand storytelling examples included Campfire's campaign for the popular HBO series *Game of Thrones* (see **Exhibit 17.2**), as well as campaigns for the films *Prometheus* and *The Matrix*. Mattel launched a transmedia storytelling campaign to unite dolls Barbie and Ken after Mattel engineered their break-up. Mattel had "Ken" post photos on Facebook and videos on YouTube, as well as check in on Foursquare in a concerted effort to win "Barbie" back. Fans could follow Ken's efforts and the narrative thread across different media.

PROMOTIONAL MIX FOR *THE HUNGER GAMES: CATCHING FIRE*

Realizing the power of transmedia storytelling, the producers of *The Hunger Games: Catching Fire* made social media the centerpiece of the film's marketing campaign (see **Exhibit 17. 3**). These social media channels served to illuminate the difference between the privileged life of the inhabitants of the Capitol and the bleak lives of citizens in the twelve districts ruled by the Capitol.

A traditional marketing campaign would have focused on creating brand awareness three to six months prior to the release of the film, using established elements such as ad placement on TV, radio, magazines, and billboards, as well as partnerships, a dedicated website, and YouTube teasers. Other traditional elements included in-person PR (interviews, red carpet), online PR (blogs and social media), and cross-marketing partnerships. The *Catching Fire* campaign was an elaborate effort that went beyond movie posters and websites to attract attention and create intrigue in curious fans' minds. Tim Palen, Lionsgate's marketing chief, who was responsible for crafting the message and the images, remarked, "This was dramatically different from anything we did for the first movie. It was brave of the filmmakers to agree we should be that bold."[5] Teaser billboards began appearing in April 2013, well in advance of the film's slated November opening, depicting futuristic fashion called "Capitol Couture" that garnered fans' eyeballs and attention (see **Exhibit 17.4** and **Exhibit 17.5**). When curious fans googled the terms "Capitol Couture," they reached a Tumblr site about the Capitol. The Tumblr site in turn led to the Capitol's links on Facebook, Twitter, YouTube and Instagram. Although fans had encountered the Capitol and its districts in the novels, these sites allowed them a much deeper engagement with life in the hard-edged city. Fans could experience the strange world of fashion in the Capitol through these sites and links, much more so than they ever could in the books and the movies. As in the books and movies, the Capitol largely was depicted as dark, mysterious and intimidating.

TUMBLR

The Capitol Couture Tumblr (http://capitolcouture.pn) allowed Hunger Games fans to engage deeply with the culture of the Capitol. Even though the Capitol formed an important part of the story's plot, it had remained mysterious in the books and movies. The Tumblr site changed this by offering fans a look into the strange world of fashion in the Capitol. The Capitol Couture Tumblr was designed like an online magazine and celebrated the "incredible achievements" of the Capitol in art, fashion, and design. Articles on fashion and culture were penned by real-life writers, who were featured on the site and given titles such as Editor-in-Chief, Fashion Designer, Capitol Correspondent and Capitol Contributor, thus blurring the lines between fact and fiction.

The online magazine, which borrowed its look and feel from real-life luxury magazines, also contained elaborate photographs of the film's characters taken by Tim Palen, a professional photographer who had led previous Lionsgate campaigns for movies such as *Saw* and *Warrior*. He was said to be as enthusiastic as the teenage fans of the film, and author Suzanne Collins felt that the film's marketing under Palen was in safe hands. Palen had consulted

---

5 Marc Graser, "Lionsgate's Tim Palen Crafts Stylish Universe for 'Hunger Games: Catching Fire,'" *Variety*, October 29, 2013.

closely with Collins before conceptualizing the campaign. Palen and his team designed the Capitol Portraits, a series of detailed and dramatic photographs that vividly depicted each of the eleven major characters in the film (see **Exhibit 17.6**). Each portrait's release became a major event and was sent to the magazine's Facebook, Twitter, and Instagram feeds. Simultaneously, the portraits were also distributed to a team of partners such as Yahoo Movies, MTV, MSN, and the Huffington Post. These media outlets agreed to refer to the images as Capitol Portraits, and similar outlets did the same.

Palen did not rely on overt product placements in the movie, knowing that such gimmicks tended to turn off fans. Instead, he gave promotional partners such as cosmetics brand CoverGirl, fashion e-tailer Net-a-Porter and nail-polish brand China Glaze space in Capitol Couture to promote their products which tied in to the film. "There's a little punk-rock, anti-establishment in the true core fans, the purists [of the franchise]," Palen told *Variety*. "There was always a strong sense we should keep [the campaign] authentic and not overtly gross."[6]

Even though the Capitol Couture Tumblr site did not add much to the film's story, it offered deeper insight into the ostentatious and fashionable life in the Capitol and served to expand the narrative and the fans' experience. The Tumblr site was clearly the showpiece of the campaign. It featured futuristic, avant-garde fashion as well as makeup and beauty (such as the CoverGirl Capitol Collection)[7] and design and architecture at the Capitol. Capitol Updates led to a Twitter page consisting of tweets and updates. The Tumblr site also served as the gateway to links on Facebook, Twitter, Google+, Instagram and YouTube.

YOUTUBE

YouTube served as another social sharing medium for *Catching Fire*. Called CapitolTV, the YouTube channel (https://goo.gl/fjoWbt) featured previews and trailers of the film and once again channeled the fervor and creative talents of the film's fan base. Fans were asked to post videos, which then aired on CapitolTV. The channel featured a number of slick videos, such as CapitolTV District Voices, which illustrated the various capabilities of the different districts—District 6's powerful assault vehicles, District 5's cutting-edge renewable energy technologies, District 8's textiles, and District 2's peacekeeping forces, to name a few.

FACEBOOK

Visitors who clicked on the Tumblr site's Facebook icon were led to the One Panem Facebook page (https://www.facebook.com/OnePanem). It featured photos, videos, and apps, and it solicited feedback to questions ("What do you hope to see in the new Panem?"). The Facebook page had an "Invite Friends to Like this Page" link as well as visitor posts.

---

6   Ibid.
7   "CoverGirl Gets Inspired by The Hunger Games for 'Capitol Beauty' Collection," *Fashion Gone Rogue*, October 28, 2013, http://www.fashiongonerogue.com/covergirl-hunger-games-makeup-collection.

The first Facebook page for the movie series was launched in October 2011, prior to the first Hunger Games film opening in March 2012. Prior to the release of *Catching Fire*, a Facebook post asked citizens (fans) to identify the district to which they belonged (see **Exhibit 17.7**). The Facebook page encouraged citizens to celebrate the "victors"—their fellow citizens—and to serve their district well. The marketing campaign also used the Facebook page to launch a video teaser of the upcoming movie, calling it "an important announcement." Finally, Facebook again was used, this time to announce the 75th Annual Hunger Games (the central event of the movie) and that all citizens were required by law to view it. Not only the Capitol but also each of the twelve districts also had its own Facebook page.

TWITTER

The marketing team regularly engaged with fans on Twitter and since the release of the first Hunger Games movie, the film's Twitter following had grown to almost one billion, a 75 percent growth over an eighteen-month period. The Twitter account (https://twitter.com/thecapitolpn) served mostly to relay public service announcements from the Capitol and post ideological messages to Panem's citizens. These messages, for example, called upon citizens to respect their district's boundaries ("movement beyond your district is forbidden") and threatened punishment to those who ignored the call. In addition, the Twitter account contained links to Capitol Couture and featured the film's official trailers and promotional pictures (see **Exhibit 17.8**).

INSTAGRAM

Many of the fashionable photographs featured in the Capitol Couture Tumblr were also posted on the Capitol's Instagram site (https://instagram.com/capitolcouture). Fashion-conscious hipsters comprised a large section of Instagram users. By focusing on fashion and design rather than the overall story, Lionsgate displayed a deep understanding of the film's niche fan base. The Instagram profile did not necessarily add to the story's plot, but it helped to create excitement among younger fans who used the site and who were expected to share the high-fashion pictures with friends and evangelize on behalf of the film and its characters. The Capitol's Instagram profile had 31,464 followers.

AUDIENCE ENGAGEMENT
TARGET AUDIENCE

The *Catching Fire* storytelling campaign catered to a very specific target audience: passionate existing fans—not newcomers. The film's producers looked to utilize the book series' already-large fan base, most of whom were men and women under 25. At the very least, fans were expected to be steeped in the world of the first movie if not the book series. The social media campaign was designed to elevate the excitement among fans and cause them to start conversations about the movie and its characters with their friends and associates. The film's marketing agency found eager fans who actively participated in the challenges thrown out by the Capitol and connected with other fans through the various social channels. As a result, fans produced a tremendous amount of user-generated content.

USER-GENERATED CONTENT

Fan engagement could be gauged from the huge amount of fan-created content on the film's social media sites. On the Capitol Couture Tumblr, for example, a section called "Citizen Activity" encouraged "citizens" to post their pictures and videos showcasing their fashion creations, thus serving, whether knowingly or unknowingly, as brand ambassadors. Tumblr's focus on images and videos made the site a go-to for fans who loved fashion, design, and creativity. The Tumblr videos were quickly devoured by fans of the film, which provided strong encouragement to fans to share and participate with their own videos. Fan art and fan videos were produced and consumed at a feverish level and helped to spread the word among non-fans.

FAN CHALLENGES AND PARTICIPATION

A hallmark of transmedia storytelling is the engagement of fans with the plot and characters, and the film's creative agency lost no opportunity to connect with devoted fans. As a result, fans weren't just watching but were actively participating in the movie's social media channels. Running the gamut of the film's social media strategy, fan challenges constituted a crucial part of the film's promotional strategy. On the Capitol Couture Tumblr site, fans were encouraged to enter the Capitol Art Challenge and submit their own fashion creations.[8] Fans were called to "toast the victors" and fan submissions were posted on the Capitol Couture site under "citizen activity."

Another challenge, labeled "Be Fabulous, Be Capitol, Be Seen" (#CapitolStyle), called upon citizens to post or tweet pictures of their Capitol-style fashion. In yet another challenge, fans chose their red-carpet style (#CapitolRedCarpet). A quartet of judges (three real and the fictional Effie Trinket) were said to evaluate the entries to choose six finalists and, ultimately, a grand winner. Here again, the fine lines between fiction and reality were further blurred. This kind of fan engagement and participation ensured that the film had an ongoing narrative that served to enhance the film's brand and the fans' overall experience.

The Ultimate Fan Challenge was a gamification of fan participation. To participate in the challenge, fans had to register, use specific hashtags, enter competitions, and earn points. If they earned enough points, they could unlock badges they could use for bragging rights and to share with their friends and community.

---

8   See Capitol Art Challenge, http://capitolcouture.pn/post/64228052448/enter-the-capitol-art-challenge-capitol-couture.

CAMPAIGN OUTCOMES

The Capitol's Facebook page had over 10 million likes and over 850,000 followers on Twitter. *Catching Fire*'s trailer was among YouTube's most watched videos, and the term "Hunger Games" was one of the most searched categories on Google. The film was also a top trend on Twitter. Its Twitter account had grown to 969,373 followers. These numbers showed that the film had a solid and growing fan base that created huge amounts of user-generated content, including blogs, photos, and videos. On its opening weekend the film took in $158.1 million at the box office on the way to a total of $864.9 million globally. *Catching Fire* became the highest-grossing film at the domestic box office for 2013 and the tenth highest-grossing film ever at the domestic box office. It also ranked as the biggest-ever opening weekend for November and outearned other movies based on popular young-adult fiction series such as *Divergent*, which earned $56 million in its opening weekend, and *The Maze Runner*, which earned $32.5 million. *Catching Fire* also went on to receive numerous award nominations.

EVALUATING THE TRANSMEDIA STORYTELLING CAMPAIGN

A key element of transmedia storytelling is whether the campaign focuses on telling a good story. Having a clear plot and main idea are central to the storytelling narrative. The Hunger Games campaign tried to create an elaborate "story world" with a real country, real citizens, and a real fashion magazine to play up the emphasis on fashion and apparel in the movie's plotline. But did all the elements hang together? Was the Capitol Couture idea coherent with the story? What about the fan challenges? What else could have been done to engage the audience in co-creation?

A second element contributing to a campaign's success is its distribution. The film's marketing agency had to determine the role each social media platform would play. Each platform typically is exploited for its unique qualities. On the surface, the film's marketing tried to follow through with this strategy. On Facebook, for example, fans could register for a district and have their own district badge, which gave them a sense of belonging to *Catching Fire*'s story world. They could connect with their communities on Facebook through active participation. On Twitter, fans were given an identity such as a district mayor or a recruiter. This encouraged fans to participate and to share with friends. "We felt that this was something that we would start with the core fans, and then we could see how much we could broaden it out from there," said Danielle DePalma, the social media strategist behind the Hunger Games campaign.[9] "People started consuming it and sharing it, and it really took on a life of its own. That inspired us to push it even further." The Tumblr blog reached out to fans with an interest in outlandish fashion, beauty, and photography.

Another key element is the involvement of the audience in shaping and sharing the story. Although fan participation and engagement was powerful, there were many questions

---

9 Quoted in Ari Karpel, "Inside 'The Hunger Games' Social Media Machine," *Fast Company Co.Create*, April 9, 2012.

regarding the campaign's impact. For example, why was the Capitol "in style," if it stood for violence, corruption, and oppression? Even fans seemed confused by the focus on the Capitol's fashion and entertainment. Some fans blogged about the confusing message—if the Capitol was unethical, they wondered, then why should fans feel good about a fashion line that ostensibly promoted the Capitol and its fantasies? As some fans noted, was it really worth aligning with the Capitol's outrageous ideals by becoming a part of the "future of fashion"? These observations led to many other questions. Did the fashion line really fit with the books' message? Why was the campaign taking a risk by promoting the Capitol's hollow glamor? Was the campaign simply selling to fans rather than selling the movie's particular message of triumph over evil? Was it meant to simply intrigue fans and make an impression for the short-term rather than build a compelling story covering the remaining films in the franchise?

Another criterion for evaluating a transmedia campaign is whether each piece of the narrative was easy to find and if each element is connected to the main plot. This is essential to ensure that the audience did not get lost or confused by the subplots and stories. The *Catching Fire* campaign employed a plethora of channels to convey the film's message and story. Did these channels really help to move the plot or did they serve to confuse and interrupt the flow? For example, the Tumblr blog Capitol Couture did not add any elements to the movie's plot, but it illustrated the world of Panem citizens. Did it do anything to expand fans' understanding of the movie's plot, or did it serve to confuse fans about the eccentricities of the Capitol's inhabitants? Did the site serve to illuminate the fact that the Capitol's citizens lived off the wealth generated by the districts and to establish the contrast between the lives of the inhabitants of the districts and those of the Capitol? Real-life writers and designers also inhabited the blog. It was, as one critic said, "a test for those trying to find the line between reality and fiction."[10]

Fan feedback provided the film's marketing team with the cues it was looking for. Fans were clear about what they did or didn't wish to see, and the marketing team did not ignore those wishes. Even though the film's fans typically skewed younger, it was careful not to ignore fans older than the under-25-year-old core target. The film's marketing tried to connect to a broader audience, but most of the efforts focused on the die-hard fans of the franchise. Was Lionsgate preaching to the choir by spending millions on advertising to an already captive audience? And how would this influence the marketing for the next movie in the series? With the kind of fan participation established by *Catching Fire*, would fans continue to be invested in and engaged with the film series?

Lionsgate introduced new partnerships with the release of *Catching Fire*. But the tie-ins with brands like Subway, CoverGirl, and Net-a-Porter did not seem to connect well with the movie's storyline, despite significant fan interest in fashion and beauty products. The

---

10   Emily Asher-Perrin, "Is the Capitol Couture Clothing Line Sending the Wrong Message to *Hunger Games* Fans?" *Tor.com*, September 18, 2013.

merchandising tie-up with Subway for a line of limited edition sandwiches seemed especially odd for a film about hunger and starvation. It was aimed at Subway customers who were already fans of *The Hunger Games*, as well as new enthusiasts. The beauty partnerships ignored men and children even though data showed many fans were hunting for men's and children's fashion pieces. Almost half of the film's fans were male, suggesting a strong potential for additional tie-ins. Another demographic to which the film did not strongly cater was mothers who shopped for themselves as well as for their children.

The *Catching Fire* campaign did not ignore traditional media such as print ads, TV commercials, and posters (see **Exhibit 17.9**). Rather, it turned those efforts into carefully orchestrated online events. For example, the release of each character's poster became an online event as fans rushed to Twitter to look at the images. Also, one of the film's lead actors, Josh Hutcherson, introduced the first trailer on the TV show *Good Morning America*, which meant the online efforts were being amplified offline. Leading magazines also cooperated with Lionsgate to release cover pictures of the characters to build buzz. Traditional was thus married with online to create a synergistic effort. With the amount of attention and details given to the posters/portraits, fashion, and beauty, how would this movement carry over to the marketing of the next movie? Could some elements of the campaign be repeated, or were they meant to be "one-off" efforts dedicated to the particular movie being released? The marketing for *Catching Fire* was designed to reach a bigger audience and was much more elaborate than the marketing for the first Hunger Games movie. Could this level of brand and world building be sustained for the next two movies in the franchise?

THE SEQUEL: *HUNGER GAMES: MOCKINGJAY PART 1*

The next installment in the Hunger Games series would be *Mockingjay Part 1*. How would the film's marketers build upon the platform created for *The Hunger Games* and *Catching Fire*? Lionsgate had stepped up the marketing for *Catching Fire* with the faux fashion magazine (Capitol Couture), the elaborate photo shoot, CapitolTV District Voices on YouTube, and the mobile app. The marketing platform of the first two Hunger Games movies had laid the groundwork for an ongoing conversation among fans and enabled them to continue to share and spread the word online. The campaign for *Mockingjay Part 1* would need to leverage that foundation and expand the storyline, as well as audience engagement. Were certain elements in the film's marketing message programmatic and able to be reused to maintain continuity?

For example, Lionsgate could retool Capitol Couture and CapitolTV to promote *Mockingjay*, but that could send a mixed message to fans. During the *Catching Fire* campaign, those media channels had been used as a propaganda machine for the Capitol, but for *Mockingjay* they would need to promote the concept of rebellion against the Capitol. Could Lionsgate again use the propaganda-style Capitol Portraits to tantalize fans? Could it successfully blur the line between reality and fiction once again by establishing partnerships with real designers masquerading as Panem citizens? Lionsgate also needed to consider whether to continue using low-cost media such as YouTube to advertise the film. Typically, it took a year or two to maximize demand for a film. In the interim, what new partnerships and storytelling techniques could Lionsgate execute to keep fans interested?

CONCLUSION

Brand storytelling has been used by successful brands to differentiate themselves and to enhance audience interest and engagement. Transmedia brand storytelling is a subset of digital brand storytelling that uses various media and distribution platforms to promote a brand. A transmedia marketing campaign is judged on its pervasiveness across all platforms at all times, on persistent story development in real time, on level of audience participation, and on a personalized and integrated experience. The transmedia storytelling campaign for *The Hunger Games: Catching Fire* intriguingly blurred the lines between fact and fiction, keeping fans at once guessing and engaged. From the designers (who were presented as Capitol citizens) and labels of Capitol Couture, to the enthusiastic participation of fans that expanded the original narrative, *Catching Fire* executed a campaign that ignited its core fans' curiosity and participation in and evangelizing about the film. Most important, the promotional social media campaign sought to elevate the Hunger Games brand and bring it closer to its fans. In the process, the film had risked overwhelming fans with too much content.

Could the ongoing promotional campaign be leveraged to keep fans connected to the saga and invested in the characters' narrative in the movie's sequels? Could transmedia storytelling for the film continue to enhance the audience experience before people even bought the tickets to the movie? Could the campaign enhance the Hunger Games brand and leave the audience wanting more?

EXHIBIT 17.1 Audi A3 "Art of the Heist" Ad Campaign

Source: "Audi—Art of the Heist Case Study," posted by Syed Abdul Karim Tanveer on November 21, 2010, https://www.youtube.com/watch?v=z5w2CNB9clw.

EXHIBIT 17.2 Game of Thrones

Source: "Game of Thrones Case Study," posted by Campfire on September 19, 2011, https://vimeo.com/29285256.

EXHIBIT 17.3   *The Hunger Games: Catching Fire* Movie Trailer

Source: "The Hunger Games: Catching Fire—Review SPOT (2013)," posted by Movieclips Trailers on November 21, 2013, https://www.youtube.com/watch?v=krWqNNyJYGw.

EXHIBIT 17.4 Capitol Couture

Source: http://capitolcouture.pn/post/58828194221/sight-unseen-capitol-couture-unveils-unique (accessed January 27, 2016).

EXHIBIT 17.5 Capitol Couture Cinna Fragrance

Source: http://capitolcouture.pn/post/58073053965/a-spritz-of-cinna-could-a-new-scent-compete-with (accessed January 27, 2016).

EXHIBIT 17.6   Capitol Portraits

Source: https://www.tumblr.com/tagged/capitol-portraits (accessed January 27, 2016).

EXHIBIT 17.7   Facebook

Source: "Citizens: Obtain Your Physical DIP Immediately," November 8, 2013, http://www.panempropaganda.com/news/2013/11/8/ citizens-obtain-your-physical-dip-immediately.html (site discontinued) and "Reminder: Respect Your Victors, November 13, 2013, http://www.panempropaganda.com/news/2013/11/13/reminder-respect-your-victors.html (site discontinued).

EXHIBIT 17.8 Twitter

Source: https://twitter.com/TheHungerGames (accessed September 1, 2015).

EXHIBIT 17.9 The Hunger Games Movie Series Posters

Source: Racheli Evanson, "Transmedia Storytelling," *Vivian's Voice* (blog), April 2, 2015, https://viviansvoice.wordpress.com/ 2015/ 04/02/transmedia-storytelling.

CHAPTER 18

Coca-Cola

Surging Ahead with Social Media Marketing Plans

Jimmy Thakkar

This case was written by Jimmy Thakkar, Amity Research Centers Headquarters, Bangalore. It is intended to be used as the basis for class discussion rather than to illustrate either effective or ineffective handling of a management situation. The case was compiled from published sources.

COCA-COLA: SURGING AHEAD WITH SOCIAL MEDIA MARKETING PLANS

CASE STUDY

> "Coke's marketing strategy is about working hard to stay ahead of the curve, and making sure that knowledge is communicated throughout the giant business. The company is fully 'wired and networked' with a view to building skills and 'shortening the learning loop.'"[1]
>
> —Joe Tripodi, Chief Marketing and Commercial Officer, Coca-Cola

> "Consumers are incredibly empowered, and what used to work to get their attention now needs a bit more thoughtfulness."[2]
>
> —Brian Solis, Principal Analyst at the Altimeter Group[3]

The birth of the internet in 1960s had revolutionised the communication pattern in the world. By 1990s, the use of internet was commercialised with the emergence of several online service providers. Internet facilitated information sharing at considerable speed and

---

1 Choueke Mark, "Behind Closed Doors at the World's Most Famous Brand", http://www.marketingweek.co.uk/behind-closed-doors-at-the-worlds-most-famous-brand/3026712.article, May 26th 2011

2 Snider Mike, "Social media is latest front of Cola wars", http://www.usatoday.com/tech/news/story/2012-04-30/pepsi-coke-social-media/54631902/1, April 29th 2012

3 A research and advisory firm.

connected people from different parts of the world who formed Online Social Networking Groups (OSNGs). The OSNGs enabled the users to share information, videos, pictures etc. and made interactions more expedient. These websites allowed people to connect with their friends and provided a platform to socialise, interact, entertain and have fun.

The OSNGs also led to development of new kind of conversation among consumers, by challenging traditional ideas about marketing and brand management and created new opportunities for organisations to understand customers and connect with them instantly. The emergence of ONSGs such as, Facebook,[4] Twitter,[5] Orkut,[6] and YouTube[7] etc had changed the meaning of marketing communication. Marketers were seen hurriedly adopting innovative technology to bind people in the networks which had become the most acceptable domain of interaction.[8] The tech savvy youth had led several companies especially the global soft drink majors to focus on digital media.[9] Homi Battiwalla, Category Director, PepsiCo[10] India mentioned that "The youth–our core target audience–spends a significant amount of time online and uses the social media space to express their views and opinions. Therefore, all our campaigns have a strong social media element built in. Digital medium is increasingly proving to be the most effective platform to create awareness around a brand's initiative as it provides an opportunity for direct consumer engagement."[11]

Realising the growing importance of Online Social Media as a new frontier of marketing and communications, Coke devised policy to achieve sustainable growth online in late 2009.[12] Joanna Allen (Allen), Global Senior Brand Manager at Coke said, "We are facing a moment of renewed belief that we can be optimistic about Coca-Cola's future and the fact that we see so much opportunity for growth."[13] In 2011, Coke envisaged to double the system revenues by 2020 by developing new beverage systems to meet the consumers' needs and preferences and convert aspirations into reality.[14] Joseph V. Tripodi (Tripodi), Executive Vice President and Chief Marketing and Commercial Officer at Coca-Cola said: "Our biggest

4   A social Networking website, operated by Facebook Inc.
5   An Online Social Networking and Microblogging service platform.
6   A video Sharing Website.
7   A social networking website, operated by Google Inc.
8   "Social Networks Overview: Current Trends and Research Challenges", http://cordis.europa.eu/fp7/ict/netmedia/docs/publications/social-networks.pdf, November 2010.
9   Change Lab Solutions, "Breaking down the Chain: A Guide to the Soft Drink Industry", http://changelabsolutions.org/sites/changelabsolutions.org/files/ChangeLab-Beverage_Industry_Report-FINAL_(CLS-20120530)_201109.pdf.
10   An American Multinational Corporation, Manufacturing, Marketing And Distribution Of Grain-Based Snack Foods, Beverages, And Other Products.
11   Khandelwal Payal, "Raising The Online Pitch", http://www.financialexpress.com/news/raising-the-online-pitch/975251/0, July 17th 2012.
12   "Online Social Media Principles", http://www.thecoca-colacompany.com/socialmedia/, December 2009
13   "Happy Birthday, Coca-Cola!", http://www.thecoca-colacompany.com/presscenter/happy_birthday_coca-cola.html, July 5th 2010.
14   "Passionately Refreshing A Thirsty Word: 2011 Annual Review", http://www.thecoca-colacompany.com/ourcompany/ar/pdf/TCCC_2011_Annual_Review.pdf.

competitor is really our past. Our biggest challenge is really our present. Fifty-seven percent of the stores in the world do not carry our products ... We can't be complacent."[15] Tripodi further stated that, "All of us can turn brand-loyal customers into true brand advocates, which becomes increasingly important in an era of social media like Facebook, where the Coca-Cola fan page has more than 40.6 million 'likes'."[16] Although Coca -Cola was able to connect the brand with the consumers successfully, analysts were wondering whether the company would able to achieve its 2020 vision given the public health concerns and social media's biggest asset and drawback–content creation and sharing.

SOCIAL MEDIA: AN INNOVATIVE MARKETING TOOL

Communication had always remained a social phenomenon since ages. With the advent of computers and internet technology, sharing information and connecting with people became easier. In 1980s, CompuServe[17] introduced e-mail and chat service by allowing incoming and outgoing messages to other Internet e-mail addresses. More companies started offering services like email, chat, forums, file sharing etc.[18] In 1997, the first social networking website—SixDegrees.com[19] was launched that enabled users to create profiles, add friends and search friends lists.[20] Since 1997, a plethora of social networking websites were launched with different features and services to connect people **(Annexure 18.1)**. In 2002, another social networking website Friendster[21] was introduced with focus on connecting strangers (friends of friends) with each other followed by MySpace[22] Orkut, Facebook, Flickr,[23] Twitter and Google Plus over the period of time.[24]

Since 21st century, Social Media Networking Sites (SMNs) such as MySpace, Facebook etc. emerged as a marketing communication tool.[25] Despite the activeness and prominence of the Traditional Marketing Communication (TMC) channels like TV, print media, physical public relations, trade fairs etc., the charisma of the Internet and SMNs utterly transformed the way individuals and business enterprises communicated.[26] Initially, the Internet was

15   Elliot Stuart, "Coca-Cola and L'Oréal Offer Ambitious Goals for 2020", http://mediadecoder.blogs.nytimes.com/2012/03/15/coca-cola-and-loreal-offer-ambitious-goals-for-2020/, March 15th 2012.
16   ibid.
17   The First Major Commercial Online Service in the United States.
18   Borders Brett, " A Brief History of Social Media", http://copybrighter.com/history-of-social-media, June 2nd 2009.
19   A Social Network Service Website that Lasted from 1997.
20   Boyd Danah M. and Ellison Nicole B, "Social Network Sites: Definition, History, and Scholarship", http://www.danah.org/papers/JCMCIntro.pdf.
21   A Malaysia Based Social Gaming Site.
22   A Social Networking Service Company Headquarter Based in California.
23   An Image Hosting and Video Hosting Website, Web Services Suite, and Online Community, Owned By Yahoo. Inc.
24   "Social Network Sites: Definition, History, and Scholarship", op.cit.
25   Nair Gopalakrishnan T.R and Subramaniam Kumarashvari, "Transformation of Traditional Marketing Communications in to Paradigms of Social Media Networking", http://arxiv.org/ftp/arxiv/papers/1206/1206.0425.pdf.
26   ibid.

perceived as a "virtual announcement board" but since 2006-07, it progressively evolved and successfully integrated the SMNs.[27] With the increasing number of the internet user base, the popularity of OSNGs surged. The total number of internet users reached nearly 2 billion globally in 2011.[28] Out of the total internet users, nearly 1, 202.2 million people were using social networking sites in 2011.[29] According to eMarketer,[30] "There will be 1.43 billion social network users in 2012, a 19.2% increase over 2011."[31] In 2011, Facebook topped as the global SMN with the market share of 64.69% followed by Twitter with 1.11% of the total market share of social networking sites.[32] The other popular SMNs were Bebo,[33] MySpace, LinkedIn,[34] Tagged[35] His[36] MyLife[37] MyYearBook,[38] and Meetup.[39] Facebook was the forerunner with over 300 million users and reached the benchmark of 750 million users in 2011.[40] According to Ralph Vega, President and CEO, AT&T Mobility and Consumer Markets,[41] "We are seeing an unparalleled adoption of technology ... Consumers are embracing new technology, particularly because companies like Apple have made technology easier to use, and social media is expediting awareness and adoption."[42]

According to David Meerman Scott, a marketing strategist, "marketers are realizing the need for sophisticated tools to harness social data and make sense and use of it. As a result, marketing departments will add a new job function that will play a role similar to that of bond traders in financial institutions in that they will rely on instant, real-time data to make informed decisions ... social data from platforms such as Twitter, Facebook, Google +, YouTube, blogs and LinkedIn; and data from websites to answer key questions such as number of people visiting your web properties, content they are interacting with, the impact of reorganizing content and presentation, and speed of response to close rates."[43]

---

27 ibid.
28 "Internet World Stats-Usage and Population Statistics", http://www.internetworldstats.com/stats.htm
29 "Social Networking and UGC", http://www.newmediatrendwatch.com/world-overview/137-social-networking-and-ugc.
30 eMarketer Publishes Data, Analysis and Insights on Digital Marketing, Media and Commerce.
31 "Social Networking and UGC", op.cit.
32 Bennett Shea, "Social Media Showdown: Top 10 Social Networking Sites Of 2011 [Infographic]", http://www.mediabistro.com/alltwitter/social-networking-2011_b12969, August 23rd 2011.
33 A Social Networking Website Launched in July 2005.
34 A Social Networking Website for People in Professional Occupations.
35 A Social Discovery Website Based in San Francisco.
36 A Social Networking Site Based in San Francisco, California.
37 A Social Network Service Founded in 2002 By Jeffrey Tinsley.
38 A Social Networking Service Founded in 2005.
39 An Online Social Networking Portal that Facilitates Offline Group Meetings in Various Localities around the World.
40 Ehrlich Brenna, "Facebook Hits 750 Million Users", http://mashable.com/2011/07/06/facebook-750-million/, July 6th 2011.
41 A Wholly Owned Subsidiary of AT&T that Provides Wireless Services to Subscribers.
42 "AMA 2012 White Paper: The Consumer in 2020", http://www.marketingpower.com/ResourceLibrary/Documents/newsletters/mtl/2012/5/consumer-in-2020.pdf.
43 "2012 Social Marketing & New Media Predictions", http://www.brandchannel.com/images/papers/534_awareness_wp_2012_predictions_01-12.pdf.

Jason Falls, the Founder and CEO of Social Media Explorer[44] while commenting about the integration of the toolsets said: "As monitoring platforms add publishing and management solutions, analytics platforms integrate with management and monitoring solutions, and social platforms evolve to include e-mail, mobile and website management, the tools will just get closer to what the customers want and need."[45] While Paul Gillin, an independent Marketing Consultant and Founding Editor in Chief of TechTarget[46] opined that "Brands are learning not to treat social media as some kind of an outlier to delegate to a junior manager or an agency. We will begin to see very large ad campaigns from some prominent companies developed with a social component at their core. This development will light the way to a new generation of integrated marketing programs that are much more sophisticated that anything we've seen in the past."[47]

From being just an online personal communication tool, the social media evolved to emerge as a powerful innovative marketing tool[48] (**Annexure 18.2**). Michael Troiano, of Holland-Mark[49] observed that "Social Marketing will become Marketing. It will just be what you need to do, when you're trying to sell something to more than one person."[50] The usage of SMNs had shown steady and continuous growth, business organisations had to relook upon their marketing strategy (**Exhibit 18.1**). The purpose of SMNs was not limited to only chatting and making friends but its usage had moved towards doing business virtually. SMNs had a vital role to play in the marketing mix of promotion. The abounding ability to connect the people in the market allured various companies to integrate with social media and online applications. SMNs like Facebook, Twitter, YouTube, offered gaming, and other applications offered opportunities for the companies to promote canvass and encourage the mass to interact, befriend and assimilate with the brands.[51] Besides, the social media also led to rise of the Online Recommendation Culture. Stacy Debroff, Founder and CEO of Mom Central Consulting, (a firm which helped companies, develop meaningful conversations, connections and communities with Moms) said, "Moms' rapid embrace of social media translates into blogs, Facebook, and Twitter becoming the new 'picket fence,' where Moms connect with one another to make friends, hear trusted recommendations, and gain first-person perspective."[52]

---

44   A digital media marketing agency.
45   "2012 Social Marketing & New Media Predictions", op.cit.
46   Online intersection of serious technology buyers, targeted technical content and technology providers worldwide.
47   "2012 Social Marketing & New Media Predictions", op.cit.
48   Boris Cynthia, "The Rise of Social Business: it's About More Than Just Marketing", http://www.marketingpilgrim.com/2012/07/the-rise-of-social-business-its-about-more-than-just-marketing.html, July 13th 2012
49   An American advertising and marketing communications agency based in Boston, Massachusetts.
50   "2012 Social Marketing & New Media Predictions", op.cit.
51   "AMA 2012 White Paper: The Consumer in 2020", op.cit.
52   "2012 Social Marketing & New Media Predictions", op.cit.

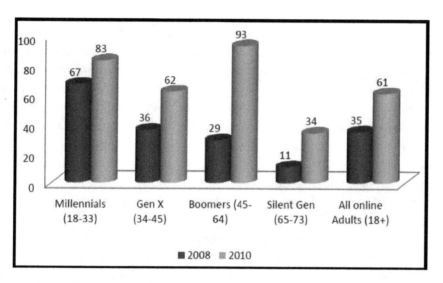

EXHIBIT 18.1   Growth (in 000 Numbers) and Usage of Social Networking Sites (Percentage)

Source: Nair Gopalakrishnan and Subramaniam Kumarashvari, "Transformation of Traditional Marketing Communications in to Paradigms of Social Media Networking", http://arxiv.org/ftp/arxiv/papers/1206/1206.0425.pdf

Jon Bridges, Vice President of Customer Experience at Chick-fil-A[53] said: "We don't view our customer base in big chunks anymore. We can overlay customer demos with their usage and referral behavior to understand their true value. The ways we market to them will change. As for the experience, we will allow customers to pre-order and pre-pay for their food, so that when they drive up, their food is ready and they're greeted by name."[54]

Food and Beverage companies such as McDonald's, Burger King, PepsiCo, and Coca-Cola were few pioneers in using social media marketing strategy. For instance, Burger King's whooper sacrifice campaign was ground breaking, where the customers were given incentive for sacrificing (unfriend) 10 Facebook friends. In return, the hamburger chain offered free premium sandwich –whopper to customers. As a result, more than 230,000 friends were ditched for a burger. The campaign attracted publicity and Burger King was able to increase foot falls at their outlets.[55]

Popular food and snack brands like Domino's, Dunkin' Donuts, Pizza Hut, Sonic, Starbucks, Subway, and Wendy's had opened Facebook pages to launch new products, perform product evaluation and obtain information about customer preferences by asking typical questions on favourite products, best pizza toppings, preferred side dishes, and ways to customise and

---

53   A Quick-service U.S. chicken restaurant.
54   "AMA 2012 White Paper: The Consumer in 2020", op.cit.
55   *Verma Ashish and Choudhari Tejas, "Burger King's Whopper Sacrifice campaign: Is friendship worth one-tenth of a Whopper?", http://www.managementcanvas.iimindore.in/icanvas/index.php?option= com_content&view=article&id=181:burger-kings-whopper&catid=34:marketing-and-branding&Itemid=56, March 21st 2012*

improve menu items.[56] For instance, Starbucks had posted seven polls on Facebook page and received 479,000 responses and more than 4,000 comments in 2010. Similarly, the Facebook page of Pizza Hut had five polls and received 58,000 responses and 270 comments.[57]

According to Heather Foster, Vice President of Marketing, ControlScan,[58] "Technology is changing everything, and not just yearly but continually. You have to quickly learn about new technology, and decide if it makes sense, and then figure out how to use it and how to interrelate with other channels (which also change in response to new ones). Just when you think you have your ducks in a row, you don't."[59]

COCA–COLA'S CONTEMPORARY MARKETING STRATEGIES: ROLE OF SOCIAL MEDIA

Over 126 years, Coca-Cola (Coke) had grown to become a world beverage company from just being a soda fountain.[60] Coke with about 500 new brands launched in 2011 and dispensing over 3,500 beverages became the world's most recognised brand.[61] The company's portfolio encompassed a wide range of regular and zero calorie beverages which include –energy drinks, still and sparkling waters, sports drinks, juice drinks, coffee based beverages and teas.[62] Allen said: "Our past has been an amazing story, as we have created connections and inspired happiness for people all around the world."[63]

Since the 1970s, advertising has been an integral part of the business and centered on 'fun' that connected the brand with the consumers. During the period, Coke thrilled its target audience with exciting and dynamic communication.[64] By the end of 1989, Coca-Cola was present in 165 countries. By 1990s, the operations were spread over 200 countries and it was also a decade of continued growth, entering new markets like erstwhile East Germany and re-entry into India. The decade also saw the introduction of Polar Bear and memorable 'Always Coca-Cola' campaign. Since 2000, Coke embarked on a global marketing journey and resolved to reach out to consumers paying attention to different needs and preferences.[65]

With changes in technology and the arrival of internet along with proliferation of media, companies were left with no alternatives to incorporate other promotional strategies,

---

56   Richardson Johanna and Harris Jennifer L., "Food Marketing and Social Media: Findings from Fast Food FACTS and Sugary Drink FACTS", http://www.yaleruddcenter.org/resources/upload/docs/what/reports/FoodMarketingSocialMedia_AmericanUniversity_11.11.pdf.

57   ibid.

58   ControlScan is the Leading Provider of PCI Compliance and Security Solutions for Small Merchants and the Businesses.

59   "The Consumer in 2020", op.cit.

60   "Our Company: Growth, leadership, sustainability", http://www.thecoca-colacompany.com/ourcompany/index.html

61   ibid.

62   "The Best Brands in the World", http://www.cokecce.com/pages/_content.asp?page_id=85

63   "Happy Birthday, Coca-Cola!", op.cit.

64   "A World of Customers", http://heritage.coca-cola.com/

65   "A World of Customers", op.cit.

besides traditional marketing tools.[66] The consumers were becoming tech savvy and were making informed decisions in their purchases.[67] According to a report by Berkeley Media Studies Group[68] (BMSG), the changing nature of advertising and marketing ecosystem forced companies redefine their strategies. The consumers, particularly the millennial youth were adopting modern digital tools and assimilating them in their daily lives.[69] BMSG report further stated that "Fifty-seven percent of online teenagers post their own 'user-generated content' on the Web, including photos, stories, art work, audio, and video."[70]

According to Russel Neuman, Professor of Media Technology at the University of Michigan, "We are witnessing the evolution of a universal interconnected network of audio, video, and electronic text communications that will blur the distinction between interpersonal and mass communication and between public and private communication."[71]

In August 2008, Dusty Sorg an aspiring American actor and his writer friend Michael Jedrzejewski, who loved Coke made a Facebook page which attracted about 3.3 million fans by March 2009.[72] From a single page consisting only high-resolution Coke can digital image, the unofficial Coke Facebook page grew to 253 pages to become number two page following US President Barack Obama's Facebook page[73] (**Exhibit 18.2**).

In November 2008, Facebook enforced the policy that brand pages must be authorised or associated by the brand owners and told the Coca-Cola page creators either to close the page or handover the same to the company. According to Michael Donnelly (Donnelly), Director of Worldwide Interactive Marketing at Coca-Cola Co, the company decided to let the creators keep the page and administer the same, but with a condition of sharing the page and allowing interactions from the senior members of the Coca-Cola Company.[74] Donnelly further added that "This page is a fan page and happens to be the biggest one, but we recognize that when you do a search you see 253. We don't want to be a big brand there doing big-brand advertising."[75]

Coke strived to portray itself as a social brand that people loved to share and bonded with consumers emotionally at all times. Moreover, since 2008, the Coca-Cola page on the Facebook attracted 5.4 million fans who shared the experiences, love, stories about the influence

---

66   Saeidinia Mojtaba, et. al, "Operation Strategies for Coca-Cola vs. Pepsi Companies to Attract Their Customers", http://www.businessjournalz.org/articlepdf/CMR_11003.pdf, January 1st -15th, 2012
67   ibid.
68   A nonprofit organization dedicated to expanding advocates' ability to improve the systems and structures that determine health.
69   Chester Jeff and Montgomery Kathryn, "Interactive Food & Beverage Marketing: Targeting Children and Youth in the Digital Age", http://ftc.gov/os/comments/foodmktgtokidspra-3/529477-00004.pdf, May 2007
70   ibid.
71   "New Media Branding", http://www.festoonmedia.com/whitepapers/images/New_Media_Branding.pdf, April 2010
72   Klaassen Abbey, "How Two Coke Fans Brought the Brand to Facebook Fame", http://adage.com/article/digital/coke-fans-brought-brand-facebook-fame/135238/, March 16th 2009
73   ibid.
74   "How Two Coke Fans Brought the Brand to Facebook Fame", op.cit.
75   ibid.

EXHIBIT 18.2   **Top 10 Facebook Pages**

S. N.	NAME	NUMBER OF FANS	DAILY GROWTH RATE (%)	WEEKLY GROWTH RATE (%)
1.	Barack Obama	5,881,499	1.45	0.10
2.	Coca-Cola	3,287,101	2.93	0.19
3.	Nutella	3,052,502	2.98	0.18
4.	Pizza	3,005,922	3.52	0.20
5.	Cristiano Ronaldo	2,730,570	3.93	0.23
6.	kinder surprise	2,581,651	3.13	0.18
7.	Facebook	2,492,881	4.22	0.27
8.	Windows Messenger Live	2,469,402	2.75	0.13
9.	Sid	2,409,639	3.25	0.17
10.	Boo	2,343,221	3.95	0.20

Source: Klaassen Abbey, "How Two Coke Fans Brought the Brand to Facebook Fame", http://adage.com/article/digital/coke-fans-brought-brand-facebook-fame/135238/, March 16th 2009

of the brand in their lives.[76] Donnelly mentioned that "By its nature, Coca-Cola has always been a social brand that consumers share with friends. In social media marketing, we want to be everywhere our consumers are, but in a contextual, non-big-brand advertiser way."[77]

In 2010, Coke slashed the traditional advertising budget by 6.6% to focus on social media.[78] To start with, Coke launched a social media site, 'Coke Zone' to integrate offline and online marketing. According to social media analysts "using social media has allowed Coca-Cola to break out of the stop-start cycle of more traditional media campaigns and to start engaging on a more frequent, ongoing basis. Coca-Cola's social media strategy is clearly about long-term sustainable engagement, developing advocacy and encouraging brand loyalty"[79] **(Exhibit 18.3).**

Coca-Cola had achieved great success with tweets, blogs, photo sharing, videos and social media apps. According to Muhtar Kent (Kent), CEO, Coca-Cola, "Coke is increasingly focusing on internet-based channels. Television advertising, while still valuable, is expensive and doesn't improve brand accessibility and overall reputation like a solid social campaign can."[80] The Company continued to invest heavily in creating awareness across the social

---

76   "Happy Birthday, Coca-Cola!", op.cit.
77   ibid.
78   Rohdes Matt, "Coca-Cola Cuts Ad Spend by 6.6% and Invests More in Social Media", http://socialmedi-atoday.com/mattrhodes/279661/coca-cola-cut-ad-spend-66-and-invest-more-social-media, March 21st 2011
79   ibid.
80   "Coke CEO: Social media marketing more than 20 of budget" http://www.brafton.com/news/coke-ceo-social-media-marketing-more-than-20-of-budget, October 24th 2011

EXHIBIT 18.3 Coca-Cola's Social Media Strategy 2020

Compiled by the author from source: "Coca-Cola's Social Media Strategy 2020: 5 Lessons SMEs Can Learn", http://www. socialmedia.ie/coca-colas-social-media-strategy-2020-5-lessons-smes-can-learn/, June 11th 2012

media sites, embedding consumer conversation and brand interaction as its core marketing strategy.[81] Coke generated about 5000 conversations a day across the social media outlets adhering to five core values–Transparency (in all its social media engagements), Protection (gave priority to consumers' privacy), Respect (regarding copyrights, trademarks, rights of publicity, and other third-party rights), Responsibility (in use of technology) and utilisation (following best practices).[82]

Wendy Clark, Senior VP-Integrated Marketing, Coca-Cola opined, "Among Coca-Cola's most powerful differentiators are the stories only our brand can tell … But we're not the only ones that can tell our story. Much of our content comes from our consumers. It's the phenomenon of social media. Consumers remind us daily that Coca-Cola is actually their brand, not our brand."[83] Donnelly in an interview said: "Social media is where our consumers are at the moment. There's no better way to amplify your message. If you're building a major

81 "Coca-Cola", http://superbrands.com.gh/pdf/case.pdf, 2011
82 "Online Social Media Principles", op.cit.
83 Zmuda Natalie, "Coca-Cola Lays Out Its Vision For the Future At 2010 Meeting", http://adage.com/article/news/coca-cola-lays-vision-future-2010-meeting/140664/, November 22nd 2009

campaign and putting a lot of time and energy into enabling social and interactive aspects, you have to make sure people know about it."[84]

In January 2010, the company had initiated a yearlong social media project—Expedition 206 to find out 'what makes people happy.' Tony Martin, Kelly Ferris and Antonio Santiago were selected based on the worldwide vote to represent Coke and visit 206 countries and territories where the company sold its products.[85] Clyde Tuggle, Senior Vice President, Global Public Affairs and Communications, The Coca-Cola Company said: "Our goal is to bring fans along for the ride, using social media platforms to make them an integral part of the adventure. The magic of Expedition 206 is in its potential to bring people together in a global conversation, highlighting the stories of happiness and optimism people everywhere are eager to share."[86] The 'happiness ambassadors' three member team arrived back in Atlanta (Coke HQ) on December 30th 2010 after travelling more than 275,000 miles covering 186 countries.[87] The team members during their 365 days journey shared their adventure with friends, Coke fans and followers in real-time on social networking sites such as YouTube, Twitter, Flickr and Facebook.[88] Tony Martin said: "It was a long and sometimes challenging journey, but what truly kept us going were the smiling faces and stories of happiness we encountered every step of the way."[89] For Coke, the Expedition gambit paid off with about 650 million media impressions, generated across SMNs around the world.[90]

Explaining Coke's social media strategy, Donnelly said: "Our strategy is to be everywhere our consumers are, but as a member of the community. That's not to say that we think there's anything wrong with big billboards in Times Square or Super Bowl commercials. There's a time and a place for that. Within the social media marketing realm, our approach is to be a strong member of the community that's enabling consumers to celebrate manifestations of the brand."[91]

In March 2011, Coke organised a 24-hour live session with Maroon 5 to create music history via the social media.[92] Joe Belliotti, Director of Global Entertainment Marketing,

---

84 "USA drinks: Coke crowdsources happiness", http://www.eiu.com/index.asp?layout=ib3PrintArticle&article_id=765066461&printer=printer, December 11th 2009

85 "Expedition 206: Traveling the World for a Year to Discover What Makes People Happy", http://www.thecoca-colacompany.com/dynamic/press_center/2011/02/expedition-206-track-their-path-with-interactive-map.html

86 "The Votes Are In! Fans Choose Three Young People To Represent Coca-Cola On Unprecedented, 275,000-Mile Journey Around The World", http://www.thecoca-colacompany.com/dynamic/press_center/2009/11/expedition-206.html, November 16th 2009

87 "Globetrotting 'Happiness Ambassadors' Conclude Year-long Coca-Cola Expedition 206 Adventure with the Secret to Happiness" http://www.thecoca-colacompany.com/dynamic/press_center/2010/12/expedition-206-finale.html, December 30th 2010

88 ibid.

89 ibid.

90 Kiley David, "Coke Wraps Up Biggest Ever Social Media Campaign", http://www.dailyfinance.com/2011/01/04/coke-wraps-up-biggest-ever-social-media-campaign/, April 1st 2011

91 "USA drinks: Coke crowdsources happiness", op.cit.

92 "Coca-Cola and Maroon 5 Set to Make Music History with the "Coca-Cola Music" 24hr Session", http://www.thecoca-colacompany.com/dynamic/press_center/2011/03/coca-cola-music-24hr-session.html, March 1st 2011

at Coke said: "Coca-Cola has a long history of using the power of music to bring people together from around the world in the most relevant and compelling ways. We are excited to be working with Maroon 5. They have a huge global following and a strong track record of producing great music. They have worked closely with us to help shape the event and ensure the session will be a fun and engaging experience for fans no matter where in the world they are."[93] The event was witnessed by fans in over 139 countries, with over 350,000 views, and generated 25,000 fan tweets.[94]

Going ahead with social media marketing strategy, the company had introduced an iconic character of polar bears for Super Bowl advertisement in 2012. Coca-Cola's Super Bowl advertising ran across three screens –television, mobile and social media.[95] Pio Schunker, Head of Integrated Marketing Platforms and Content, Coke, North America opined that "'The trick is to be everywhere consumers are' and that means having a presence on the TV broadcast, as well as on Facebook, Twitter, YouTube and other popular sites."[96] According to Alison Lewis (Alison), Senior Vice President of Marketing for Coke in North America, the largest social TV event generated 70 million pre-game impressions, the ad spots went on air across 2 million live NBC[97] screens and 9 million streams on social media.[98] Alison further added that "So, massive, massive result, and it really taught us about engagement with television. Old world was about placement of messages. New world is about movement of stories."[99]

In the digital age, mobile phones were considered as one of the most important platforms for reaching young people. It enables marketers to directly target users based on information such as previous purchase history, actual location and other profiling data.[100] Tripodi said: "Mobile is the remote control for peoples' lives and that will play an increasingly large role."[101] By using social media tool, the company wanted to gather teenage fan base by associating soft drink with events such as, football, festivals and music.[102] Tripodi opined that, "There are 1 billion teens in the world. That represents 18% of Coke's total volume. We know that 47% of them have not had a Coca-Cola in the past month."[103] In addition, Coke decided to incorporate 'My Beat Application' for smartphones to engage teens during London 2012

---

93   "Coca-Cola and Maroon 5 Set to Make Music History with the "Coca-Cola Music" 24hr Session", op.cit.
94   Brady Shirley, "Coca-Cola Releases Results of Crowdsourced Maroon 5 Tune", http://www.brandchannel.com/home/post/2011/04/01/Coca-Cola-Releases-Results-of-Crowdsourced-Maroon-5-Tune.aspx, April 1st 2011
95   Annual Championship Game of the National Football League (NFL).
96   Petrecca Laura, "Coke bears back in Super Bowl ads, social media campaign", http://www.usatoday.com/money/advertising/story/2012-01-25/coke-polar-bears-super-bowl/52796578/1, January 26th 2012
97   An American commercial broadcasting television network.
98   Hof Robert, "Coca-Cola's New World of Marketing: Facebook + TV sales", http://www.forbes.com/sites/roberthof/2012/05/15/coca-colas-new-world-of-marketing-facebook-tv-sales/, May 15th 2012
99   ibid.
100   "Interactive Food & Beverage Marketing", op.cit.
101   "Behind Closed Doors at the World's Most Famous Brand", op.cit.
102   ibid.
103   ibid.

Olympics.[104] Kim Siler (Siler), Mobile Brand Strategy, Global Connections, Coca-Cola, Atlanta said, "Mobile is at the heart of many teens' daily lives, connecting them with their family, their friends and their world. Mobile, in turn, is at the heart and foundation of our strategy for London 2012, amplifying those connections with music, relevant content and movement."[105]

According to Forester, an independent tech and market research firm, by 2014 the marketer expenditures involving several media like display, search, e-mail, mobile and social was estimated to touch $55 billion from about $23 billion in 2008.[106] Sundar Bharadwaj, Associate Professor of Marketing at Emory University's Goizueta Business School, opined that, "People are looking to divert their search spend and anything that can leverage conversions, they'll use them. It's not just about building brand awareness. It's about 'influencing behavior'."[107]

Meanwhile, Coke in February 2012 announced its plans to cut $550 million to $650 million in annual costs by 2015, to re-invest in marketing and brand building, besides addressing rising commodity costs. Kent said: "This program will further enable our efforts to strengthen our brands and reinvest our resources to drive long term profitable growth. We remain relentless in our efforts to become more efficient, leaner and adaptive to changing market conditions, while at the same time building a continuous improvement in cost management culture in keeping with our 2020 vision. The key component of how we strengthen our global brand portfolio is through innovative consumer engagement."[108]

While Julie Bowerman, Group Director of Digital Platforms Coca-Cola commented, "Content is the key to connecting the dots–a way to create a narrative that integrates each part of the customer experience, and leads the consumer down the path to purchase. Coke creates content that inspires consumers to share and continue the story."[109] According to Tripodi, "We're changing fundamentally from being TV commercial producers to content developers. ... We're leading a new and unique approach ... from purely mass marketing to one-on-one marketing."[110]

According to Bill Pecoriello, CEO at ConsumerEdge Research,[111] "Coca-Cola remains the dominant beverage company in the world, and controls nearly 51% of the global carbonated soft-drink business compared to Pepsi's 22%, according to Beverage Digest figures, it had, perhaps, been too focused on soft drinks at a time when other beverage categories

104   Tode Chantal, "Coca-Cola exec claims mobile underpins entire Olympic Games strategy", http://www. mobilemarketer.com/cms/news/content/12870.html, May 21st 2012
105   ibid.
106   "New Media Branding", op.cit.
107   ibid.
108   Zmuda Natalie, "Coca-Cola Cuts Costs, Reinvest in Marketing", http://adage.com/article/news/coca-cola-reinvests-marketing/232572/, February 7th 2012
109   "The Consumer in 2020", op.cit.
110   Toussaint Lenny, "Future Plans–Marketing Coca-Cola", http://cargocollective.com/Coca-cola/Future-Plans
111   A preeminent independent equity research boutique focused on the global consumer sector.

were on the rise. They were too inward thinking and missed a lot of trends that were happening."[112]

MAJOR ROADBLOCKS

Steve McKee President of McKee Wallwork Cleveland[113] said: "Not so long ago, it was enough to have great strategy and a big idea. Today, even the best ideas have a hard time getting off the ground as consumers' media and purchasing options–not to mention their attention spans–grow increasingly fragmented. While perfect integration is unachievable, companies that do the best job of harmonizing all their marketing efforts have an advantage."[114]

According to Ken Barnett (Barnett), Global CEO Mars Advertising[115] the digitisation of media, empowered customers and fundamentally changed how companies marketed their products.[116] Marketing had entered the 'Express-Lane' and digital marketing was the ubiquitous driving force.[117] Barnett further opined that, "speed can be scary. However well prepared, there are still plenty of speed bumps as marketers shift into high gear and move into the express lane. But speed is also exhilarating! We may not know what's at the end of the road but the opportunities seem boundless."[118]

Moreover, according to McKinsey[119] "social media may have a more specific role, such as helping to launch a new product or to mitigate negative word of mouth ... As these social-media activities gain scale, the challenges center less around justifying funding and more around organizational issues such as developing the right processes and governance structure, identifying clear roles–for all involved in social-media strategy, from marketing to customer service to product development–and bolstering the talent base, and improving performance standards. New capabilities abound, and social-media best practices are barely starting to emerge. We do know this: because social-media influences every element of the consumer decision journey, communication must take place between as well as within functions. That complicates lines of reporting and decision-making authority."[120]

Yasir Yousuff, Managing Director, Asia-Pacific, Middle East and Africa NM Incite,[121] said: "It is the consumer, not companies, that controls information on social networks such as

---

112   "Coca-Cola Lays Out Its Vision for the Future at 2010 Meeting", op.cit.
113   A strategic integrated marketing agency.
114   McKee Steve, "Integrated Marketing: If You Knew It, You'd Do It", http://www.businessweek.com/articles/2012-05-10/integrated-marketing-if-you-knew-it-youd-do-it#p2, May 10th 2012
115   A 35 year old advertising agency offering brand-building strategies key account knowledge, and shopper insights through program activation.
116   Barnett Ken, "Express-Lane Marketing", http://hubmagazine.com/html/2012/hub_49/jul_aug/237230749/mars_identity/index.html, July/August 2012
117   ibid.
118   ibid.
119   A global management consulting and advisory firm.
120   Divol Roxane,et al., "Demystifying social media", http://www.mckinseyquarterly.com/Demystifying_social_media_2958, April 2012
121   A Nielsen McKinsey Company, Helps Businesses Harness the full Potential of Social Media Intelligence to Drive Superior Business Performance across their Organisations.

Facebook and Twitter."[122] The consistent bad consumer experiences affected the projected choices and loyalty towards the brands.[123] In 2012, marketers confronted major challenges of measuring the effectiveness of social media marketing and allocating the resources.

According to Adam Brown, Director-Digital Communications and Social Media, Coca-Cola "One of the great things about digital and social-media programs is the ability to measure just about everything. This is critical for us to demonstrate ROI on an exciting and, in a way ... I also think content sharing is a critical metric to watch. ... That third-party credibility is magic."[124]

On the other hand, Kent said: "The company will focus on working across many geographies, cultures and channels, targeting the right consumers in a fragmented media environment and innovating."[125] Kent further added that "We know that winning ... is going to require new capabilities, new models and new innovations."[126] To meet this goal, Coke needed to analyse and understand the new tools for building management capabilities. The company traversed a long journey to become a global brand, cherished across continents. But the challenges were complex and variable, individual hires to capital investments, region to region and country to country.[127] Irial Finan opined, "A seemingly simple update, such as changing an SKU, could lead to downtime in the plant, leading to breakage, damage and loss."[128]

While Tripodi commented that, "When we want to double our business in basically a decade, it really requires us to look at balance between how we grow at that accelerated pace, but also how to do it in a sustainable way. One of the greatest challenges that we have is making sure that we are growing the right way, the proper way and making sure that we are living up to our commitments that we make not only to NGOs and governments around the world, but to the world community. I think that that's critical for us to be able to grow aggressively and in the right way."[129] But social media observers wondered whether Coca-Cola would be able to achieve its aim to double its servings' worldwide leveraging social media and fulfill envisaged 2020 vision given the global public health concerns and social media's biggest asset and drawback–content creation and sharing.

122   Mahpar M Hafidz, "The social media challenges", http://biz.thestar.com.my/news/story.asp?-file=/2012/4/7/business/11062253&sec=business, April 7th 2012

123   "Social Media Marketing Challenges: Resources, Measurement", http://news.accuracast.com/social-media-7471/social-media-marketing-challenges-resources-measurement/, March 8th 2012

124   "Coca-Cola Lays Out Its Vision for the Future at 2010 Meeting", op.cit.

125   ibid.

126   "Executing Coke's Roadmap for Growth", http://www.bts.com/Libraries/Case_Studies/bts-coke-system-value-creation.pdf

127   ibid.

128   ibid.

129   "Brand relevance is the challenge: Coca-Cola's Joe Tripodi", op. cit.

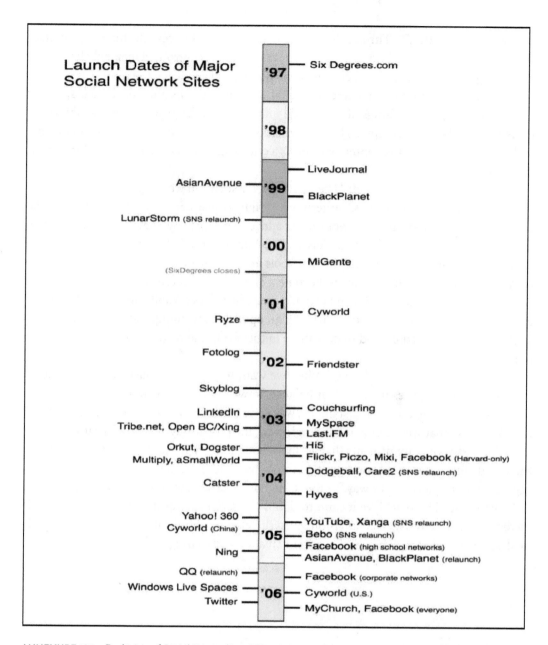

Launch Dates of Major Social Network Sites

'97		Six Degrees.com
'98		
'99	AsianAvenue	LiveJournal / BlackPlanet
'00	LunarStorm (SNS relaunch) / (SixDegrees closes)	MiGente
'01	Ryze	Cyworld
'02	Fotolog / Skyblog	Friendster
'03	LinkedIn / Tribe.net, Open BC/Xing	Couchsurfing / MySpace / Last.FM
'04	Orkut, Dogster / Multiply, aSmallWorld / Catster	Hi5 / Flickr, Piczo, Mixi, Facebook (Harvard-only) / Dodgeball, Care2 (SNS relaunch) / Hyves
'05	Yahoo! 360 / Cyworld (China) / Ning	YouTube, Xanga (SNS relaunch) / Bebo (SNS relaunch) / Facebook (high school networks) / AsianAvenue, BlackPlanet (relaunch)
'06	QQ (relaunch) / Windows Live Spaces / Twitter	Facebook (corporate networks) / Cyworld (U.S.) / MyChurch, Facebook (everyone)

ANNEXURE 18.1 Evolution of Social Networking Sites

Source: Boyd Danah M. and Ellison Nicole B., "Social Network Sites: Definition, History, and Scholarship", http://www.danah.org/papers/JCMCIntro.pdf

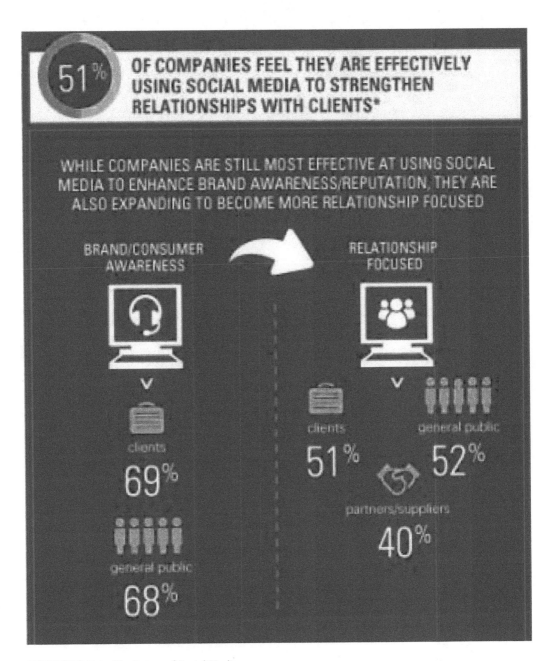

ANNEXURE 18.2 The Future of Social Media

*Percentages displayed reflect participating companies only

Source: Boris Cynthia, "The Rise of Social Business: it's About More Than Just Marketing", http://www.marketingpilgrim.com/2012/07/the-rise-of-social-business-its-about-more-than-just-marketing.html, July 13th 2012

Air France Internet Marketing

Mark Jeffrey, Lisa Egli, and Andy Geraltowski

R ob Griffin, senior vice president and U.S. director of search for Media Contacts, a media solutions provider, examined a report containing this month's numbers for the profitable paid-search campaign his agency had managed for one of its top clients, Air France. Executives at the French company were pursuing an international growth strategy and were looking to increase their share in the hyper-competitive U.S. air travel market. Although they were pleased thus far with the results that Griffin and his team had delivered during the engagement, the pressure was on Media Contacts to continuously optimize performance and return on advertising (ROA) dollars spent for search engine marketing (SEM) campaigns.

Sharon Bernstein, director of insights for Media Contacts, had recently briefed Griffin on the situation:

> Air France's revenue from online ticket sales continues to grow. Our reports demonstrate Media Contacts' success at driving a growing volume of visitors to Air France–affiliated Web sites. As we continue to make decisions regarding allocation of funds toward search marketing, my team is eager to focus our analytic marketing expertise on increasing Air France's net revenue gained through online advertising as well as ROA. As you know, the cost-per-click of search engine keywords is continuing to increase and there are more new players entering the market. I would like to see our campaigns be even more efficient at driving visitors to Web sites and converting them to customers while keeping click costs minimized.

As Griffin digested Bernstein's comments, he thought about how SEM had become an advertising phenomenon, with North American advertisers spending $9.4 billion in the SEM channel in 2006—62 percent more than they had spent in 2005.[1] But Griffin did not take this bullish growth for granted; although he was pleased with his company's performance to

---

date, Griffin wanted to make sure that the team kept its edge and could deliver the results Air France expected. Griffin agreed with Bernstein that a more effective mix of tactics could improve the efficiency of Media Contacts' campaigns and continue to deliver positive net revenue and ROA for Air France. Griffin knew the data Media Contacts had been collecting on its search campaigns for Air France could be analyzed to optimize future campaign performance; now he had to decide how to move forward.

AIR FRANCE

In 1933 five French airlines merged to form Air France, and the new company set up its hub at the main airport of the Ile de France Region in Paris. Seventy-five years later, that hub, Paris–Charles de Gaulle, had grown to be one of the most efficient in Europe, providing the largest number of connections within the shortest time span.

After the end of World War II, Air France launched its first successful flight to the United States; this inaugural flight between Paris and New York City was held on July 1, 1946, with a flight time of 19 hours and 50 minutes. By 2007 Air France had expanded its U.S. cities served to thirteen. In total that year, Air France served 185 destinations in 83 countries and its total fleet size stood at 383 aircraft.

On May 5, 2004, Air France and Netherlands-based KLM, two of Europe's oldest airlines, joined forces and created the SkyTeam global alliance. This alliance was in response to the need for a global travel offering (Exhibit 19.1). In 2007 SkyTeam employed a work force of 150,000. Combined, the two airlines carried the most scheduled international passengers, flying to 225 destinations in 109 countries (Exhibit 19.2). The new Air France-KLM group developed its strategy based on a concept of "one group, two airlines."

As Air France grew, it developed an approach to aircraft fleet management that was based on a two-prong strategy: *rationalization*, through acquisition of modern aircraft with similar technical characteristics (i.e., "family effects"), and *flexibility*, to adjust aircraft delivery dates or change models within a given aircraft family. Air France needed to be able to adapt quickly to the changing demands of its environment. If demand was low, the company had to reduce capacity by eliminating unnecessary aircraft. For this reason, a substantial part of Air France's fleet was on short- or medium-term lease, a practice known as a "progressive operating lease." Thanks to this strategy, Air France registered positive results from 1999 through 2007, despite years of crisis in the airline industry.

By the end of the 2006–2007 fiscal year, Air France-KLM continued to see growth. During this time, the global economy grew by 4.9 percent, while airline traffic increased 6.6 percent, according to the Association of European Airlines. At Air France specifically, passenger activity increased 5 percent, with 73.5 million passengers carried, resulting in Air France posting a 5.1 percent rise in unit revenue per available seat kilometer.

THE AIRLINE INDUSTRY AND ITS COMPETITIVE LANDSCAPE

Profitability is finally on the horizon. Airlines can be proud of impressive results in safety, efficiency, and the environment. But profits still don't cover the cost of capital. Air transport must continue its agenda for change.

—Giovanni Bisignani, director and
CEO of the International Air Transport Association (IATA)

The airline industry had historically been plagued with low returns, bankruptcies, and ever- fluctuating demand. But in 2006 airline profitability finally improved. After six challenging years and $42 billion in losses, airlines came within $500 million—0.1 percent of revenue—of what industry analysts considered breaking even. Furthermore, operating profit for the industry reached $13 billion in 2006, more than double the amount generated the previous year. At just over 3 percent of revenues, however, this was still far from ideal industry profit levels (**Exhibit 19.3**).

Nearly all of the $42 billion in losses accumulated in the six years prior to 2006 had been generated in the U.S. market. In 2006 the U.S. airline industry returned to profitability, excluding the $10 billion cost of bankruptcy restructuring. Outside the United States, airlines had suffered net losses in 2001 following the events of September 11, but in subsequent years, most airlines had seen the return of modest profits.

International travel had begun to emerge as the fastest growing market; in 2006 the number of international passenger kilometers grew by 6 percent, while growth in domestic passenger kilometers was less then 4 percent. Although two-thirds of air passenger journeys were domestic, when measured in revenue passenger kilometers (RPK), international travel accounted for 60 percent of airline revenues.

In addition to the general increase in demand for air travel, from 2000 to 2006 the industry saw a 50 percent rise in the number of passengers traveling on economy tickets while travel on premium tickets remained stable. In 2006 international premium traffic grew 4.3 percent, much less than the 7.4 percent growth in economy traffic.

Taking advantage of this growing demand for economy air travel was Ryanair, Europe's original low-fare airline. In 2007 the company led the market for international air travel. The airline offered services across twenty-six European countries but had not expanded its offerings to the United States. French-operated L'Avion, on the other hand, catered to the traditionally less price-sensitive business traveler. Indeed, in 2006 L'Avion emerged onto the international airline scene as a provider of business-class-only service between Paris and Newark. This route was the airline's sole offering that year.

Other airlines operating in the Air France market space included U.S. carriers American Airlines and United, as well as European carriers Lufthansa and British Airways. At the time, American Airlines carried more passengers than any other airline.

TRANSFORMATION OF TRAVEL INDUSTRY BY THE INTERNET

WORLD WIDE WEB AND THE EMERGENCE OF E-COMMERCE

The travel industry was one of the earliest to adopt e-commerce into their sales strategies. Driven primarily by the development of the World Wide Web, the Internet had evolved from its origins as an institutional and educational network into a consumer-driven network. The user-friendly interface of Web-browsing software quickly led to development of consumer-geared Web sites. Consumers could access information more readily and at their own convenience. This newly found accessibility held huge potential for increasing businesses' sales by vastly increasing their reach. As consumers grew more Web-savvy and became more trusting in the security of online services, e-commerce emerged as a very fast growing sales medium.

Having already built systems for external use by travel agents to search and book flights for customers, airlines were uniquely well suited to establish direct-to-consumer sales portals via the Internet. Further, with the adoption of e-tickets, airlines were better protected from many of the logistical problems faced by other industries as they evolved toward online sales.

THE LANDSCAPE OF THE TRAVEL INDUSTRY ON THE INTERNET

The travel industry comprised several different types of online service providers. Direct Web sites were owned and hosted by the individual airlines, and as popularity of the Web and e-commerce grew, travel providers responded quickly by establishing their own Web sites. Airlines' direct Web sites provided a number of services beyond the ability to purchase flights, which made them attractive destinations for travelers performing their own Web searches. These Web sites housed full flight schedules for the airline, real-time information on flight arrival/departure times, fleet information, and customer loyalty programs. As a result, the number of user-oriented travel tools on airlines' direct Web sites increased dramatically in just a few short years (Exhibit 19.4).

Consumers could also choose to purchase air tickets from aggregator Web sites such as Expedia.com, Orbitz.com, and Priceline.com. The aggregators existed in a pseudo-competitive position relative to the airlines' own direct Web sites but also offered services beyond flight purchase, including hotel and vacation packages. When consumers would book via the aggregators, the airlines still earned revenue, but they paid a fee to the aggregator for facilitating the purchase. The airlines' direct Web sites had difficulty competing with the convenience of the aggregators, which could perform lowest-price searches and allowed the consumer to build full travel packages with the convenience of one purchase from one Web site.

Further increasing the number of travel-booking alternatives online was a third type of service provider, metasearchers. The metasearch sites (e.g., Kayak.com, Sidestep.com) were also aggregators of information but did not offer transaction services. Instead, consumers could use these sites to search for their travel services, view consolidated results from multiple direct service providers, make their choice, and then be linked through to the airline's direct Web site to complete their purchase. Travel providers paid these sites for advertising (in a similar fashion to the major search engines) in order to be included in the search results.

CONSUMER ADOPTION OF E-COMMERCE FOR TRAVEL

According to the Travel Industry Association (TIA), the number of consumers going online to research and book travel increased 263 percent between 1996 and 2005.[2] All estimations of the online travel market predicted substantial growth rates. PhoCusWright, a travel industry marketing research authority, estimated that more than one half of all U.S. travel would be booked online by consumers in 2006, compared to 30 percent in 2005, 20 percent in 2003, and 15 percent in 2002.[3]

The intangibility of travel as a consumer product made it uniquely well suited to online purchasing when compared to other segments of the retail industry. With other products, consumer decision making could be difficult without handling the product prior to purchase. This was not the case with travel purchases. Additionally, increased access to the Internet by consumers, brought on by greater availability of high-speed connections, helped bolster this trend considerably, along with increased price competition among suppliers.[4] While overall Internet penetration approached saturation, the volume of high-speed connections was continuing to rise (Exhibit 19.5). In 2005 an estimated 32.2 million households in the United States had high-speed Internet connections.[5]

SEARCH ENGINE MARKETING

With billions of Web pages to sort through, search engines provided the primary means for navigating and organizing the Internet. SEM became a well-known method of marketing in which businesses promoted their products and services through targeted placements on Internet search engine results pages (SERPs). Search engines constructed SERPs using proprietary algorithms, which determined the most relevant sites for a given search. This provided a highly targeted space to connect consumers to exactly what they were looking for when they were looking for it. In 2006 SEM had become the most successful form of online advertising because of this targeted relevancy. SEM involved both Web site search engine optimization and pay-per-click sponsored search campaigns.

SEARCH ENGINE OPTIMIZATION (SEO)

SEO analyzed the structure and content of a business's Web site to maximize its readability and relevance to search engine "robots" indexing the content of the Internet. SEO strategies

---

2   Mintel International Group Ltd., "Internet Travel Booking—U.S.—September 2005."
3   Ibid.
4   Ibid.
5   Ibid.

looked at technical aspects of sites such as URL address structure, Web server settings, information architecture, site usability, and text content. Image- and multimedia-heavy sites required adding alternate text tagging to be readable by search engines. The goal of SEO was to organically improve a site's relevancy ranking, which meant it would naturally appear higher on a SERP.

PAY-PER-CLICK, OR SPONSORED SEARCH

In pay-per-click, or sponsored search, advertising campaigns, businesses bid on keywords for sponsored link listings consisting of a title, a short description and a display URL. Sponsored links usually appeared at the top of a SERP for a relevant search. Relevancy was determined by the match of keywords bid on by the advertiser, the amount bid for those keywords in comparison with competitor bids, the number of times an ad had been clicked on for a keyword, and proprietary "black box" algorithmic criteria from the search engine provider. Generally, an advertiser paid for an ad only when it was clicked. This cost-per-click could reduce with volume as the search engine provider determined the ad was more relevant to those keywords.

Sponsored search could be managed in terms of campaigns, keywords, and groups of keywords. Although each search engine had unique terms for its programs, most had become similar, likely due to the success of Google's program. Advertisers placed maximum bids on keywords and laid out daily budgets for campaigns. These budgets, along with relevancy, determined how much share-of-voice (SOV) the advertiser achieved. The larger search engines allowed for broad, exact, and phrase keyword campaigns to allow advertisers to cast either wide or narrow nets of impressions. Choice of keyword type depended on the uniqueness of a keyword to describe the underlying product or service. Geotargeting, a relatively new search engine feature, allowed a campaign to target a specific geographic region and language.

Emerging trends in sponsored search tended to revolve around more finely targeted relevancy. Search engine verticals had appeared in several industries, such as Kayak for travel services, to allow for more specific searches within the given industry. Local search had also achieved buzz as a means to target consumers with locally relevant search results; geotargeting was a form of local search.

Pay-per-click campaigns were considered easily measurable, due to the ability to track precise actions on the Internet. Using analytic software, an advertiser knew the number of times an ad was seen (known as impressions), which keywords were used, the number of clicks per impression or click-through rate on the ad, how many clicks were converted into transactions (known as transaction conversion percentage), and how much revenue those resulting transactions were worth.

To optimize a sponsored campaign, the campaign had to improve on one or more of the following: cost-per-click reduction, increase in bookings, net revenue, revenue per transaction, return per transaction, overall performance by engine, or other performance metrics that could improve the net revenue of a particular campaign.

Sponsored search provided more immediate traceable results than SEO and generally was more campaign driven. The instant tracking of results and on-the-fly adjustments allowed pay-per-click campaigns to be highly responsive.

SEO and pay-per-click worked together in a SEM strategy: performance of pay-per-click keyword campaigns could be used to tweak content on the home Web site, and the relevant portfolio of pay-per-click keywords could be inferred by analyzing which keyword referrals were most effective at leading a consumer to the Web site through a natural listing.

MEDIA CONTACTS AND ITS PARTNERS

In 2007 Air France operated in the fiercely competitive business of international and domestic airline travel services. Catering to both business and leisure travelers, Air France turned to Internet marketing campaigns and search engine optimization to reach large customer segments in multiple countries including the United States. To be successful, Air France had to understand how to maximize the net revenue and the ROA of its Internet marketing campaigns by evaluating alternative strategies. The airlines hired Media Contacts to help it achieve this goal.

MEDIA CONTACTS

Media Contacts was the global interactive media network of Havas Media, a group ranked sixth among communications consulting companies throughout the world. Beginning in 1997, Media Contacts had grown to operate twenty-seven offices in twenty-three countries in Europe, North America, South America, Asia, and Oceania. The company provided data-driven media solutions across all interactive channels, from direct response to relationship-based media. In addition to Air France, Media Contacts' extensive list of customers included Royal Caribbean, Fidelity, and Goodyear. John Arnott, Web and communications manager of ING Direct (UK), commented on Media Contacts' service:[6]

> One of the most refreshing aspects of working with Media Contacts is that they are genuinely passionate about our brand and delivering results for us. They constantly look to improve our online performance through innovative thinking and testing new approaches. The level of analysis and reporting we receive from them is crucial to the continuing success of our business.

---

6 Interview with the authors.

Media Contacts worked to form strategic partnerships with a number of research and technology providers in order to gain access to granular data sets, which could be integrated with the company's campaign data. One of the partnerships Media Contacts established was with DoubleClick, a company that developed and provided Internet ad services. In 2007 Media Contacts was one of three agencies in the world that transferred all impressions, clicks, and activity data from DoubleClick services to its data warehouse on a nightly basis.

DOUBLECLICK

As an Internet ad services company, DoubleClick offered technology products and services marketed primarily to advertising agencies and media companies in an effort to allow clients to traffic, target, deliver, and report on their interactive advertising campaigns. The company's main product line, known as DART enterprise, was intended to increase the purchasing efficiency of advertisers and to minimize unsold inventory for publishers.

Included in the DART enterprise system was a Web-based search system, which was integrated with leading engines such as Google, Yahoo, and MSN. With the increased Internet use for client purchases, buyers of online advertising struggled to find the best allocation of ad dollars. DoubleClick's Advertising Exchange service was designed to help customers maximize ROA through dynamic pricing and intelligent bidding. The tool allowed search specialists to set maximum bids based on past performance with specially designed bid rules. In addition, specialists were able to define budgets and time frames, as well as select cost-per-thousand, cost-per-click, and cost-per-action pricing models. Customers using the DART enterprise system spoke highly of its benefits:

> DART Enterprise has helped us to understand where users are going on our site and their buying behavior patterns so we can continually adjust offers, placements, and creatives to improve buy-through and maximize sales.
>
> —Otto Linton, ad trafficking manager, VEGAS.com

In 1999, at a cost of $1.7 billion, DoubleClick merged with data-collection agency Abacus Direct, which worked with offline catalog companies. Roles changed for Double-Click in 2007, however, when Google announced it had reached an agreement to acquire DoubleClick for $3.1 billion in cash, a decision that quickly stirred anti-competitive concerns regarding Google's power and influence in the growing SEM industry.

GOOGLE

Google began in January 1996 as a research project by two PhD students at Stanford University. Based in Mountain View, California, the company was incorporated in 1998 and received its first round of venture capital funding in June 1999. Google's advanced Internet search engine technology positioned the company for rapid growth, and following an initial public offering in August 2004 that raised $1.67 billion, the company pursued an aggressive growth strategy through new product developments, acquisitions, and partnerships. By June 2006 Google employed 7,942 full-time workers and was one of the top five most popular sites on the Internet.

Google generated revenue primarily through two programs: highly targeted advertising and online search services. Google's advertising program used auction pricing based on the value (cost-per-click) an advertiser assigned to particular keywords. The position of a particular advertisement on Google's search results page was determined by a combination of the cost-per-click and the click-through rate so that the most relevant ads were displayed more prominently. While these tactics allowed Google to display the more relevant ad copies higher on a given page, Google's page-ranking technology also utilized certain "black box" algorithms and calculations to which search engine marketers did not have access.

Powering Google's search engine technology and advertising services was an advanced technology architecture that linked large numbers of inexpensive PCs together in a highly efficient grid network. Employing highly complex mathematical algorithms, Google software conducted a series of simultaneous calculations requiring only a fraction of a second. Unlike its early competitors who relied heavily on how often a word appeared on a Web page when displaying search results, Google used its patented PageRank algorithm to determine which Web pages were most important. According to Google's Web site, "PageRank reflects Google's view of the importance of Web pages by considering more than 500 million variables and 2 billion terms. Pages that Google believes are important pages receive a higher PageRank and are more likely to appear at the top of the search results."[7]

Not surprisingly, Google's growth did not go unnoticed by competitors such as Yahoo and Microsoft. As consumers and businesses increasingly shifted a larger percentage of purchases to Internet channels, SEM and digital advertising campaigns represented a significant growth industry. Google launched the opening volley in this race for market share by announcing in 2007 that it was acquiring DoubleClick. Tim Armstrong, Google's president of advertising and commerce for North America, explained the rationale for the acquisition:

> This transaction will strengthen our advertising network by expanding our access to publisher inventory and enabling us to serve the needs of a broader set of advertisers and ad agencies.

---

7   Braintique.com, "How Google Works," http://www.braintique.com/research/topic/how.shtml.

MICROSOFT MSN

The Microsoft Network (MSN) was released in August 1995 and established Microsoft as a major player in the online world. Originally focused on Web e-mail and positioning itself as an Internet service provider, Microsoft realized by 1999 that the largely underused MSN.com domain name would require a certain level of rebranding to better challenge Yahoo for online advertising dollars. As a result, that same year MSN.com was relaunched as a Web portal and a branded family of sites produced by Microsoft's Interactive Media Group (IMG). Perhaps the most significant aspect of the relaunch was Microsoft's decision to offer the majority of content for free, compared with its previous policy of paid subscription services.

Early in its inception, MSN realized an opportunity to partner with other service and content providers in order to drive traffic to the MSN.com home page. MSN received revenue from three key sources: Microsoft adCenter, MSN Shopping, and the subscription-based Internet service to Web users. Microsoft adCenter (formerly MSN adCenter) was developed internally by Microsoft to deliver ads and to end Microsoft's historical reliance on third-party providers. As late as 2006 Microsoft had relied heavily on Yahoo for search-related advertising; now it began creating its own search product within adCenter.

Despite a comparatively late entry into the SEM world, MSN.com enjoyed at least one advantage over pure-play search engines: rich customer data gathered through its Internet hosting service. At one point, MSN.com claimed approximately nine million subscribers, second only to AOL.com in terms of registered users. By combining the technology capabilities of Microsoft adCenter with customer transaction information, Microsoft moved to differentiate itself from its competitors.

Like Google adWords, Microsoft adCenter used pay-per-click technology when serving advertisements as well as advertisement click-through rate in determining the frequency at which an ad would be displayed. Microsoft differed from Google, however, by allowing its advertisers to target ads to a particular customer demographic. In other words, by restricting ads to a given set of demographics, Microsoft could increase the bid price whenever users of a particular demographic would see an ad.

Despite adCenter's promising potential, Microsoft was keenly aware of the threat posed by Google. When Google announced its intention to acquire DoubleClick, Microsoft responded with a $6 billion tender offer for digital marketing firm aQuantive—an offer that represented an 85 percent premium over aQuantive's stock price in the days preceding the announcement. When Kevin Johnson, president of the platforms and services division at Microsoft, announced the acquisition, he erased any doubt of Microsoft's perspective of Google:

> The Microsoft aQuantive transaction will promote competition, and the Google DoubleClick transaction will reduce competition ... Consider

on the one hand that aQuantive today is in three lines of business ... Microsoft today is in none of those businesses. That's why this acquisition will increase competition.[8]

YAHOO

In early 1994, Stanford graduate students Jerry Yang and David Filo created a Web site that would later become known as Yahoo. Originally designed as a directory of other Web sites, Yahoo in time shifted course, evolving into a searchable index of Web pages. As it grew organically in size and breadth of the products it offered, Yahoo expanded into new markets by acquiring a broad mix of companies. With each acquisition, Yahoo modified the terms of service for customers of the acquired company, claiming intellectual property rights for the digital content residing on Yahoo's computer servers. By leveraging this content, Yahoo pursued a strategy of expanding beyond pure-play search and becoming a content-driven Web portal for the global Internet user community.

As the predecessor of Yahoo Search Marketing, commercial Web search services company Overture was one of the early pioneers in monetizing Internet search traffic. Its May 1999 patent application, entitled "System and method for influencing a position on a search result list generated by a computer network search engine," was used in litigations against several companies, including Google. Interestingly, it was precisely during this litigation, in 2003, that Yahoo acquired Overture. Perhaps to hasten the buyout of Overture, the Google vs. Overture lawsuit was settled the next year, with Google agreeing to issue 2.7 million shares of common stock to Yahoo in exchange for a perpetual license of the underlying patent's technology.

Yahoo pursued competitive differentiation in SEM by combining ads with "content matching." Content matching represented Yahoo's ability to marry search and non-search content into a single unified user experience. Yahoo's extensive Web portal network and digital content repositories provided the company with a unique ability to display more than just search results; context-specific content could be linked to search keywords, a function Yahoo hoped would present a greater value proposition than pure-play Internet search providers. It should be noted, however, that Yahoo received 46 percent less revenue per SERP than Google.

While Google and Microsoft had enjoyed measurable success in their respective search marketing businesses, Yahoo's performance had been comparably less positive. Yahoo responded to lackluster results in 2006 by replacing its CEO of six years, Terry Semel, with company co-founder Jerry Yang. As a first-time CEO, Yang acknowledged the challenges ahead during his first earnings conference call:

---

8   Enid Burns, "Microsoft Will Acquire Ad Company aQuantive," ClickZ.com, May 18, 2007, http://www.clickz.com/showPage.html? page=3625912.

I intend to spend the next 100 days or so focused on mapping out a strategic plan for long-term success, working with our teams to put the right organization and the right people in place, and making any necessary changes.[9]

KAYAK

Founded in 2004 by Steve Hafner and Paul English, Kayak.com was a relative newcomer to the SEM industry. The company was considered a travel aggregator of sorts, meaning it scoured the Internet for the best possible business and leisure travel services. Kayak's founders were experienced entrepreneurs with a history of successful startup businesses under their belts.

Focusing on a specific niche in the SEM industry, Kayak aimed to differentiate itself in two ways: as an alternative business model from those of established travel service aggregators such as Orbitz, Expedia, and Travelocity; and as a unique technology architecture. Long-time industry players such as Orbitz and Expedia purchased and resold airline seats and hotel rooms, in effect committing to expensive inventory holding costs in a notoriously volatile and price-sensitive market. Kayak, however, was exclusively a travel search service; rather than sell anything, it merely connected consumers with the airlines and hoteliers.

The company also intended to leverage highly advanced software application architecture that was distinct from existing competitor offerings. Instead of passing Web site data through expensive central servers, Kayak's rich Internet application (RIA) architecture transferred some of the processing load to the consumer's computer, ultimately allowing much greater (and cheaper) processing capacity. As a result, Kayak said it "provided a more exhaustive search than any other travel site, including the inventory of 551 airlines and 91,500 hotels. Its goal is to find and search every hotel on earth, which it estimates at 300,000 properties."

In addition to the company's service operations and technology architecture, Kayak.com enjoyed another distinction relative to the larger search engine providers such as Microsoft, Yahoo, and Google: Kayak's Web site search and clickstream data were not integrated with DoubleClick. As a result, advertising agencies and media companies interested in analyzing Kayak.com site activity had to rely on alternative data sources and data integration techniques for an effective comparison. Because of Kayak's comparably smaller market share position in the industry, extensive analysis of Kayak data was rare.

Kayak's historical business results were less than impressive, but the forecast was beginning to look more positive. Although monthly losses were running at $500,000, sales volume

---

9   Larry Dignan, "Yahoo To Lay Out Strategic Plan in Next 100 Days," ZDNet.com, July 17, 2007, http://blogs. zdnet.com/BTL/?p=5684.

was increasing at 15 percent per month, reaching $388,000 in September 2005. In addition, the company boasted a click-through rate of 8 percent for Kayak.com, significantly higher than the 0.8 percent industry average for online travel sites.

DETAILS OF THE CHALLENGE

The Media Contacts team had only a short time to make sense of all of its research and determine a way to optimize future campaigns. Although it appeared that using branded keywords might bring in more revenue, it was also apparent that unbranded keywords produced a larger percentage of single-click conversions. Which approach would have a higher propensity to increase ticket sales and to improve ROA? Furthermore, Media Contacts had to determine whether broad or focused keywords were more profitable for Air France. Although broad keywords occupied the majority of searches, were they as profitable as focused keywords? How could Media Contacts use assist keywords to lead consumers to a desired behavior? Note that typical Internet tracking worked by measuring the last keyword clicked, and this keyword was credited for the sale/conversion. The team's research therefore extended well beyond the examination of numerical data; it had to think about consumer behavior, considering how many searches it might take for someone to convert.

Each search engine that Air France was working with in July 2007—Google, Yahoo, MSN, and Kayak—appeared to specialize in different services and consequently might appeal to different audiences. Media Contacts needed to decide which search engine(s) delivered the most value to Air France per dollar spent. They also needed to be mindful of whether any search engines were partnered with travel aggregators, as this could create a potential conflict of interest for Air France.

Media Contacts could use DoubleClick data to analyze past performance and make recommendations for strategy optimization. The data included line item information for keywords and keyword groups for each campaign and search engine (Exhibit 19.6). To make sense of this information, it would need to be grouped and analyzed using Microsoft Excel's pivot table feature (Exhibit 19.7). Using pivot tables to show different summaries of data, the Media Contacts team could analyze campaign key performance indicators (KPI) by search engine, bid strategy, keyword group, keywords, and so on.

NEXT STEPS

As Griffin and his team reviewed the latest marketing campaign figures for Air France, he paused to reflect on potential future strategies Media Contacts should consider for increasing Air France's market share and profitability in the United States. While a quick review of the data indicated that SEM was a profitable venture for Air France, Griffin was eager to understand what a more thorough data analysis would uncover. For example, he was curious whether different search engines were attracting different consumer segments and yielding unique purchase patterns and consumer behavior from SEM campaigns. Glancing at his calendar, Griffin noticed the upcoming biannual financial planning session with the Air France marketing team to review campaign funding proposals.

- Should Media Contacts recommend a uniform strategy for Air France across search engine publishers? Or would it be more effective to tailor each publisher strategy to maximize return on investment?
- How can campaigns be improved to increase overall value gained from investment with a search engine publisher? Should keywords be added or dropped from the campaign? Should campaign tactics or copy be adjusted to improve campaign performance?
- What are the most important KPIs, and what impact will campaign changes have on these KPIs?
- How should future SEM campaigns be structured? In the past, Media Contacts had concentrated on Google, Microsoft, and Yahoo; was there now an opportunity to optimize search advertising with metasearch companies such as Kayak?

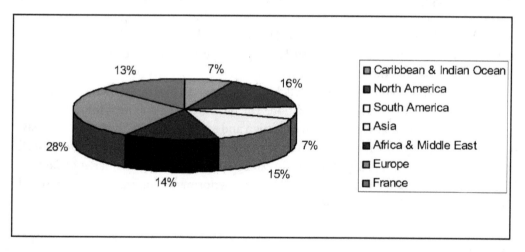

EXHIBIT 19.1   Scheduled Passenger Revenue by Destination

Source: World Air Transport Statistics (WATS). WATS provides statistics from more than 350 airlines, including low-cost carriers. This represents a complete statistical picture of the airline industry in 2006.

EXHIBIT 19.2 Scheduled International Passengers Carried in 2006 (World), left, and Scheduled Passengers Carried in 2006 (World), right

RANK	AIRLINE	NO. OF PASSENGERS		RANK	AIRLINE	NO. OF PASSENGERS
1	Ryanair	40,532,000		1	American Airlines	99,835,000
2	Lufthansa	38,236,000		2	Southwest Airlines	96,277,000
3	Air France	30,417,000		3	Delta Airlines	73,584,000
4	British Airways	29,498,000		4	United Airlines	69,265,000
5	KLM	22,322,000		5	Northwest Airlines	55,925,000
6	Easyjet	21,917,000		6	Lufthansa	51,213,000
7	American Airlines	21,228,000		7	Air France	49,411,000
8	Singapore Airlines	18,022,000		8	All Nippon Airways	49,266,000
9	Emirates	16,748,000		9	Japan Airlines	48,911,000
10	Cathay Pacific Airways	16,667,000		10	China Southern Airlines	48,512,000

Source: World Air Transport Statistics (WATS). WATS provides statistics from more than 350 airlines, including low-cost carriers. This represents a complete statistical picture of the airline industry in 2006.

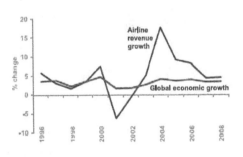

Global net profit and operating margin

Airline revenue and global economic growth

EXHIBIT 19.3

Source: International Air Transport Association (IATA). IATA, an international trade body created more than sixty years ago by a group of airlines, represented some 250 airlines comprising 94 percent of the international scheduled air traffic.

EXHIBIT 19.4 Frequent Business Travelers' Use of Online Tools, 2002 and 2004[10]

	2002	2004
Total sample of frequent business travelers:	312	304
Number of respondents that:		
Print boarding pass before airport arrival	30	77
Check in online	22	76
Receive mobile or PDA alerts	30	44
Use in-flight Internet access	7	7

Source: JupiterResearch

---

10   Mintel International Group Ltd., "Internet Travel Booking—U.S.—September 2005."

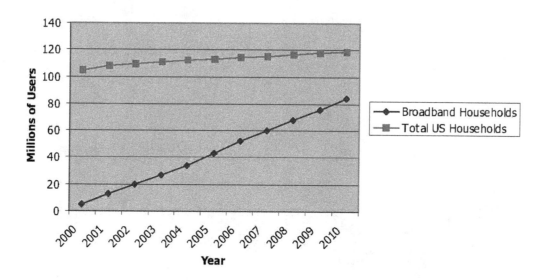

EXHIBIT 19.5   U.S. Broadband Household Projections, 2000–2010[11]

Note: Mintel estimates are based on deployment data of all high-speed Internet access technologies, including cable service, DSL, and both fixed and mobile wireless connections.

---

11   Ibid.

EXHIBIT 19.6 DoubleClick Data on Campaign and Publisher Performance[12]

PUBLISHER NAME	KEYWORD ID	KEYWORD	MATCH TYPE	CAMPAIGN	KEYWORD GROUP	CATEGORY	BID STRATEGY	KEYWORD TYPE
Yahoo - US	43000000039657988	fly to florence	Advanced	Western Europe Destinations	Florence	uncategorized		Unassigned
Yahoo - US	43000000039651113	low international airfare	Advanced	Geo Targeted DC	Low International DC	uncategorized		Unassigned
MSN - Global	43000000019452431	air discount france ticket	Broad	Air France Brand & French Destinat	France	uncategorized	Position 2-5 Bid Strategy	Unassigned
Google - Global	43000000005663331	[airfrance]	Exact	Air France Global Campaign	Air France	airfrance	Position 1- 3	Unassigned
Overture - Global	43000000005421354	air france online booking	Standard	Unassigned	Unassigned	airfrance	Position 1-2 Target	Unassigned
Overture - Global	43000000005421146	airfrance,com	Standard	Unassigned	Unassigned	airfrancewebsite	Position 1-2 Target	Unassigned
Google - US	43000000014110441	paris cheap airline	Broad	Geo Targeted San Francisco	San Francisco to Paris Sale	uncategorized	Position 5-10 Bid Strategy	Unassigned
Overture - US	43000000014278681	airfrance.us	Standard	Unassigned	Unassigned	airfrance	Position 1-4 Bid Strategy	Unassigned
Overture - Global	43000000005421374	air travel to paris	Standard	Unassigned	Unassigned	paris	Position 1-2 Target	Unassigned
Google - Global	43000000019449172	air france site	Broad	Air France Brand & French Destinat	Air France Website	uncategorized		Unassigned
Overture - Global	43000000005421298	cheap fare to paris	Advanced	Unassigned	Unassigned	paris	Position 1-2 Target	Unassigned
Overture - US	43000000014278799	air france.com	Standard	Unassigned	Unassigned	airfrance	Position 1-4 Bid Strategy	Unassigned
Google - US	43000000017532136	air france us	Broad	Air France Branded	Air France Website	uncategorized		Unassigned
Google - US	43000000017532129	airfrance	Broad	Air France Branded	Air France Website	uncategorized		Unassigned
Overture - US	43000000014278804	cdg flight	Standard	Unassigned	Unassigned	paris	Position 2-5 Bid Strategy	Unassigned
Google - US	43000000017532133	airfrance us	Broad	Air France Branded	Air France Website	uncategorized		Unassigned
Google - US	43000000014113402	france airline ticket	Broad	Geo Targeted New York	New York to France Sale	uncategorized	Position 5-10 Bid Strategy	Unassigned
Google - US	43000000013069003	airfrance website	Broad	Air France Branded	Air France Website	uncategorized	Position 2-5 Bid Strategy	Unassigned
Overture - Global	43000000005420920	airplane france ticket	Advanced	Unassigned	Unassigned	airline	Position 1-2 Target	Unassigned
Google - US	43000000014115425	france airfare sale	Broad	Geo Targeted Miami	Miami to France Sale	uncategorized	Position 5-10 Bid Strategy	Unassigned
Overture - Global	43000000005421434	air france schedule	Advanced	Unassigned	Unassigned	airfrance	Position 1-2 Target	Unassigned
Overture - Global	43000000009683629	airfare to tahiti	Standard	Unassigned	Unassigned	tahiti		Unassigned
Google - US	43000000014122527	france flights	Broad	Geo Targeted DC	DC to France Sale	uncategorized	Position 5-10 Bid Strategy	Unassigned
Google - US	43000000014201100	international airfares	Broad	Geo Targeted Detroit	International Detroit	uncategorized	Position 5-10 Bid Strategy	Unassigned
Google - US	43000000014113704	france air ticket	Broad	Geo Targeted New York	New York to France Sale	uncategorized	Position 5-10 Bid Strategy	Unassigned
Overture - US	43000000017532937	airfrance.com/us	Standard	Unassigned	Unassigned	airfrance		Unassigned
Google - US	43000000014127450	paris cheap ticket	Broad	Geo Targeted Boston	Boston to Paris Sale	uncategorized	Position 5-10 Bid Strategy	Unassigned
Google - US	43000000014118997	paris cheap flights	Broad	Geo Targeted Houston	Houston to Paris Sale	uncategorized	Position 5-10 Bid Strategy	Unassigned
Overture - US	43000000007003938	tunis	Standard	Unassigned	Unassigned	regional	Position 1-4 Bid Strategy	Unassigned

12 See spreadsheet accompanying this case for the complete data set.

(continued)

STATUS	SEARCH ENGINE BID	CLICKS	CLICK CHARGES	AVG. COST PER CLICK	IMPRES-SIONS	ENGINE CLICK THRU %	AVG. POS.	TRANS. CONV. %	TOTAL COST TRANS.	AMOUNT	TOTAL COST	VOLUME OF BOOKINGS
Live	$6.25	1	$2.31	$2.31	11	9.09%	1.27	900.00%	$0.26	$8,777.95	$2.31	9
Paused	$6.25	1	$0.63	$0.63	6	16.67%	1.00	100.00%	$0.63	$1,574.20	$0.63	1
Deactivated	$0.00	1	$0.39	$0.39	9	11.11%	1.11	100.00%	$0.39	$390.15	$0.39	1
Unavailable	$7.50	59	$2.31	$0.04	401	14.71%	2.00	3.39%	$1.16	$1,665.15	$2.31	2
Paused	$0.25	8	$2.20	$0.28	318	2.52%	2.98	12.50%	$2.20	$935.00	$2.20	1
Paused	$0.13	42	$5.25	$0.13	722	5.82%	1.13	4.76%	$2.63	$1,817.30	$5.25	2
Paused	$6.25	3	$5.21	$1.74	13	23.08%	1.00	33.33%	$5.21	$1,685.55	$5.21	1
Paused	$0.33	47	$11.80	$0.25	547	8.59%	1.18	4.26%	$5.90	$3,796.10	$11.80	2
Unavailable	$7.50	13	$5.21	$0.40	448	2.90%	1.86	7.69%	$5.21	$1,513.00	$5.21	1
Unavailable	$5.00	19	$8.24	$0.43	129	14.73%	1.03	5.26%	$8.24	$2,348.55	$8.24	1
Sent	$0.69	29	$26.61	$0.92	559	5.19%	2.33	6.90%	$13.31	$7,418.80	$26.61	2
Paused	$0.31	273	$46.35	$0.17	3,171	8.61%	1.01	3.66%	$4.63	$11,271.85	$46.35	10
Live	$10.00	231	$99.55	$0.43	1,277	18.09%	1.02	8.66%	$4.98	$23,076.65	$99.55	20
Paused	$10.00	907	$235.11	$0.26	4,352	20.84%	1.01	2.87%	$9.04	$48,551.15	$235.11	26
Paused	$0.13	18	$4.75	$0.26	169	10.65%	1.66	5.56%	$4.75	$896.75	$4.75	1
Live	$10.00	207	$30.79	$0.15	730	28.36%	1.00	2.42%	$6.16	$5,733.25	$30.79	5
Live	$6.25	2	$2.69	$1.34	24	8.33%	1.54	50.00%	$2.69	$494.70	$2.69	1
Live	$0.71	10	$9.94	$0.99	80	12.50%	1.06	10.00%	$9.94	$1,815.60	$9.94	1
Paused	$0.44	16	$8.31	$0.52	6,073	0.26%	2.46	6.25%	$8.31	$1,473.90	$8.31	1
Paused	$6.25	1	$2.76	$2.76	2	50.00%	1.00	100.00%	$2.76	$470.05	$2.76	1
Paused	$0.33	30	$10.71	$0.36	2,192	1.37%	1.52	3.33%	$10.71	$1,785.00	$10.71	1
Paused	$10.00	6	$12.27	$2.05	102	5.88%	4.16	16.67%	$12.27	$1,989.00	$12.27	1
Unavailable	$6.25	6	$18.35	$3.06	137	4.38%	1.20	50.00%	$6.12	$2,810.10	$18.35	3
Unavailable	$6.25	2	$6.60	$3.30	79	2.53%	3.01	50.00%	$6.60	$923.95	$6.60	1
Live	$6.25	12	$19.40	$1.62	116	10.34%	1.09	33.33%	$4.85	$2,706.40	$19.40	4
Paused	$7.50	17	$5.59	$0.33	98	17.35%	0.96	5.88%	$5.59	$778.60	$5.59	1
Paused	$6.25	3	$5.14	$1.71	18	16.67%	1.83	33.33%	$5.14	$676.60	$5.14	1
Paused	$6.25	21	$43.39	$2.07	174	12.07%	1.32	14.29%	$14.46	$5,638.05	$43.39	3
Paused	$11.25	36	$25.37	$0.70	832	4.33%	1.41	8.33%	$8.46	$3,254.65	$25.37	3

PUBLISHER NAME	KEYWORD ID	KEYWORD	MATCH TYPE	CAMPAIGN	KEYWORD GROUP	CATEGORY	BID STRATEGY	KEYWORD TYPE
Yahoo - US	43000000029356928	france travel agency	Standard	Paris & France Terms	France	uncategorized		Unassigned
Google - Global	43000000005663431	air france airlines	Broad	Air France Global Campaign	Air France	airfrance	Position 1- 3	Unassigned
Google - Global	43000000005663208	lyon airfare	Broad	Air France Global Campaign	Lyon	lyon	Position 1- 3	Unassigned
Overture - Global	43000000005421430	air france web site	Standard	Unassigned	Unassigned	airfrance	Position 1-2 Target	Unassigned
Google - Global	43000000005648300	cont:air france global campaig campaig	N/A	Air France Global Campaign	France	uncategorized		Unassigned
Google - US	43000000017532124	airfrance.com	Broad	Air France Branded	Air France Website	uncategorized		Unassigned
Yahoo - US	43000000027382609	airfrance.us	Advanced	Air France Branded	Air France Website	uncategorized		Unassigned
Google - US	43000000013136095	book airfrance	Broad	Air France Branded	Air France Brand	uncategorized	Position 1 -2 Target	Unassigned
Google - Global	43000000005663350	nice flight	Broad	Air France Global Campaign	Nice	nice	Position 1- 3	Unassigned
Google - US	43000000017532142	airfrance.us	Broad	Air France Branded	Air France Website	uncategorized		Unassigned
Yahoo - US	43000000039658517	rome travel	Advanced	Western Europe Destinations	Rome	uncategorized		Unassigned
Google - US	43000000007147583	rabat flights	Broad	Google_Yearlong 2006	Google|rabat	uncategorized	Postiion 1-4 Bid Strategy	Unassigned
Yahoo - US	43000000027382580	airfrance,com	Advanced	Air France Branded	Air France Website	uncategorized		Unassigned
Overture - Global	43000000005420948	air france phone number	Standard	Unassigned	Unassigned	airfrance	Position 1-2 Target	Unassigned
Overture - US	43000000014278767	airline ticket to france	Standard	Unassigned	Unassigned	france	Position 1-4 Bid Strategy	Unassigned
Google - Global	43000000005663191	airfrance com	Broad	Air France Global Campaign	Air France Website	airfrancewebsite	Position 1- 3	Unassigned
Overture - Global	43000000005421358	new york to paris	Advanced	Unassigned	Unassigned	paris	Position 1-2 Target	Unassigned
Google - US	43000000005277892	cont:google_year-long 2006::go	N/A	Google_Yearlong 2006	Google|Europe	uncategorized		Unassigned
Google - US	43000000013069225	airfrance	Broad	Air France Branded	Air France Brand	uncategorized		Unassigned
Overture - Global	43000000005421406	cheap travel france	Advanced	Unassigned	Unassigned	france	Position 1-2 Target	Unassigned
Google - US	43000000014113121	paris flight	Broad	Geo Targeted Philadelphia	Philadelphia to Paris Sale	uncategorized	Position 5-10 Bid Strategy	Unassigned
Overture - Global	43000000005421034	airfrance.us	Advanced	Unassigned	Unassigned	airfrancewebsite	Position 1-2 Target	Unassigned
Google - US	43000000013068975	airfrance airlines	Broad	Air France Branded	Air France Brand	uncategorized	Position 1 -2 Target	Unassigned
Google - US	43000000014113546	florence cheap tickets	Broad	Geo Targeted New York	New York to Florence Sale	uncategorized	Position 5-10 Bid Strategy	Unassigned
Yahoo - US	43000000027413323	air france travel	Advanced	Air France Branded	Air France Brand	uncategorized		Unassigned
Google - US	43000000005278156	rome fare	Broad	Google_Yearlong 2006	Google|Rome	uncategorized	Postiion 1-4 Bid Strategy	Unassigned

(continued)

Chapter 19—Air France Internet Marketing | 339

STATUS	SEARCH ENGINE BID	CLICKS	CLICK CHARGES	AVG. COST PER CLICK	IMPRES-SIONS	ENGINE CLICK THRU %	AVG. POS.	TRANS. CONV. %	TOTAL COST TRANS.	AMOUNT	TOTAL COST	VOLUME OF BOOKINGS
Live	$6.25	5	$15.44	$3.09	167	2.99%	1.24	40.00%	$7.72	$1,978.80	$15.44	2
Unavailable	$1.25	228	$55.31	$0.24	3,747	6.08%	1.42	1.75%	$13.83	$6,873.10	$55.31	4
Unavailable	$1.25	12	$15.02	$1.25	1,030	1.17%	1.31	16.67%	$7.51	$1,836.00	$15.02	2
Paused	$0.29	17	$5.39	$0.32	752	2.26%	2.22	5.88%	$5.39	$637.50	$5.39	1
Unavailable	$7.50	49	$11.00	$0.22	4,780	1.03%	4.84	2.04%	$11.00	$1,296.25	$11.00	1
Live	$10.00	1,260	$365.80	$0.29	6,231	20.22%	1.01	2.54%	$11.43	$42,538.25	365.80	32
Live	$7.50	242	$87.57	$0.36	1,371	17.65%	1.02	5.79%	$6.26	$10,140.50	$87.57	14
Live	$10.00	4	$6.00	$1.50	43	9.30%	1.09	25.00%	$6.00	$671.50	$6.00	1
Unavailable	$1.25	28	$36.42	$1.30	2,356	1.19%	1.55	10.71%	$12.14	$3,944.00	$36.42	3
Live	$10.00	25	$6.95	$0.28	132	18.94%	1.00	4.00%	$6.95	$751.40	$6.95	1
Live	$2.70	27	$56.41	$2.09	1,051	2.57%	2.86	14.81%	$14.10	$5,729.00	$56.41	4
Paused	$6.25	11	$14.07	$1.28	361	3.05%	1.14	9.09%	$14.07	$1,402.50	$14.07	1
Live	$7.50	48	$7.31	$0.15	298	16.11%	1.00	2.08%	$7.31	$718.25	$7.31	1
Paused	$0.13	65	$9.71	$0.15	1,831	3.55%	2.48	1.54%	$9.71	$947.75	$9.71	1
Paused	$1.26	14	$10.26	$0.73	225	6.22%	2.10	7.14%	$10.26	$991.10	$10.26	1
Unavailable	$2.50	548	$247.94	$0.45	2,919	18.77%	1.47	2.19%	$20.66	$23,041.80	247.94	12
Sent	$0.73	39	$24.44	$0.63	2,364	1.65%	3.63	2.56%	$24.44	$2,226.15	$24.44	1
Unavailable	$7.50	112	$31.65	$0.28	157,285	0.07%	2.31	0.89%	$31.65	$2,882.35	$31.65	1
Live	$27.50	11,789	$2,412.51	$0.20	78,814	14.96%	1.13	1.85%	$11.07	$216,915.75	2,412.51	218
Sent	$0.48	20	$10.40	$0.52	501	3.99%	2.12	5.00%	$10.40	$935.00	$10.40	1
Paused	$6.25	2	$4.89	$2.44	38	5.26%	1.71	50.00%	$4.89	$434.35	$4.89	1
Paused	$0.14	207	$34.87	$0.17	1,100	18.82%	1.17	1.93%	$8.72	$3,035.35	$34.87	4
Live	$0.35	116	$59.35	$0.51	776	14.95%	1.30	4.31%	$11.87	$5,146.75	$59.35	5
Unavailable	$6.25	3	$5.97	$1.99	6	50.00%	2.00	33.33%	$5.97	$490.45	$5.97	1
Live	$6.25	24	$33.79	$1.41	1,171	2.05%	3.07	4.17%	$33.79	$2,772.70	$33.79	1
Paused	$6.25	14	$20.11	$1.44	310	4.52%	1.49	7.14%	$20.11	$1,489.20	$20.11	1

EXHIBIT 19.7 Microsoft Excel Pivot Table Overview[13]

Excel PivotTable reports provide the ability to organize, summarize, and analyze data by viewing it in different ways. Views can be created that offer comparisons, reveal patterns and relationships, and analyze trends.

Use the PivotTable Wizard, located in the Data menu, to create PivotTable reports. PivotTable reports are interactive; the table is "pivoted"—that is, its row and column headers are rotated to show data in different ways and to show different summaries of the data.

To create a PivotTable report layout, click a cell in the data to be used to create the report. On the Data menu, click PivotTable Report.

Excel determines the data to include in the report based on the cell selection. By default, it creates a layout for the report on a new tab and includes the column headings as buttons on the PivotTable toolbar.

PivotTable reports are created by dragging heading buttons to different areas of the layout. The layout changes appearance as fields are dropped into it. Once the results are seen, simply drag the headings outside the layout area and try a different arrangement.

Click on Field Settings to change the mathematic operator on the data.

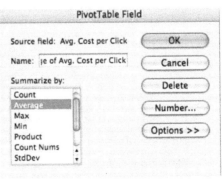

---

13 From Microsoft Excel Help, *Overview: PivotTable Reports.* Search for PivotTable reports in Excel for the most current tutorial.

Drag other heading buttons onto the table to drill into the data. Consult Microsoft Excel Help for more detailed information.

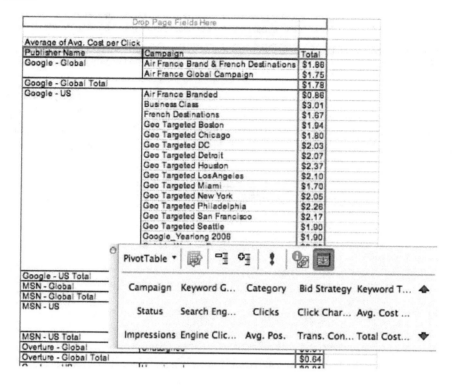

KEY TIPS ON HOW TO AVOID COMMON SOCIAL MEDIA MARKETING PITFALLS

- **Implement a social media policy for your organization.** The most important tip of all is to make sure that your business has a well-defined social media policy that is both easy to understand and readily accessible to your entire staff. Creating a social media policy is the best way to proactively safeguard your brand's image. At a minimum, the policy should do the following:

  1. Set clear limits as to what organizational information can be released, and by whom.
  2. Set organizational standards for online decorum.
  3. Set guidelines for employees concerning what they say about the company on social media, both on and off company time.
  4. Set rules governing all third-party online interactions, especially as they relate to customers/clients.

- **Never post online without a thorough proofread.** In construction, the rule is to always measure your material at least twice because you only get one chance to make the cut. For the social media, the same principle also applies—once a mistake gets posted online, it tends to live forever, no matter how many retractions or deletions are attempted. Save yourself and your organization untold embarrassment by taking the time to proofread all online content before you post it. Check for content accuracy (no fake news!), spelling errors, punctuation, or any potentially X-rated or offensive material. It is good practice to have at least two to three sets of eyes review the content before final upload

- **Take it easy on the hard sell.** If your online marketing content is too obvious or obnoxiously self-promotional, you will only succeed at turning people off and shrinking your overall user numbers. It is supposed to be social media, right, not spam media? The point of viral content is to engage an audience with unique, interactive content, not drive them away with an endless stream of marketing material and advertising!

- **Steer clear of controversy.** Gaining attention by being divisive or stoking controversy is a risky proposition, even if your ultimate goal is to connect with an edgier, alternative audience. It is important to be authentic, but understand that notoriety gained through controversy is not an optimal way to brand yourself for the long term. If your strategy is to reach as wide an audience as possible, then steer clear of content that is racially charged, features excess profanity, prurient appeals to sexuality, or that promotes chronic drug abuse. Following any of those paths is sure to get you attention, but it will engender a vocal backlash, if not outright calls for a boycott as well.

- **Stay positive about negative feedback.** Do not take negative comments left on your social media platforms personally. These comments actually present an opportunity for you to make things right with your user or follower. They have already taken the time to send you feedback representing their personal experience with your brand. Do not ignore their input, disregard its importance, or, worst of all, become defensive and combative in your response. Instead, reach out the disgruntled user as quickly as possible. Engage them in a dialogue, not an interrogation. Refrain from any type of personal antagonisms. The idea is to resolve your customer's concerns not exacerbate them.

- **Upgrade your online security measures.** Here is another way to avoid tons of negative feedback: do not ever let your online systems become compromised. Hardly a week goes by without reports surfacing of some company or organization's data being attacked by outside hackers. The list of organizations is long and includes: Yahoo, Equifax, Ashley Madison, Reddit, FedEx, and even the U.S. Department of Education. These security failures do not even include the targeted Distributed Denial of Service (DDoS) attacks that occur on websites or the release of user financial data via internal leaks. There is no surer way to lose the public's trust—and devalue your brand—than to have your organization featured in a data scandal on the nightly news. Instead, invest on upgraded cybersecurity, encrypted data storage, and improved training for all of your team members.

- **Have a crisis management plan at the ready.** If, despite all your best efforts, a negative rumor or scandal involving your company should occur, how prepared are you to respond? What if the crisis breaks suddenly in the middle of the night, or over a long, holiday weekend? What if a trending Twitter hashtag is threatening to send your stock into a freefall? Waiting to formulate a response until "after the fact" can leave your brand significantly damaged. The smart move is to think ahead and have a crisis management plan already in place; one that spells out who has decision-making authority to respond to any breaking news or negative online trends. In times of crisis, it is best to be as open and transparent as possible. Do not try to lie your way out of the problem or cover it up. If a mistake has been made, own up to it, and then find a way to prevent it from ever happening again.

- Regularly scrub your old social media accounts and websites. Not all viral marketing campaigns pay off and others simply run their course. Either way, never let an unmaintained website sit dormant, yet remain accessible to the public at-large. Once an online promotion ends or a viral campaign concludes, shut down that corresponding site. Like it or not, by leaving the site active, some prospective client is going to find their way onto this vestigial site and take note of the out-of-date layout, the dearth of user interaction, and a comment feed filled with unanswered questions and complaints. Due diligence is all that is needed to avoid falling into this potential trap.

QUESTIONS

1. Discuss some of the potential risks that a brand could face if one of their team members posts offensive content on one of the organization's social media platforms? What safeguards can a company put into place to prevent something like this from happening? Also consider this: What if a team member or company executive posts offensive tweets on their own social media site? Should a person's employment status be put in jeopardy for posting controversial content on social media? Does it matter how recent the postings are, or what the age of the person was when they posted the material? Exactly what kind of commentary or material should be deemed offensive, and why?

2. According to the case study examples presented in Section V, what are some of the preferred tactics that companies should employ when first launching a new viral media marketing campaign? Did any particular type of content or promotions outreach strategy seem to work better than the others? Why do you think that is? Which strategies seemed to be the least effective? Do the case studies reveal any commonalities about the most effective approaches brands can use to gain new online users and followers? What role does brand storytelling play in this process as it relates to customer acquisition and retention?

3. From a journalistic perspective, discuss why is it important for reporters to understand the influences that viral marketing is having on consumer tastes. From your perspective, is journalism—in any form, online or otherwise—immune from the demands of advertisers and sponsors? How do you feel about online news sites post sensational, click bait to help drive traffic? Does this practice only add to the perception that the news is biased or outright "fake"? Even for the individual journalist, how important has it become build up a lengthy list of online followers in order to advance one's career. What difficulties does this requirement place on talented young reporters who are skilled journalists but lack social media expertise?

- **Social media never sleeps—responding to a crisis in real time.** How would you react if you were the head of a company's social media team and you learned that an obscure Internet user's group is claiming to have unearthed evidence that your highly paid and well-recognized celebrity endorser (or, if you prefer, make it a high-profile company executive or big-time investor) has a history of posting racist and misogynistic tweets? Whether the claims are true or not, if the story begins to trend, the mainstream media will rapidly take note. If that happens, the negative publicity could devastate your organization's quarterly sales.

  So, time is of the essence; but if you can react quickly enough, you may be able to squelch the rumors and keep the story from spreading. You have only a few short hours, perhaps only minutes, to come up with a game plan. Using your in-class groups, discuss the benefits and shortcomings of each of the following public relations crisis response options:

  Option #1: Try and keep things quiet for now. Reach out directly to the user's group and ask for their assistance in getting to the bottom of the claim before the group releases any further information. What happens though if the information leaks out anyway?

  Option #2: Issue a press release discounting or refuting the claim as being false and merely a vindictive rumor. This might demonstrate company virtues like loyalty and camaraderie. Of course, if the rumors do turn out to be true, will you already have created a fierce backlash against your company?

  Option #3: Immediately cut ties with the endorser/executive and issue a press release clearly stating the company's zero tolerance towards discrimination of any kind at any level. This might earn you initial public support, but what if the rumors turn out to be false? Many will now see the company as being unreliable for having jumped the gun.

  What other options might you take? What are the risks involved with each of the potential choices that you have to make? Would it make any significant difference if it turned out that while the person did post these tweets, all of the most offensive comments were uploaded well in the past, more than ten years prior, and the person has since made a full apology for the tweets? In a situation like this, describe what steps either the individual endorser/executive or the organization can take to help use social media to turn public consensus back in their favor?

- **How Secure Is Your Online Privacy:** Exactly what are your personal privacy rights on the Internet? Should one even expect to have any privacy when online or is someone always watching you and the digital footprint that you leave behind? As for social media, in most instances, your privacy expectations will depend on the Terms of

Service (ToS) agreement that you agree to adhere by when you first sign up on a social media platform. For one, that ToS agreement likely allows the social media provider to access and use your personal data for a variety of promotional and marketing purposes. In many cases, your profile data, workplace information, e-mail, user-generated content, and location settings will all be open for the public to see unless deliberate steps are taken to keep that data confidential. Inadvertently exposing that information can leave an individual vulnerable to identity theft, confidence schemes, or even online harassment.

To see how safe you are when online, complete this **Cybersecurity Personal Privacy Review**:

Concerning your Internet service provider:

By and large, Internet service providers (ISPs) track your every move while online. They then take your browsing history and aggregate it with data from all of their other users. This web-browsing information is then monetized for sale to third-party marketers. So, the first issue for you to address is:

Who is your ISP and what are their stated privacy policies? Research and explain the benefits of using VPN's, proxy servers and the Tor browser.

Your online web browser:

ISPs only provide you with a connection to the Internet. To actually access specific web pages, you will need to use a web browser, like Chrome, Edge Firefox, or Safari. As with your ISP, browsers can also pose a vulnerability to your online privacy and anonymity, so it will be important to check the following: the easiest step to help ensure privacy is to simply turn off third-party cookies, but before you do that, here's another part of the exercise:

What are the current privacy settings on your Internet browser? Research and explain exactly what cookies have to do with cybersecurity in the first place, and what distinguishes third-party cookies from other cookies? Prior to the start of this assignment, take a count and report on how many cookies were present on your browser.

Now, in order to adjust your browser's privacy settings, take the following steps:

For Chrome users: select Settings> Advanced> Content settings> Cookies. From there, select the "Block third-party cookies" option.

For Edge users: select Settings> Advanced settings> Cookies. From there, use the drop-down menu to select the "Block only third-party cookies" option.

For Firefox users: select Preferences> Privacy & Security> History. From there, select the "Accept third-party cookies" toggle switch to "Never."

For Safari users: select Preferences> Privacy. Then select the "Prevent cross-site tracking" option.

(Note: there is also a setting to automatically clear cookies from your browser upon each exit.)

Your social media platforms:

Now that we have dealt with your ISP and web browser privacy concerns, there is still your social media security to take into consideration. Depending on your usage levels, social media platforms can contain a great deal of personal information, including your photos, personal information, and a list of main contacts. Even if you limit your information to friends or family, they often have the ability to download that content, which they can repost with indiscretion. Be careful what you share. Log in to your most used social media accounts and update your privacy status, as necessary.

How many social media platforms do you maintain a regular presence on? Is your online profile purely social in nature, or do you also maintain professional profiles as well? What are the privacy settings on each of your favored social media platforms? Have you been careful to restrict your profile access to just people that you know and trust?

Your password choices:

The latest research findings suggest that for passwords used to access sensitive data or web accounts, that at least 12 characters or more should be used and that the passcode should include a mixture of letters, numerals, and special characters. Experts further recommend that rather than using a single word for your password it is best to use a short phrase or expression (e.g., TheMoonI$Blue). It is also a very smart practice to assign different passwords for each different device. Moving forward, new advances in biometric technology such as facial recognition, fingerprint ID, and retinal scans may allow us to do away with traditional written passcodes,

Do all of your online devices, e.g., smartphones, tablets, laptops, and home computer have strong, secure, and individualized passwords? On average, how many passwords do you maintain across your various online sights or device applications? Do your passcodes tend to follow the safety guidelines mentioned above? Do any of the devices that you currently own contain examples of the biometric technology described above? If so, do you regularly use this technology? Why or why not?

Your online connection mode:

When you go online, are you using a wired Internet connection or are you using Wi-Fi? Wired connections offer an additional layer of security that Wi-Fi cannot. If you must use Wi-Fi, use your personal home or business network whenever possible. As a rule, avoid public Wi-Fi since it is usually not secure.

Research and report on the security dangers of using public Wi-Fi. When you are online, how willing are you to provide your personal information to the websites you visit? Does the appeal of an entry prize, a contest, or a discount coupon have any influence on your final decision to share your data?

Your data storage:

While cloud storage offers numerous benefits, it is also very susceptible to hacking. If you really want to keep data private, do not store it online! Store it locally, somewhere at your home or office and then keep it regularly backed up. When there are no other practical options and the data must be stored online, make sure that data is encrypted. This same rule applies to confidential information of any kind, including your chat and e-mail. If you must share sensitive data online, the only way to make sure that it is secure is to encrypt it.

What exactly is encryption? What is end-to-end encryption? Research and report on some of the top encryption programs now being to protect online data. Based on what you have discovered about your own online digital footprint, have you changed any of your personnel security measures or modified your online habits?

After completing the exercises above, gather all of your data into a folder and submit an analysis of your Cybersecurity Personal Privacy Review findings.